T0244460

I Dream of Things That Never Were

The Ken Kunken Story

I Dream of Things That Never Were

The Ken Kunken Story

Kenneth J. Kunken

TWELVE
TABLES
PRESS

Twelve Tables Press
P.O. Box 568
Northport, New York 11768
www.twelvetablespress.com

Cover art by Grzegorz Błażejczyk, projektportret.pl

To my incredible wife, Anna,
and our three wonderful sons,
Joseph, James, and Timothy,
who continue to make all
my dreams come true.

Life is what happens to you while you are busy making other plans.

— John Lennon, in the song
"Beautiful Boy (Darling Boy)"

Contents

◆ ◆ ◆

Foreword

◆ ◆ ◆

My brother was never the fastest athlete as we were growing up. He was never the biggest, the strongest, the tallest, the quickest. But he was always the toughest.

I am two years older than Ken. We had our share of fights over the years—never punching, mostly wrestling on the ground. I was always the winner, or so I thought. But he would never concede the fight, he would never quit, he would never stop fighting. In order for the fight to stop, I would have to run away from him, and I would ask myself afterward, "Did I really win that last fight?"

After Ken had his devastating football accident, and as he was recuperating in the various hospitals and rehabilitation centers, he received a large number of visitors—family, friends, neighbors, and teammates. They were almost always nervous and concerned prior to the visit: "How is he feeling?" "Is he awake?" "Can he talk?" "Has he had any improvement?" "What should we talk about?" After every visit, invariably, the visitor would come out of his room and say, "I feel so much better. He was smiling, he was joking, he had a positive attitude!" Ken was the one who would cheer up the visitor.

Ken had a singular goal during the months of rehabilitation—work to be as independent as possible and return to Cornell to continue his education. He returned to a campus in Ithaca that was not wheelchair accessible, had no curb cuts, few elevators that could accommodate his wheelchair, and had multiple steps to get to most of the classrooms. He persevered, becoming the first quadriplegic to graduate from Cornell. Ken went on to obtain a master's degree in counseling from Cornell, and a second master's degree from Columbia, before deciding that what he really wanted to do was study to be a lawyer, following the path that my wife and I had taken.

As he was preparing to graduate from Hofstra Law School, we talked about the type of law that he could practice, given his serious physical limitations. I suggested tax law, because he was always strong in math, and it was a field that he could have everything that he needed laid out in front of him. His decision? He wanted to be in the courtroom! He has just completed more than 40 years of service as an Assistant District Attorney in Nassau County, New York, having tried more that 50 felony jury trials to verdict—most without any written notes!

Ken has provided inspiration to everyone who has come in contact with him. He has given many motivational talks—to students, to business groups, to counseling organizations, to sports teams—and his message has always been the same: have a goal as to what you want to achieve in life, work hard and be prepared, appreciate your family, friends, and your community, and you will succeed in whatever you set out to do.

Ken's memoir about growing up, overcoming a tragic, life-altering injury, building a life, a career, and a family is a testament to his message to all who came into contact with him—never give up, never stop fighting, follow your dreams, and you can have a productive and fulfilling life.

Stephen Kunken

Introduction

◆ ◆ ◆

In 1970 I was a fairly typical twenty-year-old college student at Cornell University. I worked hard in school and loved sports. I was a member of a fraternity and had a lot of good friends. And, like many twenty year olds, I dreamed of leading a useful, productive, rewarding, and happy life.

On the night of October 30, 1970, a few of my football teammates and I decided to spend the evening at my friend Bob's cabin on the other side of Lake Cayuga in upstate New York. We all went together to the local IGA in Collegetown to shop for steak, corn, and pie. When we returned to the cabin, the question that should have been asked, before we bought all the food, was finally verbalized, "Who knows how to cook?" Since I was the only one who seemed to have any experience, I volunteered.

I put the steaks into the oven and turned the knob to *broil*. I checked on the meat five or six minutes later, but the oven wasn't even warm.

I called in Bob and said, "There's something wrong with the oven. It isn't heating up."

Bob asked me if I had lit the pilot light.

"What's a pilot light?" I replied.

Bob started laughing at me, "Are you sure you know how to cook if you don't even know what a pilot light is?"

I had never cooked on a gas stove before. I learned fast when Bob lit a match. The gas that had been building up inside of the stove exploded. Suddenly there was a bright flash of light coupled with a thunderous boom.

I instinctively looked down to see if I was hurt but there was not a mark on me. Incredibly, I was not injured. I was not burned. I was not even singed.

I remember lying in bed that night thinking how lucky I was. I remember thinking, "If I can survive an explosion like that without being injured, I can survive anything. Nothing can happen to me. I must be invincible!"

The next day I broke my neck.

All my hopes and dreams were suddenly shattered.

My very survival was now in question.

And I was only twenty.

I Dream of Things That Never Were

That Never Were

The Ken Kunken Story

Chapter 1

Growing Up

♦ ♦ ♦

I entered this world shortly before my mother left it. I was born on July 15, 1950. Twenty-seven days later, my mother, Judy, died. She was twenty-four years old.

We lived on Long Island in the village of Levittown, New York. The country was in the grips of a virulent polio epidemic. There were so many cases in our community that a mobile medical unit was going house to house to test possible victims. My brother Steve was showing symptoms, was tested, and diagnosed with polio. Fortunately, his was a mild case with symptoms confined to his right leg. However, while the medical team was in our house examining my brother, my mother became weak, was tested, and polio was confirmed.

My mother and brother were hospitalized in adjoining first-floor rooms in Meadowbrook Hospital in East Meadow. My father and my maternal grandparents stayed at the hospital around the clock. When my family was not allowed in their hospital rooms, they would move from window to window, watching the two of them from outside the building.

Steve was discharged after three days. Unfortunately, my mother's condition deteriorated, and, within days, she was breathing only with the aid of an iron lung.

My grandmother refused to leave my mother's side. Years later, I remember my grandmother telling me that, at one point,

Baby Ken, brother Steve, and their mother, Judy.
This is the last picture taken of Judy—July 30, 1950.

she observed a nurse adjusting the controls on the iron lung, after which my mother seemed to be in distress. My grandmother immediately reported this to hospital personnel who, indeed, confirmed that the controls were not set properly.

After staying at the hospital around the clock for four days, my grandmother reluctantly agreed to go home for the night to get some sleep. It was that night that my mother died. For the rest of my grandmother's life, she was wracked with guilt that she had not remained at the hospital that night to watch over her oldest daughter.

Judith Mae Kunken was buried on August 11, 1950, the same day that she died, wearing the gown in which she was married just three years before.

In all, ten people on our block on Morning Glory Road were diagnosed with the disease. My mother was the only fatality.

♦ ♦ ♦

At the age of twenty-eight, my father Leonard was a widower with me, a twenty-seven-days-old baby, and my brother Steve whose polio symptoms required six months of physical therapy.

Out of necessity, my father, brother, and I moved in with my paternal grandparents, Joe and Bea Kunken, into a large house in Lynbrook.

While we lived with my father's parents, my maternal grandmother came over every day to help with our care. Both our grandmothers became, in effect, Steve's and my surrogate mothers. Although we called both sets of grandparents "Mom" and "Pop," to distinguish them, we referred to my paternal grandparents as "Lynbrook Mom" and "Lynbrook Pop," and called my maternal grandparents "More Mom" and "More Pop."

Lynbrook Pop never attended college, but he still managed to develop a successful life insurance practice. His company was called J.E. Kunken & Company and, with time, became the family business. My father worked there, as did his sisters' husbands, Mel Danis and Sid Regen. Steve and I developed an especially close relationship with our extended family, which included not only our grandparents but our aunts, uncles, and cousins as well.

I have vivid memories of the house in Lynbrook. It had three floors, plus a basement and a large backyard. That backyard was the perfect place for Steve and me to play. At an early age, I remember my father teaching us how to throw, catch, and hit a baseball. That was the precursor to the passion for athletics that Steve and I developed over the years.

Steve and I shared a bedroom on the second floor. I suppose, as a result of our mother dying while we were so young, and being raised with our grandparents, Steve and I formed a particularly strong bond. I do know for sure that we did everything together, and my brother has always been my best friend.

Ken at three and Steve at five—best friends—summer 1953.

My time in that house was filled with day-to-day routine activities rather than dramatic events, but I distinctly remember feeling loved and secure there.

We lived with Lynbrook Mom and Lynbrook Pop until I was almost five. That was when my father married his second wife, Janis. Janis had been recently widowed. She had two children from her first marriage: Alan, who was nine months younger than me, and Hope, who was one and a half years old. My father bought a house for the six of us on Freeman Avenue in an undeveloped part of Oceanside.

Unfortunately, my father's marriage to Janis was not a happy one. They argued about everything. Even though my father adopted Alan and Hope, we never really seemed like a family. The atmosphere in the house was often so charged I couldn't wait to get away. Fortunately, both sets of our grandparents lived close by and Steve and I spent a lot of time visiting with them.

My maternal grandparents were a particularly calming influence. They never argued or even raised their voices. There was not a

Ken, age four, in the backyard of the Lynbrook house—1954.

prejudiced or mean-spirited bone in their bodies. They were tolerant of everyone and everything. Whenever I was with More Mom and More Pop, I could feel the tension and anxiety leave my body, my shoulders lower, and the knots around my neck disappear.

My grandparents' marriage was a sharp contrast to my father's with Janis. The only good thing that came from that marriage was the birth of my sister Meryl. She was born on May 2, 1960. I was not yet ten years old, and I loved having a little sister.

Over the years, I learned so much from both sets of grandparents. They helped, cared for, and supported everyone, never expecting anything in return. They gave unconditional love and

Lynbrook Pop and Lynbrook Mom with their grandchildren in 1960:
front row from left to right: Jill Danis, Roy Danis, Billy Regen, Hope Kunken;
second row: Ken, Lynbrook Pop holding Ronnie Danis,
Lynbrook Mom holding Meryl Kunken, Jeff Danis;
back row: Alan Kunken, Steve Kunken, Mark Regen.

always knew what to say or do to make me feel better. They taught me the importance of family.

When I was five years old, my father's sister Carol was diagnosed with multiple sclerosis. At the time, she was the only person I knew who needed to use a wheelchair. Because Aunt Carol also lived in Oceanside, I frequently saw Lynbrook Mom help with her everyday needs.

Unfortunately, Lynbrook Mom was stricken with colon cancer and died when I was fourteen. She suffered terribly near the end. It was painful to watch. For me, losing Lynbrook Mom was like losing a mother.

Ken with More Mom and More Pop
in the Catskill Mountains—summer 1962.

Ken, Steve, and Meryl in front of the house on
Freeman Avenue in Oceanside—1963.

Aunt Carol died the following year, adding to our family's grief.

♦ ♦ ♦

Seven boys, who all happened to be just one year older than me, lived within two blocks of our home on Freeman Avenue. They were the perfect age for both Steve and me to play with. We turned every piece of property near our home into a ball field. We played football and stickball on the street in front of our house, attached a basketball net to a telephone pole and played basketball there as well. We played wiffle ball on our driveway, miniature golf and running bases in our backyard, and jai alai against the wall of our next-door neighbor's house.

I played six years of little league football and five years of little league baseball. As long as I had a ball to play with, I was never bored.

Ken's dad, Leonard, is second from the left in the back row,
Ken is right in front of him. Ken's friend Russ Canan is
third from the right in the front row—1959.

My favorite day of the year was Halloween. What could be more fun than knocking on neighbors' doors and getting bags and bags of candy and chocolate? We would usually go trick-or-treating as a group. We would start knocking on doors at about four in the afternoon and, apart from taking a short break for dinner, a quick trip to the bathroom, and to empty our bags so that we would have room for more goodies, we wouldn't quit until close to eight o'clock at night. By that time, we had enough candy and chocolate to last us into the New Year.

Little did I know that an incident would occur on Halloween years later that would make it the worst day of my life.

♦ ♦ ♦

I spent the summer after eighth grade with Steve at Camp Birchwood in West Goshen, Connecticut. I got to play softball, basketball, volleyball, and other sports all day long. I swam in a lake a couple of times a day and even learned how to water ski. It was great to spend eight weeks away from all the tension and arguing that was taking place at our home on Freeman Avenue.

It was that summer that my father separated from Janis. My father told Steve and me the news when he came to see us on visiting day. My brother and I were happy that day had finally come. It had been so clear, for years, that their marriage was not working.

When camp ended, my father drove Steve and me to our new home. He had rented a two-bedroom garden apartment on the opposite side of Oceanside.

My sister Meryl lived with us on weekends and with her mother during the week. Unfortunately, the arguing between my father and Janis continued for many years to come, with Meryl frequently caught in the middle. It was a terrible situation for her and very uncomfortable for the rest of us. It seemed like every weekend, when my father picked Meryl up or dropped her off, he and Janis would get into an argument.

♦ ♦ ♦

Part of the Oceanside High School football team picture;
Ken, number 23—1967.

Between the family problems at home and the academic demands of school, I needed some type of release for all the stress in my life. Football was particularly effective. In addition, I loved being a part of a team. I enjoyed the competition and the camaraderie with my teammates.

When I was in the ninth grade, I was the quarterback and co-captain of the junior high school football team, co-captain of the wrestling team, played on the baseball team, and was co-captain of the boys' sports night.

During my senior year in high school, I started on both the varsity wrestling and football teams. At 145 pounds and five feet, seven inches tall, I was by far the smallest defensive end in the league. Once I had my uniform on, though, I was not afraid or intimidated by anyone, no matter how big they were.

♦ ♦ ♦

Despite the family problems growing up, I did well in my studies. In fact, I did well enough to be admitted into the National Honor Society.

I excelled in math and was certain that I would someday enter a profession that would make use of my math ability. My high school advisor told me that I should be an engineer. At my brother's suggestion, I applied for admission to the College of Engineering at Cornell University and was accepted. I decided to go there.

Chapter 2

The Cornell Experience

◆ ◆ ◆

On August 23, 1968, two weeks before I was to leave for college, my father married for the third time. His new wife, Betty Meeker, had been married once before but had no children. Because I would soon be away from home, the change in my father's life did not seem like it was going to have a big impact on me.

My father drove me to school during the second week of September.

The Cornell administration had said they would try to pair each freshman with a roommate who had similar interests. The match they made for me was uncanny. They paired me with Bob Skelly, a young man from Westfield, New Jersey. Bob and I were both majoring in engineering. We had the identical high school average and were both avid athletes. Both our fathers sold insurance and we each had a sister and a brother. To top it off, if we didn't go to Cornell, both of us would have chosen the University of Vermont as our second choice. We got along great.

Bob, however, seemed to have no problem mastering his engineering courses, while I struggled terribly with mine.

Before entering Cornell, I was considered a very good student. I only had to put in minimal effort to get good grades. Now, for the first time, I had difficulty with my studies.

I knew I could compete with anybody in math. Science was another story. Physics and chemistry did not come easy to me.

In engineering, we had to take physics and chemistry at the same time.

Many Cornell engineering students had fixed cars or designed their own stereo sound systems in high school, just for fun. I had never picked up a hammer or screwdriver in my life, nor had I any desire to. It was clear to me I was in way over my head in engineering.

Most of my classes were graded on a curve. My chemistry professor began his first lecture by putting the grade curve up on the opaque projector. Ten percent of the class was going to get an A, fifteen percent would get a B, fifty percent would get a C, fifteen percent would get a D, and ten percent would fail.

You needed to maintain at least a C- average to not flunk out. And yet, seventy-five percent of the class was going to get a grade of C or below. If you were a little below average in chemistry, you'd better be above average in physics, or you would be in danger of not maintaining a C- average. There was incredible pressure on everyone.

Somehow, with the help of my roommate and other engineering students on my corridor in the dorm, I made it through the first year without flunking out. It was nip-and-tuck the entire time.

Despite struggling with my engineering courses, I loved being at Cornell. It was an incredible experience being on my own for the first time. I met and interacted with people from all over the country. There were a lot of students from Long Island at Cornell, but far more from places I had never been. I learned so much just being around them and being exposed to different points of view, especially regarding social and political issues.

During the second semester of my freshmen year, I pledged the Sigma Nu fraternity. That was one of the best decisions I made during my college career.

The fraternity house was a great place to live. Because Cornell was such a large school, it was especially nice to have a group of close friends that I could do things with, confide in, and count on. I enjoyed the camaraderie with my frat brothers, many of whom were also enrolled in engineering.

Sigma Nu fraternity, Ken is in the front row, fifth from the left—1969.

The summer after my freshman year, I worked as a lifeguard at a pool at Nassau Beach in Lido, Long Island. I really enjoyed being outdoors. Lifeguarding made me realize how much I had missed playing a sport the past year at Cornell. I decided that during my sophomore year, I just had to participate in some kind of athletics for my psychological, as well as my physical, well-being.

Cornell had a varsity lightweight football team in addition to the heavyweight team. To play on the lightweight team, you had to weigh 154 pounds or less, two days before each game. For that reason, it was also called the 150-pound team. Now, for the first time, I played with and against people my own size. I loved being on a football team again, even though I was only a substitute and did not get to play much.

With my fraternity brothers' help, I managed to complete my sophomore year in engineering. It wasn't pretty and my grades were low, but I did it. Be that as it may, I loved the whole "Cornell experience."

Chapter 3

Injury

♦ ◆ ♦

I returned to the Cornell campus to prepare for the upcoming lightweight football season two weeks before classes were to begin for my junior year. I knew I had to be in great shape because we were about to start two-a-day practices in what was still very warm, if not hot, weather. I had worked out extra hard all summer swimming, exercising, lifting weights, and running in the sand, hoping to earn a starting position or, at least, more playing time. The previous year, my total playing time had consisted of only five plays in one game, in which we were already ahead by thirty-five points.

Coach Bob Cullen began our first team meeting by reading out loud the schedule for the season. Our first game was against Rutgers and would be on October 10. To my dismay, the Jewish holiday Yom Kippur fell on that day. Although I was not very religious, that holiday was sacred. Yom Kippur was the only day in the entire year that I would not play for religious reasons. Even Sandy Koufax would not pitch on Yom Kippur in the 1965 World Series.

Once the coach knew that I would not play in the first game, he concentrated on the players who were sure to see a lot of action. I spent the first six weeks of practice working out with the substitutes and the scrubs.

As luck would have it, one of our starting linebackers injured his shoulder in a practice and now was not expected to be able to

Ken with pool lifeguards—summer 1970.

play in our first game. A few days before the game, the coach called me into his office and asked if there was any way I could play on October 10 and observe the holiday on another day. Of course, I could not. It was not a difficult decision for me to make, just a frustrating one. I spent that day in temple.

The second game of our season was against Penn, and I would have started in that one as well. But that week, Lynbrook Pop died from a heart attack. I immediately returned to Long Island for the funeral. It was a difficult time for the entire family. We were all shocked by his sudden death. The game against Penn was the last thing on my mind.

Lynbrook Pop had visited me at Cornell just two days before his death, in seemingly perfect health. He took me out to dinner and even went to a psychology lecture with me. There were a thousand students at that lecture, but I felt special because Lynbrook Pop was by my side.

All four of my grandparents played such an important part in my growing up. Now two of them, Lynbrook Pop and Lynbrook Mom, were gone. How could I even begin to concentrate on anything else at this time?

There were only six games in the entire lightweight football season and I had now missed the first two. We had won both of those games, so the coach felt that the lineup should be kept intact for the third one. I was only to be a sub. After eight weeks of practice, I still had not played in a game that year.

Coach Cullen, referring to the circumstances that had prevented me from putting on the Cornell uniform the past two weeks, said that he had never seen a football player with such tough luck.

Our third game of the year was against Army. Right after my computer science exam on Thursday, October 22, I got on the team bus taking us to West Point. As the bus was leaving, the coach started the roll call. When he reached my name and I answered, "Here," a loud cheer came up from my teammates. They never thought I would make it. In fact, one of them cautioned me, "Don't even answer the phone if it rings, just get on the bus."

When the game finally began, on the afternoon of October 23, I was the first substitute linebacker and the middle linebacker on punt returns. I played a total of seven plays, two on defense and five on punt returns. I watched from the sidelines as Army scored with fifty-three seconds remaining, taking the lead and the game. It was a long Friday night bus ride back to Cornell.

Our fourth game was scheduled for October 31, Halloween, against Columbia. It was a home game. Cornell University had shut down for "Citizenship Recess" so that students could campaign for their candidates in the upcoming mid-term elections. The football team was practically alone on campus for ten days. Had it not been for football, I, too, would have returned home.

Because the campus was virtually deserted, a few of us decided to spend the evening before the game at a cabin on the other side of Lake Cayuga that was rented by one of my teammates, Bob

Ken with his roommate John Golasheski and John's sister,
one week before Ken's injury—October 1970.

Clark. It was that evening that the gas that had been building up
inside the stove exploded.

Strangely, in August, when football practice first started, I
had a strong feeling that I was going to get hurt that season. I
actually shared that thought with my roommate, John Golasheski.

One night in the fraternity house, I said, "John, I don't know
what it is, I just have this feeling that I am going to get hurt this
season."

"What do you mean?" John asked.

I said, "I don't know, I just have this feeling."

In all my years of participating in organized sports, I had
never had that feeling before.

My brother Steve was a terrific athlete, but seemed to get
hurt a lot. He injured his knee while at a day camp when he was
four, was hit in the head with a pitched ball while batting in Little
League, fractured his ankle playing football in high school, and
was hit in the head by a golf ball on the golf course, just to name
a few. I, on the other hand, seemed relatively lucky. I just had one

broken pinkie finger, stretching to catch a football, and a whiplash from a car accident, both when I was in the sixth grade.

I knew that many people were injured playing football. I had played for so many years I supposed I was due, but that night in the cabin before the Columbia game I no longer thought about the premonition. In fact, I thought I was invincible.

We had a late breakfast in the cabin, drove to the locker rooms, and suited up. We would play on our usual lower alumni field.

It started to rain about two hours before game time. It was the kind of day you hate to have to roll around in the mud. The wetness goes right through your uniform and stays with you until you finally take your shower after the game.

It was just about noon when we ran out onto the field to warm up.

The game began at 1 p.m. There were a number of spectators who had remained in Ithaca during the recess and braved the unpleasant weather conditions.

We lost the toss of the coin and had to kick off to Columbia. One of our players, Mal McLaren, got hurt on the play, suffering what appeared to be a concussion. The coach decided that McLaren should sit out the remainder of the game. As a result, I took his place on the kickoff squad.

We held Columbia, and they were forced to punt. I went in on the punt return team. I had my first crack at the action and finally had a chance to show what I could do.

As soon as the center snapped the ball, I hit him in the face mask with a hard-upward swing of my forearms. We had good field position following the punt and scored a few plays later. Cornell 7, Columbia 0.

Now I was in on a kickoff for the first time. A wall of blockers rapidly moved between the ball carrier and me. I ran hard into them, taking two of them down. The player behind me made the tackle. That had to look good to the coach. Again, we held them and, again, I was in on the punt return, my third play.

I gave the center a really good shot. The resulting bad hike went over the punter's head and into the end zone for a safety.

That gave us two more points: Cornell 9, Columbia 0. There was applause from the stands. I believed at least some of it was for me. It felt great!

Now Columbia had to kick to us. This time we didn't move the ball but after we punted, neither did they. As I was running out onto the field for my fourth play, Coach Cullen yelled to me, "Whatever you're doing to that guy, keep it up." I did. I gave the center a good shot to the head. Another bad hike. The punter tried to run, dropped the ball when he was tackled, and I helped recover the fumble. This play was definitely the best of my college career so far.

We had the ball on their twenty-yard line. We soon scored on a pass play. Cornell 16, Columbia 0, with only twelve minutes gone in the first quarter.

Soon, I was back on the field for my fifth play. I lined up as the first person to the left of the kicker. Just before the kickoff, I turned to Bob Clark, who was standing to my right and said, "We're going to win big!"

We got off a good kick. Columbia formed a wall of blockers on their left side of the field. The ball carrier was running between this wall and the sideline.

As I ran down the field, a Columbia player tried to block me but I was able to sidestep him. Now, I was inside the wall and had a clear shot at the ball carrier. I didn't lose a stride going toward him.

At the last second, I shot out at him, head first. I was going for the lower part of his abdomen for a hit so hard it would make him fumble. I put everything behind it.

People later told me the impact sounded really loud in the stands.

As soon as I made contact with the ball carrier, I felt an electric shock shoot through my body, followed by a stinging numbness.

The upper part of the ball carrier's body bent forward over me and then tumbled sideways and partly backward. He didn't fumble.

The ball carrier got up slowly.

I didn't get up at all.

Initially, no one knew I was hurt. The referee came up to me and said, "Great tackle, kid," and walked away. My teammates shouted, "Great hit, Kunk!"

As the teams started to change and leave the field, I yelled, "I can't move!"

I was lying on the ground at the thirty-five-yard line, not far from the sideline. One of my teammates called out to the trainer, "Kunk is hurt." The ref stopped the game.

The team doctor and two of the coaches quickly followed the trainer onto the field. I don't recall which person asked what the problem was but I replied, "I don't know. I just can't move."

"Where does it hurt?" was the next question. At the time, I was not in a great deal of pain. Mostly, I still felt the stinging numbness. I wondered if this was what a pinched nerve felt like.

I noticed there were now three doctors over me, not just one. In addition to the team doctor, a doctor from Ithaca happened to be at the game, as well as another doctor, the father of one of the players.

There seemed to be a long silence. Although I was on my side, I could see the perplexed looks on everyone's faces. I saw the look on Coach Cullen's face turn more somber as I lay there.

I thought it was just the shock of the tackle that was lingering and I would soon jump up and run off the field. I learned later that one of the doctors had been fairly certain, as he saw me lying helpless in the fetal position, that I had broken my neck.

I was conscious and cognizant. In fact, I still thought I would be up and around within minutes. Then I heard the call for a stretcher.

The stretcher appeared and was put under me.

From what I was later told, the least little jarring of my neck could have caused more damage. In fact, moving me at all could have killed me.

All that time it was raining, and I was now lying face up in that rain. I asked someone to straighten my legs but was told that my legs were straight. I was sure they were still bent. That really hit me.

The strangest sensation occurred when the stretcher was lifted. As my head rose, it felt as though my body was being left behind. I had feeling only from the neck up. It was as if I had been decapitated and they were carrying just my head off the field.

They put the stretcher down about ten yards from the sideline. It seemed I had only been moved so the game could go on.

By now, I felt a lot of pain in my neck. On top of that, my shoulder pads had been pushed up, digging into it. I asked if someone would adjust my uniform, but there was to be no more touching. No one was to do a thing for me until the ambulance came. I had to convince someone to take out my mouthpiece so I wouldn't choke on it.

To reassure myself, I asked one of the doctors, "I'll be able to move again, won't I, Doc?" It was a loaded question. I was sure he would say yes. I wanted to hear him say yes. But he didn't. He said he didn't know.

One of my friends, Mark Langweiler, came down from the stands and stood near me. Mark later told me I asked the doctor that same question a few times, but I only remember asking once.

Now reality was setting in. I can't move at all! I'm paralyzed!

"It just can't be," I thought, "It was only a football game, just a game. It was just a game!!! I've still got a whole life ahead of me."

It was a long and painful half hour before the ambulance came. I was still face up in the rain as they lifted me into it.

I asked Mark if he would ride to the hospital with me. He did. My teammates, of course, were still on the field, as the game continued.

It was my first ambulance ride ever.

I heard the attendant tell the driver, "Go slow, avoid bumps, and try not to jar." The three-mile ride to Tompkins County Hospital in Ithaca seemed endless. Every car on the road must have passed us. The attendant was right there holding my head and Mark was close by, but not much was said. I was getting more and more frightened at the thought of permanent paralysis.

Dr. Yale met me in the emergency room. I was moved slowly and carefully for X-rays. I was conscious the whole time and in quite a bit of pain. Everybody was busy.

As soon as the X-rays were read, it was clear that Tompkins County Hospital was not equipped to handle an injury as serious as mine. It was decided that I should be moved to the Arnot-Ogden Hospital in Elmira, forty miles away.

I still didn't know what was wrong with me and wasn't even sure how to ask. Dr. Yale and his staff were bombarding me with questions, even before I could get one out of my own.

"Where do you live? What's your telephone number? How can we reach your father?"

I told Dr. Yale, "Make sure you're careful how you tell my father. Tell him I'm all right and not hurt too badly." I stressed breaking the news that I was in the hospital gently because I knew the shock of my grandfather's recent death was still weighing heavily on my father. Besides, I was still trying to reassure myself. How bad could a football injury be?

Despite my request, Dr. Yale was direct, blunt, and to the point when he spoke to my father. He told him that I had been critically hurt, and, "If he were my son, I'd get up here immediately."

My father was on a plane to Elmira within two hours of the phone call.

I was soon surprised and a little relieved to see a familiar face in the emergency room. It was Kathy, the fiancé of my fraternity brother Ed Reifler. She was a nurse at Tompkins County Hospital. As luck would have it, Kathy was working that day in the emergency room.

They cut off my uniform, which did not pose too many problems, but getting my helmet off was another matter. I was wearing a big, birdcage face mask. They couldn't pull it off. They couldn't cut it off. As a last resort, four nurses "inched" it off as another held my head as steady as possible. It must have taken three to four minutes. Considering how critical my situation was, it was truly a life-or-death precision operation. As they worked, I was in severe pain all over, from the neck up, which was all I could feel.

I asked repeatedly if they would give me something for the pain or put me to sleep. Dr. Yale said no. He said he still needed more information from me. I had to be in full control of my senses to help him. Later, he said I needed to be fully alert when I arrived in Elmira to speak to the doctor there. The pain was getting worse. I was wrapped in sheets and blankets but received no pain medication.

I was placed back in an ambulance and the slow drive to Elmira began, with Kathy holding my head between her hands during the entire trip.

The trip to Elmira took well over an hour. The driver was slow and careful. A bump could have been fatal. I couldn't tell if it was still raining outside. All I could see was the ceiling of the ambulance. My neck was broken. Nobody needed to tell me that now. The pain was excruciating.

I kept telling Kathy, over and over again, "Tell my father I love him very much." I believed there was a strong possibility I would never get to say those words to him myself.

If I wasn't in shock before, I certainly was now. The doctors couldn't help me. The nurses couldn't help me. The hospital couldn't help me. The pain continued to get worse and nobody could help me. I thought I was going to die.

Kathy tried to calm me down. She kept trying to reassure me that everything would be all right.

My friend Mark later told me that, while he was still at the hospital, he spoke with Dr. Yale about my X-rays. The doctor told him that I had broken two vertebrae in my neck.

I was hurt between the fourth and fifth cervicals. If I had broken one vertebra higher up, I would not have been able to breathe on my own. I probably would have died on the field. There would be times later when I would wish I had.

By now, the football game was over. Final score: Cornell 36, Columbia 14.

Chapter 4

In Critical Condition

◆ ◆ ◆

When I arrived in Elmira, I was met by the neurosurgeon, Dr. Rossman. He usually practiced at a second hospital in Elmira but was covering for Arnot-Ogden's vacationing specialist.

I was brought right into surgery, where Dr. Rossman drilled two holes into my skull, one on either side. The doctor then screwed Crutchfield tongs into my head.

The tongs looked like those used to carry large blocks of ice. Twenty pounds of weights were hung from the opposite end of them, stretching me in a prone position so that the dislocated bones in my neck would realign. The traction was also to prevent my neck from moving.

I lay motionless on an eighteen-inch-wide bed called a "Striker Frame." I had to be turned every two hours to prevent bedsores, aid circulation, and lessen the chance of congestion developing in my lungs. To turn me, the nurses would strap another bed on top of me. They would then quickly flip the bed over. I went from being on my back to being on my stomach. It felt like I was being turned on a medical barbecue spit. The turning was done in a split second and was tremendously painful. Twenty pounds of weights were swinging around with me. It felt as though the weights were tearing my head off. The rapid movement made me nauseous and dizzy. I was turned on that bed every two hours, twenty-four hours a day.

One of the doctors told me there actually was a more comfortable bed called the "circo-electric bed." It was relatively new, very expensive, and only a few places had it. The hospital would look into trying to get one for me.

My father arrived at the hospital three hours after I did and was probably in as much shock as I was. Before my father saw me, he had an extensive conference with the neurosurgeon. My father was so upset and unnerved by my injury he wasn't able to follow a thing the doctor said.

My father's first conversation with me was brief and superficial. What could he say to his twenty-year-old son after such a catastrophic event? Were there really any words that could make me feel better?

I must have been heavily medicated by then because I don't remember my father saying that he loved me, though I am sure he did. I know he certainly felt it, wanted to say it, as well as so many other things at that time. Or maybe I just wanted and needed to hear it.

I also don't remember telling him I loved him, though it had been the one thing I kept saying I wanted to say during the ambulance ride. Unlike when I broke my finger playing football and my father took me to the hospital, this time I knew he could not help me. Still, it was comforting to see my father and have him by my side.

Everyone was keeping a close watch on me in the intensive care unit.

As a result of my injury, my chest muscles were no longer working. My breathing was weak and shallow. I was breathing almost exclusively with my diaphragm. My cough was almost nonexistent. Had I been injured one cervical higher, I would have needed a respirator to breathe.

The doctors considered giving me a tracheotomy. Had they done so, I would have had difficulty speaking as well. To this day, I cringe at the thought of it.

Any upper respiratory infection, even a common cold, could cause my condition to deteriorate further. My visitors at Arnot-Ogden had to wear masks.

My breathing, temperature, fluid intake and output were all being monitored. As with everything else that was being done to my body, it was not discussed with me. Because I had no feeling below my shoulders, I did not know what or how many needles or other objects were inserted into or sticking out of my body. I found out later that I had a suprapubic catheter placed inside me. The catheter consisted of a tube going through my lower abdomen, directly into my bladder.

My head and face itched terribly. They were pretty much the only parts of my body I could feel. No amount of scratching was enough to stop the itching. I had to be scratched until I bled to get any relief. That pain felt better than the itching.

I was later told that other recently injured quadriplegics experienced the same problems with itching. I am not sure whether it was another effect of the spinal cord injury or that our other senses became magnified to the point that a slight itch became a huge problem.

There were no clocks in the room. The days seemed endless. For the entire time I had to lie totally flat, either on my back or on my stomach. I just lay there, not knowing whether it was day or night, raining or sunny outside.

I was surrounded by a roomful of strangers, doing God knows what to me. No one told me the extent of my injury, or even what exactly my injury was. I was kept in the dark about everything. All I knew was that the doctors didn't know if I would ever be able to move again. I was terrified!

My brother Steve learned of my injury from my father's wife Betty. She called him in Boston, where he was attending law school, when my father was already on the plane to Elmira.

Steve immediately booked a flight to Ithaca. He had to borrow money from his law school roommate, who drove him to the airport. Once in Ithaca, Steve rented a car and made the one-hour drive to Elmira. He arrived at the hospital about 9 p.m., had a brief conversation with my father, and then entered my room.

Steve was devastated by my injury. He became so upset when he saw me in the intensive care unit that he had to leave the room. He returned the next morning.

The next day, my maternal grandparents, More Mom and More Pop, flew up from New Jersey, where they had been living for the past six years. My Uncle Mel and Aunt Lorraine arrived by car from Long Island.

I still had cakes of mud in my hair from playing in the rain. More Mom tried to comb it out but didn't have much success. She had to be careful not to use too much pressure. Any movement of my neck had to be avoided. Still, it was good to feel her loving hands on my head.

Having my family near helped tremendously. Being in the intensive care unit, however, limited the time they could visit with me.

A social worker at the hospital suggested my family stay at a nearby boarding house. It was close by, so the appropriate arrangements were made.

My father and Uncle Mel got busy making phone call after phone call to doctors in the fields of neurology and neurosurgery. They must have been on the phone for hours.

One of those doctors suggested that my family speak with Dr. Allan Russek, one of the top doctors at the Rusk Institute in New York City. The Rusk Institute was considered the most prestigious rehabilitation center in the world.

Dr. Russek told my family that Dr. Rossman appeared to be very knowledgeable and competent. In fact, he was quite impressed with him. He said that Dr. Rossman seemed to be quite experienced as a surgeon. Dr. Russek indicated that Dr. Rossman was doing exactly what they would be doing for me in New York City.

As a result of my Uncle Mel's phone calls, Dr. King, the chief neurosurgeon of the Guthrie Robert Packer Hospital in Sayre, Pennsylvania, came to Elmira to consult with Dr. Rossman on my condition. Dr. King visited me either that Monday or Tuesday. I must have been asleep or just out of it at the time because I don't remember seeing him.

My family gathered in the hospital chapel when Dr. King came in and spoke with them. He confirmed the seriousness of my injury. Dr. King didn't think I would make it through the week because there was a serious risk of developing a fatal infection.

When my family asked what type of future I could look forward to, Dr. King replied, "If you're thinking in terms of a lifetime, don't. Think in terms of days, maybe hours." He told my family that, if I were to survive, my life expectancy would be between five and nine years and I would probably end up spending that time in a nursing home.

Dr. King then said, "If he was my son, I would just let him go." My family was too stunned to say anything in reply.

In my more lucid moments, I asked questions. I felt things were being kept from me and that my visitors knew more than I did. Still, no one told me anything about my condition or prognosis.

I knew I had been hurt very badly. I knew I had broken my neck. I knew that I was paralyzed from the neck down. What I did not know was if the paralysis was going to be permanent.

No one explained the ramifications of a spinal cord injury to me. In fact, no one even told me that I had injured my spinal cord.

I constantly asked my relatives about my condition. They kept changing the subject. I asked the nurses. They said, "Ask the doctors." I asked the doctors. They said they weren't sure. They all kept telling me to be patient.

I was convinced the doctors would have told me if the paralysis was just going to be temporary, but they hadn't.

My mind was racing. I couldn't get it out of my head that the doctors weren't sure if I would ever be able to move again. The thought of going through another week, another day, another hour, another minute in my condition was overwhelming.

Would I lie helpless in bed for the rest of my life? I was an athlete, damn it! If I couldn't be active, what was the point of going on?

All that time, I was in a lot of pain. It seemed like every minute lasted an hour.

I begged my family, doctors, nurses, attendants, anyone who would listen, to put me out of my misery.

I kept pleading, "Why are you torturing me? Why do you want to keep hurting me? Don't you see that I am in agony? I don't want to live in this condition. Why won't you just let me die?"

I was constantly being told, "Don't talk like that. You've got to keep hope."

But I could tell by the way everyone was acting, there wasn't any hope that I would ever get better.

I was told that a surgical procedure was being scheduled. The "cure-all" operation was supposed to take place in a few days.

I was now convinced that I was paralyzed because my neck was broken. I kept hoping that, once the break in my neck was repaired, I would be back on my feet. I wanted to believe that "be patient" meant to be patient for two, possibly three, more weeks.

Whether I was awake or asleep, I was turned every two hours. I had no idea what day it was. I dreaded every minute. It seemed like one long nightmare.

Steve wanted to be with me but soon developed a fever and bad cold. He was not allowed to see me until he got better. He was finally told to fly back to Boston and recuperate there.

Aunt Lorraine remained with me in Elmira through most of my stay. She treated me as though I was her own son, though she did have five children of her own. Her oldest son, Jeff, was a sophomore at Syracuse. Her daughter Jill was sixteen years old at the time, Roy was fourteen, Ronnie was ten, and Jeanie was seven. I knew her own family needed her, but I asked Aunt Lorraine to stay and, without hesitation, she did. She only left my side to sleep at the boarding house.

My relatives felt it would be good for me to also have some visitors from outside the family. Hopefully they would take my mind off my condition.

My coach, Bob Cullen, was my first visitor. He arranged for some of my teammates to come to see me as well. Among them were the three Clemente brothers: Jeff, who was an assistant coach; Rod, one of my teammates; and Mark, the team manager.

Mark needed to use a wheelchair as a result of a freak accident "tray sliding" at Cornell the previous winter. He broke his back when a person sliding down behind him ran into him. Mark had become a paraplegic, paralyzed from the chest down. I guess he was supposed to be an inspiration to me.

At the time, I never even associated Mark's injury with mine. After all, Mark might be in a wheelchair for the rest of his life, while I was still expecting to be back on my feet soon after the surgery.

My fraternity roommate John Golashesky cut short his "citizenship recess" break when he heard about my injury. He rushed to Elmira, only stopping for a speeding ticket along the way.

As the rest of my fraternity brothers returned from their break, they gathered at the hospital.

Dave Gilbert, my closest friend from Oceanside, immediately drove up from Harpur College in Binghamton.

Rich Gilman and Russ Canan, two other close friends from Oceanside, came as well. They had heard about my injury from Dave. Rich had been attending the State University of New York at Buffalo and Russ was studying at Syracuse University.

All my visitors had been instructed not to say anything depressing or demoralizing. My father told my visitors not to even mention that I was paralyzed.

One day, as I was lying on my stomach, a lifeless arm suddenly seemed to fall from the ceiling. A left hand was now dangling menacingly eighteen inches from my face. It looked like a claw, ready to attack. It scared the hell out of me. It took a while before I realized it was my own arm. It had fallen off the bed. That really shook me up.

Four days after my injury, I developed a bad bladder infection and my temperature went up to 105 degrees. Soon the close watch on me turned into a deathwatch. Perhaps Dr. King was right.

My surgery had to be postponed. The doctor would not operate on me while I was running a fever. After two days, my fever began to go down. The doctor insisted, however, that my temperature be normal for at least two days before surgery.

About a week after my injury, my grandmother commented on how smooth my hands felt. She moved my left hand against my face, so I could feel it. All the calluses and rough skin had peeled off. My hand felt as smooth as a baby's bottom. For some reason, that embarrassed me. Mine was no longer the hand of a football player. It didn't feel like my hand at all. It felt like the hand of a helpless child.

On Saturday, November 7, I remembered that my football team had a big game against Navy. I still felt that I was an integral part of the team, so I asked my family to send my teammates the following telegram: "With you in spirit. Beat Navy. Kunk."

The coach read it to the team right before they left the locker room to run onto the field. The Coach told me later that everyone was incredibly moved.

On Sunday, November 8, the weights that had hung from the Crutchfield tongs for the past eight days, were reduced from twenty to fifteen pounds. The removal of those five pounds lessened some of the strain on my neck. Unfortunately, it didn't reduce the excruciating pain I experienced every time the weights swung around with me when I was turned.

On Monday, November 9, I finally had my surgery. I thought or hoped—maybe a little of both—that all my movement would be back when I awakened in the recovery room. Nobody had told me that, but I had convinced myself that a cure was coming.

All I knew about surgery was what I saw in the movies or on television. No one explained to me what was going to happen or even what the surgery entailed.

I had expected to be put to sleep with anesthesia before I left my room. Instead, I was put on a stretcher and wheeled through the halls, past my family. I remember seeing my father, my grandparents, and Aunt Lorraine in the hallway. They, too, seemed surprised I was still conscious. I told them, "Don't worry, I'm tough. I'll be okay."

I was then wheeled through the doors of the operating room. I remember thinking, "When you're wheeled into the OR, you're supposed to be asleep." I was wide awake. I was worried the anesthesia wouldn't knock me out.

The room was crowded with doctors and nurses. The operation seemed to begin right before my eyes.

A long tube was inserted through one of my nostrils. When it reached the lower part of my throat, I started to gag. The tube continued to be pushed, and the further the tube was inserted the more painful it became. They kept pushing it downward to my lungs.

I tried screaming to the doctors, "I'm not asleep yet!" I was convinced they were starting the surgery. Of course, my "screaming" could not have been very loud at that point, considering how weak my breathing was.

They told me to relax and said, "Everything is fine."

They started suctioning me. They were trying to remove the congestion that had been collecting in my lungs for the past nine days.

It is common for a person's lungs to fill with congestion as a result of lying flat for a lengthy period of time. In addition, I did not have a strong enough "cough" to bring up the phlegm.

The suctioning felt like a vacuum was pulling everything out of my lungs, not just the congestion but all the air as well. I was both gagging and gasping for breath, trying to scream louder and longer that I still wasn't asleep. The suctioning procedure seemed endless. At some point, I lost consciousness. They must have given me some type of anesthesia intravenously.

The operation took five hours and consisted of two parts.

Dr. Forrest, the orthopedic surgeon, handled the first part. He removed a piece of the tibia bone, several inches long, from my left leg. That procedure took about an hour and left me with a five-inch scar.

Before the procedure, Aunt Lorraine was concerned the upstate doctors were not qualified to handle my surgery. She questioned Dr. Forrest about his experience.

Dr. Forrest replied, "Kenny isn't the only important person I've operated on. I also did surgery on General Eisenhower in the fifties."

That helped put Aunt Lorraine a bit more at ease.

Dr. Rossman, the neurosurgeon, then performed an "anterior" cervical laminectomy. He fused the removed part of the tibia with the third, fourth, fifth, and sixth cervicals in my neck, to make sure the vertebrae stayed aligned. That would eliminate the need for any more traction. Dr. Rossman worked for four hours on my neck. I now have a noticeable three-inch scar to the right of my Adam's apple.

The next thing I remember was waking up in the intensive care unit (ICU). I no longer had the Crutchfield tongs screwed into my head. There were no longer any weights pulling on my neck. When I opened my eyes, I was on my back, lying in some sort of metal Ferris wheel. It was the circo-electric bed, ordered specially for me.

The bed enabled the nurses to turn me without causing much additional strain on my neck. I was told that being turned on the circo-electric bed would be less painful than on the Stryker frame. The first time I was turned that was true, perhaps partly because I no longer had twenty pounds of weights swinging along with me. Later, however, the turning became very painful again.

Just like on the Stryker frame, before I was turned on the circo-electric bed, another bed was strapped on top of me. A face mask, similar to a baseball catcher's mask, was placed over my face. The mask was the only support for my head while I was lying on my stomach, as the bed ended by my shoulders.

The two beds were bolted together and, at the push of a button, the bed began to move in a semicircle. My feet lowered toward the floor while my head went up toward the ceiling to a standing position. When the rest of the 180-degree turn was completed, I was lying on my stomach, on the new bed. The old bed, which was now on top of me, was unbolted, unstrapped, and removed. My head was supported by my chin and forehead pressing against the face mask.

When I was turned, as I approached the vertical position, the blood rushed from my head to my feet, frequently causing me to pass out. When that happened, I remained unconscious for various lengths of time.

The slightest buckling of my knees, or improper positioning of my feet against the footboard, put a lot of strain on my neck. The resulting pain was excruciating.

When I woke up after the surgery, I couldn't move a muscle. I was still paralyzed. I thought the operation hadn't worked. I was devastated!

Everyone tried to reassure me, "It takes time."

The doctors told my family that, after a spinal cord injury, patients sometimes go through a period of spinal shock. The shock could last for up to six months. As the shock to the cord starts to wear off, some patients get some muscle return. The quicker the return, the more promising the outlook for recovery. The longer a patient goes without some return, the less likely the patient will ever get more movement back.

I later learned that spinal shock could last for years but, in most cases, six months was the guideline.

There were some hopeful signs. I seemed to have some feeling around my shoulders, which I didn't recall having before my surgery, but I wasn't sure. Everyone had been so careful when moving me, I just might not have been touched in those places before the surgery.

More Pop told me he had read my full surgical report. It stated that there was no breakage in the dura, the outside covering of the spinal cord, and no spinal fluid leakage. That was good news. Breakage or leakage might mean that the spinal cord was severed.

Now all I could do was wait and hope.

The operation left my throat so sensitive, just swallowing my own saliva was torture. The slightest movement of my neck, and now even my jaw, was agony. Yawning was incredibly painful and I was constantly yawning as a result of being severely sleep deprived, heavily medicated, and awakened every two hours to be turned.

One of the doctors' biggest concerns was my inability to cough up the phlegm that was continuing to congest my lungs. Pneumonia could easily result.

When I was on my stomach, the nurses would hit on my back with cup-shaped hands, trying to loosen congestion to help me cough it up. It didn't help. The nurses kept telling me that, if I didn't cough up the phlegm, they would have to suction me.

I had never experienced anything more frightening and painful in my life than the suctioning that took place on the operating table. I made up my mind that I would never let them suction me again. I told the nurses, "You are not going to stick those tubes down my nose again. I don't care if I get pneumonia or drown in my own phlegm. You are not going to stick those tubes down my nose."

Because I was not able to cough up the phlegm, I tried to make them think that I had. I would take a drink of water, hold it in my mouth, and then spit it out slowly while the nurses were pounding me on my back. I tried to spit out as much saliva as I could, but I couldn't fool them. The nurses and doctors listened to my lungs with a stethoscope. They could tell that my lungs were still congested.

Not long after my surgery, they woke me up and started to suction me.

"Don't do it!" I yelled. They did it anyway.

This time was even more painful because the passageways were still sore from the prior suctioning. I screamed. I was gagging and gasping for air. The more I fought it, the worse it was.

The pain in my neck was still very intense but, after a few days, the pain in my throat started to lessen. The healing process had begun.

About a week after the operation, the doctors decided I could now be fed by mouth. Apparently, I had been fed intravenously this whole time. I had no appetite whatsoever but being fed by mouth seemed to be the next step toward my recovery.

One of the doctors suggested that, rather than feeding me while I was lying flat on my back, it would be better if I were turned on the circo-electric bed to an angle of approximately 135 degrees. I would now be looking at the floor at a forty-five-degree angle. The rationale behind that move was that it would be easier for me to swallow my food the closer I was to an upright position. In addition, two hours were up and I was due to be turned anyway.

I didn't think I would be able to eat that way and I told that to the doctor. For that matter, I couldn't eat in any position. The turning alone made me nauseous. But the doctor insisted, so I tried to be a good patient. I took one bite from the nurse's spoon, possibly two, when I started to choke.

The food wasn't going down. It got caught somewhere in my throat. I gagged. I had trouble breathing. I tried coughing but I couldn't. The nurses pounded on my back to no avail.

The doctor immediately ordered suctioning, this time through my mouth. As the technicians rushed in with the necessary equipment, the doctor left the room. He didn't want to wait around for the unpleasantness. I watched him leave when I needed him the most.

I couldn't yell. I couldn't breathe. I thought I was going to die. The suctioning did its job, though.

My father was furious at the doctor for insisting I eat in that position and then for leaving the room before I was out of danger. My father chased after him screaming a barrage of criticisms and complaints.

Intravenous feeding was restarted. The subject of solid foods didn't come up again for another three days.

I absolutely hated the nurses in the ICU. They seemed cold-hearted, cruel, and uncaring. They stayed distant. I suppose they had to be that way in order to take care of the many critical cases that were on their unit. Still, I wanted to be moved out of the ICU as soon as possible.

The doctors said they would not transfer me until my family found private duty nurses to watch me around the clock. It took two days before my family could find a "special" for the third eight-hour shift.

Chapter 5

The Healing Has Begun

◆ ◆ ◆

Finally, I was moved into a large private room on the second floor. It was a tremendous boost for me. In addition, my family was now allowed to stay in the room with me twenty-four hours a day.

More Mom stayed by my bedside every night from then on. She had never forgiven herself for leaving my mother's side that fateful night, twenty years earlier, when my mother died. More Mom was not going to let that happen again.

It was a great comfort to have her with me during those long sleepless nights. More Mom had a loving touch and manner about her that helped me to relax. Everything always seemed like it would turn out all right when she was around. Still, I knew even More Mom could not make things better this time.

My mind wouldn't stop racing. Like More Mom, I worried about the doctors making mistakes. I was helpless and at everybody's mercy. Every day seemed endless. I only knew what time it was by seeing who was in the room with me.

Within a few days post-surgery, I became extremely sensitive to loud or sudden, unexpected noises, as well as to light. If someone so much as closed a drawer, I don't mean slammed it, just closed it, I experienced intense pain. The slightest vibration seemed to go right through me. If a nurse dropped a tray, I went through the ceiling. My head pounded, my body stiffened, my neck hurt. Any unexpected noise made my eyes dart toward the door. I wanted to run out but I couldn't even flinch.

Although my room was kept fairly dark, a ray of sunlight would sometimes sneak through the blinds. The least bit of light caused me severe headaches. At times, I had to have a washcloth placed over my eyes to shield me from the light from the window or from the hallway. I couldn't cope with anything at that point.

In addition, I still itched nonstop, and the itching drove me crazy, especially because I was unable to scratch it myself.

I had a terrible time trying to get any sleep during those days. Sleeping pills did not work well on me. It usually took almost two hours for me to finally become drowsy and ready to fall asleep, which, of course, meant that it was now time for me to be turned, waking me up, again.

The turning was getting worse. Now, every time, as I reached the standing position, I would suddenly be hit with the same sensations I had experienced when I made the tackle: a painful electric shock shooting through me and a stinging numbness all over my body. I had to relive the nightmare of my accident every two hours.

My mind would get hazy and everything would turn blurry. A feeling, partly of euphoria, but mostly of discomfort and pain, would take over. Then I was "out," sometimes for seconds, sometimes for minutes. I would regain consciousness when my head was returned to the same level as my heart and the blood was able to flow back to my head.

I would hear the nurses asking, "Kenny, are you all right?" I could hear and see them, but I couldn't answer.

Moments before my faculties returned, I would enter a different dimension. I would become disconnected from my paralyzed body. Peculiar thoughts and events would flash through my mind. Later, I would enter that "twilight zone" with greater frequency.

I never had given much credence to an "out-of-body experience," until I had my own. It occurred during one of those turns on the circo-electric bed. At some point, after I blacked out, I found myself floating near the ceiling of my hospital room, looking down. I could see a lot of nurses surrounding a patient who was lying in bed. I couldn't see who the patient was, though. I knew that someone close to me had been seriously hurt but I couldn't remember who. I kept moving around in the air, trying to see past the nurses, who the patient was. I kept hearing nurses ask, "Are you all right? Are you all right?" but there was no response. Finally, I was able to move to a position from which I could see between the nurses. It was me! I was hovering above in the air, looking down at myself! I was not able to talk or, for that matter, do anything but look.

Suddenly, I was back in my body, lying in the bed, looking up at the nurses. Now I kept hearing them ask, "Kenny, are you all right?" But I still couldn't respond. Finally, after a few more seconds, I was able to talk.

I never thought of that incident as a near-death experience. I was not afraid of dying, just of being in more pain.

Late one afternoon, there was an accident at the construction site for a new addition to Arnot-Ogden Hospital. An electrician had fallen onto a live wire. He was rushed into the emergency room in critical condition.

The accident caused a power failure. Everything in the hospital went out for three hours, including the auxiliary equipment in the intensive care unit. A special respirator was rushed into the room opposite mine to substitute for the no longer functioning breathing apparatus that patient was on.

Fortunately for me, I was on my back when the power went out. Being on my back was more comfortable than being on my stomach. The power failure meant that I couldn't be turned for a few hours. Initially I felt good about that. Then suddenly it occurred to me. What if the bed had been in motion? What if it had stopped while I was in the upright position, certain to black out? I could be left there in the dark, hanging unconscious for hours.

And what if that were to happen at some other time? Now I became afraid of the possibility of power failures. It was a great relief when the lights finally came back on.

There were some additional benefits of being out of the intensive care unit. I now had a television in the room. Unfortunately, because I was usually lying flat, either on my back or my stomach, I was not able to watch it.

Dr. Forrest happened to stop by my room on Sunday, November 15. Seeing my predicament, he put wooden boxes under the television to raise its height. Dr. Forrest lifted the heavy television onto the boxes himself.

Dr. Forrest was one of the few doctors I came to admire. He seemed to really care about me and how I was feeling. I had a lot of confidence and trust in him. In fact, throughout all my initial hospital stays, I never had a doctor as helpful and concerned as Dr. Forrest.

Being Sunday, and now with a TV in the room, the first thing I wanted to watch was football, much to my family's dismay. I still loved the game and hoped that I would be able to play again, someday.

My family had become very sensitive to the whole subject of football. Some of them left the room. They didn't want to watch me watch the game.

I watched a New York Giants football game. I thought the game was great.

I knew that the game in which I had broken my neck, as every one of our football games, had been filmed as a matter of course. I decided to ask Coach Cullen to show me the game film. Along with many of my teammates, he had watched it dozens of times already. The coach told me they couldn't tell why I had been injured. Now I wanted to see for myself. I needed to know what I did wrong and why I got hurt.

Within the week, Coach Cullen brought the film and a projector to the hospital. More Mom left the room before the film was even threaded. She couldn't stand the thought of watching me being injured.

An attendant elevated my bed to a thirty-degree angle, so I could see the screen better. He then left. Now, just my father, Coach Cullen, and I were in the room. As the coach started to thread the projector, my stomach became queasy. I didn't know how I would react, watching myself break my neck.

The projector started to roll. The film began with the opening kickoff of the game. I was growing more and more nervous.

I didn't know if I could handle it. Would I black out? Would it traumatize me?

It was still five minutes before my tackle. It was easy for me to spot myself on the screen. I saw some nice shots of me in action. I could even recall the thoughts that were going through my head as I was playing.

We had just scored another touchdown and taken the lead 16-0. My tackle was about to be shown. The closer it got, the more I felt I would pass out. I tried to hide my uneasiness for fear that they might shut off the projector and call the doctor. As it turned out, I didn't have to be concerned about them stopping the film. The coach and my father were focused on the screen, not on me. It was almost as if they had forgotten I was in the room.

Now we were up to the start of the kickoff. I saw myself lined up immediately to the left of the kicker. The camera caught me running the first five yards down the field before it switched to the ball carrier. Seconds later, it showed the last five yards of my approach to the ball carrier.

I could feel the blood rushing from my head. I almost looked away, but I couldn't turn my head even if I wanted to. I thought about closing my eyes but I didn't. Then, boom! I saw myself make the tackle.

It was a good hit. The ball carrier seemed to bend in half over me, and then fell partly to the side and back.

"Would you please play it again," I said. This time I was concentrating on my head. I wanted to see if it moved when I hit the ball carrier. I needed to see why I got hurt.

Coach Cullen rewound the film. I watched it for the second time. My head looked like it remained straight. Had it jerked up, down, or to the side, I would have understood why my neck snapped. But my head didn't seem to move. It was a pretty good tackle.

"Again," I said, and the coach didn't hesitate to rewind the film. I still couldn't detect any movement in my head. I was running almost full speed and hit the ball carrier hard. It still seemed like a really good tackle.

"Again. I would like to see it again," I said.

That afternoon, I watched the tackle five times. It didn't seem like I did anything wrong. The others in the room agreed it was a good tackle. I didn't know whether to be happy or upset by that. If the tackle was good, why did I get hurt?

◆ ◆ ◆

The wounds from my surgery were starting to heal. Dr. Forrest decided that the stitches could now be removed from my leg. Early one morning, he came into my room for the procedure.

I nervously asked, "How much pain will this involve?"

His reply was direct, to the point and depressing, "You have no feeling below your shoulders." It was as if he was saying, even if he were to cut off my leg, I wouldn't feel it. Why worry about a few stitches?

He was right. I didn't feel a thing.

A few days later, Dr. Rossman entered my room with a pair of scissors in his hand. He informed me he was going to remove the stitches from my neck.

Because I did have feeling in my neck, I nervously asked, "How much pain will this involve?"

The doctor replied, "You won't even feel it."

At that time, my neck was still super sensitive but he was right. Removing the stitches was not painful.

The fact that the doctor felt the stitches could come out that soon bolstered my hope for a speedy recovery.

Dr. Rossman decided I could now be put in a new position, rolled manually by an attendant onto my side. I would then be allowed to stay on my side for the two hours I would normally spend on my stomach.

I quickly found out it was way too soon. It caused a great deal of pain in my neck and I became very dizzy. Turning onto my side would have to wait a few more weeks.

I was ready to have some range of motion exercises on my arms and legs but there was no Physical Therapy Department at Arnot-Ogden. Instead, every other day, I had an electric current applied to different parts of my body.

When the current was applied, my arms would jump, my fingers would spread apart and then come back together. Everyone thought that was a very good sign. I was encouraged as well. It appeared that my nerves were still intact and just needed to be stimulated for me to move my arms and legs again.

Right about that time, I had my first muscle spasm. My arms and legs shook involuntarily. The doctors said that, too, was a very good sign. It could mean that the nerves were being activated on their own, not by an external electric current. Those spasms were often painful to my neck but it was a pain I looked forward to having.

Things seemed to be progressing faster than the doctors had anticipated, which shortened the time I would have to stay in Elmira.

Plans were being made for my move to the Rusk Institute in New York City. My father had been told that Rusk was the place for me to go to for my future therapy. It would be where my recovery, if it were to come, would happen. Telephone calls were made, medical reports were transferred, and consultations took place. My father visited the Institute as well.

By now, I was watching every football game that was shown on TV. For the Ohio State–Michigan game, I arranged to have the turn to my stomach delayed until half time. Then, through the ingenuity of my nurses and attendants, I was able to watch the rest of the game by looking into two mirrors rigged up to the bed.

Throughout the days and evenings, I had many visitors. I received many get-well cards from schoolmates as well as friends from home. My accident had been a big story in all the papers. I received a flood of mail from people all over the country. In fact, the mail from strangers outnumbered the mail from friends.

Coach Cullen continued to be one of my most frequent visitors. One evening, he appeared holding a football in one hand and a jersey in the other.

My team had decided to give me the "game ball" from the Columbia game. All the players signed it. The ball had a big red star on it. That star would have been placed on my helmet for helping recover a fumble during the game.

The jersey was my "away" game jersey—number 66, white, with red stripes. My red "home" game jersey had been cut off in the hospital.

The team decided that my number was to be retired. I was very touched.

But I was then hit with a setback. I was not going directly to Rusk. The doctors at Rusk had advised my father I needed more hospital care before I would be ready to undergo the intensive rehabilitation at Rusk. Instead, I was going to be transferred to South Nassau Communities Hospital in my hometown of Oceanside.

South Nassau Communities Hospital was just two miles away from our house. After researching other hospitals on Long Island and in the surrounding metropolitan area, my father discovered that our hometown hospital had a good Physical Therapy Department. Furthermore, South Nassau's physiatrist (doctor of physical therapy), Dr. Mickey Holtzman, had been a college classmate of my father's, at the University of Vermont.

Dr. Holtzman said that the Oceanside community would like to see me at the local hospital. South Nassau had never had a case like mine before. I was a big thing for them, so Dr. Holtzman actively recruited me as a patient.

Dr. Holtzman promised he would remain in constant contact with the Rusk Institute concerning the proper therapy and equipment for me to use. If there was a need for any special equipment recommended by Rusk, South Nassau would purchase it. According to Dr. Holtzman, South Nassau's therapists had undergone the same schooling and training as those at Rusk.

I was furious. That decision had been reached without my knowledge, consent, or approval. I felt strongly that that "interim" step would slow down my recovery.

I lost that battle, one of many that bore directly on my care.

In hindsight, the move to Oceanside really did make the most sense. I was not physically ready for the intensive rehabilitation at Rusk. I still needed significant hospital care.

Regardless, I was anxious to start my physical therapy treatments, even if it was at South Nassau. The sooner I started, the quicker I would recover. To me, any additional days spent in

Elmira would be wasted time. I wanted to be transferred as soon as possible. I kept telling the doctors I felt fine, whether I did or not.

The date of my departure to Oceanside hinged on my temperature. All I needed was for it to remain at 98.6 degrees for three straight days. I had to be free of headaches and any other discomforts.

My temperature was taken rectally at least four times a day. Unfortunately, my temperature kept fluctuating from close to normal to a few degrees above. It would be normal for six straight readings and then go up a degree, once again delaying my trip for at least three days.

It took ten days before my temperature was normal for three consecutive days. What the doctors considered a fever seemed to me like my normal body temperature. My temperature stood just a little below 100 degrees on any given healthy day, but the doctors were strict about 98.6.

On Saturday, November 28, exactly four weeks to the day I had entered Arnot-Ogden Hospital in Elmira, I was moved to South Nassau.

My brother Steve and my night nurse, Millie, rode in the ambulance with me. My father followed in his car. My grandparents said goodbye at the ambulance door. I had told Aunt Lorraine she could return home to her family the week before.

We left at 7 a.m. It was still dark outside. I would remain motionless, staring directly at the ceiling of the ambulance, for the more than five-hour drive. I could not see outside the windows, because I was still unable to turn my head more than a degree or two. We traveled slower than the regular highway speed, making one brief stop for the others to stretch.

I was given a sedative and was groggy during the entire trip but sleeping was difficult. I couldn't doze off for more than a few minutes at a time. I became very uncomfortable remaining in one position. I had not been turned for so long a period of time since my injury.

Although I couldn't see much, it still felt good to hear the wheels rolling, cars passing, and even horns honking. I was outside of a hospital for the first time in four weeks.

Chapter 6

A Behavior Problem on a
Circo-Electric Bed

◆ ◆ ◆

We arrived at South Nassau Communities Hospital shortly after noon. I was taken to a double room on the surgery ward. As soon as I was wheeled into my new room, I saw suction apparatus attached to a wall. That apparatus remained by my bedside in every hospital room I would be in and was a constant reminder that it still could be used on me at some point in the future. Just looking at it gave me chills.

A circo-electric bed was waiting for me there as well. While I was not looking forward to being back on it, I was so uncomfortable by then that I couldn't wait to be turned. I felt as though I had been tied to a board for the past six hours.

I was exhausted, but couldn't sleep. Despite not eating for most of the day, I had no appetite.

On the bed next to mine was a thirteen-year-old boy reading a comic book. He was in the hospital for some routine tests. It didn't take long before I discovered that he had a very bad cold.

A few hours earlier, I had been reminded that a cold could be fatal to me. Now that danger was just five feet away. I immediately told the nurse about how serious catching a cold could be.

The nurse told the boy that if he had to sneeze he should turn his head the other way. Then she pulled a curtain between our two beds as if that was going to give me the appropriate protection. I couldn't believe it! For weeks, my visitors in Elmira were required to wear masks. Now, I was to stay in a room, twenty-four hours a day, with a boy who had a bad cold.

Within forty-eight hours, I was moved to a different room. During the first four weeks following my arrival at South Nassau, I was moved five times, sometimes without any explanation. It was no easy task. The circo-electric bed was very difficult to move, especially with me in it.

By my second day, I had met many of the medical personnel who would be responsible for my care: Dr. Mickey Holtzman, the physiatrist, would be in charge; Dr. Michtom, who also happened to be my father's doctor, was to be my internist; and Dr. Katz my urologist. There were to be many floor nurses, private duty nurses, respiratory therapists, physical therapists, and orderlies.

The day after my arrival, my brother Steve came to the hospital at 9 a.m. to explain to the day nurses how to turn me. Steve knew most medical personnel were not familiar with using the circo-electric bed. He wanted to show them how to operate it in a way that would be most comfortable for me. Even at Elmira, many of the nurses had learned how to do it while working with me.

That morning, at South Nassau, Steve started to give some helpful suggestions when Dr. Holtzman directed him to leave the room. Dr. Holtzman told him, "I'm the doctor and we know what we're doing. We don't need your help."

I said I would feel better if Steve could stay. However, hospital policy and the doctor's order demanded that my brother leave.

A second bed was strapped on top of me. The nurses surrounded the bed, in case I slipped out the side, and the turning process began.

I was now in the hands of a skilled doctor, at least three nurses, and one or two up-and-coming trainees. Everything had been set. With decades of experience under their belts, one medically trained finger pushed the button.

The bed began turning in a semicircle. I started to feel dizzy as I approached the upright position. When I got close to ninety degrees, the bed just stopped. I blacked out and, from what I was later told, was out for a long time.

The finger remained on the button but the bed wouldn't turn further. Someone had forgotten to release the brakes at the bottom of the bed. The brakes were a safety feature to protect me from being accidentally turned too far.

I was unconscious and my breathing was shallow. The medical staff could not tell exactly what my problem was. They probably had difficulty checking my pulse because I was strapped in so tightly.

An aide ran to the nurses' station and told the nurses there to dial 2-2-1. That was the hospital's code for an emergency. Immediately, it was announced over the loudspeakers for everyone in the hospital to hear, "Medical team! Medical team! Room 2721."

While this was going on, my father and brother were in the waiting room, speaking to my internist. When they heard the call, they all rushed to my room.

Someone finally had enough sense to put the bed in reverse, which returned me to my original position, and allowed the blood to flow back to my head. I gradually regained consciousness.

Soon my eyes began to focus on more than just the group of nurses. My room was now also crowded with doctors, therapists, and some lifesaving equipment.

It didn't take long for me to realize what had happened. They had thought I might be in cardiac arrest. They were about to start working on me. If I hadn't come to when I did, I don't know what they would have done next.

I thought about the movies I had seen involving cardiac arrests and the brutal manner in which patients were treated while they were being brought back to life. I could almost feel the strong electric shock being applied to my chest.

What if they had decided my breathing was so shallow I needed a tracheotomy? Who knows what they would do to my body during an emergency?

To the staff at South Nassau, this had been just a false alarm. To me, it was far more than that. My life was in the hands of doctors and nurses who were too stubborn and full of themselves to let my brother help them.

It took a while before the room cleared. Only Steve remained. The excitement seemed to be over for everyone but me.

"They don't know what they're doing! I'm completely dependent on them and they don't know what they're doing!" I finally broke down and cried like a baby.

My brother put his arms around me and remained by my side, hugging and comforting me until I finally stopped crying. There was nothing else he could do at that point but it really helped having him there.

After that incident, I was petrified of being turned. I began to worry that it would happen again. In fact, it might happen two hours from now, or two hours after that.

♦ ♦ ♦

Not long after I arrived at South Nassau, many rabbis, as well as other members of the clergy, visited me. I never asked for them to come, they just came on their own. They would always ask me how I was doing.

I would reply, "Terrible!" I would then ask them why I got hurt. Since they were supposed to have a special relationship with God, perhaps they could give me the answer.

They usually answered with phrases like, "There is no way of knowing the ways of God, but there's always a good reason in the end." Or, "God works in mysterious ways, but I am sure that He has a plan for you."

I never found much comfort in those responses.

Rabbi Rosenthal, my rabbi from Oceanside, read me the sermon he had delivered to his congregation on Yom Kippur, two months earlier. It was a good sermon but, again, brought me no comfort.

Yom Kippur is the Jewish Day of Atonement. My understanding was that it is also the day that the Book of Life is closed for the next year. Jews believe that, on that day, your fate is determined for the next year.

So why did I get hurt? I didn't play football on Yom Kippur. I spent that day in temple. What did I do wrong? Why would anyone continue to believe in a God that would allow this to happen?

The rabbi couldn't give me an answer. No one could.

♦ ♦ ♦

My father arranged, through a registry, for me to have three private duty nurses who would work eight-hour shifts.

My afternoon nurse, Mrs. Jones, was not only competent, she was young, pretty, easy to talk to, and, in general, pleasant company.

Mrs. Jones and I started every afternoon trying to keep my mind sharp by doing the *Readers Digest* vocabulary tests. At least, we did so for four days. Then Mrs. Jones told me that she was five months pregnant and had to leave. My luck. A nurse I had grown to like was already signing off my case.

Mrs. Nona Foster, a woman in her sixties, became my night nurse. She was a very nice, warm, and caring person. She did not take one night off the entire time I was there.

Mrs. Foster was the only nurse who seemed to know how to operate the circo-electric bed in the most comfortable way for me. When she was turning me, I never passed out nor did I experience those frightening sensations that had first occurred during my accident.

The problems began when Mrs. Foster's shift ended. So far, none of the other nurses were able to duplicate her skill. I implored Mrs. Foster to show them how to turn me. I know that she would have gladly done so but "hospital etiquette" frowned upon one nurse telling others, supposedly her peers, how the procedure should be done. Of course, my brother could have also demonstrated the process, but his suggestions were even less welcome. That meant that I was still at the staff's mercy sixteen hours of the day.

My morning private duty nurse, Miss Joanne "A," was a young woman who appeared to be in her twenties. Regardless of the discomfort I was in, or the position in which I was left, she would leave to take a one-hour break for lunch in addition to two fifteen-minute breaks during her shift.

"That's how nurses work," she said.

By that time, I was scared to be left alone. I still couldn't talk loud enough to call for assistance.

I asked Miss "A," as she was about to leave on one of her breaks, to have another nurse, volunteer, or even a young candy striper stay with me in the room while she was gone. She indignantly replied, "I can't disrupt every other person's routine just for you."

Whenever Miss "A" would turn me on the circo-electric bed, my knees would buckle, causing me to slide a bit, resulting in a lot of neck pain.

In addition, Miss "A" would invite student nurses into the room to observe her working on me. I was uncomfortable with that, to say the least. She would wait until the students were inside the room before she would ask me, "You wouldn't mind, would you?"

Here I was, lying in bed with just a flimsy hospital gown partially covering me, a urine-filled bedside drainage bag attached to a railing on the side of the bed, scared out of my mind, while a group of young female nursing students were observing me in all my discomfort. Did she really think I wouldn't mind or feel embarrassed at being stared at as if I was some sort of exhibit?

I repeatedly asked my father to replace her with somebody else but he dismissively would reply, "It's very difficult to get specials. Besides, she's qualified and doing what's best for you." According to my father, I was the one who should adjust to her. I shouldn't be "rocking the boat" and causing unnecessary trouble.

I can sum up my early experience with some of the private duty nurses, as well as the floor nurses, by describing an incident that occurred about a week after my arrival.

I woke up from a nap at about 3:15 p.m. My morning private duty nurse had already left without waiting to be relieved. My afternoon nurse was late in arriving. I was alone in the room except for my current roommate, an eighty-nine-year-old man.

I was in terrible pain. I tried calling for a nurse, but no one on the floor could hear me. My voice was still very weak. I couldn't understand why my roommate didn't try to help by calling for assistance for me. It was not until later that I learned he was deaf.

I lay there moaning for at least fifteen minutes when, luckily, my sixteen-year-old cousin Jill appeared. I asked her to get a nurse because something was wrong. Jill ran to the nurse's station.

Eventually a nurse walked into my room and, in a big huff, demanded, "What seems to be the problem?" When I told her I was in a lot of pain, she replied indignantly, "The call button is just two feet away from you. Next time just push it. Don't send someone to the station."

Whether the call button was two feet or two inches away, it didn't matter. I couldn't reach it. I could barely turn my head let alone move my arm, or even a finger. The floor nurses should have been aware of that. I was too upset to reply.

◆ ◆ ◆

On Monday, November 30, my third day at South Nassau, I was disappointed to hear that I was not going to begin physical therapy. Instead, pulmonary function tests needed to be done. Those tests were to evaluate my breathing.

Two pretty respiratory therapists, both about my age, entered my room lugging some heavy equipment. They told me the tests would be long and tiring. If I felt faint, at any time, I should tell them and they would temporarily stop the procedures.

For one of the breathing tests, I was to take in as deep a breath as I could and then blow all the air out as long and hard as I could, into a tube.

I took in a deep breath but exhaled almost immediately. I could not hold it. I tried again but had little success. The scores I received on that test were not those of a football player, lifeguard, or, for that matter, any other healthy person. They were more typical of someone who had severe breathing problems.

For another test, I was instructed to breathe in and out of a tube very rapidly a few times, then hold my breath and finally exhale into the same tube. I began to feel a bit faint and had to take frequent breaks. My scores on that test were even less satisfactory. My diaphragm certainly was not a good substitute for my no longer working chest muscles.

As a result of those tests, I was to receive Intermittent Positive Pressure Breathing (IPPB) treatments. Those treatments would be repeated twice a day, for at least fifteen minutes each time.

The treatments involved breathing in and out through a tube. When I took in a breath, the machine would force more air into my lungs than I would normally take in. The air had a misty saline solution in it which made me very thirsty and left a terrible taste in my mouth.

It was difficult keeping the tube in my mouth. Some of the technicians would hold it there for me, but others would leave it unsupported.

Those treatments continued throughout my stay at South Nassau.

As it turned out, most of the technicians were young women with whom I eventually became good friends. Although I didn't look forward to the treatments, I would often turn the allotted fifteen minutes into a half hour to give me more time to visit with them.

After I had been at the hospital a few weeks, the respiratory therapists used to drop by my room on their own, without that awful IPPB machine. They would come just to talk, relax a bit, and sometimes, I believe, to hide from their supervisor.

♦ ♦ ♦

On Tuesday morning, December 1, I finally had my first physical therapy session.

Jimmy, the head physical therapist, came to my room with a student named Mike who was majoring in physical therapy. It was to be Mike's first practical demonstration.

After Jimmy introduced himself and Mike to me, we engaged in some small talk. Mike said he had heard a lot about me. He was a student at Ithaca College, which is located just two miles from Cornell.

Jimmy explained that what they were about to do were called "range of motion" exercises. The therapist would bend and straighten my arms and legs and also move them out to the side and back in again. The exercises were to keep my muscles from developing contractures and keep the joints loose and lubricated.

I was very anxious to begin. The first exercise that Jimmy did was to bend my leg at the knee. Before he began, Jimmy said, "This is probably going to hurt, Ken."

I wasn't able to see him working on my leg as I was lying flat on my back. I could only see the ceiling above me. I felt nothing. Jimmy bent and straightened my leg a few times and then switched to the other leg. Still, I felt nothing.

Jimmy seemed surprised that it was not painful, because my legs had not been moved in almost five weeks. For most people, it probably would have hurt or at least been very uncomfortable. Although it meant I was spared the pain, my complete lack of sensation was, nevertheless, depressing. I know it must sound a bit strange, but I was actually looking forward to that kind of pain.

I began to worry that physical therapy might not help me at all. I was also concerned that the head therapist did not seem to know I had no feeling below my shoulders. The range of motion exercises would only have been painful for me if there were some strain on my neck.

I hoped the therapists at Rusk would be able to do something for me that the Oceanside therapists couldn't. When I questioned Jimmy about that, he said that all physical therapists had the same training, regardless of where they worked. He and his staff were just as qualified as those at Rusk.

Beginning the next day, however, I no longer even saw Jimmy, only Mike. I was being limited to one session a day, with a student, rather than the two sessions I had expected, with a licensed therapist. I felt they weren't doing everything they could to help me get my movement back.

During my second week at South Nassau, I was assigned a new physical therapist named Yvonne. She was a good-looking redhead who appeared to be in her late twenties. Yvonne told me she was extremely interested in my case. She had read quite a bit about my accident and wanted very much to work with me. Yvonne was also a graduate of Ithaca College.

During our first few sessions together, we worked on range of motion exercises for a half hour and then would spend about ten minutes on "resistance" exercises. Those were exercises in which I would try to move my arms and shoulders, with the therapist either assisting or resisting me. At that time, all I could do was shrug my shoulders. To strengthen them, Yvonne would push down on my shoulders, while I would try to pull them up. We did similar exercises with my neck, though my neck was still in a very delicate state and we needed to be extremely careful.

By the end of each forty-five minutes, I was always left completely exhausted because, during every session, I exerted myself well past my limits.

One day, I fell asleep during the range of motion exercises. Yvonne woke me up by saying, "That's the first time a male patient ever fell asleep on me." I looked forward to seeing Yvonne every morning.

Unfortunately, my physical therapy didn't seem to be bringing any positive results. It didn't help to be told to tighten my bicep and loosen my triceps, because I had no feeling in them. It was as if I was being told to move a chair that was on the other side of the room just by thinking about it.

About a week after we began exercises, Yvonne paused in the middle of the session and said, "There is a chance that these exercises may not bring back any movement at all." That was the first time I was told that physical therapy might not help.

"They've got to," I said.

"I can't guarantee anything," she replied.

"That's not fair. Why am I going through all this, then?" I complained.

Just then, Rabbi Rosenthal entered my room. As usual, he asked me how I was doing.

This time, in front of Yvonne, I replied, "Lousy. Yvonne might not be able to help me and it doesn't seem like your efforts at the synagogue have done me much good either." I immediately felt bad about being so disrespectful to the rabbi.

The rabbi responded, "God doesn't seem to listen to me. If he did, you would have been back up and walking the day I heard about your accident."

I decided to end the exercises for the day and just sleep on that one. I said I was tired and asked the two of them to leave.

♦ ♦ ♦

Whether as a result of my condition, or the hospital care I was receiving, I was a wreck, both physically and emotionally. Because no one seemed to be giving me much hope for improvement, what was the point of me going through so much physical and mental pain?

Half of every day, I lay on my stomach, staring at the floor. In order for me to see visitors during those times, they would have to sit on the floor under the part of the bed where my head was. Tubes hung from many parts of my body. Saliva dripped from my mouth and mucus ran from my nose. I felt sorry for those below me.

My friend "Puddy" Kelly came by one day to visit. Less than four months earlier, she and I had worked together as lifeguards. Puddy asked me a lot of questions about my condition, including how I went to the bathroom. Puddy never seemed to have any inhibitions. I was taken aback by her question. I knew I had a suprapubic catheter tube to empty my bladder but I didn't know how I moved my bowels. I had been hurt for five weeks by then, and I never knew or thought about how I did that. Apparently, I was being given enemas. No one had ever told me.

♦ ♦ ♦

In Oceanside, I depended on my father to be my advocate, so I complained to him about my doctors, roommates, and even about my hospital room. He usually told me not to say a word.

I begged my father to move me to Rusk, as originally planned. He emphatically told me, "No." This was where I would stay. Rusk could do no more for me than South Nassau.

One evening, while my father and his wife Betty were visiting, I was in tremendous pain. The doctor prescribed two Darvon painkillers but there was no relief. I was still in agony, "Give me something! Call a doctor."

A phone call from my father brought me more medicine but, again, no relief. A second phone call, this one to Dr. Holtzman, resulted in Dr. Holtzman's curt response, "He has to learn to take the pain."

Dr. Holtzman felt that they had given me too much narcotic pain medicine while I was in Elmira and I needed to stop taking it. He thought I was addicted to it.

By now, I was ranting, raving, screaming in pain.

How Betty heard the announcement that visiting hours were over, I will never know. But she told my father it was eight o'clock and time for them to leave. And they left. Nobody came to chase them out. They just left. I will never forget watching my father walk out of my room that evening.

I needed my father more than ever but he just left me there in the hands of the uncaring hospital staff. I cried myself to sleep that night.

This may be the appropriate place to talk about my father.

My father had dealt with a lot of misfortune in his life. He saw extensive combat in Europe during World War II, including fighting in the Battle of the Bulge. Many of his fellow soldiers were killed around him.

My father married when he was twenty-five but, by the time he was twenty-eight, he was a widower with two very young children, one with polio. He remarried when he was thirty-two and then suffered through ten tumultuous years in an unhappy relationship before finally being granted a divorce.

For Steve and me, their separation was a welcomed change. For my father, there was guilt, loneliness, and helplessness as a result of his new marital status. He was now father and mother, breadwinner, and housekeeper. Because he had legally adopted his ex-wife's first two children, my father was financially responsible for five children, his former spouse, and two residences.

During the mid to late 1960s, life with my father in our bachelors' apartment was far more pleasant than living in an unhappy household with his second wife. However, as is probably the case in many situations like ours, Steve and I were the ones who suffered the brunt of my father's misfortunes. We were the ones who were yelled at when he became frustrated. We were the ones who bore the anger of a despairing man permitted to see his daughter only on weekends and after an argument with his ex-wife at that.

Things started to improve for my father around the time my brother left for college. My father dated and eventually married for a third time. I looked upon Betty, the new woman in my father's life, as his wife, not as a replacement for my mother. Near the end of my freshman year at Cornell, they moved into a large house, right around the corner from our garden apartment.

Unfortunately, once they got married, Betty's relationship with the rest of the family created some tensions not experienced before.

Betty never expected to have to contend with problems associated with her husband's children. After all, his two grown children were away at college and his daughter only visited on weekends. Our school vacations were tough enough on her. She was unaccustomed to having young people around.

Perhaps because of that, things weren't as good as I had hoped between my father and me. I had more disagreements with him than during his bachelor days. Whenever I returned from Cornell on breaks, I found it difficult to accept the newcomer in our household. As long as I could come and go as I pleased, and knew my return to school was never far away, I tried to make the best of the situation. We all did.

The shock of my grandfather's death on October 14 hit us all hard, but briefly brought my father and me closer.

My accident changed a lot of things.

Sitting in the emergency ward of a hospital once again was torture for him. My father was beside himself. He had not gotten over his father's sudden death or his mother's and sister's slow painful deaths. Despite his good intentions and all that he tried to do for me, he gradually antagonized me and the rest of the family through his anger, self-pity, and despair. Those emotions had been building up inside of him during my entire stay in Elmira and finally burst through when I was in Oceanside.

Even with everyone's support, getting adjusted to a new hospital and staff would have been difficult for me. I had expected, once in Oceanside, to be surrounded by my grandparents, Aunt Lorraine, Uncle Mel, their five kids, and my many friends. I was counting on their support to help me adjust to my new condition not only physically but emotionally as well. Now, according to my father, I was to have no visitors outside the immediate family. By immediate family, my father meant himself, who worked during the day; his wife Betty, who also worked and with whom I did not get along; Steve, who was away at law school in Boston; and my sister Meryl, age ten, who could only come on weekends. Visitors, when they did decide to defy my father's initial ban, were discouraged from staying.

My relatives insisted on visiting me whenever they could. Finally, they just ignored my father's wishes.

My father told me I should be treated without a single deviation from the normal hospital routine, no matter how ridiculous some of the rules were. He was afraid that the hospital might discharge me if the family didn't follow the hospital rules. Then where would I go?

Why was my father like that? Was he truly afraid of the doctors or any repercussions from bending hospital rules? Did he really believe that the best way to treat me was to be strict with me? And why, suddenly, were there such vast disagreements between my father and the rest of the family?

I believe it was Betty who pressured my father into what seemed like harsh treatment. Betty openly frowned upon all the extra attention I was getting from my relatives. She told me I shouldn't be babied and that I must learn to live with the situation.

During my first few weeks at South Nassau, numerous family meetings took place outside the hospital. My condition, treatment, care, and possible plans for my future were discussed. My maternal grandparents were pushing for my move to Rusk, but my father remained adamant that I was to remain at South Nassau. I heard rumors that, instead of me going to Rusk, my next move might be to a nursing home.

Where could the idea of a nursing home have come from? Even though my father never mentioned it to me, there were others who did. My hope was still to return to school. Now that prospect was growing dimmer.

The family was starting to divide more and more.

The change in the relationship with my father, during the weeks that followed my accident, while certainly understandable, was disillusioning and disheartening. I sympathized with his predicament but I began to dread his visits. They only seemed to make me more uncomfortable.

Chapter 7

To Barbara, with Love

♦ ◆ ♦

I asked Aunt Lorraine to work on my father to at least get him to change my morning nurse. After a couple of days of what I'm sure was hard work, Aunt Lorraine finally convinced him to replace her.

My father contacted the registry, which then went down their list of nurses. Nobody wanted to work with me, though, because, according to my last nurse, I was "a twenty-year-old quadriplegic, who is a behavior problem, on a circo-electric bed."

The registry called seven nurses. They all turned the job down, one after another. On December 9, I woke up early in the morning and saw a young nurse of about twenty-five, cheerful, and pretty. She was eighth on the list. Her name was Barbara Crook.

Barbara told me later that the case didn't sound appetizing, but she needed the money. She decided to take it and put up with the "behavior problem" for ten days or so. Miss Foster helped convince Barbara to take the job and, lucky for me, she succeeded. Barbara was an excellent nurse: kind, considerate, and caring. Unfortunately, back then, I found her to be the exception, rather than the rule.

That same morning, I was transferred to a regular hospital bed. My neck was now stable enough to allow me to be turned manually onto my side. It was a great relief knowing that I was not going to be flipped on the circo-electric bed ever again.

The next day, Barbara waited for Aunt Lorraine to arrive before Barbara took her lunch break. Not long after Barbara left, I became uncomfortable in the position I was in, so I asked Aunt Lorraine to turn me. Just as Aunt Lorraine was doing so, Barbara returned.

In light of our experiences with my former nurses, Aunt Lorraine started to apologize, but Barbara said, "If Ken is more comfortable that way, then that's fine."

Barbara and I talked quite a bit. She had grown up in West Hempstead, Long Island, and earned her nursing degree from the State University of New York at Farmingdale. She had been married for two years, and her husband David was currently a law student at Brooklyn College. We talked about college, about her husband, her old boyfriends, and my old girlfriends.

At the beginning, Barbara worked a five-day week, but it wasn't long before she started taking her two days off every two weeks. I looked forward to seeing Barbara every morning.

In addition to her regular duties, Barbara would watch my physical therapist exercise me and then she would do it herself, giving me range of motion exercises on weekends when the therapists were not working.

I don't remember my hair being washed the entire time I was in Elmira. In Oceanside, Barbara would shampoo my hair while I was in bed. My head would rest on a rubber contraption that looked almost like the inner tube of a tire. It had a plastic bottom and was open on the opposite end. It had a long rubber flap there, which would allow water to drain into a garbage pail positioned at the end of the bed.

Barbara had never shaved anyone before. She learned on me how to do it. Barbara also cut my hair. She would cut the hair on one side of my head one day, while I was lying on my side, and the next day she would cut the other side, while I was lying facing the other way.

Barbara later told me that, when she got together with other nurses in the cafeteria during her breaks, they would often ask her, "How is the brat?"

Apparently, Miss "A," my former nurse, had complained about what a difficult patient I was. Everybody expected Barbara to tell some horror stories about me as well. It took a while for Barbara to convince everyone that I was not a "behavior problem," that I was actually a nice guy whom she enjoyed working with. Not long after that, it seemed everyone in the hospital started treating me better. There was a different air about the room. It was amazing how much Barbara did for me. So, this chapter is dedicated to Barbara, with love.

♦ ♦ ♦

I did my best to maintain a positive attitude and be optimistic. Although I was never told it, I believed that once the surgery repaired my broken neck, my movement would return and my getting muscle spasms meant that my movement was, in fact, returning. I expected that once I started physical therapy and regained some movement in my shoulders, more movement would soon follow. I believed that once I was able to sit up in a wheelchair, the rehabilitation process would accelerate. If all else failed, I still believed the therapists at Rusk would be able to help me.

For more than six weeks, though, the doctors, nurses, and therapists tried to avoid the subject of my chances for recovery. They never said that I would recover some or all of my movement, although they also never said that I wouldn't. Because they seemed reluctant to discuss it, I tried to look for clues in whatever they said.

One day I received a get-well letter from a stranger upstate. The letter included a newspaper clipping discussing my condition. Barbara started to read the article out loud to me. It stated that I was "paralyzed indefinitely."

"What do they mean, 'paralyzed indefinitely'?" I shouted at Barbara.

Barbara immediately crumpled up the article. I again asked her what the words meant. Barbara replied, "They have to write 'indefinitely.' Nobody knows the exact day that you will get your movement back."

I was so desperate, I fell for that line. I grew more suspicious the next day, however, when I asked to see the article. Barbara told me that she couldn't find the clipping. I became angry and frustrated.

My body, by now, had drastically deteriorated. I had lost a lot of weight. At the time of my injury, I weighed just under 150 pounds. Barbara later told me that, during my stay at South Nassau, I dipped below 100 pounds.

One weekend day in mid-December, Martin, a floor orderly, came into the room to turn me, while my fourteen-year-old cousin Roy and my Aunt Helen, my mother's youngest sister, were visiting. Martin asked my guests to wait in the hall until he was finished. As they were leaving, Martin started doing some range of motion exercises on my legs. He bent and straightened my right leg rapidly a few times. My leg must have looked especially thin and lifeless as it flopped back and forth.

Roy was visibly upset seeing that. Within a minute of Roy and Helen going out into the hallway, Roy leaned against the wall and collapsed onto the floor. He fainted while Helen was talking to him. Fortunately, he was okay and continued to visit me frequently.

♦ ♦ ♦

By the third week of December, my therapy program and schedule intensified.

In addition to the exercises in my room, an hour a day of therapy in the Physical Therapy Department was added. Part of that therapy included being on the tilt table. It was going to be my first of many encounters with what I later called "the moving torture rack."

The purpose of the tilt table is to acclimate a patient who had been lying flat in bed for a long period of time to the sitting or standing position. While the therapists never explained any of this to me, I thought I had some idea what to expect. The day before, I had had a visit from my Uncle Moe, one of More Mom's brothers. He told me about an old Army buddy of his who was injured in the war. Uncle Moe's buddy was put on a tilt table during his physical therapy. "He was screaming in pain his first few times on it," my uncle told me, "but after a couple of weeks, he started to enjoy the sensation of being elevated and lowered." I know my uncle said that to encourage me but his story left me petrified of the tilt table, which I still had not even seen at that point.

The day I was to be put on the tilt table for the first time, I had a stomach binder fastened securely around my abdomen. Both my legs were tightly wrapped in ace-bandages, from the arch of my foot to the middle of my thigh. My arms were also ace-bandaged. The ace-bandages were to try to keep my blood pressure from dropping as I was being elevated on the tilt table. I no longer had the muscle tone necessary to keep my blood pressure up. Just prepping me took more than ten minutes.

Four people, using a pull-sheet, slid me onto a gurney. We then took the elevator down and I was wheeled through a maze of corridors. It was one of the few times I was moved, other than being turned. It was a very strange feeling. Being spun around and making left and right turns without any warning made me really dizzy. The lights in the hallway were far brighter than those I had been accustomed to for the past several weeks. Usually, just opening the door to my hospital room caused me to squint. Now the light hurt my eyes. I needed Barbara to cover them with a towel.

Once in the Physical Therapy Department, my "blindfold" was partially removed and I was able to make out a large room filled with various pieces of equipment. About a dozen patients were there, most of them outpatients. There were elderly people who had had strokes and some who were suffering with arthritis. There were also some children with mobility issues.

I was left lying in the middle of that large room. A tilt table was wheeled out and put beside me.

A number of therapists grabbed the pull sheet and slid me from the gurney onto the tilt table. My feet were securely placed against the footboard to assure that I wouldn't slide down. Straps were placed above my knees and chest and one of the therapists tied me tightly to the board. I felt like she was trying to prevent me from leaping off the table once the pain started.

The therapist turned a crank located near my left hip. Much like the circo-electric bed, my legs lowered and my head rose. For encouragement, the therapist called out the degrees of elevation I was reaching.

"We're getting close to ten degrees. Now, we're closing in on fifteen. Now we're at twenty."

Suddenly, I became very dizzy. The blood rushed from my head to my legs. I got a throbbing headache. My eyes started to hurt.

"Now we're approaching twenty-five degrees."

Each degree of elevation increased my discomfort. Barbara was to my right. She had a blood pressure cuff on my arm and her hand on my pulse. That probably was not necessary, because my face told the whole story. First it was red with pain and then white, as I was close to passing out.

"You'd better lower me back down!"

The therapist replied, "No, this is important. Try to stand it as long as you can."

"As long as you can" turned out to be thirty minutes before she finally lowered the tilt table. It didn't compare to the pain of suctioning, but again, it made it clear to me that I had no control over what was being done to me or my body.

I was untied, slid off the tilt table onto the gurney, "blindfolded," spun around a few times, transported through the maze of hallways and elevators, slid back onto my bed, where my bandages were removed and the stomach binder taken off. I had a wicked headache, was very nauseous, and felt totally miserable.

Just then, a young girl from the kitchen came in and said, "Your lunch tray is here." Is it any wonder I lost fifty pounds?

It was an enormous effort for me to reach forty degrees on the tilt table without passing out. I plateaued between forty and fifty degrees for about a month. Many times, the therapists wouldn't lower me until I was about to black out.

♦ ♦ ♦

At some point, Barbara got word that a private room was available. I could finally get away from my third roommate, who had asked me to call him "Uncle Max." He was a sixty-five-year-old man with diabetes and a heart condition. He constantly talked to me and anyone else who would listen. Uncle Max was also legally blind. He would turn the radio on and play it loud in the middle of the night and wander around the room, touching everything.

Later, I learned that it was in fact Uncle Max who had been responsible for my move. He had been complaining about my nurses. I didn't care. The important thing was that "Kenny and Barbara" were being moved.

The single room on F Wing turned out to be too small for me, though. They couldn't even get the bed through the door without removing parts of it, with me still in it. My bed and dresser barely fit inside.

The respiratory therapy machines couldn't be plugged in there. In fact, it was difficult to bring any equipment into the room.

The air in the room was stuffy and stale. No one could open the window, because if someone did steam would come pouring in from the hospital laundry below. To get fresh air, the bathroom door and the window inside had to be opened.

Within a few days of me being moved into those tight quarters, Dr. Holtzman came by to see if I would be able to tolerate sitting in a wheelchair. He brought with him a semi-reclining one from the physical therapy department. The hospital obtained a Stryker gel cushion for the chair to reduce the risk of me developing bedsores while sitting on it. The back of the wheelchair could be lowered to a forty-five-degree angle. That was the lowest it could go.

Before I even attempted to sit on the wheelchair, the doctor needed to see whether I could tolerate lying in bed with the head of the bed raised to a forty-five-degree angle. Barbara was to crank up my bed to that angle, but the bed did not have a gauge to measure it. Barbara came up with the idea of folding a piece of paper into an isosceles right triangle. As we all learned in high school math, the two small angles of an isosceles right triangle both measure forty-five degrees. Why didn't I think of that?

Barbara raised the head of the bed slowly until it finally reached forty-five degrees. It was a higher elevation than I was used to, but I was able to tolerate it.

My legs were again wrapped in ace bandages from my ankles to my thighs. Dr. Holzman lifted me from the back while Barbara moved my legs. As soon as I was in the wheelchair, I blacked out. They put me right back into bed. I regained consciousness fairly quickly.

The next day we tried again. I got really dizzy but didn't pass out. Barbara opened the bathroom window wide and gave me ice-cold water to drink. Somehow, I stayed conscious in the wheelchair for twenty minutes. It felt good to get out of the bed, but I was dizzy the entire time.

The day after that, as I was being lifted into the chair, I said, "I'm getting dizzy." The next thing I remember I was back in bed.

Because I wasn't feeling too bad on the chair the following day, Barbara wheeled me into the lounge area. This time, it felt good moving around. I was in the chair for an hour but, by the end of that time, I couldn't wait to get back into bed. It was exhausting.

After that, I slept on and off for seven hours. Apparently, Mrs. Jeffries, my then afternoon nurse, had given me a shot for nausea. I don't remember complaining that I was nauseous. It really bothered me that I was given that shot without asking for it.

It was so difficult lifting me in those tight quarters that even Dr. Holtzman felt I needed a bigger room. The hospital administration agreed. Barbara checked to see if there were any larger private rooms available in the hospital and found one on the surgery wing. Apparently, the last occupant of the room had just died. That wing was strictly for surgical patients but Barbara knew how to outsmart the system. Because I still had a suprapubic catheter inside me, Barbara met with my urologist and asked, "Isn't that enough to consider Ken a surgery case?"

The urologist said, "Well . . ."

That was enough for Barbara. She got in touch with the right doctors, pulled the right strings, and figured that, once I was in the room, they wouldn't touch me. She was right.

It was a nice private room across from the nurses' station. Barbara was there with me from 7:00 a.m. to 3:00 p.m., almost every day. I stayed in that room from the end of December to the day of my discharge from South Nassau.

Shortly before I changed rooms, my afternoon nurse quit. She didn't give any reason. She just never showed up again. Another ornery nurse temporarily replaced her. Two days after that new nurse started, the registry replaced her with another nurse, Mrs. Andrews. She also wasn't easy to deal with. I was stuck with her, however, until the middle of January.

Throughout my hospital stay, I had to take a lot of pills. I was given a small Dixie cup filled with eleven of them, three times a day; hence, I needed to swallow thirty-three pills every day. Because I was still lying almost completely flat on my back, I had a great deal of difficulty swallowing even one. I took them one at a time and had to rest after each pill for a few minutes. By the time I was finished taking my morning pills, it was almost time to begin taking my afternoon pills.

One day, Mrs. Andrews dropped the cup with my pills on the floor. She probably didn't realize that I could see her as she picked them up, put them back in the cup, and then tried to give them to me. I refused to take them. So much for the sterile environment of the hospital.

On another afternoon, the fire alarm went off. The nurses and orderlies closed the doors in all the patients' rooms, as well the doors at the end of each hallway.

Initially, I didn't know what the loud ringing sound meant. When Mrs. Andrews told me it was a fire drill, I became really concerned and asked her what would happen if there was a real fire.

Mrs. Andrews told me not to worry. She was trained to handle that emergency. She would take the bottom sheet I was lying on and pull it and me off the bed, onto the floor. Mrs. Andrews would then drag me, on the sheet, out of my room and down the hall. I could just imagine what the fall from the bed to the floor would feel like. If I didn't re-break my neck from the fall, I certainly would have seriously injured it being dragged down the hall.

I have been worried about the possibility of a fire ever since.

♦ ♦ ♦

At some point during my stay at South Nassau, I started to feel very warm. I was hot when everyone else was cold. The window in my new room was opened a crack through most of the winter. Nurses kept an extra pillow on the windowsill so that the one that was under my head could be constantly replaced with a cooler one.

One of the side effects of my spinal cord injury was that my body thermostat was thrown out of whack. A few months later, I was cold when everyone else felt hot.

I remained severely depressed throughout my entire hospital stay. Visitors tried to take my mind off my condition but it really wasn't very helpful having them there, especially when the visitors were complete strangers.

Cornell alumni who didn't know me, but who had read about me in the *Cornell Alumni News*, would come to visit. They wouldn't know what to say, which meant I had to be the one to keep the conversation going.

When I wanted to have the visitors leave, I would give Barbara a certain look. She understood my signal and would then ask them to leave, often telling my visitors that I needed to get some more rest.

Many times, I either didn't know or remember the names of my visitors. I would usually try to pretend that I recognized them and hope that Barbara would get them to say their name sometime during the conversation. Usually the person would say his or her name when I introduced Barbara to him or her. Barbara could immediately tell whenever I was faking it and she would cover for me.

One day, a man came into my room, said hello, and asked how I was doing. I immediately went into my routine of pretending to know the person and gave Barbara the look indicating I needed her help.

To my embarrassment, rather than helping, Barbara said, right in front of the man, "You don't know his name, do you?"

I replied, "Of course, I do."

Barbara then said out loud, "What is it?"

I whispered, under my breath, "Barbara, what are you doing?"

Barbara continued to put me on the spot, "Say his name."

Again, I whispered, "What are you doing?"

Finally, Barbara started to laugh and told me that the man was her husband, David. We had never met before.

Over the previous couple of months there had been a lot of publicity about me. I received cards and letters from strangers from all over the country. A number of elementary schools had their classes write to me. One teacher must have told her students that spending months at a time in a hospital must feel like being in prison. Almost every letter from that class began with the words, "If you think you're in a prison, you should see our school."

One afternoon, I had a visit from a man who had come all the way from New Jersey. He had read about me in the newspaper. He told me he had been a high school football coach. One day, while he was demonstrating to his team how to block, he ran head first into the blocking sled, breaking his neck. He became paralyzed as a result. While he was in the hospital, a stranger visited him and gave him a plaque with the prayer from St. Francis of Assisi on it. The prayer was:

> Lord grant me the serenity to accept the things I cannot change
> The courage to change the things I can
> And the wisdom to know the difference.

My visitor eventually regained his movement and walked out of the hospital. He thought that the prayer had helped him. He hoped it would have the same effect on me.

Barbara put the plaque on the wall, right behind my bed, and kept it there throughout the rest of my stay at South Nassau. Unfortunately, it did not have the same effect on me.

Marcia Kagan, a speech therapy student at Hofstra University, visited a number of times. Although I was not receiving speech therapy, Marcia had heard that a college football player had been injured and was a patient at the hospital. She snuck into my room

Ken's hospital room in Oceanside—1971.
Photo by Leonard Kunken.

one day to meet me by pretending to help a physical therapist carry in some hot packs for my shoulders.

Marcia took a liking to me and, apparently, told her mother a lot about me. When her mother asked Marcia what I looked like, Marcia replied, "I can tell you this. He looks great in bed!"

Marcia made a large computer printout on perforated paper that said: "Kenny—Wishing You Well—The World." That printout filled the top portion of one wall of my room.

My friend Joannie Schwartz, whose father was one of the artists for the Archie comic books, brought me a poster-size picture her father had drawn. It showed Archie in bed with Betty and Veronica, with the caption underneath: "Having Betty on one side and Veronica on the other makes it hard for a guy."

I didn't grasp the hidden meaning of the caption until Barbara said that that poster would never make it into the comic books. It still took me a while.

Yvonne, who was even more innocent than I was, couldn't seem to get it. Barbara kept trying to explain it to Yvonne, by emphasizing certain words in the caption. Yvonne still didn't get it.

Barbara, who was a bit frustrated by now, kept repeating: "Yvonne, makes *it hard* for a guy! Makes it *hard* for a *guy!*" Finally, Yvonne turned beet red. It was pretty funny to watch when the light came on in her head.

Other people either sent or brought me posters, collages, drawings, and photos. Now that I had a large private room, the walls were covered with them. There were four portraits of my ten-year-old sister Meryl, each about twelve-by-fifteen inches. I particularly loved looking at those pictures.

◆ ◆ ◆

During one of my physical therapy sessions in late December, Yvonne said to me, "Try to move your arm out to the side." Whenever she would ask me to do that, she would move it out for me while I was trying to move my arm as well. On this particular occasion, Yvonne barely touched me. I was able to move my left arm out to the side a little bit, though I couldn't move it back.

I gradually strengthened my left arm to the point where I could move it out to the side without assistance. Soon, I could even move my left arm off the bed by myself. It felt pretty good. Maybe I would start to get back more movement. At least now I had some hope.

Yvonne and I tried different things after that. We worked on externally rotating my left shoulder. If my arm was positioned just so, I could flip my left arm back toward my head while I was lying down. I started to develop some muscle function in my left bicep. When I was on my right side, I could even move my left arm a little bit. Later on, if I was positioned just so on my right side, I could almost touch my chin with my left hand.

If I could touch my chin with my hand, perhaps soon I would be able to feed myself or brush my teeth.

During one of my internist's days off, a Dr. Randall came in to examine me. I had never met him before. I showed Dr. Randall what I could do. He seemed very impressed. He asked me if my feeling had moved down my body at all.

I said, "Yes, from my shoulder, to three inches down below it."

Dr. Randall then told me that the feeling should continue to go down to my toes.

Apparently, Dr. Randall then told Dr. Holtzman about my progress. Dr. Holtzman came by to see for himself. I showed him what I could do. He seemed enthused.

In January, my physical therapy routine was changed. I was now sitting up in the wheelchair one day and spending time on the tilt table the next. Previously, I had been going on the tilt table five days a week.

Sometime in January, I confronted Yvonne and asked her what type of improvement I could expect. She told me there wasn't much hope for more muscle return.

I was devastated, but I figured that intensive physical therapy at Rusk still offered some hope.

♦ ♦ ♦

If I was ever going to return to school, I would need to find a way to read on my own. Because I was not able to turn the pages of a book, a number of different electronic page-turners were brought in for me to try. None of them worked well. They either turned too many pages at once or didn't turn a page at all. I also had difficulty reading what was on the page-turners because I was only able to tolerate the head of the bed being raised to a forty-five-degree angle.

Someone suggested that the page-turner might work better on a magazine rather than on a thick book. One of my visitors brought in a *Playboy* magazine and put it on the page-turner. The device turned a few pages until it got to the centerfold. It "got so excited" seeing the picture, it lost control and ripped the page to shreds. Even machines react to *Playboy*.

A large cassette player was purchased for me. My psychology professor, Jim Maas, as well as my Development of Human Behavior professor, Urie Bronfenbrenner, taped the remainder of their lectures for the fall semester and sent them to me. I had hoped to still get credit for those courses by listening to the lectures on the tape recorder. However, as soon as the tapes were turned on, I would inevitably fall asleep. I found listening to music far more enjoyable and soon developed a nice collection of music tapes.

◆ ◆ ◆

By mid-January, my family and I decided we would no longer continue with Mrs. Andrews. In fact, I wanted to try to get through the 3:00 to 11:00 p.m. shift without any specials. We received permission from the hospital to have family members and friends stay with me for the afternoon. The hospital floor attendants still turned me and gave me pills but the floor nurses didn't really have to do much more for me. The arrangement usually worked out fine.

Many times, either Aunt Lorraine or one of her children, Jill or Roy, covered the afternoon shift. My Aunt Honey, More Mom's sister, occasionally took a shift.

Even though Barbara's shift was supposed to end at 3:00, she never left at that time. Sometimes she didn't leave until 5:30, after deciding at 3:30 to shampoo my hair.

My favorite "nurse" was my ten-year-old sister Meryl. Barbara showed Meryl what to do. Meryl fed me and sometimes even gave me my pills. She did everything well and felt bad when the time came for her to be relieved.

Not having an afternoon special was one way to cut back on the medical bills, which were adding up. Despite the fact that my father had a major medical policy, which had covered me at the time of my injury, a lot of my expenses were not being reimbursed.

The policy was with Mutual of New York, the insurance company at which my father had been an agent for the past twenty-three years. It initially had a cap of $25,000. That cap had been exceeded fairly quickly but, fortunately, Mutual of New York increased my coverage.

Everyone was concerned about the enormous costs for my care. To help with the expenses, Coach Cullen created a Ken Kunken Fund in Ithaca, while the Oceanside community started the Ken Kunken Medical Fund. Both funds held numerous fundraisers, which also generated a lot of publicity about me.

◆ ◆ ◆

Barbara had arranged to go to Washington, D.C., with her husband for a week during his school vacation. Before she left, she made certain that she found a suitable replacement to help me. She chose Doris Glier, who had a good sense of humor and was nice to have around.

Barbara left Doris with four full pages of written notes to make sure everything went smoothly during her absence. Nobody but Barbara would have done something like that. She wrote exactly what Doris was to do every minute of her shift. Doris carried that set of notes around with her as if it was the Bible. From that point on, whenever Barbara needed to have a day off, she would arrange to have Doris as my morning special.

On Doris's first day, I became very uncomfortable. I had a terrible headache and upset stomach. I was hot, my blood pressure was high, and my temperature was elevated. My bladder wasn't draining properly. Something was blocking the suprapubic tube. The floor attendant tried to irrigate the catheter, but still my bladder wouldn't empty. Even though the urologist had been changing the tube every three weeks, it had corroded inside of me. The attendant called the resident doctor to change the tube but it took a couple of hours before it was done. Once it was, I felt much better.

The day Barbara returned from Washington, I got a letter from J. Edgar Hoover. I thought Barbara had put someone up to that, but she denied having anything to do with it. Later, I learned that Hoover was a friend of one of Lynbrook Pop's friends.

The letter was dated January 28, 1971.

Dear Mr. Kunken:

One of our mutual friends, Mr. Theodore Diamond, has informed me of your injury and I want to join your friends in extending best wishes for a complete recovery.

I know it will be difficult for you to remain in the hospital while your classmates continue the school year; however, let me urge you to follow your doctor's advice and never lose heart. Your friends are all rooting for you and I know the same courage and determination you displayed on the football field will see you through.

Sincerely yours,

J. Edgar Hoover

Everybody was very impressed that I got a personal letter from the Director of the FBI.

♦ ♦ ♦

Around February 15, South Nassau obtained an old electric wheelchair for me to try. It had a bar overhead supporting my left arm in a sling. Because I was now able to move my arm slightly out to the side, but not across my body, the sling was adjusted to enable me to move my left arm a little bit to the right as well.

The wheelchair's joystick was missing, so they ended up taking a pen from my brother Steve, who happened to be visiting me at the time, and inserted it there. The fingers of my left hand were then tied around the pen to enable me to work the wheelchair.

I moved the wheelchair into the hallway by myself. It took quite a while to do so. Barbara and Yvonne followed. Dr. Holtzman and many nurses were watching, cheering me on. It went relatively well.

I practiced riding on my own to the therapy room. It was really difficult. Unfortunately, that wheelchair didn't recline. When

I was sitting close to the upright position it was very hard for me to hold my head up. My neck was still very weak. It also was very tiring, having my left arm in the sling for so long.

Things were moving along slowly but I was happy to be making progress.

One day, in late February, the *New York Daily News* sent a reporter to write a story about me. The reporter came with a photographer, who took lots of pictures.

The *Daily News* article appeared on Sunday, February 28. I was disappointed with it. The article misquoted parts of the interview and misspelled some names as well. Nevertheless, the South Nassau Communities Hospital personnel were very impressed.

On February 20, Dr. Holtzman asked me if I would still like to go to the Rusk Institute. Of course, I said yes. I always felt that, if anyone could help me, it would be the people at Rusk.

Dr. Holtzman tried to convince me, again, that South Nassau would be able to fit me with the same braces, splints, and wheelchair they would at Rusk. He encouraged me to continue my rehabilitation at South Nassau but I was still determined to go to Rusk as soon as possible.

Dr. Russek, one of the doctors from Rusk whom Uncle Mel had spoken with while I was in Elmira, came to South Nassau and examined me. He found that I was making progress, was now stronger and was ready to go to Rusk sometime in March. A couple of days later, I was informed I would be going on March 1.

Before I left, the physical therapists threw a surprise party for me in the therapy room and the respiratory therapists made a party for me in my room. Barbara told Yvonne that strawberry shortcake was my favorite cake, so Yvonne baked one especially for me.

I said my good-byes to the doctors, nurses, and other specialists. I had gone from being considered a "behavioral problem" to being a well-liked celebrity.

Many thoughts raced through my head that last night in South Nassau. Things had been getting better there for me. It almost seemed a shame to give it up now. I was leaving some good and close friends. The move was actually kind of sad for all of us.

In addition, I knew it would be far more difficult for my relatives and childhood friends to visit me in New York City as often as they did in Oceanside.

My last night at South Nassau, Mrs. Foster gave me a sleeping pill to make sure I would get some rest. Barbara came in early the next morning. She gave me an enema and bathed and dressed me.

My cousin Jill came in while I was getting ready and asked for help with some trigonometry problems because she had a big math test coming up. It was really strange trying to cram in some tutoring while I was getting into my "good clothes" for the first time in seventeen weeks.

I hadn't been outdoors in months. It happened to be a beautiful, spring-like day. Aunt Lorraine, Jill, Roy, Ronnie, and Jeanie stood outside South Nassau, crying. I don't know why, but everybody was very emotional.

I was leaving with the hope of getting my movement back. I was also a little apprehensive: suppose even Rusk couldn't help me?

Chapter 8

Rusk—The Best in the World?

♦ ♦ ♦

Rusk was located on 1st Avenue and 34th Street, in New York City. It was an easy address for me to remember. All I had to do was to think of the movie *Miracle on 34th Street*. After all, Rusk was where miracles happen. I was convinced mine would soon be one of them.

As it turned out, at that time, there was no facility called the Rusk Institute. Dr. Howard Rusk was the head doctor at the Institute of Rehabilitation Medicine. Hence, the reason everyone referred to it as the Rusk Institute. In 1984 the name was officially changed to the Rusk Institute of Rehabilitation Medicine.

My father met us in front of the building. I was lifted out of the ambulance and wheeled, on a gurney, through the front entrance, into the lobby, up the elevator, and onto the fourth floor.

I wasn't able to see much because I was lying flat on my back. The ceiling of that "great institution" looked unremarkable. When I was able to turn my head, I saw that the hallway was lined with wheelchairs.

I was wheeled into room 415. Three other patients were already there. The room seemed too small to accommodate four people.

Immediately to the right of the door was the bathroom. I was slid onto the first bed past the bathroom. Another patient was in the bed to my right, next to the window. To the left of the entrance door there was a sink and two other beds.

Once I was in bed, I could not see the door. I was hidden from view from the outside of the room by the bathroom wall. I didn't like that.

It felt like the temperature in the room was over eighty degrees. My bed, tucked away in the corner, seemed to have no ventilation. I asked if we could open a window but the patient to my right, closest to the window, complained that, if we did, there would be a draft on him. I was roasting.

During the afternoon that first day, a steady stream of doctors was in and out of the room. One of them, Dr. Barard, asked me what I hoped to achieve at Rusk. His question seemed silly to me. Of course I told him, "I want to get my movement back."

Dr. Barard replied that I wasn't being very realistic.

I was surprised he said that. Why else would I have come to Rusk? Of course, I wanted to get my movement back. How could he respond that way before he even examined me?

Soon, another doctor came into the room and asked me to show him what I could do. Now, I had my chance to show a doctor at Rusk all the progress I had made since the injury.

I demonstrated that I could not only shrug my shoulders but also could move my left arm slightly out to the side. If my left arm was bent at the elbow, I could externally rotate my shoulder a bit and move it a little. Those accomplishments had really excited the doctors at South Nassau. I was looking forward to getting my first favorable feedback from one of the experts in the field.

To say that the doctor was not impressed would be an understatement. He came right out and said to me, "That's not very much."

Not only didn't I get the compliment I was expecting, he as much as said I hadn't accomplished anything. I was devastated. Apparently, all my hard work during the past four months amounted to nothing.

Whenever I yawned, my right arm moved a little bit out to the side. As the doctor was leaving, he told me to make sure to keep my right hand on the bed. As soon as he left, my right hand fell off the bed. There was no aide nearby to put it back and I, obviously, could not ring the call button. How harmful was it, if my hand was off the bed for any length of time? The doctors at South Nassau had never even mentioned that, which just confirmed what I thought: they really didn't know enough about patients with spinal cord injuries. When I was at South Nassau, I never even noticed where my right hand was. Who knows what damage I might have already done? I started to feel panicky.

I didn't find out until much later that, aside from my hand getting a little more swollen, there were no ill effects from having my hand hang over the side of the bed. Of course, if my entire right arm were to fall off the bed, it would pull on my shoulder, which was weak and sore to begin with, and cause me a lot of pain.

That doctor had no idea how much he needlessly scared me. His visit was followed by an unfortunate comment made by a nurse a few days later.

Before that nurse came into the room, Mike, one of my new roommates, had complained about how much his Foley catheter was bothering him. He asked me if I had the same problem.

I told him, no, because I had a suprapubic tube. My catheter wasn't inserted through the urethra but, rather went right through my lower abdomen, directly into my bladder.

Mike thought that that sounded much better, so he asked Mr. Whelan, the nurse who worked with the urologist, about getting that type of catheter.

Mr. Whelan, while standing just a few feet away from me, and unaware that I had a suprapubic tube, told Mike, "A suprapubic tube is only inserted as a last resort. A patient has to be in really bad shape to need it." Again, I couldn't believe it. I knew I was in bad shape but I guess I didn't know exactly how bad I actually was.

The one positive comment I received was that I must have had tremendous nursing care to go without bedsores for so long. Some of the other patients at Rusk had to have skin grafts to help their bedsores heal.

I had clung to the hope that the medical personnel at Rusk would put me back on my feet. Now I was confronted with the realization that there were people who remained paralyzed from a spinal cord injury for years and even the Rusk Institute was not able to help them. If Rusk was not able to help them, why should I believe that Rusk could help me?

The patient in the bed to my right was in his late twenties. His name was Richard and he was at Rusk for his annual checkup. Richard had broken his neck diving into the shallow end of a pool. He previously had been a patient at Rusk but they couldn't help him regain his movement. He had been a quadriplegic for more than eight years. Richard had some use of his arms down to his wrists. His wrists and hands both looked deformed to me.

Richard told me that he was an alcoholic before his accident. He said he didn't drink at all now. Richard didn't have a job and still lived at home with his family. It took him an hour just to dress himself.

Richard was a talker. I, however, was in no mood to talk. Just spending time with Richard was depressing. I couldn't imagine being in his condition for eight years. However, within two months, I would be told that my condition would never even be as good as Richard's. I would never have as much movement as he had, since I was hurt higher in the neck.

Dave was in the bed opposite me. He was twenty-two years old and had been paralyzed three years earlier, diving into the ocean. Dave had a little more movement than Richard, even though they both had injured their necks at the same level. Dave, like Richard, didn't seem to be doing anything productive with his life. Dave drank often and smoked marijuana as well.

Apparently, drinking was permitted in the rooms at Rusk, or at least no one seemed to try to stop it. I also heard it was not uncommon for some of the patients to go up to an open outdoor area on the roof and smoke marijuana.

My third roommate's name was Mike. He was twenty-five years old and had been injured in January 1971, less than three months after me. Mike had been in a car accident, which left him a paraplegic. He had full use of his arms but no use of his legs.

I started to think that, if I was ever fortunate enough to be able to progress to Mike's condition, a paraplegic, I would be thankful.

Mike had been a heroin addict before his accident. He had dealt drugs to support his $100 a day habit. Since his accident, Mike hadn't been able to get hold of any heroin but he told me that he would start again if he could. He said he had no willpower.

Before my accident, I was straight as an arrow. I had never been drunk and never even seen marijuana, let alone heroin. Now here I was, confined to bed and totally helpless, living just a few feet away from a heroin addict, an alcoholic, and a marijuana smoker who drank often.

I was nervous, uncomfortable, and I suppose, a little bit scared. In fact, I was almost thankful that my roommates were paralyzed. Who knows what they might do to me in the middle of the night if they weren't.

I spoke to a social worker and told her I wanted to be in a private room. She told me it would be better for me if I had roommates.

I also told my father I wanted a private room. He said that was not going to happen at Rusk. I was going to be treated like everyone else.

◆ ◆ ◆

By my second day at Rusk, I was really upset. Even though they had all my medical records from both South Nassau and Elmira, they insisted on redoing all the tests. X-rays were taken of my neck, an intravenous pyelogram test (IVP) to check my kidneys, and an electro cardiogram were done. There was also another round of pulmonary function tests. With the exception of going for those tests, I was confined to my bed. For the first four days, there was absolutely no therapy, not even range of motion exercises.

By the time I went for the pulmonary function tests, I had reached the end of my rope. Why was my body left so broken and my mind fully intact? I was so disgusted, frustrated, and depressed I actually tried to "will" myself to lose my mind. I was convinced that, if I no longer knew what was happening to me, I would be better off. But, just like everything else, I was not even able to do that.

As if I wasn't feeling bad enough at that point, the pulmonary function technician felt it important to tell me that my roommates didn't like me. She told me they were complaining about me.

Because there was no privacy whatsoever in our room, my three roommates could hear everything I said. They knew I had asked to be in a private room. They were probably saying among themselves, "Who does he think he is? Does he think that he is too good to share a room with us?"

It didn't help matters that my roommates had seen the article about me in the *Daily News* the day before I arrived. They had never received that kind of publicity. What made my spinal cord injury more important or newsworthy than theirs?

Rather than having private duty nurses, as I had had at South Nassau, I had two private attendants, each working a twelve-hour shift. My night attendant's name was Mike. He was in his late thirties. Working with me was Mike's first position at Rusk.

When company was around, Mike tried to act like he had a lot of experience and knew exactly what he was doing. He seemed very attentive to my needs then. But when my visitors left, Mike did almost nothing. He didn't even stay in the room with me. He would return every two hours only to turn me.

My morning attendant's name was Stanley. He was a large man, around forty years old. For some reason, we just didn't get along. I don't remember why.

Every morning a team of doctors, nurses, therapists, and students would make their rounds in one big group. They would come into the room, turn to my attendant, and ask, "How is Ken today? Did he have a good night?"

After a while, as soon as the medical team came into the room, I would immediately turn to my attendant and anxiously await his response to the question about how I was feeling. I didn't know whether I was having a good day or a bad day until my attendant answered the question.

You would think the doctors would have known enough to ask me directly but, apparently, they didn't. That was typical of the attitude and treatment at Rusk. The patients were treated like they didn't know anything. The doctors didn't like answering patients' questions either, even when someone was bold enough to ask.

Just four months earlier, I had been studying engineering at one of the most prestigious schools in the country. I had injured my neck, not my head, and yet, from the moment of my injury on, I was treated like I didn't have a brain.

Rusk was "an institution" in every sense of the word. The patients were either reduced to a stereotype or, in effect, given a number and treated like sheep. Sometimes a doctor would bring a group of visiting medical professionals involved in rehabilitation right up to my bedside. Without saying a word to me, the doctor would simply say to the people he was giving a tour, "Kunken. High quad. Football injury." He would then move to the next bed. Apparently, those few words described everything there was to know about me. I felt like I had lost my identity.

As at South Nassau, I was supposed to get IPPB, Intermittent Positive Pressure Breathing, treatments, two times a day, fifteen minutes at a time. I didn't receive them at all for the first week I was at Rusk. When the treatments were given to me, they were done by nurses and attendants, rather than by specially trained respiratory therapists. The nurses and attendants giving the treatments were sometimes not familiar with the equipment. I had to explain to them how to do it.

At Rusk, the breathing tube for the IPPB machine was attached to a bar. The staff didn't even need to hold it for me. Someone would start the machine, then leave the room for fifteen minutes before returning to turn it off. Sometimes the tube fell out of my mouth almost immediately and there was nobody around to put it back in before the fifteen minutes were up.

When my physical therapy finally began, I was again scheduled to spend time on the tilt table. The first time I was on the tilt table at Rusk, I got dizzy at thirty-five degrees. When I had left South Nassau, a few days earlier, I had gotten to sixty degrees. I was worried I was regressing.

I was also supposed to spend some time each day sitting in a wheelchair. Rather than being provided with top-of-the-line equipment, I was given an old, broken-down wheelchair to use. I needed to sit reclined, because I couldn't tolerate being upright. I needed a headrest to support my neck and head because my neck muscles were still too weak to hold my head up unassisted. It wasn't long, however, before an orderly took my headrest and gave it to another patient. It took a while for me to get it back. The first time I was lifted into a wheelchair at Rusk, I only lasted an hour.

My first physical therapist's name was Sandy. She was with me for a few weeks before I was switched to another therapist. It was supposed to be helpful to continue with the same therapist during your entire time at Rusk, but I had five different physical therapists while I was there. It seemed the therapists only wanted to work with the patients that had a chance to improve. It made them look better. I suppose it was obvious to everyone, early on, I was not going to be one of their success stories. Quite often, only students or physical therapy aides were working on me.

One day, while a student was moving my right leg out to the side, doing range of motion exercises, there was a loud pop. The student immediately ran to get her supervisor. The supervisor hurried over, felt my hip, and moved my leg out to the side the same way the student had. My leg moved without making a sound this time. The supervisor told the student I was fine.

Apparently, the student thought she had just broken my hip. When she ran for her supervisor, I started to think so as well. It was certainly nice to know that she hadn't, but it was not very comforting for me to continue to be worked on by students, especially believing they could, in fact, break my bones.

I began spending some time each day on the tilt table and one to two hours a day on the wheelchair. Either way, I was still getting dizzy. My blood pressure would drop whenever my head was higher than my feet. When I was on the tilt table, the table was usually in the hallway, not in the therapy room. There was constant traffic walking past me as I struggled with dizziness. Sometimes, the therapist or an aide would move the tilt table to a small corridor, near a window overlooking the East River. That certainly provided me with a better view but there were now fewer people around to call to for help when I needed assistance, which was often.

University Hospital, which was attached by a tunnel to Rusk, sometimes showed movies at night. Patients from both Rusk and University Hospital attended the shows. Two weeks after I arrived at Rusk, the movie *Charley* was being shown.

My evening attendant, Mike, really wanted me to go. I was not in the mood but Mike tried to convince me that it would be good for me to get out of the room and do something different. I believe that he just wanted to see the movie.

My grandparents were visiting, as they did almost every day, and they also encouraged me to try it. They offered to go with me.

I had been lying in bed at the time. From the moment I was lifted into the wheelchair, I was dizzy. The entire time I was wheeled to the theater, I was dizzy. We frequently had to stop so that Mike could tilt me back. I needed to have my legs elevated and my head positioned on the same level as my heart.

I was still extremely dizzy when we got to the theater. Mike asked me to try to stick it out. I sat tilted back, leaning against the back wall, for the entire movie. The dizziness never went away.

The movie was based on the book *Flowers for Algernon*. Cliff Robertson played Charley. Charley was a developmentally disabled man who underwent an experimental procedure, which turned him into a genius. Unfortunately, the improvement in his mental condition was only temporary. Charley could tell he was regressing. He tried to fight it but there was nothing he could do to stop the backward slide. By the end of the movie, Charley was back to his original cognitive state.

When the movie ended, I was still extremely dizzy. As Mike wheeled me out of the theater, I told him I needed to be tilted back again. Since a crowd of people was leaving the theater right behind us, Mike told me, "Wait till we get around the corner."

I couldn't wait. I blacked out and had another out-of-body experience. I was floating and dancing, effortlessly, in outer space. It felt great. I was free from all my physical limitations, if only for a few seconds. I did not want to return to my paralyzed body.

Suddenly, a force seemed to be pulling me back. I tried to resist it but I couldn't. I felt like it sucked me right back into my body. I felt like Charley must have felt near the end of the movie, when he was regressing and could no longer fight it. Like everything else that had happened to me during the past four and a half months, I had no control over it.

As I was coming to, I heard my grandparents saying, "Ken, are you all right? Are you all right?" It took a while before I could respond.

I was in unfamiliar surroundings, with strangers walking past me as if nothing had happened. I wasn't sure I would be able to make it back to my room without passing out again. I was terribly upset by the experience, especially having my grandparents witness me in that condition. I know it worried them a great deal.

Mike finally got me back to my room and into bed. It still took a while before I started to feel better, physically. It took considerably longer before I felt better emotionally: "I can't do anything. I can't go anywhere. No one can help me. Maybe I should just stay in bed and not even think about doing anything productive. What's the point of even trying?"

Shortly after that evening, I stopped having Mike as my night attendant. Because he didn't do much more than turn me every two hours, I decided I might as well just have the floor orderlies do that. I didn't notice much of a difference once that change was made.

◆ ◆ ◆

Not long after the movie theater incident, an orthotist fitted me with a lumbar sacral support, which everyone referred to as a corset. It was put on me when I was being dressed in the morning. I then wore it for the rest of the day.

The corset had a number of benefits. It improved my posture while sitting in a wheelchair. Without it I couldn't sit up straight and would fall over whenever I leaned the slightest bit to one side.

The corset helped my breathing by putting some additional pressure on my diaphragm. It was supposed to prevent my blood pressure from dropping too low by putting some pressure on my blood vessels as well. The corset helped, but wasn't enough to keep me from getting dizzy whenever I sat up.

A few weeks later, I attempted to take my first shower in almost six months. I passed out when I was lifted into the shower wheelchair without my corset on. I never made it to the shower the next few times either. I always had to be returned to bed almost immediately.

Sometime in the middle of March, Mr. Whelan removed the suprapubic tube. The doctors wanted me to get used to my bladder emptying on its own.

I had what they called a neurogenic bladder. When my bladder reached a certain level, the sphincter valve at the end of it would, hopefully, open and allow the urine to drain. My bladder never emptied completely though. It always kept a high residual of urine inside. That high residual became a breeding ground for bacteria, resulting in frequent urinary tract infections.

I wore a condom that had a hole at the end of it. It was attached to a tube that connected to either a leg bag, during the day, or a bedside drainage bag at night. The doctors referred to that type of bladder management as condom drainage.

To attach the condom, my penis was first painted with a beta-dine solution to protect the skin. Special glue called "skin bond cement" was spread over the shaft of the penis. The condom would then be rolled over it to adhere to the glue. Unfortunately, as my penis changed size throughout the day, the condom would leak or come off entirely. As a result, I would quite often be left sitting in a puddle of urine.

Sometimes my bladder just wouldn't empty on its own. I either had to be bent forward, to put pressure on it, or reclined, to take pressure off it. Sometimes nothing worked. When my bladder filled beyond a certain level, I would get a terrible headache, sweat profusely, and my blood pressure would go extremely high.

I asked one of the floor nurses what would happen if my blood pressure went too high. He matter-of-factly responded that I could have a stroke. Because I had trouble emptying my bladder every day, I constantly worried that, someday, I was going to have one.

Managing all my bodily functions was a major chore. The staff tried to get me on a regular bowel routine. Before my injury,

I usually had a bowel movement every day. Now, every bowel movement seemed to take hours, which was just too difficult, disruptive, and uncomfortable for me to do every day. Instead, I tried to get used to having a bowel movement every other night. It was accomplished while I was lying on my side in bed, by inserting a suppository into my rectum. The bowel movement would end up on chux and paper towels, and be cleaned up while I was still in bed on my side. Although the directions for the suppositories said they took fifteen minutes to work, it usually took at least an hour and a half for me to have a movement.

In addition to the many pills I had been taking ever since South Nassau, the doctors at Rusk added Valium to the list. Valium was supposed to help lessen my muscle spasms, of which I had many. I was also told that Valium would help the sphincter valve at the end of my bladder relax, to enable it to empty easier.

Most of my days and nights at Rusk were extremely boring. Typically, I would wake up at 3 a.m. and lie there staring at the ceiling, wondering what it would be like had I not been hurt. I would remain awake for hours, finally dozing off around 6 a.m. I would soon be awakened to take pills, to be turned, and then awakened again for more pills.

One day, while I was still lying in bed, waiting to be lifted onto my wheelchair, my black-and-white television happened to be on and tuned to the PBS station. I was not able to turn the channel by myself, so I started to watch the next program. It was *Sesame Street*, which had been on for about a year by then, but I had never seen it before. It actually was very entertaining. I am sure the nurses and attendants who were going in and out of the room must have thought it a bit strange that a twenty-year-old college student seemed mesmerized by a children's show. At the end of the half hour, the announcer stated, "Today's show was brought to you by the letter 'I' and the number '5.'"

For some reason, that struck me as incredibly funny. I started laughing hysterically. Whoever was nearby probably thought that I had finally flipped out and lost my mind.

I saw a number of patients at Rusk who seemed to have mental breakdowns while there. Perhaps the staff did not think my behavior was so unusual after all.

♦ ♦ ♦

Gradually, I started different therapies. In addition to physical therapy and spending time on the tilt table, I was now going for occupational therapy (OT).

The name "occupational therapy" is misleading. OT was not intended to help me get a job, it was to help me develop more functional use of my arms, often by utilizing the aid of braces and splints. The therapy took place in a large room, often filled with senior citizen stroke patients who seemed to be mostly doing basket weaving. A good deal of the time, other than the therapists, there was no one in the room within forty years of my age. Being surrounded every day by elderly stroke patients made me feel even more miserable.

During OT, a therapist would put my left arm in a splint that extended from midway up my forearm, down to the middle of my hand. A stick would be placed into a special clip that slid into a slot in the splint. My arm would then be placed in a sling.

The sling was needed to support my arm, because I was not strong enough to lift it in the air, or to hold it there, for any length of time. The sling was angled to make it a little easier for me to move my arm even a short distance.

Eventually, the sling was replaced by a set of braces called a balanced forearm orthosis (BFO). The BFO involved three different metal pieces, which fit together and then were inserted into a bracket attached to my wheelchair. Those braces supported the weight of my arm and could also be angled to allow me to move my arm more easily. The BFO protruded about eight inches to the side, making it almost impossible for me to fit through doorways with it on.

I used the stick to try to move a small block across a table. I worked on that movement, over and over again, for weeks. Sometime later, I worked on trying to feed myself. To do that, I used a fork, the end of which swiveled. The fork was attached to a long piece of metal, which was inserted into my wrist splint. With my left arm in the BFO, and with the fork in my wrist splint, I would try to push food against a metal rim attached to the side of a plate and eventually spear or scoop the food with the fork.

The splint had to be angled perfectly for me to have any chance of getting the end of the fork near my mouth. The food frequently ended up on the floor, my lapboard, or shirt, rarely in my mouth. Occasionally, I would stab my face with the fork. I didn't know eating could be so dangerous. It was extremely tiring as well. I burned up more calories trying to eat than I took in with food.

Sometimes, instead of inserting the swivel fork into my splint, the therapist would insert a clamp-type device that could hold a donut or sandwich. In trying to learn how to use that splint during those first few weeks, I must have eaten more donuts than I had during my previous twenty years.

After a number of weeks of OT, I began receiving prevocational therapy. There, I learned to type and turn the pages of a book, using a stick with a rubber tip on the end. The stick was inserted into the same wrist splint I used in OT. While in prevocational therapy, I also learned to write a little bit by inserting a pen into my wrist splint in place of the rubber-tipped stick. Whether I was typing, turning pages of a book, or writing, I still needed to use the BFO for support.

Fortunately, I was left-handed before I was hurt. All of those tasks would have been even more difficult had I been right-handed, since I had no movement in my right arm.

I was now receiving a half hour of range of motion exercises, a half hour of progressive resistance exercises, one hour of occupational therapy, one hour of prevocational therapy, and one hour on the tilt table each weekday. Most of the other twenty hours were spent in bed. Later, the prevocational therapy was increased to one hour in the morning and one in the afternoon.

One morning, as usual, during the doctors' rounds, they gave me my therapy schedule for the day. I was surprised to see that they scheduled me for "mat class." The last time I had been on a mat was when I was wrestling in school. In mat class at Rusk, the

Ken in prevocational therapy—1971.
Photo by Don Hightower.

therapist would lay me down on a mat, part of the time on my back and part of the time on my stomach. When I was on my stomach, the therapist would try to prop me up on my forearms. It was uncomfortable and difficult for me to support my head. I was also worried that one or both of my arms would collapse under me and my face would slam against the mat.

Breathing was also very difficult when I was in that position. As a result of the surgery in Elmira, I could no longer turn my head all the way to one side because the operation had decreased the range of motion in my neck.

When I was on my back in mat class, the therapist would sit me up and let go to see if I could maintain my balance. I couldn't. We tried it a number of times, without any success.

Mat class seemed like a complete waste of time and energy. After a week, the therapist finally agreed and took me out of the class.

Before I left, one of the patients there, a man in his sixties who also had a spinal cord injury, sarcastically said to me that I better take advantage of whatever publicity I was getting now, because "Nobody gives a damn about you when you get older."

He didn't intend to be mean. He was just frustrated and depressed about what he was going through. Still, it made me worry about what things would be like when I got older.

The gentlemen had been referring to publicity I had been receiving for both the Oceanside and Cornell Fund drives.

Following my spinal cord injury, I had more than enough to worry about, without also being concerned about the financial aspects of my care. Fortunately, my father took care of all of those details. The hospital expenses and medical costs were astronomical. There were numerous other expenses as well.

The Ken Kunken Fund at Cornell and the Kenny Kunken Medical Fund in Oceanside were started to help cover some of my medical expenses. A fund was even started at Columbia University, the school against which I was playing when I got hurt. Partly as a result of all those fundraisers, there were even more human-interest stories about me in the newspapers.

A reporter from the Long Island newspaper *Newsday* came to Rusk to interview me for a story. A reporter from the *New York Daily News* came the day after to do a similar one. The *New York Post* sent a reporter soon after that.

A few days later, a woman I had never met before awakened me from a brief nap. She appeared to be in her late forties and had read the story about me in the *New York Post*. She told me that her son had been hurt in a car accident, two years before, and that he, too, had been paralyzed from the neck down, for five days. He refused medical treatment. He prayed instead. Miraculously, he was up on his feet within a week. She said my paralysis was all in my mind and, if I believed strongly enough in both God and myself, I, too, would be up on my feet in a short period of time. Of course, that wasn't so. If it were, I would have been up and running the day of my accident. Her son must have had a different type of injury than mine. After the initial shock of his accident, all his movement returned. It was no miracle, no result of prayer to God.

Anyway, I heard virtually that same story about wonder religions, from many different people, many different times, over and over again. And over and over again, I tried to explain the medical aspects of a spinal cord injury as best I could. And over and over again, they refused to listen. It was hard to make some people understand that, no matter how hard I tried to move my arms and legs, they would not move.

While I enjoyed having unlimited visitors, that did not extend to unannounced strangers. How could I be sure someone more dangerous than that eccentric woman wouldn't, one day, pay me a visit?

We were all warned not to keep any valuables in our room. It just wasn't safe. My small television had to be chained to a table, to ensure it didn't vanish.

♦ ♦ ♦

Around the beginning of April, I was finally able to change my daytime attendant. I was able to replace Stanley with Mary, a woman in her forties. Mary left a lot to be desired, but she was an improvement over Stanley.

One day, when Mary was turning me from my back to my right side, she let go too soon and I started to fall out of bed. My upper body was dangling over the side and my left forearm had hit the floor. My head was only inches away. Mary caught me just below my knees and held on until help arrived.

When I later related that incident to Barbara Crook, with whom my family kept in close contact during my entire stay in Rusk, she became very upset: first, that it happened at all, and, second, that I wasn't immediately checked out by a doctor to see if I had injured myself during the mishap. I had no feeling a few inches below my shoulders, so I could have broken a bone and not even known it.

♦ ♦ ♦

On Friday, April 9, Aunt Lorraine called the hospital and asked if I'd like to come to her house in Oceanside the next day, for the first Passover Seder. Barbara, who was not Jewish, offered to pick me up in her Volkswagen, drive me both ways, and stay with me during the Seder.

That would be the first time in more than twenty-two weeks that I would be away from a hospital, doctors, and emergency care. My family and I were all really nervous but we figured that, since Barbara would be with me, we could try it.

We checked with the doctors at Rusk to make sure it would be okay. They said that I could go, but at the first sign of a headache or any trouble, I would have to be brought back immediately.

I was still almost constantly dizzy and didn't know if I could tolerate sitting in a car seat for any length of time. I was worried we would be stuck in New York City traffic for hours. Barbara's car had bucket seats in the front, so at least my seat could be reclined. Barbara brought along smelling salts, just in case.

Lifting me in and out of the Volkswagen was not easy, so my still-fourteen-year-old cousin, Roy, helped with the lifting and traveled with us both ways. A manual wheelchair was folded up and squeezed into the back of the car, with Roy beside it.

Once we arrived in Oceanside, Barbara and Roy lifted me into the wheelchair and pulled me up the four steps to get into the house. We all, basically, held our breath for the couple of hours I was in Oceanside. We made it through the evening without any mishaps and I didn't pass out. *Success!*

♦ ♦ ♦

Within a relatively short period of time after my arrival at Rusk, two of my roommates were discharged. I was able to move my bed next to the sink. That gave me, and my visitors, of which I still had many, more space. I had some room on both sides of my bed, as well as a partial view out the door. Unfortunately, above the door was the air conditioning vent. In the spring, the air conditioning at Rusk became unbearably cold. Because the vent was now so near, it constantly blew on me. The staff couldn't turn the air off. They tried taping cardboard and Saran Wrap over it but the force of the air blew everything right off.

While at Oceanside, I felt very warm, even with the windows open and the thermostat at fifty-five degrees. But at Rusk, it all changed and I was now constantly cold. In addition to my body thermostat being out of whack, low blood pressure and lack of movement made it even worse. Frequently, I had chills and often shivered uncontrollably. It could take hours before I warmed up and was comfortable again.

I still have tremendous problems keeping my body temperature regulated. While I am usually cold, there are times when I become too hot. When that happens, my body is not able to cool itself down, because I don't seem to perspire properly. As a result, the heat builds up inside me, so much so that I can get heat stroke when the temperature around me is above eighty-five degrees.

And yet, when either my bladder or bowels have trouble emptying, I break into heavy sweating a few inches below my shoulders and up. I frequently can be having chills while I am sweating profusely at the same time. I just can't win.

Chapter 9

The Senate Health Subcommittee Hearing

◆ ◆ ◆

On April 13, the Long Island newspaper *Newsday* featured an editorial titled "The Kunken Case." It described my accident and how much my care was costing. One of Senator Edward Kennedy's aides saw the editorial.

At that time, Senator Kennedy had been conducting Senate Subcommittee hearings on health care in different parts of the country. The health care system in America was dysfunctional and, clearly, needed to be fixed.

On April 14, at 4 p.m., the senator's aide came to Rusk. My grandparents and father were visiting. I was on the tilt table in the hallway, looking out over the East River.

The aide told us that Senator Kennedy would be at Hofstra University on Long Island the following day conducting hearings concerning health care issues. The aide asked if my father and I would be willing to go to Hofstra and speak to Senator Kennedy.

We said we would.

I had the impression that Senator Kennedy wanted to speak with me informally, just one-on-one. That sounded great.

When I went to sleep on April 14, I had really bad chills. I spent a miserable night, shivering through most of it, and woke up feeling terrible.

I told the doctors at Rusk how I was feeling, expecting them to tell me I shouldn't go to Hofstra that day. To my surprise, they said, "You'll get over it." They clearly wanted me to keep my appointment with the senator.

I am sure they felt that, if one of their patients had the opportunity to speak to Senator Kennedy about health care, he or she shouldn't pass it up. It may also have crossed their minds that Senator Kennedy's father, Joseph Kennedy, had been a patient at Rusk in the early 1960s, after he had suffered a stroke. Having Joseph Kennedy as a patient greatly enhanced the Rusk Institute's reputation. Having one of Rusk's patients take part in the Senate Health Subcommittee proceedings had the potential to provide good publicity for the Institute once again.

I was scheduled to be at Hofstra at 10:30 a.m. on April 15. However, I was not bathed, dressed, and ready to go until after 11:00 a.m. The car that was supposed to take me to Long Island didn't leave Rusk until noon. We finally arrived at Hofstra's campus, in Hempstead, at 1:15 p.m.

While at Rusk, I would normally dress in jeans, a button-down shirt, and sneakers. I didn't have much closet space for clothes. I certainly did not keep a jacket and tie there. So, because I didn't have much notice before I was to speak with Senator Kennedy, I tried to put together what I thought were the nicest pants and shirt I had. The resulting outfit was horrendous. I chose a pair of checkered bell-bottom pants and a shiny royal blue shirt. I looked like I was dressed to go to a disco.

My hair had not been washed for some time. It looked dirty and slicked down. I had a scraggly goatee and wore big metal wrist splints on both hands. I did not look like the conservative, straightlaced, twenty-year-old college student athlete I had been. I certainly did not look like a young man that people would feel compassion for. Instead, I looked scuzzy and sinister. I suppose it was fortunate for me that I was not able to look in a mirror before I left. I would have been far more self-conscious than I already was.

I was transported in a Lincoln Town Car. I sat in the back seat. Mary, my attendant at Rusk, and Stanley, my former attendant, were assigned to take care of me.

We drove into the parking lot on Hofstra's North Campus.

The driver asked a guard where Senator Kennedy's hearings were being held.

The guard replied with a question: "Are you the party from New York?"

When the driver responded that we were, the guard said, "Then come this way." He directed us to drive right up onto the pavement, next to the Student Center. As they started to lift me out of the car, I saw a lot of reporters running toward us and filming. I didn't know that we were considered such important people.

I still had a bad chill. I was also dizzy and worried that I was going to pass out.

I was surprised to see a high school friend, Mike Greenberg, greet me by the car. He asked what had taken us so long and then asked, "Where's your speech?"

I didn't know what he was talking about, so I asked, "What do you mean?"

"Kunk, don't kid around." Mike said, "Everybody who has spoken has had his or her speech all written out. What are you going to say?"

"Mike, I don't even know what I am doing here."

Mike had been sent out by my family to try to keep me calm. Instead, he was making me really nervous.

My father was already in the hearing room giving his testimony. By all accounts, he was excellent. He spoke without notes and with a lot of passion. My father told the subcommittee about my injury, hospitalization, and the enormous costs that went along with it. The bills were continuing to mount with no end in sight. Despite having me well covered under his major medical policy, it still was not enough. In fact, the insurance was about to reach its limit.

My father told the senators that he had been working in the insurance industry for close to twenty-five years and, to his knowledge, there was not a policy out there that would provide sufficient coverage for my type of injury.

That was the testimony the senators needed to hear. Finally, they had an expert, a highly respected insurance agent, saying that the system needed to be changed. My father's testimony may have been the most important the subcommittee heard while conducting their hearings throughout the country.

Now they needed me to put a human face to it.

I was wheeled from the car into the cafeteria. I was sitting with a jacket on, still shivering. Someone asked me if I wanted something hot to drink.

That sounded like a good idea. I asked for a cup of tea, which was soon provided.

Kennedy's aide came over to greet me, followed by a few reporters. Paul Schrieber from *Newsday*, who had written some articles about me in the past, was among them. We were all talking as if we were good friends. Then I noticed that Paul was writing everything down. It suddenly occurred to me that I was speaking with reporters. I immediately became more guarded about what I was saying.

People from the Oceanside Ken Kunken Medical Fund, as well as a few others I didn't know, came by to say hello and ask how I was doing.

Kennedy's aide asked me to let him know when I was ready to be taken into the hearing room.

I was still cold and had a half-cup of tea left in front of me. I said, "Thank you. I will be just a few more minutes."

I thought that other people were still testifying before the subcommittee at that time and, when I was ready, I would be wheeled into the back of the hearing room to wait for my turn. No one told me that the testimony in the hearing room had already come to a halt.

When the aide finally told me that the senators were all just sitting in silence, waiting for me, I apologized profusely. Although I was still shivering, my jacket was taken off and Mary started wheeling me into the hearing room. As we entered, I saw that the gallery was filled with people. I tried not to look at them. I then noticed the biggest tape recorder I had ever seen. I couldn't get over it. It now hit me that everything I said would be recorded.

There were lights and a CBS TV News camera pointing at me. I was wheeled past Senator Edward Kennedy, Senator Peter

Ken testifying at the Senate Health Subcommittee hearing—April 15, 1971.
Photo by Arscott.

Dominick from Colorado, and an aide from New York Senator Jacob Javitz's office. They were all sitting behind a long table.

Senator Javitz and Senator Claiborne Pell, from Rhode Island, were not able to make it, although they were a part of that subcommittee.

As Mary slowly wheeled me by the table, I hesitantly muttered, "Hi" to Senator Kennedy and he replied, "Hi" back to me.

I was left sitting behind a small table less than fifteen feet away from the senators. The table had three microphones on it.

Radio, TV, and newspaper reporters were present. After all, this was a senate subcommittee hearing! This was really a big deal! How could I not have known?

Now I was cold, dizzy, and nervous. I felt like I was about to pass out. I also worried that the slightest movement on my part, including taking a deep breath, would probably result in my having a big, uncomfortable, and embarrassing muscle spasm. I tried to stay as still as possible.

Senator Kennedy thanked me for coming in from New York City. He tried to put me at ease. Senator Kennedy asked me to tell him about my accident and injury.

I wasn't sure how much detail I should go into and the senator didn't specify. I could give an answer that would take one minute or I could talk for hours. I decided to go through it pretty quickly: accident, operation, different hospitals, therapy, progress, and so on. I also told him about my need for attendants around the clock.

The senator asked some more questions. Then he asked, "Did the accident affect you mentally?"

I told him there was no brain damage but that the accident has had a big psychological effect on me.

Senator Kennedy asked, "Would you like to return to school?"

I replied, "I'd love to, especially to Cornell."

The Senator asked me if I would be able to keep up with my studies. Wouldn't it be too difficult?

I told him that I wasn't sure how I would be able to do it. I couldn't turn the pages of a book and the automatic page-turners that I tried didn't work well.

Then the senator asked, "Did you read a lot, before?"

That was a tough and potentially embarrassing question. My friends and relatives knew that I had rarely done any reading for pleasure. What should I say? Everything was being tape-recorded. I had to be truthful.

I was proud of how I handled the question, "Outside of my studies, I did not do that much reading."

By then, I was very thirsty. My mouth was completely dry. There was a water pitcher sitting on the table in front of me but the straw was too far away for me to reach it.

I asked if someone would please give me a drink. There was dead silence. No one knew what to do. Everyone just sat there looking at me. Finally, Mary, my attendant, walked slowly from the back of the room and put the straw into my mouth.

Senator Kennedy, and then Senator Dominick, asked me a few more questions. "Were there other people in the rehab center in a similar condition to yours?" "What was the average age of the patients there?" "How did they get hurt?"

I was in the hearing room for about twenty minutes. When it was over, Senator Kennedy thanked me and I thanked him.

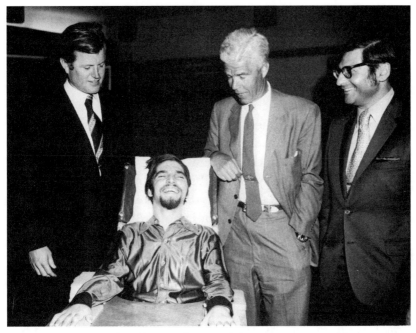

Senator Edward Kennedy, Ken, Senator Peter Dominick,
and Ken's father—April 15, 1971.
Photo by Arscott.

Then Senator Kennedy got up and walked over to me. He
lifted my hand up in his and held it. I was later told that there was
a tear in his eye.

People said that the senator had paid close attention during
my entire testimony. Apparently, he did not stay nearly as focused
when others were testifying.

When all was done, Senator Kennedy and Senator Dominick
came outside and posed for pictures with my father and me. They
could not have been nicer or more genuine.

Senator Kennedy's aide asked if my father and I would go
down to Washington, D.C., to appear before the full senate committee when it met. Of course, we said yes.

I didn't see anything on the CBS News that evening but on
Channel 4 at 6 p.m., and on Channel 11 at 10 p.m., they reported
about the hearings and my father's and my testimony. All the next

day, there was more coverage. People told me they'd heard me speaking on WOR, WGBB, and CBS radio. I never heard or saw any of it. There were big write-ups in the papers as well.

The following day, April 16, I was told that Dr. Howard Rusk wanted to see me in his office.

I could not believe it. One day I was speaking with Senator Kennedy, one of the most famous men in the country, and the next day I am invited to speak, one-on-one, with the most famous rehabilitation doctor in the entire world.

Being asked to talk with Dr. Rusk was unheard of for a patient, unless that patient was either very rich or very famous. I was neither, or at least I thought I was not famous. Apparently, now I was.

At noon, I was wheeled up to Dr. Rusk's office on the sixth floor. Most patients never even get to see the sixth floor, let alone Dr. Rusk's office.

When I arrived, Dr. Rusk asked me how I was and then engaged me in some small talk. He seemed genuinely interested in how I was doing. It was strange because, for the month and a half that I had been a patient at the Institute, none of the doctors had shown much interest in me or concern about my needs. In fact, they treated me as if I was a problem patient. They didn't like that I had been constantly asking questions. They always acted like the less the patient knew, the better.

Now, here I was, sitting in Dr. Rusk's office, having a nice conversation with the head doctor himself. After a few minutes of pleasantries, Dr. Rusk said, "By the way, I heard you spoke with Senator Kennedy yesterday."

When I answered that I had, Dr. Rusk started with rapid-fire questions, "What did he say?" "What did you say?" "What did he say?" "What did you say?" "What else did you talk about?"

Obviously, it was not just a coincidence that Dr. Rusk chose to meet with me the day after I spoke with Senator Kennedy.

When I came back to my room, the nurses and therapists were buzzing. It was interesting to see their reaction. Now, I would constantly hear, "If there's anything you need, don't hesitate to ask." How quickly the hospital staff had changed their attitude toward me.

The next week, I received two items of mail from Senator Kennedy. There was a long letter thanking my father and me for our testimony and telling us how much he appreciated it. Later came a package, containing a glass paperweight with an inscription on it, and a short letter to me. The letter stated:

Dear Ken:

I thought you may like to have the enclosed, a quotation that Senator Robert Kennedy loved and that symbolized his commitment to the belief that one man *can* make a difference.

With my best personal wishes,

Sincerely,

Ted Kennedy

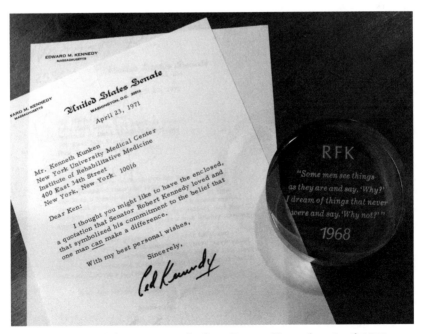

The letter and glass paperweight from Senator Kennedy—April 1971.

The quotation was:

> Some men see things as they are and say, "Why?"
> I dream of things that never were and say, "Why not?"

I also received a letter from President Nixon, who was looking into changing the health care system as well. The president and Senator Kennedy had different ideas about how to do it. On April 26, 1971, President Nixon wrote:

Dear Kenny:

A news item concerning your bravery and determination came to my attention, recently. I understand that, despite paralysis as the result of a football accident, you have been making remarkable progress and that there is hope that you will eventually return to your studies. Your perseverance is a splendid example for all our fellow Americans and I commend you on what you have been able to accomplish.

With best wishes for the future,

Sincerely,

Richard Nixon

I received a letter from Senator Jacob Javitz, which was also written on April 26. Senator Javitz apologized for missing the hearing. He had been out of the country at the time. His letter went on to say, "However, my staff has briefed me on your excellent testimony in support of legislative enactment of national health insurance."

"... I do want you to know that your courageous testimony regarding your tragic accident will, I believe, make an outstanding contribution on behalf of all Americans who unfortunately suffer catastrophic illness ..."

More letters from Senator Kennedy followed. One came to me a year later. It was clear that the senator really wanted to keep in touch with me. He even forwarded a letter he had received, talking about page-turners that may be of use to me.

Senator Kennedy wrote to my father as well. In addition, he sent a $100 donation to the Oceanside Kenny Kunken Medical Fund. I was very touched.

A few weeks after I testified before the senate subcommittee, *Time* magazine ran a story about Senator Kennedy and mentioned my testimony at the hearings. In August, *Look* magazine did a similar article. A magazine in Cincinnati did the same. I was amazed at how much publicity our testimony received. I might actually have an impact on important legislation!

In 1972, Senator Kennedy published his book, *In Critical Condition: The Crisis in America's Health Care*. He personally inscribed a copy for me: "To Kenneth Kunken whose story is a true profile in courage. With admiration—Ted Kennedy, Oct. 1972."

When the Sunday *New York Times* book review section reviewed Senator Kennedy's book, mine was the testimony they quoted and wrote about.

My friend Dave Gilbert heard that Senator Kennedy was going to appear on Dick Cavett's late night television show to promote his book. Dave asked me if I thought Senator Kennedy was going to talk about me.

I laughed at my friend and made fun of him for even asking that question. "Do you really think that everywhere Senator Kennedy goes he talks about me? Are you crazy?"

To my surprise, Dave was right.

As soon as Senator Kennedy and Dick Cavett started talking about the book, Dick Cavett said to the senator that he was "particularly impressed with the part about the injury to the young college football player."

Senator Kennedy immediately responded, "Oh, Kenny Kunken." Then Senator Kennedy began talking about me.

I was dumbstruck.

In late April-early May 1971, there was another round of human-interest stories about me in the New York papers.

On May 2, 1971, the Sunday *New York Times* published an article about me: "The Cost of One Shattered Career Is Placed at $75,000 a Year."

"One Shattered Career." That's what almost everyone thought. Someone with a significant disability could not be expected to ever hold a job, much less have a career.

Seventy-five thousand dollars a year, that's how much my physical care was expected to cost back then, and that seemed to be the most important part of any discussion about someone with a disability. How much was it going to cost to take care of him or her? That was the attitude in 1971.

Soon I was back to being treated like a regular patient by the staff at Rusk. My moment of fame came and went fairly quickly.

Chapter 10

No Miracle on 34th Street

◆ ◆ ◆

In late April, Gordon Kent visited me at Rusk. Gordon was a childhood friend of my brother. After we exchanged some small talk, Gordon told me that he was getting married in a month.

Wow! I wasn't expecting that.

If Gordon was about to be married, how much longer would it be before Steve would take that same step?

Steve was the same age as Gordon. They had done everything together when they were growing up, including skipping the fifth grade, sharing the haftarah for their Bar Mitzvah, going to the same sleepaway camp, and graduating high school.

I couldn't stop thinking about it.

Steve and I had always been extremely close. We were more than just brothers, we were best friends. Not only did we spend every free moment together when we were growing up, Steve was one of the few people I could confide in, talk to about my fears, and express my frustrations. I always felt I could count on Steve for whatever I needed, whenever I needed it.

I assumed that, when I was finally discharged from the hospital, I would live with Steve. I was counting on him to take care of me. If Steve were to get married, how could he ask his wife to take in someone paralyzed from the neck down?

I knew I would need most of Steve's time and energy. I couldn't afford to share him with someone else. To make matters worse, if Steve married a girl from Boston, where he was attending law school, perhaps he would remain there. Where would that leave me?

I couldn't even talk to Steve about it because he was more than 200 miles away. It was very difficult for me to speak on the telephone while at Rusk. I had to be wheeled to the nurses' station and have someone hold the phone to my ear. Because of that and the lack of privacy, I almost never did it.

I had to try to put that whole marriage situation out of my mind and deal with my day-to-day problems until I could speak with Steve in person.

♦ ♦ ♦

One day, I caught Dr. Barard as he was passing in the hall. I asked if he would take a look at my ankles because they were very swollen. I told him that I had a friend from home who was a nurse (Barbara) and she said that it was "pitting edema."

Dr. Barard asked indignantly, "Is she a doctor?"

I told him that she was a nurse.

He repeated, "Is she a doctor?"

I responded, "No."

Dr. Barard stated that I should just listen to my doctors, not anybody else.

I said, "Okay. Can you take a look at my ankles?"

He said that he did not have time and stormed off.

It probably would have taken five seconds. Instead, he preferred to spend the time asking me if Barbara was a doctor rather than looking at my ankles.

One of the most frustrating things about being at the Rusk Institute was that the staff wouldn't answer any of my questions. Their policy seemed to be: "Don't tell the patient anything." They seemed to feel that the less the patient knew, the better.

One day, when one of the physical therapists was "rating" some of the muscles in my arms and shoulders, I asked her what rating she gave to a particular muscle. Her exact words to me were: "That is none of your concern."

I told her that I wanted to know and she continued to refuse to tell me. I asked to see the chart that she was filling out on me but she refused that request as well.

I questioned my attendants, therapists, nurses, and head nurse without receiving much information about my condition and prognosis. I spoke to a psychologist and a social worker, also without receiving many answers.

At some point, someone gave me a pamphlet, published by the Institute of Rehabilitation Medicine (Rusk), about spinal cord injuries. The pamphlet seemed very thorough. It was divided into sections describing different aspects of spinal cord injury. Each description was broken down based on the level of injury. My injury was considered C 4/5, which meant my spinal cord was damaged between the fourth and fifth cervicals in the neck. By then, I was only able to move my left shoulder and bicep a little bit. I had sensation from about three inches below my shoulders, up. I was incontinent, meaning I had no control over my bowels and bladder.

There was a page describing what muscles I should be able to use at my level of injury. I was surprised how accurate it was. There was a page describing where my level of sensation would be. Again, it was right on the money. There was a page describing how my bodily functions would be affected. Once again, it was accurate.

There was also a page describing what careers people with different levels of injury could pursue. When I looked at my level, the only job I remember seeing was "selling magazine subscriptions over the telephone."

I was devastated. Because the rest of the pamphlet had been so accurate, I had to assume that selling magazine subscriptions over the telephone was the best that I would ever be able to do. Six months earlier, I had been studying engineering at Cornell, and now selling magazine subscriptions seemed to be the best I could aspire to.

I lay in bed thinking about that for hours. The more I thought, the more depressed I became. To make matters worse, I tried to picture myself doing that job. At that time, I could not dial a telephone, take notes, or write much of anything. Now I started to think that even that job would be out of reach for me.

In late April, I became increasingly frustrated at not being able to find out more about my condition. I had been hurt for almost six months. I needed to know. The pamphlet provided a lot of information about spinal cord injuries in general, but I wanted to hear from a doctor specifically what my condition was and what type of future I could look forward to.

I asked to speak with Dr. Sel, one of the head doctors on my floor. It took a while, but, finally, I was given that opportunity.

It wasn't easy to get this appointment and, if I forgot any questions that I had wanted to ask, another chance might not come. I was not used to going into a conference without notes. As I entered Dr. Sel's office, I kept turning over and over in my mind all the questions I wanted answered. I was desperately trying not to forget any.

Dr. Sel seemed upset that I had requested this meeting and he was very cold and distant the whole time.

The meeting went something like this:

Question: "Doctor, can you tell me exactly what condition I'm in and what I can expect in terms of future muscle return?"

Answer: "Your spinal cord has been clinically severed and you will get no more return."

Question: "How do you know that?"

Answer: "I know."

Question: "How do you know?"

Answer: "I am a doctor."

Question: "Doctor, how could you possibly say, 'it was severed.' Even the neurosurgeon didn't actually see the cord. I was told his surgical report said there had been no breakage in the dura (outside covering of the spinal cord) and no spinal fluid leakage."

Answer: "I know it was severed by all the symptoms you display."

Question: "I have heard that, after a person has received a traumatic injury to the spinal cord, he goes into a state of spinal shock, which may last six months, a year, a year and a half, or even longer. It has been less than six months. How can you tell by the return I now have that it's been severed?"

Answer: "You're out of spinal shock."

Question: "How do you know?"

Answer: "I know."

Question: "How do you know?"

Answer: "I'm a doctor."

Question: "I was told that the Rusk Institute would not accept someone if it felt it could not help the person."

Answer: "That doesn't mean that we expect you to get more muscle return. We feel we can help you by fitting you with braces and splints and helping you learn how to use them."

Question: "During the last month, I feel I have gotten more movement. I don't understand how you can make the statement that I won't get any more."

Answer: "What you have is not new muscle return. What we have done here, thus far, is strengthen the affected muscles. There is a chance they will get stronger but you will not get the use of other muscles."

Question: "Where do I go from here?"

Answer: "That's up to you."

My blitzkrieg of questions ended with that answer. I was at a loss for words.

When I was wheeled back into my room, one of my roommates at the time, Jim Graham, asked me why I was in such a "blue funk."

I told him that, after five and a half months, they were just telling me now my cord was severed and this was it. I might as well give up hope for any more improvement.

"That's a tough break," Jim replied. Jim added that he knew a person in my condition doing well in the outside world. That did not cheer me up. At this point of my rehabilitation, I wanted to hear that that person got better physically.

That long afternoon, I just lay in bed and stared at the ceiling. My mind wandered from the past, to the present, to the future. I couldn't believe it.

It seemed like from the moment I was injured, the doctors had felt it was important to take away any hope that my condition would improve. I still clung to that hope though. After all, what was the point of working so hard in therapy if my condition was never going to change?

I had always felt that I had Rusk as a last resort. Now what?

I certainly did not want to live in this condition for any length of time. But what can I do? I am only twenty years old. It's too soon to give up on life, but I don't want to end up like most of my roommates, not doing anything productive.

The doctors recommended that I meet with a psychologist once a week. I didn't know whether they recommended that for every spinal cord–injured patient or just for those who were severely depressed, like me.

I went to a psychologist at Rusk a number of times but did not find it comforting or helpful. I didn't discuss anything with her that I hadn't already talked about with Steve or Barbara many times before. The psychologist could not help me get my movement back and that was all I wanted at that time.

Near the end of my stay at Rusk, the psychologist actually was able to be of some help. I had been extremely concerned that Steve was scheduled to enter the Army when he completed law school. At my father's suggestion, Steve had participated in ROTC (Reserve Officer Training Corps) throughout his four years at college. When Steve graduated from the University of Vermont, he was commissioned as a second lieutenant in the Army but was granted a deferment for law school. Now, in 1971, the country was still in the middle of the Vietnam War.

I knew I desperately needed Steve to remain close by to help me. More importantly, I was scared to death that Steve would be injured or killed in Vietnam.

Following my injury, I applied for a hardship discharge for Steve. I had to supply the government with extensive medical records on my condition as well as a letter from the psychologist, stating how important it was for me to have Steve close by. It seemed to take a long time for my application to be considered, but the government finally approved my request.

From that moment on, I always felt that, if it took my spinal cord injury to keep Steve from getting injured or killed in Vietnam, it was worth it. I still feel that way.

♦ ♦ ♦

In May 1971, I started meeting frequently with a vocational counselor named Joyce Mesch. Joyce was one of the few people at Rusk I really liked. I knew I could both trust and confide in her. We talked a lot about what I could and should do, once I was discharged. Joyce encouraged me to return to school and get my degree.

Joyce also saw the way my father treated me during his visits. She told me that, while I had a significant physical disability, my father was treating me like I was an invalid. I shouldn't let that happen.

I agreed. After all, I was twenty years old. I could make my own decisions about my future.

During one of my sessions with Joyce, she told me that they had tutors at the hospital to help the children on the pediatric ward with their studies.

I asked Joyce if I could participate in the tutoring classes. Joyce misunderstood me and said that, unfortunately, they did not have anyone that could help me with calculus or engineering.

I told her that what I meant was that I wanted to be one of the tutors. I had helped tutor many members of my family in math and I wanted to offer my services.

Joyce thought that tutoring the children was a great idea. She put me in touch with the teacher on the pediatric ward, who was very pleased that I offered my help.

Soon, however, I was sorry I had volunteered because the pediatric ward was very depressing. It was heartbreaking to see so many young children with all types of serious physical disabilities. Nevertheless, three days a week, I went up to the pediatric ward and tutored two young girls in ninth grade math. Both of the girls were paraplegics and lay on their stomachs on gurneys during our sessions. It was difficult for me to see their books during those meetings but the girls did their best to wheel close enough to turn pages of the textbook, which was resting in front of me.

The kids really liked having a young person help them. They seemed to enjoy the sessions with me.

Tutoring was a challenge, but good stimulation. I began to think that maybe I should become a teacher. I thought that I might enjoy teaching calculus on the college level, although I would probably have to do the problems in my head.

It felt great to be able to help the kids, but I had to stop after just a couple of weeks. The doctors scheduled me to spend more time on the tilt table. They had stopped putting me on the tilt table some time before. Now, for some reason, they wanted me back on it.

♦ ♦ ♦

On May 29, I met briefly with a twenty-three-year-old man named Glenn Higgins. He had broken his neck at the same level I had, fooling around wrestling on a beach six years earlier. He was the first person I met who was in the same condition as me.

Glenn had just graduated from Hofstra University, where he majored in psychology. He was going to be married in July. His fiancée had previously been his occupational therapist. Glenn said they were going to live in Suffolk County, Long Island. He was at the Rusk Institute that day only for a checkup.

After our short encounter, I lay in bed thinking about both Glenn's future and my own. I couldn't picture myself ever getting serious with a woman, much less thinking about marriage. What woman would ever want to spend the rest of her life with me? And if one would, wouldn't it be incredibly selfish on my part to have her do that?

How could I ever support anyone?

♦ ♦ ♦

Beginning in the late spring, and throughout the summer, I went on a number of "out trips" with some of the other patients and therapists. I was still using a manual wheelchair. We would all pile into a large bus that had a hydraulic lift on the back. People were constantly staring at us wherever we went, particularly when we were getting on and off the bus.

I felt very uncomfortable going on those trips. Most of the other patients were much older than I was and had been recovering from strokes. In addition, being constantly stared at made me feel like a freak. Still, the "out trips" were among the few opportunities for me to escape the confines of the hospital and the boring day-to-day routine.

♦ ♦ ♦

There was a day in June when my physical care hit a new low. It happened at night. A floor attendant had trouble inserting a suppository into my rectum so that I could move my bowels. He discovered that there was a thermometer inside me.

My day attendant claimed that she didn't insert it. My night nurse said that she never took my temperature. Somehow, the thermometer just slipped in there.

How long had the thermometer been in me? Twelve hours? Twenty hours? Days?

I suppose I got off lucky that the thermometer didn't break inside me.

♦ ♦ ♦

There was no therapy on the weekends at Rusk. During my first two months there, I would just lie in bed and stare at the ceiling most of the day. Occasionally, I would doze off, only to be awakened every two hours to be turned or to take pills.

By late May-early June, I started to spend the weekends at Aunt Lorraine's in Oceanside. Steve or Barbara would pick me up after therapy on Friday, from Rusk. Barbara would spend the weekend at Aunt Lorraine's with me, making sure that I was still receiving the proper medical care. Barbara and Roy would carry me up and down the dozen steps every day, to get me to and from the upstairs bedroom.

Barbara slept in a bed that was a few feet away from me. She turned me every few hours and gave me drinks of water throughout the night. Every other night, she would give me a suppository to move my bowels.

One weekend night at Aunt Lorraine's, I had a very strange dream. In the dream, I was at Cornell playing football. I ran down the field on a kickoff and tackled the ball carrier just like I did on October 31. This time, though, I broke my back and became paralyzed from the waist down. I couldn't move my legs. I remember thinking in my dream, "How could I live this way? I can't run. I can't walk. This is horrible."

When I woke up, I felt as if I had just awakened from a nightmare. My first reaction was, "Thank God, it was just a dream!"

I tried to get out of bed but suddenly realized that I couldn't move at all. Only this time it was not a dream. At that moment, I would have given anything to be in as good a condition as I was in that dream. At least then I had the use of my arms and hands.

On Saturday night, July 31, while spending another weekend at Aunt Lorraine's, I dreamt that the attendants at Rusk were plotting to kill me. I told people, but nobody believed me. I was convinced that it was just a matter of time before their plot succeeded. That was the first time I had a dream in which I was sitting in a wheelchair, paralyzed. Until that night, I always dreamt that I was on my feet, doing something active, not dependent in any way on others. I woke up at five in the morning and couldn't get back to sleep.

I suppose my distrust of the people at Rusk was expressing itself through my subconscious. I used to be able to escape from them in my sleep. Now, I would have to wait until I was discharged to feel safe.

It was always very depressing to be driven back to Rusk on Sunday evenings.

♦ ♦ ♦

In June, I had another conference with Dr. Sel, this time at his request.

I met Dr. Sel in his office at 1:30 p.m. He got right to the point. He told me that I was going to be discharged in a couple of months.

"Look into returning to school in September," were his words. It was his way of telling me that they could not do anything more for me at Rusk. He was pretty sure that I would have no more muscle return. That was it.

It was quite a shock.

I had recently gained new hope for more return of muscle function. I thought that I had a trace of movement in my triceps. Two physical therapists, as well as Dr. Barard, also thought that might be the case.

For the past few weeks, when I tried extending my left arm, a movement controlled by the triceps, I thought that I was having some success doing it. I had learned that the triceps muscles were controlled by nerves branching off the spinal cord lower down than where my break was. To me, that was proof that my cord was *not* severed.

But Dr. Sel said that it was impossible for me to have use of those muscles. When I specifically asked him to check it, he refused. He said that me extending my arms was the result of substituting other muscles for the triceps. The deltoids in the shoulder region, as well as gravity, were probably responsible for my arm moving.

I knew that if I could prove my triceps were functioning, there would be a whole different outlook on my case. In addition,

I had been under the impression that the doctors were very pleased with the improvement I had been making the past few months. I had been told that as long as I showed progress, they would continue to work with me. I was also told that the average stay for a quadriplegic at Rusk was ten months. It seemed that they were now cutting my therapy time in half. Now it was as if they were saying, "Not only are we not able to help you, but we will no longer even try."

It took a few weeks before I could convince the doctors to do an electromyogram (EMG) on my left arm. Unfortunately, Dr. Sel was right. I did not have even a trace of triceps functioning.

The meeting with Dr. Sel, as well as the EMG results, erased all my hope for my rehabilitation under the guidance of doctors and therapists in a hospital setting. The experts now said it was hopeless. The experts said that I would spend the rest of my life living in a wheelchair, almost 100 percent paralyzed. I would never be able to dress myself, or even roll over in bed.

Good luck. Have a nice life. Don't let the door hit you on your way out.

It seemed like everyone had been continually trying to crush all my hopes for improvement. They finally succeeded.

Now I had to make the best of a bad situation. Just surviving wouldn't be enough for me, though. I needed to learn how to live in that condition. I had to find a way to overcome it, and lead a semi-normal life.

Chapter 11

Planning for the Future

♦ ♦ ♦

One afternoon in July, Sir Reginald Mehling, an engineer from England, gave a talk to the doctors and therapists at Rusk about the latest equipment he had invented. An article had recently been published about him in the *Readers Digest*. I asked for permission to attend. The hospital allowed me, as well as one other patient, to sit in for his talk.

Sir Reginald demonstrated some devices that could be used to type, as well as to dial a telephone, just by breathing in and out of a tube. All the things he showed us were fascinating.

After the lecture, I asked Sir Reginald whether, if I continued my studies in engineering, I would be able to pursue a career doing the type of work he was doing. He didn't see why not, and he encouraged me to do so.

I now spent time in prevocational therapy, trying to both type and dial a telephone using the sip and puff equipment that Sir Reginald had demonstrated. It was fascinating but slow, even though the speed could be adjusted. I much preferred trying to do those tasks using my wrist splint, rubber-tipped stick, and BFO.

Later, I was one of the first patients to try an electric wheelchair that could be controlled simply by moving one's eyes. It used technology developed for the space program. Frames for glasses, which had photo cells attached on the top of both sides, were placed on my head. When I moved my eyes to the left, the chair would go forward. When I moved my eyes to the left again, the chair would stop. When I moved my eyes to the left a third time, the chair would go in reverse. When I moved my eyes to the left again, the chair would stop.

If I moved my eyes to the right, the chair would keep turning in a circle, as long as I kept my eyes in that position. As soon as I moved my eyes straight ahead, the chair would stop turning.

The wheelchair never worked well. There were problems whenever I went under some of the lights in the hallway. It certainly didn't help matters when a pretty girl walked by and I tried to sneak a glance at her. How could I explain turning in circles at that point? Obviously, more work needed to be done, on me as well as the wheelchair.

Sometime at the beginning of the summer I was invited to go up to the sixth floor again. I met with Dr. Rusk and representatives from some large firms located in New York City. The hospital had a program under which those representatives would come to the Institute once a month and speak with individual patients in the presence of Dr. Rusk. The meetings were intended to expose patients to possible jobs in their field of interest.

When it was my turn for the interview, Dr. Rusk asked me, in front of the group, what I would be interested in doing for a career.

I replied that I was good at math and science and felt I should continue with what I did best. I wanted to go into a field where I would be working with those subjects. I mentioned that I had been studying Industrial Engineering and Operations Research and had done extremely well on a computer aptitude test.

Soon the representatives started firing questions at me: "Have you thought about accounting?"

"Yes, but I don't know too much about the field."

"Have you thought about becoming an actuary?"

"Yes. In fact, I had even registered to take the first actuarial exam. Ironically, I was supposed to take the test November 4, four days after I was hurt."

"Do you think you'd like to work in City Planning, with the School Board, for example?"

I answered, "It never entered my mind, but I wouldn't rule it out."

For some reason, my vague answers came across well. Within two weeks, at least five different firms called the Rusk Institute and invited me to visit their offices for further discussion.

The first interview was at Chemical Bank's Main Office, near Wall Street, on the thirty-second floor. I spoke with a Mr. Merrill, who was in charge of recruiting for Chemical Bank. Mr. Merrill and I shared common interests in lacrosse, football, and hockey. After some small talk about sports, he and I discussed what positions would be available at the bank for someone like me, after I graduated from college. His list was a long one. It included careers in all areas of management and computer work, as well as other areas in the banking field.

One of the interviews I went on took place at Pfizer Pharmaceuticals. At one point, the interviewer went off on a tangent. He started complaining about how some of the new health care proposals would hurt the Pfizer Company. He particularly singled out Senator Kennedy's. I immediately became uncomfortable. I wasn't sure if he knew I had testified before the senator's subcommittee on healthcare a few months earlier.

Neither the representative from Chemical Bank nor Pfizer Pharmaceuticals ever mentioned any specific jobs someone in my condition might do at their companies or how someone in my condition would be able to perform any of the tasks that they required. There were no desktop or laptop computers back then. I did not see one person in a wheelchair at either office. In fact, I did not see one person in a wheelchair within ten blocks of their offices.

◆ ◆ ◆

On July 15, I was awakened at the normal time for my pills, but this was not an ordinary day for me. It was my twenty-first birthday, and certainly my most unhappy one.

One of the nurses saw on my chart that it was my birthday and a chain reaction of good wishes began from the rest of the staff. A floor attendant brought in pizza from down the block. My roommates and I finished it quickly. I think that was the first time I had pizza since my accident.

My grandparents came, of course, as well as Steve, two friends from Cornell, my Aunt Dorothy, my friend Dave Gilbert, his girlfriend, and a few others. Later that evening, my relatives and friends took me out for Chinese food at a restaurant two blocks from the hospital.

I had spent my past three birthdays working at swimming pools. On those days, I celebrated with my fellow lifeguards. Somebody would bring in a cake. There would be a lot of joking around and some crazy five-cent gifts. I would, inevitably, be thrown into the pool. It was always a lot of fun.

Most of my twenty-first birthday was spent in a hospital ward, undergoing token therapy.

There was a popular television commercial constantly being played at that time. It showed a husband, looking lovingly at his wife on her birthday, and saying, "You are not getting older. You are getting better."

For me, just the opposite was true: I was not getting better, just older.

The one bright spot of the day was Betsy Ross. She worked as a summer aide at Rusk and was majoring in physical therapy at Ithaca College. Betsy was a pretty, blue-eyed blonde, tall, and very lively. She poked her head in the room, wished me a happy birthday, and then ran off down the hall.

A few days later, a male summer intern literally dragged Betsy into my room and formally introduced us. That was when Betsy told me that she had actually been at the game at which I was injured.

Shortly after that, Betsy convinced me to go on an evening "out trip" with some of the other patients, to Central Park, to see Roberta Flack in concert. I had never heard of Roberta Flack, but Betsy said that she was great. The big selling point, for me, was that Betsy was going to be there.

Since my injury, I felt terribly uncomfortable and insecure in crowds. My head seemed to be at the same level as most people's elbows, so it was frequently bumped and some people would inevitably trip over my feet. On top of that, I was still dizzy quite often. I felt helpless and vulnerable. This time, though, the outing was, indeed, great, mostly because Betsy stayed by my side the whole time.

◆ ◆ ◆

I was going to be discharged from Rusk in August. I knew that because of my physical limitations, I had to make the most of my mental abilities. I needed to go back to school and get the best education possible if I was going to have any chance of making something out of my life. But what should I study? Would more schooling help me be able to work or would I just be wasting everyone's time?

In any event, I now had less than two months before school started and I couldn't even begin to think where to start. I worked closely with Joyce Mesch, the vocational counselor, with whom I had numerous discussions about the many obstacles I would have to confront.

Could I even return to school? was still a question in my mind. Schoolwork itself was the least of my worries.

Medically, I still had many problems. I developed bladder infections frequently. I was on a lot of medication and had difficulty swallowing pills. I got dizzy each day, sometimes to the point of blacking out. I had to worry about catching a cold and being exposed to other bugs, just to name a few of my concerns.

I had trouble operating the electric wheelchair. If I wasn't set up with my braces and splints just right, or if I wasn't sitting high and straight enough in the wheelchair, I couldn't operate it at all. Often, the first time I pushed the joystick, my wheelchair would jerk. I would then have a muscle spasm. My fingers would spread apart, my arms would shoot forward, and my head would jerk back. I would slide down in the wheelchair and end up slumped for the rest of the day. It sometimes took me as much as ten minutes just to go ten yards, the length of a first down on a football field.

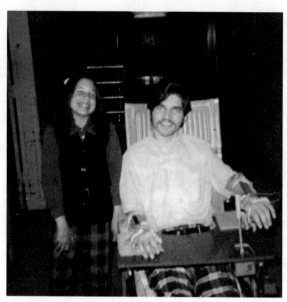

Ken operating his electric wheelchair with Meryl by his side—1971.
Photo by Leonard Kunken.

What school could I attend? Only a few were wheelchair accessible. I shouldn't be too far away from the hospital or from my family. Would I even be admitted to any school, especially at such a late date? My past academic record in engineering at Cornell was only a C average. That alone could be grounds for many schools to reject me.

I didn't even know what I wanted to study. Could I function as an engineer, or lawyer, or accountant, or whatever? Would I eventually be hireable in any of those fields? I would need a lot of help, from many people, with whatever I chose to do.

My biggest problem, though, was my need for an attendant, seven days a week, twenty-four hours a day. I would have to depend on that person for everything. I would need an attendant to be with me all the time. I would never have any privacy, ever again.

How would I go about finding an attendant? Should I go through a medical registry, like in a hospital to find a private duty nurse, or just pick a person off the street? How much would I have to pay him or her? Could my family afford it? Why would anyone want to take that kind of job? Certainly, anyone that I had anything in common with would not be interested.

It was clear to me that, before I looked for an attendant, I had to decide where I was going to be living and which college I would be attending.

Hofstra University was five miles from Oceanside. Its campus was flat and relatively accessible for someone in a wheelchair. I probably would live at home if I went there but where would home be. Would it be at my father's house in Oceanside? Only my father and his wife Betty would be there. They were not able to take care of me. I would still need an attendant to live there with me. Where would I sleep? Where would the attendant sleep? Was Aunt Lorraine's house a possibility? I would still have all those same problems there, and neither house was wheelchair accessible.

Apart from that, how would I get back and forth to college? If I did go to Hofstra, I probably would not live on campus.

I did not want to just go to classes, though. I wanted to go to college and take part in all the extracurricular activities that college had to offer. It did not sound like Hofstra was the place for me to do that.

To my surprise, Columbia University offered me the opportunity to go to school in their engineering program. Columbia's campus was in New York City, not that far from Rusk and my doctors, if I needed them.

Columbia was really going out of its way to be helpful. As nice as that offer was, I really did not want to be in New York City. I didn't like the City to begin with and being near Rusk was not a big selling point for me. Besides, just hearing the name "Columbia" always reminded me of the game in which I was injured.

The only college I really wanted to go to was Cornell. I had loved it there. I also thought, or I guess at least hoped, that if I just ignored my injury and did everything that I was doing before I got hurt, maybe it would just go away. As best I could, I wanted to resume the life that I had had before I was injured.

Many people were telling me I was crazy to even consider going back to Cornell. My father was especially adamant. He didn't want me to have anything more to do with Cornell, other than a possible lawsuit.

Cornell was 250 miles away. It had been known to snow there seven months out of the year. Cornell had a very hilly campus and most of its buildings had steps in front of them. There were no ramps or curb cuts. Additionally, Cornell was a tough school academically. I was having difficulty with my studies before I was injured. Now it would be 100 times harder.

Joyce Mesch believed strongly in doing what I thought was best. If I was the one who made the decision, Joyce felt that I would do my best to make it work.

Against most people's advice, I decided to go back to Cornell.

♦ ♦ ♦

About 4:30 one July afternoon, I was having a particularly frustrating day. I was so fed up with everyone and everything at Rusk that, for the sake of my own sanity, I had to get away for a while. I needed to be alone.

I decided that, rather than getting into bed after my last therapy class, I would stay in my electric wheelchair and just take off. However, there really weren't many places I could go. I decided to take the elevator up to the seventh floor, to the roof.

I had been up on the roof many times before but always accompanied by other people. Now, because it was late in the day and it looked like a storm was coming, I had the chance to be up there by myself.

When the elevator door on the fourth floor opened, I caught the operator's attention and told him where I wanted to go. He took me up and let me off on the roof. He then took the elevator back down.

The roof was often used by visitors to talk with their disabled relatives and friends, as well as for occasional cookouts for the patients from the pediatric ward. Although the roof was normally well occupied, the ominous weather left me its only visitor that afternoon. For that, I was happy ... but not for long.

Within ten minutes it started to rain. I managed to maneuver my wheelchair back near the elevator, where I was shielded from the rain by a very small portion of an overhang. Unfortunately, there was no one to push the elevator button for me.

I decided to try to swing my left arm as high and as far out as I could, aiming for the button. Not only did I miss, I fell partly out of the chair in the process. My right arm slipped off the other side of the chair. I was not able to lift it back up. I was sitting by the elevator, in a contorted position, hanging onto the wheelchair with the back of my head.

It was now 5 o'clock, which meant the elevator operator was going off duty for the night. No one else knew I was up there. Because of the weather, probably no one else would go up to the roof that afternoon. The sky was getting darker and the rain heavier.

I was completely helpless. I was in physical pain, frustrated at being trapped in that uncomfortable position, and I feared that with me hanging over the side, the wheelchair would topple over.

"Well, I guess this is what it's like being on my own now," I thought.

I was mentally preparing myself for spending the night on the roof. To my surprise, the elevator door opened and a maintenance man stepped out. He was there to replace a small broken window next to the elevator. He didn't even seem to take notice of me.

"Can you push me back over in the wheelchair?" I asked, "Can you lift my right arm back onto the chair? Can you straighten me up? Can you put my arm back in the brace (BFO)? Can you get me back into the elevator?"

He didn't say a word but did what I asked. I then asked him to push the button for the fourth floor, which he did, and then he stepped out of the elevator.

The doors shut behind me. I was now riding by myself, with my back to the door. I couldn't see the numbers indicating which floor I was approaching, so I wasn't sure when I had to move the wheelchair in reverse. When I heard the doors open, I moved quickly. I just barely made it out, when the doors shut.

Unfortunately, I was now on the sixth floor, on which there were just offices. Because it was after 5 p.m., there was no reason for anyone to be there until the next morning. To my great relief, someone finally did come along and helped me get to my floor.

◆ ◆ ◆

Near the end of July, Betsy stopped by my room to tell me that her internship was ending and that she would be going to her home in Pawling, New York. She would be returning to Ithaca College in September.

I told Betsy that I was hoping to return to Cornell in the fall. I surprised myself by then saying that I would like to see her up in Ithaca if I did. Mind you, we barely knew each other at this point. And yet she seemed very enthusiastic about seeing me up there.

Because the Institute was planning to take an "out trip" to see the play *Hair* on Monday night, August 2, I asked Betsy if she would stay in New York a little bit longer and go with us. She agreed to stay. Unfortunately, on the day of the scheduled "out trip," everything was canceled.

Before I thought about what I was saying, I asked Betsy if she would like to go to a movie that night, instead.

Betsy said she would.

Now what do I do?

More Mom happened to be visiting at the time. She told me that there was a movie theater just a few blocks from the hospital. She checked in the newspaper and found that the movie *Bananas*, starring Woody Allen, was playing there, so I asked Betsy if she would like to see it. She said yes.

Now I was getting really nervous. What had I just done? The more I thought about it, I realized what I had asked Betsy to do. In order to see a movie with me, she had to pick me up, wheel me a few blocks to the theater in a manual wheelchair, pay for the tickets with money my grandmother put in my pocket, sit next to me for an hour and a half, and then wheel me back to the hospital. How could I have just asked her to do that? And yet she seemed excited about the whole idea.

Betsy returned in the evening and pushed me to the theater. She bought the tickets and wheeled me inside. To our dismay, we were then confronted with three steps. Betsy tried to pull me up, but couldn't do it alone. She asked an usher for help and he obliged. Almost immediately, the usher's supervisor started yelling at the usher that that was not his job and that he shouldn't be pulling me up the steps.

That made me extremely uncomfortable. I didn't want to get the usher in trouble and I felt bad for Betsy because I put her in a difficult position as well.

Now I started worrying about how I was going to get back down those steps at the end of the movie.

I sat in the aisle, to Betsy's left. As soon as she sat down, I realized that the back-left side of my wheelchair had broken and the back of the chair would no longer stay level. As a result, I kept falling toward the left side of the chair, away from Betsy. Every thirty seconds or so, I needed "my date" to pull me back up. I felt terrible about all of that.

At least the movie was funny.

When the movie ended, Betsy somehow got me down the steps. She wheeled me out of the theater and back toward the hospital. On the way, she asked if I would like to stop at the corner liquor store, get a bottle of wine and go back to her dorm room. Of course, I said yes!

Betsy left me sitting on the corner, outside the liquor store. I felt very uneasy. It was dark out and we were not in a particularly safe part of the City. Sitting alone, I was an easy target for drunks and other strangers passing by. Being in a broken manual wheelchair made it even worse. Not only couldn't I move, I couldn't even sit up straight.

It seemed like Betsy was gone for a long time. I felt very relieved when she finally returned. Nine months earlier, I was a rugged football player. Now I was afraid of my own shadow, depending on a girl to protect me.

Betsy's dorm room was very small. There was just enough space for my wheelchair to fit in. Betsy opened the bottle and poured us each a glass of wine. She held a glass up to my lips so I could take a drink. It tasted strange. I was not a drinker and, with the exception of a Passover Seder, almost never had even a sip of wine.

Being shy, rather than looking Betsy in the eye I looked down. To my horror, I saw that my leg bag was totally full and looked like it was about to burst. It never occurred to me to have an aide empty the bag before we left Rusk. I knew that, if the bag wasn't emptied right away, the condom would start to leak.

Betsy must have seen the anguished look on my face and asked what was wrong. I was embarrassed to tell her but felt I had no choice. It would be worse if my pants were suddenly soaked with urine. Finally, in a low voice, I told her that my leg bag was full.

Betsy didn't bat an eye. She asked if I would like her to empty it. Again, I was embarrassed but felt I had no choice. I said yes.

Now another problem arose. We had nothing to empty it into.

Betsy came up with a solution. She would empty the bag into the wine bottle. I am not certain how Betsy disposed of the rest of the wine but soon the bottle was empty. Looking back on it, Betsy must have finished it. She did seem a bit tipsy afterward.

Because the wine bottle had such a small opening, it was difficult to empty my leg bag into it, but that did not deter Betsy. I felt even worse when I saw that some of the urine ended up on Betsy's hands. She was great about it, though.

We didn't stay in Betsy's room long because it was getting late. She wheeled me back, through a connecting tunnel, to Rusk.

The attendants and nurses were in the process of changing shifts. I told Betsy to just leave me in my room and an attendant would soon come and put me to bed. My three roommates were already asleep.

Betsy left me sitting near my bed, said good-bye, and left. I had to wait for more than a half hour before an attendant finally showed up.

I didn't get much sleep that night. I turned over in my mind every detail of the evening. I had not dated much before my injury. Still, I didn't remember it being this difficult. However, if Betsy was willing, I would be ready to try it again. Of course, I wouldn't know the answer to that until I saw her up in Ithaca in the fall.

♦ ♦ ♦

On Wednesday, August 4, I was weighed. I was 124 pounds clothed, about 120 pounds stripped. When I was hurt, I weighed 153 pounds stripped. Still, I was twenty pounds heavier than when I was at South Nassau.

Also, on August 4, I tried taking a shower again. Because the shower wheelchair did not recline, I had to sit straight up. I wore a tight stomach binder to keep my blood pressure from dropping. I felt dizzy and was nervous the whole time but, I wanted to shower so badly, I practically talked myself out of passing out. It was the first time in nine months I had had a shower.

♦ ♦ ♦

Before I actually started looking for an attendant to help me at Cornell, Coach Cullen got in touch with my father and indicated that he had found one for me. His name was Dave McMurray. Dave had heard about my injury and approached Coach Cullen to offer his help. Dave was a year older than me and had played on Cornell's 150-pound football team the year before I joined. He had injured his knee and could no longer play football. However, he was still very active and even taught tennis.

Dave adamantly opposed the Vietnam War. He had graduated from Cornell with a degree in Chemical Engineering but did not want to work in that field because he was concerned that his work might, potentially, be used in Vietnam. He did not want to earn more than a certain amount of money, either. If he did, he would have to pay taxes, which might be used to support the war. Because of his knee, he did not have to worry about being drafted into the Army.

Dave came down from Ithaca one weekend in July, to meet me in Oceanside and learn how to take care of me. Barbara showed him what needed to be done. Dave picked everything up very quickly.

♦ ♦ ♦

My family, Joyce Mesch, and I agreed that we should take a trip to Ithaca, meet with representatives from Cornell, and figure out the logistics of my return to school.

On Sunday afternoon, August 15, my father, Steve, and I took the 5:10 p.m. flight from LaGuardia to Ithaca. At the LaGuardia airport, Steve and an employee of the airline carried me onto the plane. They put me in one of the seats and strapped me in like everyone else. Fortunately, the flight was uneventful.

We arrived in Ithaca about 6:30 p.m. and Coach Cullen met us at the airport. I was lifted into his car. My wheelchair was folded and put into the trunk. The coach drove us to the Statler Hotel, located on the Cornell campus. We ate in the main dining room. The coach fed me himself. It was a good meal.

Cornell looked different to me now. Before my injury, I never noticed how many steps there were in front of virtually every building. I knew that the campus was hilly but never realized how steep the hills were. The campus was even bigger than I had remembered.

We stayed at the Statler Hotel that night. I had a lot of trouble sleeping, partly because I was freezing and had a bad chill. I woke Steve a number of times to help me.

The next morning, my father, Steve, and I had breakfast in the cafeteria at the hotel. A number of people stopped by to say hello and to tell me that they heard I would be returning to Cornell. By then, I had lost my chill and was feeling much better.

We had our first meeting at 9:20 a.m., at the Statler, with the Cornell provost, the acting president, and Mr. Herman, the head of the hotel. Things went well until the subject of money came up.

The acting president put a written agreement on my lap. Page one was fine. Cornell was willing to give me up to $7,000 a year, for up to five years of schooling, for a total of $35,000. Tuition at that time was somewhere between $2,400 and $3,000 a year. Any funds that came my way for education from other sources, such as a Regents scholarship, would be deducted from that amount.

On page two, however, it stated that Cornell was not liable for my injury and there would be no other payments.

My father and I wouldn't sign that agreement. At the time, we were considering suing the university. We asked the representatives from Cornell if they would still allow me to return to Cornell and provide the $35,000 for education if we didn't sign the paper. We also wanted Cornell to pay for my attendant's room and board as part of the package.

They said that they would have to ask the Board of Trustees. They seemed willing to help in every other way but, obviously, were concerned about being sued.

Our next meeting was with Howard Kramer, the Dean of Students. We talked about continuing with my studies in industrial engineering.

For our third meeting that day, we met with Professor Allen, the Assistant Dean of Industrial Engineering. We discussed my class schedule for the fall. I decided to take three engineering courses for ten credits: Computer Programming, Probability, and Deterministic Models.

At lunchtime, we met Joyce Mesch and the Home Planning Counselor from Rusk. They had flown up that morning.

Dave McMurray also joined us on campus. We walked around the Engineering Quad to check out its wheelchair accessibility. Unfortunately, the building that had the most steps in front of it, was Upson Hall, the Industrial Engineering building. Just my luck!

We spent a good deal of time that afternoon trying to find the best place for me to live when I returned in September.

We had originally thought that I would be staying in one of the rooms in the Statler Hotel. We had looked at a beautiful room on the fifth floor, but I knew that it wouldn't be big enough for me, my attendant, two wheelchairs, and other equipment.

Another possibility was to stay in Sage Hall, the graduate dormitory. Sage was right across the street from the Engineering Quad. We looked at a large sitting room, about eighteen-by-twenty-two feet. It was located just opposite the cafeteria. The bathroom was a distance down the hall though. While that was not a problem for me, it would be very inconvenient for my attendant.

We asked the administration if they could install a sink in my room. They said yes and agreed to do so.

Unfortunately, there were ten steps to get into Sage Hall and four steps to get up to the cafeteria. A representative from Cornell showed me that, if I took the freight elevator down to the basement and went to the other side of the building, there would only be two steps to get out.

We certainly were not thrilled at the prospect of all those steps, but the room and the location at Sage seemed to make the most sense. We decided that that would be my home, starting in September.

Steve then wheeled me around some more of the campus. Everything looked great. There was no doubt in my mind that Cornell was where I wanted to be.

My father, Steve, and I took the 6:30 p.m. flight to LaGuardia and I was driven back to the Rusk Institute.

I was thoroughly exhausted but too wound up to sleep. It had been great being back at Cornell during the day and very depressing being at Rusk in the evening. I couldn't wait to be discharged on August 20.

A few days before August 20, however, I learned that both my manual and electric wheelchairs, which had been ordered for me well in advance, would not be ready when I was scheduled to leave Rusk.

The representative of the wheelchair company told me that he still would have to fit the chairs to me, then make some adjustments and make a lapboard. He agreed to let me borrow a manual wheelchair until mine arrived. I would have to pick up my wheelchairs at the warehouse in Queens the following week.

Steve picked me up late in the afternoon on August 20. I spent the next eleven days at Aunt Lorraine's in Oceanside before being driven to Cornell.

When I left the Institute of Rehabilitation Medicine, there was no fanfare or big party to say good-bye. A year later, there was a picture and whole page article about me in their yearly promotional brochure. In addition, there was a large photograph of me using my BFO braces and splints hanging on a wall in the hallway of the Institute.

Chapter 12

Cornell—A Steep Learning Curve

♦ ♦ ♦

More Mom and More Pop drove me to Cornell on Tuesday, August 31. Steve followed, with a large U-Haul attached to the back of his car.

When we arrived, Steve got the key to my room, which had been fixed up the day before and looked very nice. It did not have a sink yet but had two dressers, two beds, and chairs in it.

My new attendant, Dave McMurray, had been living in Ithaca. Steve called him and Dave soon joined us.

I called my fraternity brothers to help us unpack. They were surprised I was back at Cornell. They had thought I would be attending Columbia. Apparently, they had read that in a newspaper.

Steve stayed until Saturday to make sure Dave knew how to take proper care of me. Because there were only two beds in the room, Steve slept on the floor.

The day after we arrived, Steve went to the Cornell bookstore to purchase some school supplies for me. I asked him to also buy the Red Key Society calendar. The Red Key Society was the junior men's honor society. Every year they published a desk book calendar filled with many pictures taken at Cornell, with amusing captions accompanying each one. I bought a copy every year, as did almost every Cornell student.

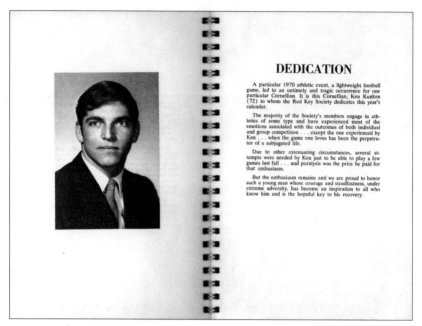

DEDICATION

A particular 1970 athletic event, a lightweight football game, led to an untimely and tragic occurrence for one particular Cornellian. It is this Cornellian, Ken Kunken (72) to whom the Red Key Society dedicates this year's calendar.

The majority of the Society's members engage in athletics of some type and have experienced most of the emotions associated with the outcomes of both individual and group competition . . . .except the one experienced by Ken . . . when the game one loves has been the perpetrator of a subjugated life.

Due to other extenuating circumstances, several attempts were needed by Ken just to be able to play a few games last fall . . . and paralysis was the price he paid for that enthusiasm.

But the enthusiasm remains and we are proud to honor such a young man whose courage and steadfastness, under extreme adversity, has become an inspiration to all who know him and is the hopeful key to his recovery.

Dedication in the Red Key Society's Cornell calendar 1971–72.

When Steve returned with the calendar, I asked him to flip through the pages for me. We were both surprised when Steve turned the cover page. On the back of the cover was a list of the 1971–72 Red Key Society members and my name was included as an honorary member. A couple of pages later was a photograph of me. The page beside my photo talked about my accident and recovery. The 1971–72 Red Key Society calendar had been dedicated to Ken Kunken. At the time the calendar was published, the Society did not know I would be returning to Cornell that fall.

Steve wanted to help me adjust to being back at Cornell, which included straightening out some administrative matters. We met with the provost and assistant dean to discuss finances again. Then we spoke to people in the Housing and Dining Department. After that, we talked with the fire department and the phone company. We also met with people in charge of the dormitory.

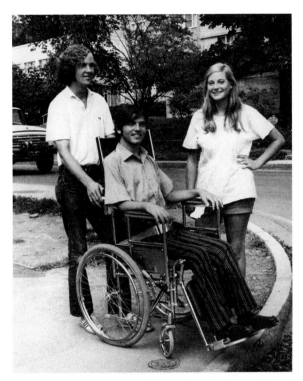

Ken with Dave McMurray and Betsy Ross—September 1971.
Photo by Jim Hanchett.

I registered for three industrial engineering courses for ten credits, as well as the Introduction to Psychology course I had been enrolled in when I got hurt, for three more credits.

I was hesitant to sign up for four courses but the psychology course didn't seem like it would require that much work. I also decided to add that course because one of Dave's friends, Chris Eddy, a psychology graduate student, was a teaching assistant for that class. Chris said she would be happy to help me with the course and would give me her notes as well. That sounded great and, besides, Chris was beautiful. How could I not take her up on that offer?

I saw Betsy a few times that week. She was now a sophomore at Ithaca College, which was located just a couple of miles away. Mostly, Betsy and I just walked around the campus and talked.

In addition, I had a steady parade of visitors from my fraternity and football team. My room was really crowded that first week.

There was also a constant stream of reporters wanting to do stories on me. The *New York Daily News*, *Newsday*, the *Ithaca Journal*, and the *Cornell Daily Sun* all interviewed me.

The publicity made me extremely uncomfortable. I didn't like doing the interviews but I knew the articles were helpful raising money for both the Oceanside and Cornell funds. Still, I didn't feel at ease with all the attention.

I felt embarrassed almost every time I read one of the articles. My words seemed to be either taken out of context or twisted. Maybe that was my fault. During the interviews, I tried to display a positive attitude and, as a result, many of the articles made it sound like everything was going great and I didn't have a care in the world. That was far from the truth.

On Tuesday, September 7, my classes started. I will never forget my first morning.

I had scheduled two classes, back-to-back, in the same lecture room in Upson Hall, so I thought attending classes my first day wouldn't be that difficult.

The lack of ramps and curb cuts at Cornell necessitated me using a manual wheelchair to get around. The electric wheelchair was too heavy and unwieldy to be pulled up steps.

Because Sage Hall had ten steps in front of it, I decided to take the freight elevator down to the basement and go out the back door, which had just two steps. That door happened to be directly across the street from the Engineering Quad.

The freight elevator was located midway down the hall from my room. It was old, very small, and basically only used by the maintenance help to bring the garbage and cleaning supplies to and from the basement.

In order for me to fit in, Dave had to take the leg rests off my wheelchair and back me into the elevator. Even then, the elevator was too small to allow Dave to ride with me. He had to push the button to the basement for me, close the gate and the door of the elevator, walk to the end of the hall, go down the steps and walk halfway down the basement hallway. He would then open the elevator door and gate, pull me out, and put my leg rests back on.

I was claustrophobic in those cramped confines and nervous riding alone. If the elevator got stuck between floors, I would be in big trouble. I worried that if anything happened to Dave, no one would know I was there. It could be days before I would be found.

Dave bounced me down the two steps by the back door of Sage Hall. In order to go up or down steps, Dave needed to tilt the wheelchair back into a wheelie position, while I had to keep my chin tucked tightly against my chest. That was quite a strain on my neck, as my muscles were still weak and sore from my injury ten months earlier.

Although Dave never dropped me, over the years my wheelchair has flipped over backward a number of times. I still get nervous every time I am pulled up or bounced down steps.

Once outside Sage Hall, we had to cross the street, which meant going down a curb on one side of the street and going up a curb on the other. Going up and down a curb is not as difficult as going up or down stairs, but it was still uncomfortable for me.

Once we arrived at Upson Hall, Dave pulled me up about ten steps to get to the door. Because there was no landing by the door, Dave had to hold the wheelchair with one hand, open the door with the other, and pull me inside. I was afraid the wheelchair was going to topple back down the steps at any moment.

When we finally reached the classroom, there was a sign on the door saying that the class had been moved to the basement of Kimball Hall.

Dave bounced me back down the ten steps of Upson Hall and wheeled me over to Thurston Hall, which connected to Kimball. I was then pulled up the two steps that stood in front of Thurston. Dave pushed me to the freight elevator, the only elevator in the building, which provided access to the basement of Kimball Hall. Unfortunately, the elevator was completely filled with desks, chairs, and other furniture. There was no room for me.

I did not want to miss the first class of my first semester back at Cornell. So, Dave and a few other students, who were attending

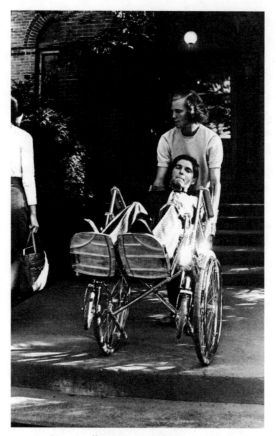

Dave pulling Ken up steps—1971.
Photo by Jim Cunningham.

the same lecture, bounced me down the twenty-eight steps to the basement in Kimball Hall.

The classroom there had stadium seating. Out of necessity, I had to sit in front of the front row, off to the side.

I hated sitting in the front. I was constantly being stared at. That was probably because I had received some publicity but also because my classmates had never seen anyone in my condition on a college campus, or anywhere, for that matter, before.

I must have spent half that class worrying about how I was going to get back up the steps. Fortunately, when the lecture ended, the freight elevator was empty and we were able to take it up to the first floor.

I was then bounced down the two steps in front of Thurston Hall and wheeled back over to Upson, where I was again pulled up its ten steps. When we reached the classroom, there was another sign on the door, indicating that that class had also been moved ... to the first floor of Olin Hall.

I was the only student in those classes that used a wheelchair. The administration was well aware of my schedule and my telephone number. However, no one had thought to notify me about those changes.

I was bounced back down the ten steps of Upson Hall and then wheeled across the street, once again going down and up curbs. When we reached Olin Hall, I was pulled up eleven steps to get into that building. That classroom also had stadium seating so, again, I had to sit in front of the front row.

When class ended, rather than going back down the eleven steep steps where we had entered the building, I was pulled up about a dozen steps that were inside the classroom. That way I could go out the back door, which was closer to the front entrance of Sage Hall. I then had to go down a curb and up another one and was finally pulled up the ten steps in front of Sage Hall to get inside.

Dave and I were both thoroughly exhausted. I had Dave put me in bed and I just lay there, staring at the ceiling. How was I going to make it through the semester? It seemed impossible. What was I thinking, going back to Cornell? I had to be crazy!

Just to attend my first two classes, I had to be either pulled up or bounced down close to a hundred steps. In addition, I was so distracted by all the physical obstacles, I had absolutely no idea what the professors were lecturing about. And I had no notes either.

That first morning was a nightmare, but I decided to continue and try to make the best of it. What else could I do? I did not see any viable alternative.

The second day of classes that semester did not look like it would be any easier. My first lecture that day was for my Psych 101 class in Bailey Hall. Bailey Hall was the only facility at Cornell

Ken being pulled up the steps in front of Bailey Hall.

large enough to hold the thousand students attending the lecture. It was on the other side of campus, quite a distance from my dorm, and had sixteen steps in front of it. I had to ask students passing by to help pull me in my wheelchair up the steps. That lecture met three times a week.

Once inside the building, I had to stay behind the top row of seats, way off to the side of the huge auditorium. The aisles were too steep and narrow for me to sit comfortably and not block other students from getting back and forth to their seats.

Professor Maas taught the course. He used many slides and short film clips throughout his lectures. Occasionally, he had some well-known guest speakers and his course was, far and away, the most popular course on campus. From where I sat, though, it was difficult for me to even see the professor or his presentation.

Any time I had a non-engineering class, it made more sense to go down the ten steps in front of Sage Hall, rather than using the elevator and going out the back door. The front door was closer to the main part of campus where the rest of my classes took place. It saved about fifteen minutes, between getting in and out of the elevator, going down the back steps, and then being wheeled up a steep hill and around the corner, just to get back to the front of Sage Hall. That meant, of course, that, on the three days a week that I had my psych course, even if I didn't go to any other classes those days, I had to be pulled up or bounced down at least fifty-two steps, not counting curbs.

My second class that day was uneventful. All of my labs were canceled the first week. As a result, after completing my two Wednesday lectures, I had now attended the first lectures for all my courses.

I was already lost! Everything had gone completely over my head. I was so preoccupied with worrying about going up and down steps, as well as with physical problems related to my condition, I couldn't concentrate on the lectures at all.

Fortunately for me, the weather was nice during those first days. I was afraid to think what it was going to be like in the rain or, even worse, in the snow and ice.

I knew my situation was unique and I didn't want to inconvenience anyone because of my special needs, so I was hesitant to ask the administration for special treatment. Back then, I actually felt grateful to Cornell for allowing me to return to school there, for contributing to the cost of my education, and for converting the lounge at Sage Hall into a dorm room for me.

On the other hand, while they had promised me some things before I came up, nothing much materialized until midway through the semester. I had meetings, on and off, with lots of people, with virtually nothing getting done. We continued discussing installing a sink in my room, as well as a different type of phone setup to enable me to contact campus security in case of an emergency.

Later, I asked the administration if they would put in some curb cuts and install a ramp in front of my dorm so I would not have to go up and down those ten steps a few times each day. They politely denied my request for the ramp. They told me that building a ramp there would necessitate removing two bushes and they were worried that students might protest if they did.

This was the fall of 1971 and the country was in the midst of the Vietnam War. Students were protesting not only the war but also many other controversial issues. Who knew what else they might protest?

I knew the school administration was not trying to be difficult. They just did not understand the needs of people with disabilities. It was all new to them, as it was for me. It was the classic example of the blind leading the blind.

There were no special counselors or advisors I could turn to for help or guidance. There were no disability services back then. This was more than twenty years before the Americans with Disabilities Act took effect.

♦ ♦ ♦

The second day of the semester happened to be date night at Sigma Nu. Betsy, Dave, Chris Eddy, and I went to my fraternity that evening for dinner. The brothers ate in jacket and tie and the "House" looked very impressive.

That was the first time I had put on a jacket and tie since the accident, ten and a half months earlier. It felt really strange. It was also the first time I was back inside my fraternity house since that fateful day last October.

I hadn't remembered that my fraternity had six steps in front of it. There was also a long flight of steep steps to get from the entrance hall down to the dining room.

It didn't feel the same being back in the House. The brothers from the class before mine had graduated and were now gone. One-third of the House was made up of last year's pledge class, which I had never met.

Nevertheless, I returned two days later, to attend the Freshman Tea.

My fraternity held the Freshman Tea every year after the first week of classes. The brothers invited the prettiest freshman girls they could find. On September 10, they ended up with close to a hundred girls. Considering there were only forty-five guys in the fraternity, and ten of them were either engaged or pinned, it was a pretty good ratio for the rest of the brothers.

It was a very awkward situation for me though. Apparently, few, if any, of the girls had read the article "Kenny Returns to Cornell," which appeared that day in the *Cornell Daily Sun*. I saw many of the girls looking at me, trying to figure out who I was and what I was doing there. I felt very conspicuous and out of place.

Occasionally, my brothers would bring girls over to introduce to me, but that also felt awkward. Frequently, after they spent some time with me, though, they would comment, "You are still the same old Kunk." That was always nice to hear.

My fraternity had a great band playing. There was a lot of dancing and drinking going on until one in the morning. I sat quietly in a corner most of the evening.

My fraternity brothers were really caring, concerned, and thoughtful. At the beginning of the semester, they tried to be especially helpful. Each night, one of the brothers would come up to visit me, giving my attendant Dave some time off. They took turns, so it was a different person each night. As a result, I spent a major part of every evening talking with whoever was visiting at the time, to either get acquainted or reacquainted. I was, therefore, not able to get much studying done at night. I needed to do it all in the afternoon, before they came. It was challenging to try to keep up with my schoolwork, even without any distractions.

One of the unplanned benefits of having my fraternity brothers come up each night, was that the fraternity cook, Calmar Handlin, insisted they bring me the dinner she had cooked for the fraternity that evening. She was a really good cook and her dinners were a lot better than those from the dorm cafeteria.

Cal had liked me a lot when I lived at the fraternity before my accident. I used to go to the back of the kitchen just to spend some time visiting and talking with her. She even visited me once when I was at Rusk. She was a tough old lady and nobody at the fraternity ever dared to cross her. When she told them to bring me dinner, I could be sure they would.

After about a month, though, I decided to bring an end to my fraternity brothers' nightly visits. It was the only way I could get any work done. They still stopped by to bring me Cal's dinner and for occasional brief visits. It worked out better that way. Besides,

I had many visits from Barbara McPherson, who worked in the dorm, Joanie Schwartz, whom I knew from Oceanside, and, of course, Betsy, whom I could never see enough of.

♦ ♦ ♦

Many times, Dave would leave me alone "studying" in the room for an hour or so, while he did some errands or took a walk. I would have him set up a textbook for me, resting at an angle on a book rack on my lapboard. My lapboard, at that time, was just a wooden board that attached with straps to the armrests of my wheelchair. It had been made for me while I was at Rusk.

I would use the eraser of a pencil to turn the pages of my textbooks. The pencil was inserted into a spring clip that was attached to my left wrist splint. My left arm would be placed in the BFO, which held my arm about eight inches above the lapboard. Because my right arm was still resting on the lapboard, I was always sitting at an awkward angle.

Studying in Sage Hall dorm room—1972.
Photo by Roger Archibald.

Many times, it would take me a few minutes just to turn one page. Sometimes the book would fall off the book rack or the book rack would fall off the lapboard.

Inevitably, my left arm would fall out of the trough of the BFO, especially when I had a spasm or even just yawned. When I did yawn, my right arm would often fall off the side of the lapboard. Either way, I would end up leaning to the left or right, hanging over the side of the wheelchair. Just as I had on the roof at Rusk, I had to try to keep from falling over by clinging to the headrest with the back of my head. All I could do then was wait for somebody to come along to straighten me up and put my arm back in the BFO.

There had been no therapists or seating specialists to advise me when I had ordered my new wheelchairs while still a patient at Rusk. I had relied on the wheelchair company's representative's recommendations. The representative said that I did not need an electric wheelchair that reclined, so I did not order one. As a result, my electric wheelchair was not very comfortable.

My manual wheelchair was a semi-recliner but not very stable. It could easily flip over backward. Neither of my wheelchairs was equipped with side lateral supports or safety straps to keep me sitting up straight. It was very uncomfortable sitting at an awkward angle for lengthy periods of time. I frequently experienced a lot of pain in both my shoulders.

Still, I liked the moments of privacy. I liked to be left alone to just think. It also made it easier for me to focus on my studies, since there were no other distractions. Being alone was often very frustrating, though, because I was virtually unable to do anything by myself.

Eventually, Cornell built a special desk for me. It took up a whole corner of the room. The desk had cutouts for my right arm and the wheelchair joystick, providing me with three workstations. Since I couldn't use my electric wheelchair outdoors because of all the architectural barriers, the only time I used it at Cornell was when I was trying to work at that desk, which, as it turned out, was only when I was typing my papers. I had an IBM Selectric typewriter set up on the desk. The typewriter was too heavy and too big to fit on my lapboard.

The first time I tried working at that desk in my electric wheelchair, I smashed my foot against the back wall. I didn't initially realize it, since I had no feeling there. I only discovered it when I backed away from the desk and saw my bloody foot. I wasn't wearing shoes at the time and I didn't know that my feet protruded farther in front of my wheelchair than the depth of the desk. I couldn't see through my wooden lapboard.

I don't know where my hands or feet are at any given moment unless I look at them. In order for me to operate my electric wheelchair, I have to be able to see my hand on the joystick. Because I cannot feel it, or even move my hand, I need to watch my whole arm make every little subtle movement, while also being prepared to quickly move my arm off the joystick in case of an involuntary muscle spasm, which I cannot control very well either.

By the same token, at every moment of the day and night I need to be aware if any part of my body could be in danger of being injured. I never know if the position I am left sitting in is going to cause a bedsore to develop. Sitting too long on a wrinkle in my pants can be enough to cause my skin to break down. Once, I burned my left elbow because I couldn't feel that my arm was too close to a portable heater.

Overcoming the physical problems would have been hard enough, but the coursework was so difficult in itself that, even when I could read a few pages, I had trouble grasping the subject matter.

I had originally planned to have my attendant, Dave, take notes for me while in class. After all, Dave had majored in chemical engineering when he was a student at Cornell. He was used to attending technical lectures. It didn't take long for me to realize, though, that that was not going to work out.

First, Dave's handwriting was totally illegible. Second, it was hard enough for the students who were enrolled in the classes to remain focused on those extremely boring lectures. To ask someone who was not even taking the course to try to pay attention would have certainly fit the definition of "cruel and unusual punishment."

After a while, Dave would just drop me off at the lecture hall and come back to pick me up when the class was over.

I eventually arranged to have my freshman roommate, Bob Skelly, as well as one of my fraternity brothers, give me a copy of their notes. I would give them carbon paper, as well as extra notebook paper, to put under their notes as they were taking them and hope that, at the end of each lecture, the carbon copy was not too smudged for me to read.

Some people had suggested I tape the lectures, but they were difficult enough to sit through once. There was no way I would have the time, energy, or desire to sit through them a second time.

I never seemed to be able to get enough sleep. I was always tired and constantly yawned while in class. Every time I yawned, my arms would move out to the side. My right arm would eventually fall off the armrest and bang against the side of the chair. That drew even more attention to me than the usual stares.

My level of alertness was certainty not helped by the fact that I was still taking a lot of Valium to control my muscle spasms.

Another constant problem was the functioning of my bladder. It was not emptying the way it was supposed to. When the urine in my bladder exceeded a certain level, I would break into heavy sweating. It seemed to happen a number of times each day. Sometimes the sweating was so profuse, I felt as if I was sitting under a waterfall. I would sometimes have difficulty seeing because the sweat would get into my eyes. My fellow classmates didn't know why I was sweating so much and probably thought I was hot. That certainly was not the case. In fact, frequently, I would be having chills and shivering uncontrollably, while sweating at the same time.

I looked at one of my old pamphlets from Rusk to see if they discussed the bladder problem. The medical staff at Rusk never really told me what to do about it, apart from that memorable warning about the possibility of getting a stroke due to high blood pressure created by the condition. I learned I was experiencing something called "autonomic dysreflexia." The pamphlet said that this is an emergency condition, could be life-threatening and I should get medical help immediately! I couldn't believe it. Even if

I had a way to get to the hospital, it would not have been practical for me to go every time I started to sweat.

I found out, on my own, that if someone reclined the back of my wheelchair or lay me down in bed my bladder would usually empty. Interestingly, one of the suggestions in the pamphlet was that, when you become dysreflexic, you should sit straight up. When you become dysreflexic, your blood pressure goes very high. Lying down or reclining could raise it even more.

Soon after my return to Cornell, a student approached me outside Upson Hall and asked if I was Ken Kunken. When I replied that I was, he asked, "Aren't you supposed to be in the hospital?" I was very tempted to reply, "Yes, but I escaped. Please don't tell anyone," but I thought better of it.

However, I started to think that maybe the student was right. Maybe I should have just stayed in the hospital or at home with my family. What was I thinking, returning to Cornell so soon after my injury? Clearly, I was not ready, physically or mentally, to resume my studies.

In spite of my numerous physical problems, I tried desperately to keep up with my schoolwork.

My first homework assignment was in Deterministic Models. It took me eight hours to complete it and that was only after getting someone to help me do the last four out of the five problems.

I couldn't do assignments on my own, in any event. I needed someone to do the writing for me. It certainly wasn't easy having another person sitting by my side, pen in hand, while I had no clue how to tackle the problems. It was disheartening to know that the assignments were only going to get more difficult as the semester wore on.

To do my Computer Science homework, I needed to go to Upson Hall to keypunch computer cards. I couldn't fit closely enough to the keyboard to do that by myself. I needed someone to do it for me or give me so much help it was as though that person was doing it all anyway.

My psychology course required only one ten-page paper for its written homework. Fortunately, I was excused from that assignment, because I had already written a paper for that course before I was injured.

Within two to three weeks, I was getting little out of the lectures in my engineering classes, nothing from the books, and even less from the homework. I was nervous and scared. There were so many doubts in my mind as to whether I would ever be able to do the work.

All my professors told me that if I was having trouble I should ask for help. The problem was, I didn't even know what help to ask for. I wanted to say, "I know absolutely nothing. Explain everything to me."

Near the end of the third week of the semester, I had my first preliminary exam. I was glad that it was in Probability. That was the one engineering course in which I had a decent knowledge of what was going on.

I discussed with Professor Weiss, my instructor in the course, how I was going to take the exam. We agreed I would take it orally, in his study, with him writing my responses on the blackboard. I felt confident going into the test, since I thought at that time that I knew my stuff.

I realized I was in trouble as soon as Dave wheeled me into Professor Weiss's study. Professor Weiss put the exam questions on my lap and stood by the blackboard with his hand in the air, holding the chalk, ready to start writing. I read question number one out loud. As he waited for me to start dictating my answer, I went blank. I read the question again, but still had no idea how to start.

I decided to move on to question number two. Again, nothing. I read question number three and then number four and finally question number five. Still, nothing was clicking in my head. I didn't know how to answer any of them. The professor was still standing by the blackboard, chalk in hand.

I had fifty minutes for the exam. If I blew it, there was virtually no hope I would do any better on any other tests. I was very close to panicking. The professor stood in silence by the blackboard for what seemed like an eternity.

I went back to question number one and, suddenly, a light went on in my head. Words started flowing and the professor had to write feverishly to keep up. Questions two through five went pretty much the same way. I finished the exam in twenty minutes.

Professor Weiss graded it right in front of me. I got an eighty-five. Initially, I felt pretty good about that grade, but soon I became upset with myself. I should have gotten an A. I knew my stuff and should have done better.

My next exam was in Computer Science. A fraternity brother helped me study for it. Going into the test, I knew I did not have a good grasp of the material, but at least it was an open book exam. The test was, again, taken orally, in my computer science professor's study. It was a one-and-a-half-hour exam.

It didn't take long for the professor to realize I didn't have a good handle on the subject. After I read a problem, I seemed clueless how to proceed. The professor encouraged me to go back over my notes to find the answer. Unfortunately, that was the one class in which Dave had continued to take notes for me. I couldn't read his handwriting. Somehow, I managed to get a grade of seventy-eight. The class average was only seventy-nine. So, because the course was graded on a curve, seventy-eight was not such a bad score.

The toughest exam was yet to come. It was in Deterministic Models. The instructor was Professor Eisner. Deterministic Models involved an advanced way to solve problems mathematically. Calculus was a prerequisite for the course and the course was only given for engineering students. I knew nothing!

Two days before the exam, Professor Eisner asked me how I was doing. I responded, "Fine." I was too embarrassed to tell him the truth.

Bob Skelly and a fraternity brother, Sal March, came to my dorm room and helped me study for more than ten hours during the next two days. From 7:00 p.m. to 12:30 a.m., we went over all the homework assignments for the previous three weeks. In those two days, I learned almost everything we had covered in the course so far. I went to sleep confident and relieved. I felt I had a good grasp of what was going on.

However, when I awoke the next morning, everything seemed to have gone out of my head during the night. Once again, I was

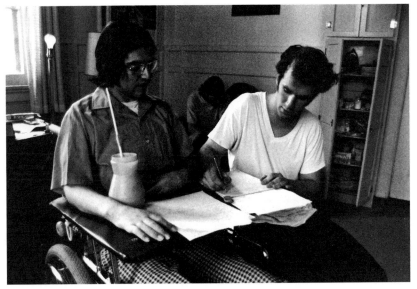

Bob Skelly helping Ken study, with Dave in the background—1972.
Photo by Roger Archibald.

ready to panic. Fortunately, during the exam, it all came back and I got an A.

Bob Skelly and Sal March helped me study for all the exams for that course. It was always the same scenario. Two days before each exam, I felt like I didn't have a clue what the course was about. By exam time, I felt I had a competent knowledge of the material. However, as the semester progressed my grades for that course got steadily worse.

On my next Probability exam, I received a ninety-eight, my highest grade yet.

I studied especially hard because my exams were mostly one-on-one, just me and the professor. If I didn't know my stuff, it was obvious. Before each exam, I felt I didn't know a thing. I crammed, did decently, and then went on to the next test. That was how it went the whole semester.

Chapter 13

A Very Different Cornell Experience

♦ ♦ ♦

I tried to participate in campus life and become involved in extra-curricular activities. Unfortunately, it usually was too difficult physically for me to do. Most of the facilities in which the activities were offered were not accessible.

Many times, I felt as if I was on exhibit at Cornell. Everywhere I went, I was constantly being stared at. Some students probably wanted to be friendly but didn't know how to approach me and start a conversation. Because I was always in a manual wheelchair, I could not approach them on my own. It didn't help that I was shy to begin with. The attention only made it worse.

The first two weeks of school, I tried to eat most of my meals in the cafeteria, right opposite my room. Usually, Dave fed me, but one afternoon I had Dave set me up with my BFO braces and splints so I could feed myself. I had to concentrate really hard and be totally focused, to have any chance of getting food into my mouth. At one point, I looked up from my plate only to find everyone in the cafeteria staring, watching me eat. I don't mean just a few people, I mean everybody. I became so uncomfortable and self-conscious that, for the rest of the year, I ate most of my meals in my room.

♦ ♦ ♦

Dave McMurray wheeling Ken on the Engineering Quad.
This picture appeared on the cover of the July 1972 issue
of *Cornell Alumni News*, with the article "The First Year Back."
The picture and the story were by Roger Archibald.

To raise money for the Ken Kunken Fund, a rock concert featuring the groups Rare Earth and Mandril was scheduled to take place in Barton Hall on October 9. The concert was being recorded live for a new Rare Earth album. Neither of those bands were well known at that time, although Rare Earth did have the hit songs "Get Ready" and "Celebrate."

Before the event, there was a lot of publicity about me and the concert. It was constantly announced on the radio and in the newspapers. Tickets were being sold at Cornell, Ithaca College, and in the city of Ithaca.

I was uncomfortable with all the attention, and, like my father, embarrassed at the fact that money was being raised for my benefit. I didn't like being the focus of a charity, but certainly was grateful for everyone's generosity and desire to help me.

Steve, who came up for the weekend, Chris Eddy, Betsy, and I sat in the center of the front row during the concert.

One of the members of the Rare Earth band began by announcing, "As you all know, this concert is to raise money for the Ken Kunken Fund. We just heard that Kenny Kunken has returned to Cornell, and we think that this is a reason to celebrate." They then started singing their hit song "Celebrate." That was really cool.

Later in the year, many other fundraisers were held. My fraternity sponsored a Steak and Brew Party. It was completely sold out. There was also a hockey game between two Canadian B teams. Half of all the admission proceeds went to my fund. Those events raised about $2,000 each.

The fundraisers gave me an excuse to spend more time with Betsy, since she always accompanied me to them. Still, I most appreciated the time that I got to be alone with her. Betsy was always bubbly and enthusiastic, no matter what we were doing. We spent some really nice weekend afternoons together. Sometimes we hiked around campus or just sat in the gardens writing letters to my relatives and listening to music on the radio. Betsy soon learned how to take care of me and would stay with me when Dave took some time off. She was great with my care.

I watched the lightweight football team practice a few times and even went with Betsy in her car to Cortland, a half hour drive from Cornell, to watch the team scrimmage.

I went to all of the lightweight football team's home games as well. Players and coaches would come by while I was there to say hello and see how I was doing.

Usually, being at the games was not easy for me. It was frustrating watching from the sidelines and not being out on the field with the rest of my teammates. I didn't want to just watch them play, I wanted to be on the field with them.

I knew the exact spot on lower alumni field where I had been hurt. Frequently, my gaze would focus on that spot, to the exclusion of everything else that was taking place around me.

At the end of the season, I attended the lightweight football team's sports banquet. The team presented me with the game ball from the Army game. The game had been played on October 8, 1971, and was Cornell's most significant win of the year.

Barbara McPherson, Ken, Chris Eddy, Sigma Nu fraternity brother
Dan Galusha and cousin Roy Danis at Cornell's Schoellkopf Field—fall 1971.
Photo by Jim Cunningham.

The inscription on the ball read: "Cornell 150s, 1971, presented to
Kenny Kunken by the team." Just like when I received a game ball
a year before while in Elmira, I was very touched by the gesture.

I went with Betsy to the home heavyweight football games as
well. A lot of people would walk up to me and introduce themselves. One of them was a campus patrolman who had been at the
game at which I was injured.

On Saturday, October 30, fifty-two weeks to the day I was
injured, I went with Betsy to the heavyweight football game. As
luck would have it, Cornell was playing Columbia. It was a beautiful day and the stadium had a large crowd. I sat in front of the
front row, on the fifty-yard line.

There was a two-page article about me, written by Jim Hanchett, in the football program that day, titled: "Ken Kunken—A Year
Later." It even had a picture of me watching a game at the stadium,
which was taken earlier that season. It would have been hard for
any of the thousands in attendance not to see the article or me.

At one point during the game, a Columbia receiver jumped
high in the air to try and catch a pass. A Cornell defender then

Ken with Chris Eddy and Dave McMurray at a
Cornell football game—October 1971.
Photo by Jim Cunningham.

took the receiver's legs out from under him. The receiver flipped over and came down on his head. He had been knocked unconscious. He lay on the field motionless for a considerable length of time. No one knew whether the Columbia player had just suffered a spinal cord injury, like I had a year earlier. Fortunately, he had not. It seemed like everyone in the stadium turned to look at me to see my reaction.

I felt terrible. I couldn't believe I almost witnessed another tragedy on the last Saturday in October, on a Cornell football field, in a game against Columbia. Talk about déjà vu! What a relief to finally see the player walk off the field. I couldn't wait for the game to end.

♦ ♦ ♦

Sunday, October 31, was not an easy day for me. It was the one-year anniversary of my injury. It had been a long, frustrating, depressing, and painful year. I was still almost totally paralyzed. I never imagined I would be in this condition a year later.

Now every time I heard anyone even mention the word "Halloween," I became more depressed. Seeing pumpkins everywhere throughout the fall made it worse. Halloween went from being my favorite day of the year to being the one I dreaded the most.

At least I was out of the hospital and back at Cornell with the rest of my classmates. While the doctors and medical researchers felt that it was impossible to fix a damaged spinal cord, and, as a result, didn't appear even to be trying to do anything toward that end, I was still hopeful that a cure for my paralysis was just around the corner. I wasn't going to remain sedentary, waiting for it to come, though. I was trying to make something out of my life until that eventual cure finally came about.

♦ ♦ ♦

Late in the semester, I developed a bedsore. I couldn't feel or see it, but either Dave or Betsy noticed it. Despite their best efforts, every time I would get back up in the wheelchair, the bedsore got worse.

I called Barbara Crook. She recommended that I stay in bed for at least a week, lying on my side. It was very uncomfortable for me to remain in that position most of the day. In addition, it was incredibly frustrating. It was tough enough trying to keep up with my studies when I was sitting in the wheelchair. It was almost impossible to do so lying in bed.

Barbara was very concerned about the lack of medical care I was receiving. In addition to visiting me one weekend, she kept in constant contact by telephone. The campus doctor assigned to me was not very helpful or accommodating. He seemed to feel I was an extra burden. Barbara arranged to have Cornell switch me to a different campus doctor, Dr. Young, who took a genuine interest in me. He even came to my room to see me once a week and was very helpful the rest of the time I was at Cornell.

Barbara also got in touch with the Tompkins County public health nursing service and arranged for a public health nurse to see me twice a week while I was at Cornell. Thanks to Barbara, I now had a nurse and a doctor in Ithaca to call in case of any medical problems.

Generally, I stayed in pretty good shape throughout the semester. I had to. I was very worried about ending up back in the hospital.

Fortunately, the weather during my first semester back was pretty good. By Ithaca standards, it was one of the best falls ever. There was very little snow and it rained mostly while I was inside. Still, I was constantly cold.

Incredibly, my grades were far better than my grades my first two years. I finished my first semester back at Cornell with the following grades: Introduction to Psychology, A; Computer Programming, B+; Probability, B; Deterministic Models, C+.

I had completed a total of thirteen credits, for a grade point average of 3.08. A few months earlier, I would have been happy just to pass. Now I was demanding a lot more from myself.

♦ ♦ ♦

Sometime in late November, Betsy invited me to spend a few days with her and her family, over the winter break, including Christmas, at her home in Pawling, New York. I was surprised when she made the offer.

I had never spent Christmas Eve or Day with any family that celebrated that holiday. Then, again, I had never really spent any amount of time with any girl's family before I was injured and certainly never considered sleeping over at someone's house. I also wondered how much Betsy had told her parents about me, my needs, and about us. What would they think of Betsy taking care of me: bathing me, dressing me, changing the condom, giving me a suppository, etc.? What would they think of their daughter dating a quadriplegic? Betsy was just kooky enough not to say a word and totally surprise her family.

Knowing I was extremely concerned, Betsy assured me that her parents knew enough about me to know what inviting me for an overnight stay involved. Betsy said that she would be responsible for my total care anyway and I didn't need to be so worried. I was apprehensive but Betsy was very insistent. With a great deal of trepidation, I agreed to go.

After my last exam, Dave and Betsy lifted me into Betsy's car. I was now ready to leave Cornell for a month's vacation, first at Betsy's and then at Aunt Lorraine's. I was really looking forward to getting away from Ithaca. Dave and I got along well but, because we spent so much time together we both needed a break.

Betsy's parents were warm and very welcoming.

Betsy really enjoyed everything involved with Christmas, and her enthusiasm was contagious. The first night there, I watched her decorate the tree. For the next few days, she continuously played records of Christmas carols.

On Christmas Eve, we went to Betsy's brother Bob's house, which was about a twenty-minute drive into Connecticut. Bob was married and had two young daughters. Bob also happened to have multiple sclerosis. His house was built to be wheelchair accessible. There were no steps. The carpet in every room was perfectly even with that of each adjoining room. The halls were wide and the cabinets were low. There were sliding doors and the bathrooms were equipped with grab bars.

It really got me thinking about the type of house I would like to eventually own. But even more so, it started me thinking again about what kind of family life I might someday have. Bob's kids were born before he was diagnosed with multiple sclerosis. His family situation had developed before his illness. How could mine possibly begin?

My stay at Betsy's worked out better than I ever imagined. What could have been better than spend my first Christmas with Betsy?

After an enjoyable three days, Betsy and her parents drove me to Aunt Lorraine's. I felt a bit uncomfortable about them doing so much to accommodate me.

Steve was in Oceanside as well, but his arm was in a sling. He had dislocated his shoulder skiing. As badly as I felt for Steve, I was also upset with him. I had been relying on him to be my arms and legs when we were together. Steve's hurting his shoulder limited my activities as well.

I started to realize that I had to be concerned with not only my health but also the health of everyone else on whom I was in any way dependent. If my attendant got sick or injured his arm, leg, or back, I would be in big trouble. Every time one of my care-givers went out without a coat or engaged in any kind of physical activity, I worried about the consequences for me.

Fortunately, I did not need to rely on Steve's help when I was in Oceanside. Ever since I was discharged from Rusk, when I was not away at school, Aunt Lorraine and my cousins took over my care. Steve was usually staying at our father's home or away in Boston.

A few days into that winter vacation, Betsy came back to Oceanside to spend some additional time with me. Barbara Crook made arrangements for herself and her husband Dave, several of their friends, and Betsy and me to go to a restaurant on New Year's Eve. It was the first time I had ever had a date for New Year's Eve. As much as I enjoyed the evening and the company, it was frustrating for me to be so limited.

♦ ♦ ♦

Armed with the confidence the previous semester's 3.08 cume had given me, I decided to push myself a bit further. I registered for three engineering courses and an elective for a total of sixteen credit hours, an ambitious undertaking.

Jim Maas, my Introduction to Psychology professor, thought that clinical psychology might be a viable field for me. He felt I could make a significant contribution in that area. Professor Maas offered me the opportunity to take an independent study course in Counseling and Clinical Psychology with him.

I was very flattered that Professor Maas had singled me out. His encouragement made me think seriously about pursuing a career in psychology.

♦ ♦ ♦

Ken talking with Professor James Maas—1972.
Photo by Roger Archibald.

Other than classes, the one activity that kept me out of my dorm room during Ithaca's frigid cold and snowy winter was attending Cornell hockey games. The Cornell-Harvard hockey game was postponed from a Saturday afternoon to the following Monday night because twenty-four inches of snow had fallen. The snow was so deep that the administration even canceled classes for a day, a real rarity at Cornell.

The snow didn't prevent me from going to the game though. Four fraternity brothers volunteered to carry me, in my wheelchair, the one-quarter mile uphill through the knee-deep snow, to Lynah Rink, the hockey arena. I was shivering for hours afterward but really enjoyed the event.

♦ ♦ ♦

One night, during my second semester, there was a fire drill. Everyone had to evacuate the building. The next day, one of the school administrators asked me how I had managed during the drill. I told him, being honest, that while I was able to get out, by having my attendant bounce me, in my wheelchair, down the ten steps, I felt bad because I had slowed down some of the other students exiting through the same door. Wouldn't you know, within two weeks they installed the ramp I had asked for at the beginning of the previous semester. It was obvious to me that the ramp was built not for my convenience, but rather for the other students' safety. That was still fine with me. At least now I had a ramp to use.

By the way, not one student complained about removing the two bushes to make room for the ramp. In fact, many preferred using it to walking up and down the ten steps. I suppose there is a lesson there somewhere.

♦ ♦ ♦

Much to my dismay, I was seeing less and less of Betsy now. She was the first girl that I ever really had strong feelings for. The gradual ending of our brief relationship was difficult for me to accept. While it would probably have ended just as quickly had I not been injured, I remained convinced that my disability was a major factor in Betsy's choosing to date other students. It was a difficult pill for me to swallow.

Betsy was special. Few others had her sensitivity and compassion. Maybe because she was studying physical therapy, she was more attuned to my special needs. Or maybe she was just a very rare and unique woman. In any event, we were now only good friends.

In late March, Steve suggested that I contact the Ithaca College Physical Therapy Department to see if some type of arrangement could be made that would be mutually beneficial to both the physical therapy students and me. Betsy put me in touch with one of her professors, Bob Grant, to discuss it.

Bob Grant and I arranged for Betsy to come to my room with four different physical therapy students each day, four days a week. Most were sophomores, like Betsy, while a few were juniors.

I would tell the students a bit about what the physical therapists had done for me in the hospital and then Betsy and I would show them how to do range of motion exercises on me. Sometimes, I had four students, each working on one of my limbs, at the same time.

Mostly, it was a lot more work for me. Different students came over each night and I had to provide them with the same lengthy explanations and demonstrations. Still, it enabled me to see more of Betsy. A silver lining in every cloud . . .

At the end of the semester, Bob Grant invited me to speak at Ithaca College, before the physical therapy students as well as anybody else that wanted to attend. On May 2, approximately 175 people came to hear me speak.

I sat in the front of a large lecture room, with a microphone on a table facing me. Bob Grant sat to my right. I was pretty nervous at the beginning. I had been under the impression that it was just going to be a question and answer session. I was surprised when I was asked to deliver a talk, but even more so when the words flowed out of my mouth with ease. I told the audience about the treatment I had received in various hospitals from the doctors, nurses, and therapists and how disappointed I was with much of the care. I told them what I thought could have been done better and gave examples of some of the few medical professionals who were particularly helpful, and why.

The next issue of the Ithaca College newspaper had a nice article about my talk and a picture of me speaking.

♦ ♦ ♦

Final exams, as usual, were a traumatic experience. I did manage to finish the semester with the following grades: Probabilistic Models, D+; Computer Science, B-; Statistics, B+; and Clinical Psych, A.

That worked out to a cume of 2.83. Not great, but still respectable.

Steve drove up in his car and, after some awkward good-byes to both Dave and Betsy, Steve and I left Ithaca.

I had completed my first year back at Cornell. Nobody had thought I could do it. I probably would have made a lot of money if I had bet against the odds. Certainly, the struggle wasn't over. In fact, it was just beginning.

Chapter 14

The Summer of '72

◆ ◆ ◆

Before I left the campus, Bob Linden, a fraternity brother who was completing his first year at Cornell Medical School in New York City, asked if I would address his class. He wanted me to talk about myself and my experiences in the hospital.

Addressing a class of medical students was too good an opportunity to pass up. This would be my chance to influence prospective doctors before they became so immersed in the medical aspects of their job they lost sight of the human side of it.

On May 22, 1972, Betsy drove from Pawling to Oceanside. With assistance from Aunt Lorraine, she lifted me into her old and somewhat dilapidated car. We took off, with Betsy holding my left shoulder with her right hand to keep me from sliding at every start, stop, and turn.

There were five doctors and approximately ninety students present to hear me talk. One of the students had played with me on the lightweight football team. In fact, he had played in the game I was injured.

I was a bit nervous at the beginning but the talk went well. Just like at Ithaca College a few weeks earlier, I described the treatment I received from various doctors while I was in the hospital. There were many questions from the students afterward.

Most of the feedback from the students was positive. However, a few said I was just bitter about my experiences because I didn't get my movement back. I did my best to convince them that, bitter or not, the treatment I was given was not nearly as good as it should have been. Much of it had been outright bad. Some of the students, though, felt it necessary to defend the medical profession. Maybe if I had spoken to them a few months earlier, they would not have already become so jaded.

♦ ♦ ♦

The previous April, I had received a call from the principal of Dryden High School, which was located not far from Cornell. I was taken by complete surprise when he told me the senior class had voted to have me be the commencement speaker at their graduation on June 26. I had no idea they even knew who I was, let alone that they would want me to speak at their graduation.

The Dryden High School students were curious and wanted to learn more about me and how I was able to function with my limitations. They rarely came in contact with someone who had such a visible and significant physical disability.

The principal told me that he would like me to speak for about fifteen minutes, on any topic I desired. There would also be a $75 honorarium for me.

The whole idea made me nervous. There were 125 graduating seniors. I figured each student would bring two parents, adding 250 people, for a total of 375, certainly a sizable number.

I worried: "How could they possibly expect me to prepare a speech?" "Don't they know that I'm in Engineering?" "We can't write, or do virtually anything that requires verbal skills. That's a given!"

I hope that you are not all nodding in agreement as you read this.

A few days before my Dryden High School talk, Russ Canan happened to stop by to visit with me at Aunt Lorraine's. Dave Gilbert, Rich Gilman, and Russ Canan were the three high school friends I still stayed in touch with.

I was really nervous about the upcoming graduation ceremony. Russ offered to help me with the talk. I went over all the points I wanted to cover in my speech with him. Russ came back the next night, three days before the speech, with a handwritten draft he had prepared, adding a few little tidbits of his own. Russ was leaving the next morning to go to North Carolina, where he was taking a job working with migrant farm workers.

I rehearsed the speech with Dave and Rich and made a few changes. Rich offered to type up the finished version that night at his house. Because I didn't have another copy, I was leery about letting the speech out of my sight for even a second. Still, I very much appreciated the offer and took Rich up on it. Rich brought back the finished copy Friday, one day before the speech.

I knew I could count on my three friends from Oceanside. Dave, Rich, and Russ always had my back.

I still wasn't sure if I liked the speech. I didn't think it sounded like an appropriate commencement address. Now it was really time to panic. Why did I agree to give that damn speech?

My Aunt Betty, one of my mother's younger sisters, volunteered to drive and take care of me while we were upstate. She was understandably nervous about assuming that responsibility for the first time.

Betty was thirty-three, only twelve years older than me. In fact, she was actually closer in age to me than she had been to my mother, Judy. Since my accident, Betty and I had become very close. She was more like a sister to me than an aunt. Betty, along with Steve and Barbara, became part of my unofficial support group I relied on for years.

The graduation was to take place on Saturday night. I arranged to drive up Saturday morning and, after the speech, spend the night in my dorm room at Cornell. My friends Dave Gilbert and Joanie Schwartz made the trip with us.

During a good deal of the car ride, Dave kept after me to rehearse the speech. I made the mistake of letting him hold on to the typed copy during the way up. A couple of times, Dave held the pages of the speech out the car window and made believe that the speech flew out of his hand while we were on the highway. Needless to say, he greatly added to my anxiety.

We arrived upstate with enough time to stop at my dorm room at Cornell and rest for a few hours before the speech. I don't remember ever feeling as nervous as I did during the fifteen-minute car ride to Dryden High School. Why had I ever agreed to do this? My stomach was in my mouth.

To make matters worse, when we got to Dryden High School, I found out that, rather than the 375 people I had been expecting, there were more than 1,000 people there. Where they came from, I'm still not sure. But it seemed like the whole town turned out.

I vowed to myself to never again do any public speaking.

After the class president's speech, the program listed "Introduction" and then "Commencement Address." I had no idea that "Introduction" meant that they were going to introduce me. I thought there would be another speech for me to sit through before it was my turn. I was very surprised when, after just two sentences, I heard my name. My name was followed by some loud applause and, before I knew what hit me, Dave Gilbert wheeled me up to the microphone.

I managed to get out one sentence before my mouth went completely dry. For the next seven and a half minutes, I was smacking my lips together, trying to draw up whatever moisture I could.

When I was two sentences into the speech, a baby started to cry. The baby continued to cry throughout the remainder of my talk.

Within another few sentences, I felt a big muscle spasm about to come on. Just like during the subcommittee hearing, that was one of my big fears: to get a spasm while talking before such a large group. I took a long but, I hoped, unnoticed pause. I spoke more softly for the rest of the speech and tried to avoid taking any deep breaths. It worked, and the spasm was, at least for the time being, avoided.

With a dry throat, a crying baby, a loud air conditioner rattling in the background, and the constant fear of a spasm, I proceeded through the speech. When I finished, I was given a long and loud standing ovation.

Both the graduates and people from the audience came up to me at the conclusion of the ceremony and told me they had really enjoyed my talk. It was music to my ears.

The principal extended his congratulations, then apologized for not having my check ready and said he would mail it. A few days later, I received a check in the mail for $150, twice the agreed amount, along with a very complimentary letter.

Over the past two months, I had spoken at Ithaca College, Cornell Medical School, and Dryden High School. I had delivered my first two talks without even preparing my remarks ahead of time. I still couldn't believe that words actually came out of my mouth. Who knew I could do this?

I had always thought I would pursue a career working with numbers, not with people. I had rarely raised my hand in class because I didn't like drawing attention to myself. Now here I was, speaking before hundreds of people—about myself no less. I was even more surprised that my talks were so well received. Perhaps I should consider a career that would make use of my newly discovered speaking ability.

♦ ♦ ♦

Engineering students were expected to take five courses a semester. Because I had taken only four courses during each of my past two semesters, I needed an additional two electives to keep pace with the rest of the class. I arranged to take two summer courses at Hofstra University, beginning in June. One was a course in educational psychology and the other was an introductory course in sociology. By taking five courses during the next two semesters, I would graduate in May 1973, only one year behind my original class.

The New York State Office of Vocational Rehabilitation provided a small compensation for my cousin Jill to take notes for me. Jill had just graduated from Oceanside High School and was going to be entering her freshman year at Cornell in September.

They also paid for a van to take me back and forth to Hofstra. The van's door was too low for me to enter it comfortably. I was wheeled up two steep boards, which they called a ramp, and, after inevitably bumping my head, the driver would recline my chair and chain it to the floor. My manual wheelchair still rocked back and forth a lot during the ride.

Hofstra was far more accustomed to having students in wheelchairs than Cornell ever was. The Hofstra campus was almost completely accessible, a luxury that would have been easy for me to get used to.

For my sociology course, I had to give a number of oral presentations. I knew that it was important to develop my ability to speak without notes, especially in light of my inability to take notes. I tried to work on improving both my skill and my confidence speaking without anything in front of me. I would think about what I would like to say when I was lying in bed in the middle of the night and couldn't fall back to sleep. I never practiced out loud.

One day, I gave a persuasive talk to the class on the need to make euthanasia legal. Euthanasia was a topic that I had thought about fairly often ever since I'd lost the luxury of being able to take my own life if I chose to do so.

Soon after I finished, I had to leave because the van was already waiting to pick me up. Before I was wheeled out of the classroom, the professor only had time to say that my talk had been very "cogent."

I wasn't sure what that word meant. During the entire ride home, I didn't know whether he liked it or not. As soon as I arrived, I asked Jill to look up the word in the dictionary. Cogent means "powerful." Apparently, the professor really liked my talk.

The sociology course was graded satisfactory or unsatisfactory. I received a grade of satisfactory. I received an A in the educational psychology course.

Chapter 15

Some Sort of Cruel
Exotic Torture

◆ ◆ ◆

My next endeavor that summer involved acupuncture treatments.

During the summer of 1971, while still a patient at the Rusk
Institute, I received a newspaper clipping from Barbara Crook's
mother-in-law. It stated that the Chinese claimed acupuncture
helped and could possibly cure paraplegics. It said that it even
worked on a man paralyzed for eighteen years.

Because acupuncture was relatively unknown in the United
States at that time, my family was convinced I should go to China
for it. Hoping to get me there, More Mom wrote to everyone she
could think of who had any possibility of making that happen.
Unfortunately, all her efforts were unsuccessful.

At some point, my grandparents came across an article in
Time magazine about a Chinese acupuncturist, trained in Singa-
pore, who was purported to be excellent. He was currently living
and working in London. The London acupuncturist responded to
my grandmother's inquiry that he would be willing to try to see if
he could help me.

The doctor could arrange to treat me for three weeks before
he was to leave for vacation. He felt that it was enough time to tell
if the treatments were to work and, if they did, I could return for

more sessions. By the time we received his letter, it was the summer of 1972.

Traveling to London for acupuncture seemed pretty far-fetched but even a remote chance that the treatment could help me regain my movement was more than enough for me to pursue it.

More Pop, my seventy-three-year-old grandfather; Roy, my sixteen-year-old cousin; and I were to fly to London at the end of July 1972. My brother Steve would join us two weeks later, after he took the New York State Bar exam.

Roy was to be responsible for my total physical care, including all the lifting, until Steve arrived. It was a lot of responsibility to put on a sixteen-year-old kid, but Roy knew very well what that involved. He had frequently assumed that responsibility while I was living at his house in Oceanside. He was very good at it. In fact, he was much better than most of my attendants had ever been.

I really didn't know what to expect from acupuncture treatments. A few days before we left, I read an article in the *New York Times* about the use of it as an anesthetic during surgery. One of the places the article indicated the needles were inserted was in the eye sockets. That was all I needed to hear. If I wasn't good and scared before, I certainly was now.

We flew to London and stayed in a hotel. We arose early the next morning. The taxi ride to the doctor's office took twenty minutes. By then, I was really nervous. About five yards from the office door, I could make out the lettering on the sign in the window: S-U-R-G-E-R-Y.

Wait a minute. I didn't know this would involve surgery!

I learned later that in England, many doctors referred to their medical offices as their "surgery."

As if I didn't have enough on my mind to worry about, we encountered an unexpected obstacle. My wheelchair would not fit through the doorway into the office. I had to be carried into the waiting room. Roy seated me on one of the semi-comfortable chairs there.

After a long half hour wait, I was carried into the doctor's room and seated on a small, unsteady chair in the middle of it. Roy had to hold me or I would have fallen over.

The doctor was a man of few words. That was just as well because he spoke with a thick Chinese accent and it was often difficult for us to understand what he was saying. I took the attitude that I would let the doctor do whatever he thought best. If it would help me get my movement back, I was sure that I could put up with any amount of pain.

I was also leery of asking too many questions, for fear of offending the doctor. Clearly, questions seemed to offend most of the American doctors. I wasn't certain if the acupuncturist really understood my English and I certainly did not want him to think I was questioning his competence. I wanted him to try everything he normally would try on someone in my condition.

Before the doctor inserted each needle, he would dab the spot on my skin with alcohol. I watched as he inserted the first needle between the thumb and forefinger of my left hand. I was relieved when I felt no pain. That reassured me that what I had heard about acupuncture being painless was true. I had forgotten that I didn't have any feeling in most of my arms, so, of course, I didn't feel anything.

After the doctor inserted the needle, what seemed to be dangerously far into my hand, he would twist and twirl the needle back and forth with his fingers. He would then, again, dab the spot with alcohol. That procedure was repeated a number of times, as the doctor gradually worked his way up my arm.

When the doctor inserted a needle into my left shoulder, however, I felt pain, which I had previously been spared because of my lack of sensation. I was shocked! It felt like someone was sticking me with a needle, pushing it in a few inches, twirling it around once in, and finally pulling it out. It really hurt. In fact, it seemed like some sort of cruel exotic torture. And now it was to be repeated again and again. Something did not seem right.

After going through that same procedure on my right arm, the doctor started on my neck. He stuck needles into the back and sides of it. It hurt like hell! He was going in so deep that I worried the needles would go right through to the other side. As if that wasn't bad enough, the doctor was now starting on my face.

All I could think about was the article I had read before I left the United States. The one that said that one of the places the needles were inserted was in the eye sockets. I was petrified.

The needles were very painful but I gritted my teeth and tried to bear them. I didn't think I could handle a needle in the eye socket though. Still, I was determined not to say anything.

There was little warning as to where the doctor was going to stick the next needle. The doctor certainly didn't say anything and often the alcohol and the needle arrived at the same time.

The doctor stuck the next needle just above my upper lip, right below the middle of my nose. He then stuck some needles by my ears and a few others around my face. All the areas the doctor was now hitting seemed unusually sensitive and all were very painful.

Now came the moment of truth.

It looked like the next needle was headed straight for my left eye. At the last possible moment, the needle's destination dropped slightly. He inserted it just above my left nostril. It wasn't much below the eye socket. It was too close for comfort.

Soon, another needle was rapidly approaching the middle of my face. This time it looked like my right eye was the target. Suddenly, the needle dropped slightly and landed just above my right nostril. Still, the doctor wasn't finished.

Now the next needle seemed like it was coming a little too high to suddenly drop down. It was headed right between my eyes.

I was struggling to keep from passing out. My face had to be white as a ghost but the needle kept coming. It finally found its mark, just above my nose, right between my eyes.

I could feel my blood pressure dropping. I was desperately hoping the doctor would stop for a minute to give me a chance to untense my muscles, if even just for a few seconds. They were tight as a drum and straining harder with each passing second. By now, the color was completely gone from my face. I was barely clinging to consciousness. Still, there was no break. Finally, the doctor finished with my face and went back down to my shoulders. At last, there was a bit of a reprieve.

This time, though, the doctor didn't take the needles out of my shoulders and arms. He left them in there, sticking out. I could see him reaching for a box that had some wires attached to it.

When I summoned up enough courage to look, I saw the doctor attaching the wires to the needles. Then he turned on the current.

At first, I felt only a mild current running between the needles. It wasn't very painful. I breathed a sigh of relief at being spared the horror I was anticipating. Then the doctor started increasing the current.

With every slight turn of the dial, the pain increased. Finally, the current became so strong my arms began dancing wildly and uncontrollably in the air. It was a scary sight to behold.

I felt like I was being cruelly played with, as some high school biology student might do while dissecting a frog. Fortunately, that torture didn't last long.

No, the treatment wasn't over. The doctor stuck me in the back a few more times. Then he took what looked like a cigar, lit it, and held it near the needles that were sticking out of my back.

It smelled like the burning herbs I had previously read about in one of the articles concerning acupuncture. The doctor asked if I felt anything. Initially I didn't. Soon, though, it felt like my back was on fire. How much more of this?

Now there was a short stoppage, just long enough for Roy to lay me on the examining table and remove most of my clothing. Needles were then inserted into my chest, stomach, legs, and toes. It looked incredibly painful but, because I had no sensation below my shoulders, I felt virtually nothing.

When the treatment finally ended, about thirty minutes after it began, I had been stuck with approximately seventy-five needles. Many of those needles were terribly painful. While we were leaving, I was surprised to hear the words "thank you" coming out of my mouth as I was carried past the doctor. That man had just used me as a human pincushion and here I was, thanking him and making arrangements to come back for more tomorrow. What in the world was I doing?

After the treatment, I didn't feel like doing much of anything. I was physically and emotionally drained. I was also depressed. It all seemed so futile. I had always been a very practical person and it made no sense for me to travel to Europe to see a Chinese doctor, just to have him stick me with needles. I was grasping at straws and I knew it. It was not only painful, it was a tremendous waste of time and money. If the acupuncturist had been in New York City, I probably would not have returned for a second treatment. But he was in London, so I was back the next day.

The second treatment was virtually the same as the first and equally as painful. As the doctor was forcing a needle deeper and deeper into the back of my neck, I let out a quick gasp of pain. That was immediately followed by a loud thud to my left. A slight turn of my head revealed Roy lying on the floor, spread-eagled and unconscious. He had fainted. My grandfather quickly grabbed on to my shoulders, or I would have fallen over as well.

It seems that Roy didn't know that the needles hurt. He was able to watch the treatments as long as he thought I was not experiencing any pain. The sight of the needle going deeper into my neck, and me grimacing in pain, was too much for him. Roy went down with a bang. Who would have guessed that a long needle stuck into my neck would cause Roy to pass out?

Roy didn't want to leave the room, though, as we suggested, and he remained throughout the rest of the treatment.

The routine altered just slightly from the day before. This time, I was laid down on my stomach and needles were stuck in my back, buttocks, and the backs of my legs and feet. At the end of the treatment, I again graciously thanked the doctor for putting me through another half hour of hell. I meekly added that some of the needles had hurt, as I wasn't sure the doctor was aware of that.

The doctor responded that it was good that they hurt. It meant that they might be working. Apparently, unlike acupuncture used for anesthesia or pain relief, this treatment was designed to stimulate nerves, not deaden the sensation.

"Oh great," I thought. "Now every time the doctor sticks me with a needle, I'm supposed to hope that it hurts. I just can't win."

After a couple of more painful treatments, I received a pleasant surprise. The switchboard operator at the hotel called to say that I had a visitor. It was Betsy!

Betsy had been spending most of the summer working on some sort of commune in Amsterdam. My grandmother had managed to get Betsy's address from Betsy's mother and wrote to her in Amsterdam. My grandmother explained that I was in London for acupuncture and either hinted or asked outright if Betsy would join me.

Betsy did! We all needed a lift and Betsy was just the ray of sunshine to do it. Things were picking up.

I had mixed feelings about Betsy watching me get the acupuncture treatments. While it would be a great feeling of comfort and support having her there, I felt uncomfortable at her seeing me wince in pain. Some stupid macho thing, I guess. Anyway, with Betsy around, the days went much faster and were much more enjoyable.

During the fifth treatment, I felt pain from one of the needles as it was stuck in the upper part of my chest. It was one that I hadn't felt before. I know that I actually felt it this time because it really hurt. I asked the doctor if he had inserted the needle in the same place he had always inserted it. The doctor replied that he did.

It was the first positive result from the acupuncture treatments. It meant that my level of sensation was starting to progress down my body.

At the beginning, we all had agreed that if by the tenth treatment I didn't have any positive results, they probably were not working and should be stopped. Now, we had some positive results. If the treatments were working, how much more improvement could I expect?

So far, there were no changes in my movement, only in my level of sensation. If I got my feeling back and not my movement, it would still be a tremendous benefit. For example, I would know when I was in danger of getting a bedsore before my skin started to break down. And certainly, far better than being able to feel pain, I would also be able to feel *pleasure*!

Knowing that the treatments were helping, it was easier for me to withstand the pain of the needles.

Betsy could only stay for a short time before she needed to return to the United States. She left after the second week of treatment. Fortunately, Steve arrived the same day that Betsy left.

The acupuncture treatments became uneventful again. After feeling the needle in my chest during the fifth treatment, my level of sensation remained unchanged. Now I questioned whether it had moved down at all. We never actually measured the level and any changes would have been very slight. Maybe it wasn't working.

Around the fourteenth treatment, after the doctor inserted needles into my left arm and shoulder, he told me to lift my left arm. As I did, my arm seemed to just fly up over my head. It easily went higher than I had ever lifted it since my accident. Maybe there was something to this acupuncture after all.

Over the next few days, I tried to repeat raising my arm to that same height, but without success. When I asked the doctor about that, he said that I was probably just tired and that, when I was more rested, I should be able to do it again. But I couldn't. Now, what do you make of this voodoo medicine? I was on an emotional roller coaster.

In all, I had seventeen treatments before my acupuncturist left for vacation. What were the results of those treatments? I thought I felt a needle in my chest that I hadn't felt before but now I wasn't sure. I once raised my arm higher than I had ever done before but I couldn't do it again.

Was the trip worth it? Probably not, but I had had to try.

Chapter 16

Senior Year at Cornell

♦ ♦ ♦

I needed to find a new attendant, so I placed an ad in the Help Wanted section of *Newsday*, the largest newspaper on Long Island. After I conducted a number of interviews at Aunt Lorraine's house, I decided to hire a young man named Doug. Doug had just graduated from Ithaca College and had been accepted to the Yale Divinity School. He wasn't certain he wanted to be a minister though. He wanted to take a year off to think about it but didn't want to leave an academic environment.

Steve drove me to Cornell in late August. My new attendant met us there.

Because my original class had graduated and many of my close friends were no longer in Ithaca, I knew this year would be even more difficult for me to get the help I probably would need.

I was determined to graduate in May 1973, just one year behind my original class. It meant taking a total of eighteen credits this semester. The previous year, I thought sixteen credits was a heavy load. Now, I registered for a four-credit course in Cost Accounting, a four-credit course in Industrial Engineering Analysis, a three-credit course in engineering entitled Introduction to Bionics and Robots, and a three-credit course in Public Speaking. I was to earn an additional four credits by serving as a teaching assistant (TA) for Jim Maas's Introduction to Psychology course, where I was to lead my own seminar.

During the previous semester, Professor Maas had asked me to be one of the thirty-two TAs for his Introduction to Psychology course. It was quite an honor for me, because those positions were usually reserved for psychology graduate students or senior psychology majors who had done exceptionally well in the professor's introductory psych course. It seemed like an interesting challenge and I was enthused to learn that I had total control of the curriculum for my seminar. I planned to encourage discussions on the psychology of the physically handicapped.

I was assigned a class of seven students, almost all of whom were freshmen and sophomores. A few of my students had a close relative or friend who had a disability. One girl spoke of her stepbrother, who had become a paraplegic as the result of an automobile accident. I asked her what he was doing now. I could see that I hit a sore spot. She stammered a bit and looked very uncomfortable. Then she told me, in a very soft voice, that her stepbrother had died. She quickly pointed out that he hadn't died as a result of his paraplegia. She was concerned that her brother's death might cause me to worry about my own fate. She did not want me, or the class, to think that all paraplegics die at a very young age.

Back then, I was not very worried about that possibility, despite the fact that Dr. King had predicted my life expectancy would be between five and nine years. I no longer thought that I was invincible, but I was still convinced that I was going to prove all the doctors wrong about my prognosis. I appreciated the student's concern, nevertheless.

By the end of my course, I realized there probably is no unique "psychology of the physically handicapped." By the same token, there probably is no unique psychology of "the able-bodied" as well. We all basically have the same needs, desires, fears, hopes, and dreams.

◆ ◆ ◆

During the fall of 1972, my stepsister Hope transferred to Ithaca College for her sophomore year. It had nothing to do with me being back at Cornell. We hadn't been very close since my father's divorce. In fact, I barely remember even seeing Hope during those previous eight years. Janis had remarried soon after the divorce and moved to Suffolk County, about an hour's drive from Oceanside.

In early September, Hope introduced me to her friend, Mary, who was a junior, majoring in psychology at Ithaca College. My attendant Doug took a liking to Mary and asked her out once or twice. It soon became apparent that Mary really liked me and preferred to be just friends with Doug. Mary was an attractive, kind, caring, and compassionate, soft-spoken girl, who was ideally suited to go into one of the helping professions.

It was obvious, by the way Mary looked at me, talked to me, and her general demeanor with me, that I had now "found" a new girlfriend.

On our first date, we went to a Cornell football game. It seemed appropriate, because on my first date ever, in tenth grade, I had taken a girl to an Oceanside High School football game.

♦ ♦ ♦

In late September, I began having a lot of trouble with my bladder, so much so that I had to go to Tompkins County Hospital in Ithaca to have it checked out. It was the first time I had been back at that hospital since the day I broke my neck.

The hospital urologist who treated me was not very sympathetic to my problem. He seemed upset that I had even seen him. I guess he felt that he shouldn't have to take on a patient with medical issues as severe as mine.

When I returned to the hospital with the same bladder complaint later that week, that same urologist had to catheterize me. He felt that the catheter should be left in for at least a couple of weeks and, possibly, permanently.

I didn't like having that tube inside me. I was worried that the catheter would be pulled out of place, for instance, when my attendant moved me between the bed and wheelchair, or when I was being lifted during the day. Some real damage could result from that. In addition, I wasn't very enthused about having someone as untrained as my attendant handling it.

Needing a catheter seemed to indicate that my condition was getting worse, not better. I can never expect to be free from doctors and hospitals, because I will always have to deal with some more or less serious medical problem related to me being paralyzed. I now had a new reason to be depressed.

The catheter had been in for a little more than a week, when I started to experience the same problems with my bladder. This time, the catheter had become blocked with sediment. No fluid would pass through, no matter how much the catheter was irrigated.

Doctor Young, my doctor at Cornell, felt that I should be admitted for a night to Sage Infirmary, the college hospital. Once I was in the infirmary, Doctor Young removed the catheter.

Mary visited me there. It was good to see a friendly and concerned face. She offered to spend the night with me in the hospital room. That way she could turn me and get the nurses if I needed them for any reason. It was nice for me not to have to sleep in a hospital room alone. Mary ended up sleeping slouched between two chairs.

Mary was genuinely interested in helping me in any way she could. Now seemed like the appropriate time to show her what was involved with my care.

◆ ◆ ◆

As if it wasn't enough for me to be struggling with five courses and dealing with medical problems, I also had to start thinking about what I was going to do the next year. It was clear by then that I would not be able to work as an engineer.

There must be something that I could do. I thought I should consider graduate school but I wasn't sure in what field. There still was the lingering question: who would ever employ me in my condition?

Both Doug and I registered to take the law boards, which were given toward the end of October.

I skimmed through some practice questions but did not put in anywhere near the time or effort preparing for the exam that Doug did. He had worked himself up into such a frenzied state that he was virtually impossible to live with. I had friends over every day to give Doug some extra time off, so that he had the opportunity to study in the library. The night before the test, Mary stayed over, allowing Doug to get a good night's sleep elsewhere.

I wasn't able to sleep much that night. Ever since my accident, I had had a great deal of trouble sleeping. In whatever position I tried to go to sleep, whether it was on my back or on my side, I usually became uncomfortable and had to be turned. It was happening at least twice a night now.

I was to take the test in a separate room from the rest of the test takers, with an instructor from the Cornell School of Industrial and Labor Relations doing the writing and turning the pages for me. The Law Boards wouldn't give me any extra time.

The instructor, being curious, kept trying to read the questions over my shoulder during the entire test. That made it very difficult for me to concentrate. To make matters worse, when I gave an answer, for instance, #2 is B, he would often respond with the question, "Is that B or D?" I would inevitably have to say, "B as in boy," and then watch him to make sure that he checked off the right box. It definitely slowed me down.

I had met with the dean of the Cornell Law School, before the test, to discuss my application for admission. He was impressed with all I had accomplished since my accident. He also felt that the grades that I had received since my return to Cornell were good enough to prove I could do the work. He said that, if I scored a 600 on the Law Boards, I would pretty much be assured admission to Cornell Law School. I received a score of 597, which would probably have gotten me in.

Doug, apparently, was so nervous during the test that he got flustered and didn't do well. In fact, he didn't even turn his test in to be scored. Needless to say, Doug was very upset, and even more difficult to live with after that.

I wasn't convinced that law was the best field for me, and Steve did not seem to be encouraging me to pursue a career in law either. He had already graduated from Boston College Law School and was now working for the Legal Aid Society in Nassau County, Long Island, as a public defender. Steve and I never spoke in detail about it but I was convinced that if Steve thought law was the right field for me he would have said so.

I was also contemplating a career in psychology at that time. Jim Maas seemed to feel that I had an aptitude for it.

♦ ♦ ♦

Keeping up with my coursework in engineering was difficult, but I was managing. I was glad I had decided to take a course in public speaking. Before my injury, I never considered entering a profession that would require me to do much of it. Now, even with all my physical limitations, at least I could still speak. Despite still getting nervous and generally hating preparing a talk, I knew my verbal skills were the area I most needed to develop now. It was very important that I get good at it.

My best talk that semester was probably my persuasive speech. I repeated the talk I had given at Hofstra for my sociology class the summer before, in favor of euthanasia. I remain convinced, more than ever, of the need for personal choice in the matter. My public speaking professor also thought that my speech was "cogent."

I finished the semester with my best grades yet: Teaching of Psychology, A+; Introduction to Bionics and Robots, A-; Industrial Engineering Analysis, B-; Cost Accounting, C-; Public Speaking, A-.

That was a grade point average of 3.17. It was still below the 3.25 necessary for Dean's List, but not by much.

♦ ♦ ♦

Near the end of the semester, I was really surprised when I received a call from a girl named Nancy, inviting me to her sorority Christmas party.

Nancy was a Cornell senior, majoring in psychology. She played the drums in the school band. She also used to lead the pep band in a rousing rendition of "Sweet Georgia Brown" between the second and third periods during the Cornell home hockey games. I sat right near the pep band during the hockey games and sometimes Nancy and I made eye contact and smiled at each other. I had never learned her name or even spoken to her before she called. Nancy was a great-looking girl and every guy in the arena stared at her when she was leading the band.

It was an awkward phone call. It was on the speakerphone and Mary was in the room at the time. Mary heard everything. She nodded to indicate that I should go to the party with Nancy. What else could Mary have done in that situation?

A few nights later, Nancy came to my room with her roommate Sue to pick me up. Sue happened to be dating Bob Skelly, my freshman roommate. Both girls were wearing long coats and had hats pulled partly over their faces. I couldn't tell who was who. I sort of stammered as I said their names, because I wasn't sure whom I was greeting. Nancy told me, later, that this had really scared her because, at that moment, she thought I had a speech impediment as well.

Soon after we arrived at their sorority, Nancy got me a glass of punch. She held the glass for me to drink but missed my bottom lip. She proceeded to pour most of the punch down my chin and shirt. She was very embarrassed. Nancy refilled my glass and proceeded to make the same mistake. I was soaked. She was about to cry. I wasn't too enthused about the second glass of punch either.

Still, it turned out to be a very nice evening.

The next night, Nancy invited me to go to the Glee Club's Christmas Choir Concert that was taking place at Sage Chapel, just a short distance from my dorm. As Nancy was wheeling me through the door of the chapel, the minister, who was standing by the entrance, said how glad he was that I could attend and how he would really like to see more of me at Sunday services. Nancy was really impressed, thinking that I must be a good Christian boy.

As the singing progressed, the audience joined in. Nancy thought I was just being shy when I wasn't singing along with the others. She kept trying to get me to sing but I kept telling her I didn't know the words. Near the end of the concert, the Glee Club sang "The First Noël." Nancy again told me to sing, and again I replied that I didn't know the words.

"Everybody knows the words to 'Noël, Noël,'" she said.

"I don't think I ever heard that song before," I replied.

Suddenly Nancy turned beet red. With a look of extreme surprise, she blurted out, "You're Jewish!"

I was amused by all this but it took Nancy some time to regain her composure.

When Nancy wheeled me back to my dorm room, my cousin Jill, who was now a freshman at Cornell in the Hotel Management School, and my stepsister Hope, were waiting there. Without thinking twice about it, I introduced Nancy to "my cousin and sister." Nancy told me later that she didn't believe the two pretty girls in my room were my cousin and sister. I guess that even when a guy is telling the truth, a girl still may not believe him!

♦ ♦ ♦

Near the end of the fall semester, my attendant Doug told me he did not want to return for the second semester to take care of me. Barbara McPherson, who worked at the coffee shop down the hall from my room, asked if she, along with her boyfriend, Bill Ochester, could be my attendants for the spring semester. They would take turns. As the semester progressed, Barbara and Bill got engaged.

During this time, I had been seeing both Nancy and Mary.

Because Nancy had now invited me out a couple of times, I thought that I should reciprocate. I didn't know where I could take her, so I invited Nancy to go with me to my fraternity's big winter party, in February.

Unfortunately, I didn't realize that Mary had been expecting to go to that party with me. There was no good way to tell Mary that I had asked Nancy. I certainly did not handle it well, and Mary was very hurt. It pretty much ended our relationship.

I started seeing a lot of Nancy and virtually stopped seeing Mary during the spring semester. I still liked Mary a lot and wanted to keep seeing her. I also wanted to see Nancy. I felt terribly guilty about it.

I always thought that every guy wanted to have a choice between two pretty girls. I had never been in that situation before so I was really surprised that a decision as to whom to take to a party could cause so many problems.

I really didn't mean to hurt Mary's feelings but I know that I did. For that I will always be sorry.

Nancy stayed over one weekend in February, to give Barbara and Bill some time off together. It was Nancy's first time handling my physical care. Things did not go very smoothly. In the middle of the night, the condom leaked and the whole bed got soaked. Nancy had to clean me up and change the bedding, with me still in it. Not an easy task. It was long, hard, and exhausting for her. Two hours later, the condom leaked again and the whole process had to be repeated. Nancy was practically in tears and, I must admit, I was pretty close to tears myself. Not the best way to start a budding relationship.

◆ ◆ ◆

To satisfy the requirements to graduate in May 1973, I took four courses during the second semester, for fourteen credits. I had to take two engineering courses: Industrial Engineering Design and Introduction to Game Theory. I also took two psychology course electives: Personality and Social Behavior, and Human Behavior Theory.

I enjoyed the study of psychology and found it very interesting. I was attracted to being in one of the helping professions. Besides, Jim Maas thought it would be the right field for me and I valued his opinion. He encouraged me to pursue a career in counseling.

Most importantly, I felt I could be fairly self-sufficient working as a psychologist. It was a job that was mostly verbal and, in that respect, with the exception of my Long Island accent, I was not handicapped.

In early March, I received my acceptance to the Master of Arts program in Counseling and Student Personnel Administration at Cornell.

I was still debating between psychology and law, though. My brother was already a practicing lawyer and, although we never discussed it, I thought we would someday open a practice together.

It was a difficult decision but I ended up picking psychology. About a week before I was to be officially notified, I called the Cornell Law School admissions office and withdrew my application.

♦ ♦ ♦

As graduation approached, I couldn't wait for classes to end.

My grades for my last undergraduate semester were: Personality and Social Behavior, B-; Human Behavior Theory, A-; Introduction to Game Theory, C; Industrial Engineering Design, B-.

That yielded a cume of 2.84 for the semester. During my last two undergraduate years in engineering, the two years of study since my injury, I earned a cumulative average of 3.03.

The official ceremony took place on May 25, 1973. I had quite a crew turn out to see me graduate. It included Steve, Meryl, my father, More Mom and More Pop, Aunt Lorraine and Uncle Mel, my Aunt Betty, and some of my cousins. There were 2,401 graduates. I was the only one in a wheelchair.

I donned my cap and gown and took my place in the processional. With a photographer friend, Jim Cunningham, snapping pictures, I was pushed along the processional path by John Reynolds, a fellow graduate and 150-pound football teammate of mine.

The graduation was held inside Barton Hall, a huge armory-type building. Once inside the building, I sat in the front row, left of center. I was covered with sweat, not from the heat, but because my bladder was acting up and wouldn't empty. Some things never seemed to change.

My family and friends were confident that the president of the university would say something at graduation about my accomplishments. I didn't know if Cornell had ever had a student graduate before me who had used a wheelchair. Certainly, they never

Graduation day with More Pop, More Mom, Nancy on Ken's lap, and
Aunt Betty behind them—May 25, 1973.
Photo by Jim Cunningham.

Graduation day with Nancy (second from the left) and
John Reynolds (third from the left)—May 25, 1973.
Photo by Jim Cunningham.

had a quadriplegic graduate from the College of Engineering. It
seemed like it would be an accomplishment they would think was
worth recognizing.

I told people I really wasn't expecting the president to say
anything about me. It might sound strange, but the one thing I
wanted at that time was to just blend in with the rest of the graduates and not stand out. Just like with the past newspaper articles
written about me, I didn't want to be embarrassed by whatever the
president might say in front of all those people, my friends and
family included. Inside, however, I was fairly certain he would.
After all, with all the publicity I had received since my accident, I
couldn't see how the president could ignore me or not to at least
acknowledge me. But he did.

Graduation photo—spring 1973.

I suppose I was both relieved and disappointed at the same time.

Not a word was mentioned about me, or any other student for that matter. Instead, the president spoke about the day's marking the one-hundredth anniversary of the first women graduates at Cornell. I guess it takes a while to get recognition. I wondered if a hundred years from now they will be talking about the first quadriplegic engineering graduate.

My bladder troubles were getting worse. Shortly after the graduation ceremony ended, I had to lie down in my dorm room to see if that would help my bladder empty. It didn't! After lying down for a half hour without my bladder emptying, I was moved to Steve's car. I was in agony during the five-hour car ride from Cornell to Boston. Steve drove there because, the next day, Steve's girlfriend Nicky was graduating from Boston College Law School. My bladder finally emptied later that evening.

Graduation brought me a lot of media attention. Pictures and stories about me appeared in a number of newspapers, including the *New York Daily News*, *Newsday*, the *Ithaca Journal*, and the *National Enquirer*. That's right, even the *Enquirer*.

Although my graduation had been the day for which I had been preparing for the previous few years, it had not been an enjoyable day for me. Somehow, all my hard work seemed to have lost much of its meaning.

Nancy was also graduating and leaving Ithaca. We both agreed we would part ways after graduation. It was a lot easier to bear than when my relationship with Betsy ended.

I would be returning to Cornell in the fall, to continue with my studies in Counseling and Student Personnel Administration.

Chapter 17

One Depressing Summer

◆ ◆ ◆

About ten days after my graduation, I went to East Brunswick, New Jersey, to spend a few days relaxing with my Aunt Betty.

Late Friday afternoon on June 8, I began feeling some congestion in my lungs. By early evening, I was having trouble breathing. Soon, I was gasping for air.

To help me bring up some of the congestion, Betty tried doing postural drainage on me. She laid me on my stomach, with my head and shoulders hanging over the edge of the bed. Then she began hitting me on the back with her hands cupped. This time, the congestion was so tight and thick I couldn't cough any of it up. Now, I felt like I was suffocating, drowning in my own phlegm. It was clear that I needed to go to the hospital.

Betty made some calls but found that it would be tough getting the proper attention and treatment for me in a local New Jersey hospital, especially on the weekend. Instead, we decided to drive to the emergency room at South Nassau Community Hospital in Oceanside, where I had previously been a patient. Betty made the appropriate phone calls and we left.

The car ride to Long Island took an hour and a half, but seemed endless. I was gagging and gasping for air the whole time. I often went more than thirty seconds without being able to breathe at all.

There was little that could be done for me in the car. It was starting to look like a life or death situation. I began to think that I would not make it to Oceanside.

We arrived at the emergency room at about twenty minutes to eleven. I was laid down on one of the beds and soon attended to by Janice, one of the inhalation therapists. I knew Janice from my initial stay in the hospital in 1970–71. She started doing postural drainage immediately but again, without success. I just couldn't bring the congestion up. I continued to gasp for air.

It was a long twenty minutes before the clock turned eleven and the shifts changed. Judy, another inhalation therapist I knew, relieved Janice. Judy said that I needed to be suctioned.

Oh God, no! Anything but suctioning! I had undergone many painful procedures since my accident but suctioning was the worst. I was terrified, but there was no escaping it.

A tube was inserted into my right nostril and pushed farther and farther down toward my lungs. The pain was excruciating.

As the tube reached my throat, it triggered the gagging reflex. The more I gagged, the more it hurt. The tube was still pushed farther down. When the tube finally reached its destination, the suctioning was turned on.

It seemed like every last drop of oxygen was vacuumed from my lungs, along with a sizable portion of phlegm. The tube was slowly pulled out along the already irritated passageway, while the suctioning and pain continued. Finally, a reprieve: the tube was out.

I still couldn't breathe well though. It would have to be repeated!

My brother Steve arrived at the hospital and joined me in the emergency room.

Steve tried to keep me calm and did all he could to get me to relax. It was more difficult and painful to insert the tube when I was tense but relaxing was impossible. Every muscle I had was pulled tighter than a drum. I still couldn't breathe. The tube was inserted again.

My brother remained by my side, with his hand on my shoulder to lend support and comfort. I started to feel sorry for him.

Hearing me gasping for air and crying out in pain would be difficult for anyone. Watching that torture had to be torture in and of itself. Steve kept talking and comforting me during the entire ordeal.

The tube was withdrawn, another reprieve. I still couldn't breathe well. It would have to be repeated again.

By now, I hated Judy with a passion. I had thought she was my friend but now she was about to suction me for the third time.

It wasn't until much later I learned that Janice couldn't bring herself to suction me. Janice did all she could to delay the inevitable until the end of her shift. Judy had no choice. It needed to be done.

The tube was reinserted. Each time was more painful than the time before. The passageway became more and more irritated. Pushing the tube through was like rubbing sandpaper on a bruised and sensitive area. It was agony!

I could see the bottle next to the suction tube, filling up with the thick, brown, mucous-like substance that had been coming out of my lungs.

Now Judy was about to start the fourth round of suctioning. This time she decided to insert the tube through the left nostril because the right one was so sore. That was a big mistake. I had such a badly deviated septum, the tube couldn't pass through. The fourth round would have to be repeated through the right nostril.

You would think that the pain would let up a bit. That it wouldn't be as bad as the first couple of times. But it didn't! It just kept getting worse.

My brother remained by my side throughout. His presence was a great help.

In all, I was suctioned ten times that night.

My return to South Nassau turned into an impromptu family reunion. We were joined at the hospital not only by my brother Steve and his girlfriend Nicky but also by my friend Dave Gilbert, my Aunt Lorraine, and some of my cousins. Perhaps they thought I was going to die that night.

After the last round of suctioning, I was lifted into my wheelchair and taken for a chest X-ray. When I returned to the emergency room, Dave joined me.

As Dave and I were talking, one of the receptionists said that she didn't know why they didn't just give me a bronchoscope. She said the bronchoscope was far more effective and suggested that I ask for it before they suction me again.

Interested, I asked her how painful that procedure was.

Hesitantly, she replied, "Well, let me put it to you this way. You'll only need it once!"

Dave and I looked at each other in horror. That pain must be excruciating. Then we burst out laughing hysterically. "You'll only need it once!" As if suctioning wasn't painful enough, now the receptionist wanted me to ask for a bronchoscope. For some reason, the prospect of my going through an even more painful procedure struck Dave and me as funny, and the idea of me asking for it was hilarious.

At about four in the morning, I was finally moved to a ward upstairs.

By that time, I was really weak and tired but it was nice to be able to breathe again. Dave came with me. He spent the rest of the night sitting by my bedside.

The next day, I was moved to a private room. I, again, had to hire private duty nurses for two of the three shifts. Dave stayed with me every night and covered the 11 p.m. to 7 a.m. shift. He made the long nights go a lot faster. He certainly was a true and loyal friend, and remained so for more than fifty years.

Unfortunately, the congestion kept returning, often faster than the treatments could remove it. The prospect of more suctioning was constantly on my mind. I didn't think that I could handle even one more round of it. The suction equipment stayed in my room twenty-four hours a day, reminding me of the possibility. Fortunately, it did not need to be used.

The entire ordeal—congestion, suctioning, and hospitalization—was not only painful, it was terribly depressing. Just two weeks earlier, I had graduated from college. Now, I was fighting for my life. I was back in the hospital as if I had never left.

I felt like I had accomplished nothing.

This time my diagnosis was bronchitis with a touch of pleurisy but, for me, I was still being hospitalized for my broken neck in 1970.

Janice was usually the inhalation therapist that performed the postural drainage on me. She was a beautiful girl, and I was very attracted to her. It was so embarrassing for me to be turned over for postural drainage, wearing one of those half open hospital gowns, while Janice was there.

One day, while Janice was pounding on my back, the ultimate indignity happened in her presence. I had a bowel movement! I just wanted to crawl into a hole and die.

I spent a terribly long week in the hospital before I was discharged on June 16, my father's fifty-first birthday. He picked me up and wheeled me the few blocks to Aunt Lorraine's. I was so upset and depressed that I forgot to even wish him a happy birthday.

◆ ◆ ◆

I did not want to just sit home for the entire summer without doing anything. I applied for a job with the Nassau County Department of Recreation and Parks. I had worked for the Recreation Department as a lifeguard for two summers before my accident.

I had just graduated college with a degree in engineering. Soon, I would start graduate school in counseling. Surely there must be something I could do. But what? It was difficult trying to sell myself when I didn't even know what I could do.

My father drove me to the interview and then, embarrassingly, stayed with me in the room for the interview, which was very awkward.

I felt especially disabled, sitting there motionless. Why should anyone be expected to hire me? How could I function at a job? What extra help would I need? Would I always need to have an attendant with me? How could I do counseling with an attendant there? How could I possibly do anything?

Fortunately, the interviewer was very supportive. He really wanted to give me a job. Nassau County tried to hire people for the summer who had disabilities probably because the County Executive, Ralph Caso, had a child with a disability.

Two possible positions were discussed. One was announcing softball games at night. Something could probably be rigged up to hold the microphone button down when I wanted to talk. My father really liked that idea. He had been telling me for some time that I should become a sports announcer. He thought that I had a good speaking voice and was knowledgeable about sports in general. This seemed like a possible choice.

While I had loved participating in sports, I could not see myself making a career out of being a spectator. In addition, I would have felt uncomfortable talking about some meaningless, rinky-dink softball game. There just had to be something more that I could do with my life.

The other possibility would be to work with Nassau County's Recreation for the Handicapped Unit. That sounded like it might be an appropriate work experience to prepare for a career in counseling. It also sounded far more challenging. I decided to take that position.

Ken with Aunt Lorraine in her backyard—summer 1973.

I hired an attendant through an ad in *Newsday*. He would take me back and forth to work in his car and help me on the job. As usual, Aunt Lorraine and my cousins took care of me the rest of the day and night.

It didn't take long for me, and everyone else, to realize there wasn't anything I could do at that job. Clerical work was certainly out. When paper work was assigned, it just meant me watching my attendant do the menial, rote tasks.

I was asked to do a lot of repetitious and useless phone work. I often had to struggle to hear what was being said, because my attendant wasn't holding the phone close enough to my ear.

The job was terribly frustrating. It showed me how vocationally handicapped I really was. There seemed to be absolutely nothing I could do in an office. Sitting helpless and motionless by a desk made me feel worthless. I felt guilty being paid just to sit there. What was even worse than that, though, I was paying more money to my attendant than I was actually netting each week on the job. I was losing money on this fiasco.

Part of my job involved accompanying people with disabilities, twice a week, to Nassau Beach. Those outings were even more depressing for me. I had worked at Nassau Beach as a lifeguard prior to my accident. They were great summers. I was in excellent shape and proud of the way I looked in a bathing suit. Now I felt like hiding. It was tough just trying to hold a conversation with some of the same lifeguards I used to like working with.

While I was at Nassau Beach that summer, I saw a woman who had polio when she was younger and, as a result, was not able to walk. She was swimming and playing with her two children in the pool. When I was a lifeguard, not so long before, I used to help that same woman. I carried her in my arms from her wheelchair to the side of the pool and, later, back to her wheelchair when she finished her swim. I had always felt sorry for her. Now I envied her. What I wouldn't give to have just some of the arm movement she enjoyed. Her lot in life now seemed to be a hundred times better than mine. She was married and had two children. She was functioning virtually independently. She was swimming and smiling.

Now, I was the sad onlooker. How fickle life can be! One never knows what the future holds.

I was almost relieved when the summer finally ended. While I was looking forward to pursuing a new career in psychology, I had to question whether I could actually work in that field when I graduated. All my schooling might prove to be meaningless.

Chapter 18

Graduate School

♦ ♦ ♦

Once again, I had to find an attendant before I left for Cornell to begin my graduate studies. I dreaded having to go through the process of advertising, interviewing, and training someone new. It always seemed to take forever and was embarrassing as well, because I had to explain details about my most intimate needs to a total stranger.

My attendants usually had no medical training, or any other skills, for that matter. The people I was interviewing now seemed to be drifting in and out of unskilled jobs and just happened to be unemployed when I was looking for my next aide. There was rarely a good applicant, so I usually ended up hiring the least objectionable one.

After interviewing a number of prospective attendants for the fall 1973 semester, I decided to try hiring a female. She would, hopefully, be more meticulous with my personal care and appearance than a man, and be more cheerful and pleasant to be around, in addition to keeping our room cleaner and more orderly.

Boy, was I wrong! It did not work out well at all. For some reason, we quickly developed a personality conflict, resulting in so much tension in the room it could have been cut with a knife. In addition, my female aide had trouble lifting me, despite the fact that she was able to do so without much trouble when I interviewed her at Aunt Lorraine's. She also had difficulty wheeling me around the campus. My classes were now located mostly in the Agriculture Quad, quite a distance from my dorm, and uphill as well.

My relationship with my attendant became so strained it necessitated making a change in mid-semester.

The coursework for the master's program in Counseling and Student Personnel Administration was considerably easier than Engineering. I only took ten credits the first semester and, more significantly, the courses were far less demanding and challenging.

I had written very few papers for my engineering courses and, as a result, I felt as if I was entering graduate school with only a high school English background. What a difference it was for me, compared to the other graduate students who didn't even blink when they heard the professors assigning term papers, yet were all petrified at the thought of taking a statistics course.

I typed all my assignments myself. My top typing speed was only twelve words per minute. It was rare, though, that I could keep up that pace for more than a few minutes. By the time I had typed one page I was thoroughly exhausted. My left arm, despite being supported by the BFO, was so fatigued I could barely move it. After typing two pages, I would have to stop and rest.

Correcting typing errors was arduous and time-consuming. Whenever I made a mistake, I would either put a series of Xs over the word, which looked terrible, or tried to cover up the mistake by rewording the sentence, which never really sounded right. Retyping the whole page was out of the question.

It was not an enjoyable semester. In addition to struggling with an unhappy attendant, bad weather, steep hills, and an inaccessible campus, I was pursuing a new major at a school at which I now knew very few people. Most of my friends had graduated and left Ithaca. My social life was virtually nonexistent. The thrill of being back at Cornell was gone.

Somehow, I managed to finish my first semester with the following grades: Guidance and Testing, B-; Student Personnel Administration, B+; Counseling, A; Seminar in Student Personnel Administration, S (satisfactory.)

My cume was 3.33.

The second semester I took on a heavier course load, consisting of fourteen credits.

In April, during that lonely and depressing school year, my brother called to tell me he was going to get married to his long-time girlfriend Nicky. The wedding would be in August and he would like me to be his best man.

Ever since Steve's friend Gordon had told me, while I was in Rusk, that he was getting married, I'd known that sooner or later my brother would follow. I really wanted what was best for him and hoped he would be happy. Steve deserved it. Still, I was worried that his marriage would inevitably change our close relationship.

♦ ♦ ♦

For the past three and a half years, I had been lifted, like a sack of potatoes, into and out of cars. In addition to the lifting being terribly uncomfortable for me, inevitably, someone would bump my head, trying to squeeze me through the limited opening of the doorway. It was time for me to finally get an accessible vehicle. I decided to order a van with a raised roof and a hydraulic lift, from a company in Missouri. The van was driven to Ithaca in late April. During the trip, the two men that drove the van locked themselves out of it and had to break a window to get in.

I could only enter the van backward. If I faced forward on the lift, my feet would get caught between the lift and the floor of the van.

Once inside, I had difficulty making the turn to face the front of the van. It took a lot of time to secure my wheelchair to keep it from moving. In addition, I sat up too high to see out the windows. All I could do was look downward and straight ahead at the mesmerizing yellow line in the middle of the road. That gave me a wicked headache every time. I also needed a special belt around my chest tying me to my wheelchair to keep me stable during starts, stops, and turns.

♦ ♦ ♦

My cume for the second semester was 3.36.

I was glad to finally leave Ithaca. It wasn't going to be much of a reprieve because I was now going to a new acupuncture clinic in Washington, D.C., for more treatments.

There were no positive results from those treatments, so I finally stopped after twenty fruitless sessions. I had had to at least try it. Now, once and for all, I could rule out acupuncture as a possible cure. Between London and Washington, D.C., I had undergone a total of thirty-seven treatments and been stuck with well over a thousand needles.

◆ ◆ ◆

In early July, I started working at the same recreation position I had worked the summer before. A year of graduate school did not help me perform any better though. In fact, there was still little I could do.

I couldn't even do as much as the disadvantaged CETA (Comprehensive Employment and Training Act) high school students who were also working there that summer. The goal of the CETA program was, among other things, to help those students develop a marketable skill, which would hopefully help them get a full-time job in the future. Those high school students looked like they would be far more employable than I ever would be after completing my master's degree.

In late July, I developed a bad bedsore. Despite spending more than two weeks lying down, the sore didn't look any better. I finally called work to let them know that I would not be returning that summer.

My supervisor had two summers to evaluate my work. I suppose I shouldn't have been surprised when she recommended that I not be rehired. She was right, of course. I had missed half of the summer and, when I had been at work, there had been very little I was able to do. With my limited skills and seemingly high propensity for medical problems, it didn't seem realistic to believe an employer would ever hire me. Even if one did, I probably wouldn't be able to keep the job for long. Still, my supervisor's recommendation really bothered me.

◆ ◆ ◆

On August 17, my brother was going to marry Nicky at her parents' house in Dedham, Massachusetts.

I lay awake the night before the wedding for hours. I still wasn't sure how I felt about my brother getting married.

The death of my mother and my father's subsequent marital problems had made Steve the one constant in my life. My

Ken, Meryl, Steve, and Nicky at Steve and Nicky's
wedding—August 17, 1974.

brother was always there for me. When we were younger, Steve and I played together every day. In fact, we played ball together every free moment of every day. Whenever I had a question, I asked Steve. Whenever I needed help or needed someone to teach me something, I asked Steve. When my accident happened, Steve was the person I depended on for help and support. When my attendants needed to be trained, Steve often did it. He was the best at it.

Despite our two-year age difference, I felt my brother and I had a relationship paralleling that of twins. Well, now half of our pair was getting married. There was little hope the other half would ever follow. My future seemed to offer little promise for a happy personal life. I could not imagine ever getting married. I hadn't even had a date in more than a year.

The wedding ceremony took place in Nicky's parents' living room. Steve was characteristically calm, his bride was beautiful, and the atmosphere was warm and loving. I was proud to serve as Steve's best man and felt assured that I would always be an important part of not just his, but their, life. They would remain living on Long Island, never far from me.

♦ ♦ ♦

At the end of August, I returned to Cornell to begin my second year of graduate school. I still hadn't completely healed from my bedsore, so I had to be careful not to sit in my wheelchair for too long. I hired an attendant who had just completed a hitch in the Navy as a paramedic. His name was Kris and he was six feet, four inches tall.

I registered to take a course in psychopathology, a seminar in student personnel administration, a course in research writing, an independent study course in psychology with Jim Maas, and a practicum.

It was difficult for me to find a practicum in which I could actually do anything useful. I chose to do it with the Director of Student Activities. To get into his office, however, I had to be pulled up about thirty steps. A couple of desks had to be moved as well. It was a good thing my attendant that semester was strong.

Not surprisingly, once in the office, there was nothing I could do. The director was very nice and really wanted to help me but I couldn't do anything productive. It was similar to my two summer jobs with the Nassau County Recreation Department. I had no reason to believe it would be different on any job.

My bedsore just wouldn't heal. Going to classes every day was aggravating it even more. Public health nurses were trying different remedies, without success. The only cure seemed to be for me to stay in bed, lie on my side, and not put any pressure on it.

It soon became apparent that my attendant Kris was both incompetent and unstable. I knew I had to let him go but kept postponing the inevitable.

During one of my brother's visits, it was decided that I should be admitted to Sage Infirmary. Two days later, Kris came into my room in the infirmary, smiling sheepishly. He had broken his hand in a fight the night before. I finally fired him.

Now, without an attendant, I was pretty much stuck in the hospital for the month, until I was to go home for Thanksgiving. My hospital stay included October 31, the anniversary of my accident. It was now four years later and nothing seemed to have changed. Here I was, completely helpless, back in the hospital.

My brother interviewed some prospective attendants down on the Island, while I interviewed some from my hospital bed in Ithaca. Based largely on my brother's recommendation, I hired a person named Steve, who turned out to be a Jesus freak. Despite his strong religious beliefs, he was one of the most prejudiced and intolerant people I have ever met. He also was totally incompetent and didn't seem all there mentally as well.

When I returned to Cornell after Thanksgiving, I discovered that my former attendant Kris had forged checks of mine, totaling close to $300. He also stole $50 in cash from me and ran up a big food bill on my Cornell credit card. Despite reporting those facts to the police and the Tompkins County District Attorney's Office, as well as providing them with pictures of Kris, his social security number, and his military service number, Kris was never found.

I knew I was an easy target for crooks but what could I do? It was almost impossible for me not to entrust my attendants with my wallet, checkbook, and valuables. After all, I was entrusting them with my physical care and my life in general. I had to trust somebody.

The fall of 1974 was also the time I started applying for admission to doctoral programs. To play it safe, I applied to twenty schools: thirteen for clinical psychology and seven for counseling psychology.

Due to my month's stay in the hospital, I had to drop my course in research writing. Still, I was able to finish the semester with a cume of 3.65.

I returned to Cornell for the spring semester, with my third attendant of the year. He lasted about two months before a previous leg injury started acting up and he needed to leave. I hired my fourth attendant and was praying I would make it through the semester without having to look for a fifth.

In March, rejection letters from the doctoral programs started pouring in. Letter after letter came, all saying "no."

It wasn't until late May that I had received decisions from all of the schools. Nineteen schools rejected my application. The twentieth, Teachers College at Columbia University, said that, while they couldn't admit me to their doctoral program at this time, they invited me to enroll in their master's program in vocational rehabilitation counseling. They said that, after successful completion of that program, they would reconsider my application for the doctoral program.

Because I had no other plans for the fall, Columbia was now my only option. I decided to enroll at Teachers College for the fall 1975 semester.

I spent a lot of time in the spring of 1975 working on my thesis for my Master of Arts degree. I decided to do my thesis on the sleep patterns of college students. Sleep was my one and only true escape from the world, so why not write about it? Jim Maas and William C. Dement had recommended the topic. William Dement was a well-known sleep researcher at Stanford University, to whom Jim Maas had introduced me my first year back at Cornell.

My cume for the semester was 3.42, which gave me a two-year graduate cume of 3.43.

I knew I wasn't going to finish my thesis by May. I had to make arrangements to spend the summer in Ithaca to continue working on it.

Although Ithaca was beautiful in the summer, it was not pleasant for me having to stay up there. The campus was deserted. Virtually everybody I knew was gone.

In early June, I developed an acute case of bronchitis and was barely able to breathe. I ended up at Tompkins County Hospital in Ithaca.

After two days of feeling near death's door, I told my brother I needed him, and he and his wife drove immediately from Long Island.

The hospital staff at Tompkins County administered some type of medicine by IV to try and loosen the congestion in my lungs. It made me terribly nauseous.

When my brother arrived, he felt it would be better for me if I were back down in Oceanside, at South Nassau Communities Hospital, where they were more familiar with my care. I agreed.

Postural drainage was performed on me one more time before we left Ithaca, but, again, was unproductive. Just as they were about to turn me back over, I threw up. I really threw up a lot. I thought I was going to choke on the vomit before I was able to get it all out. If I had been alone in the room, lying on my back at that time, I probably would have choked to death.

Once I was able to leave the hospital, I rode lying down in my van, with Steve driving and Nicky sitting beside me in case I needed anything.

The doctor at the hospital in Ithaca arranged that I be admitted to the intensive care unit at the hospital in Oceanside. When we arrived at the ICU, the charge nurse seemed actually upset that I was feeling a little better. She was making us feel terribly guilty for taking up the ICU nurses' time. My brother felt like he had to apologize to her that I wasn't dying.

I was in ICU for two days before I was moved to a bed on another ward. I remained there for another four days. I was still coughing up phlegm but at least I didn't need to be suctioned.

The day I was released, my fifteen-year-old cousin, Ronnie, came to the hospital, gathered my belongings, and wheeled me the half mile to Aunt Lorraine's.

I was extremely depressed at how little things had changed. After getting my bachelor's degree, I had ended up in the hospital with respiratory problems. Now that I had just about completed my master's, I was back in the hospital for the same problem. If I ever do get my doctorate, I'll probably just end up in the hospital again. What's the use!

After spending a week at home recovering, I returned to Cornell. I wasn't there for long before my attendant hurt his back practicing judo. I hurriedly undertook a frantic search to find a replacement.

In the middle of August, after working feverishly typing two complete drafts of my thesis by myself, I had a meeting with my graduate committee. They were not satisfied with the work I had done. They indicated that my initial questionnaire, which had been administered to college students, did not yield enough valuable information and, as a result, would not be acceptable. I had to do it over, questionnaire and all. I was crushed!

Two years of graduate work, and now I would be leaving Cornell without my master's degree. I vowed to complete my thesis while I was in New York City but I really didn't know how I would be able to do that. Maybe I had finally reached my limit.

◆ ◆ ◆

My father and brother scouted out the area near Teachers College, Columbia University, for an appropriate place for me to live. They finally arranged for me to rent a one-bedroom apartment on Morningside Drive, in Manhattan, two blocks from the school.

My bedroom was really small and the hallway was just barely wide enough for my wheelchair. My attendant had to sleep on a bed in the living room. I couldn't fit into the bathroom or kitchen. As a result, I had to have my hair washed in the basement laundry room.

The front door to my apartment building in New York City was up three steps. For me to get to school, I had to cross just one street, Amsterdam Avenue. However, there were no curb cuts there. My experience getting a ramp built for my dorm at Cornell emboldened me to call and write to the New York City Mayor's Office to ask them to put in two curb cuts. To my amazement, the City agreed to do so. Keep in mind, this was still about fifteen years before the Americans with Disabilities Act.

Because of accessibility problems, I was not able to use my electric wheelchair to go to class. I often had to rely on other students to wheel me from one class to another.

Decent attendants were, again, difficult to find. During my first year in the City, I had about ten different aides. Few worked out well. My helpers included a couple of people with drinking problems and at least one individual who was developmentally disabled. One or two of my attendants threatened to just take off and leave me alone in the apartment. All too frequently I had to rely on my family or I would have been left alone in the City for who knows how long.

My classes at Teachers College began in early September 1975. My first meeting with my faculty advisor did not go well. He told me I had virtually no chance of ever being admitted to the Teachers College doctoral program no matter how well I did in the master's program.

Because my advisor was also on the admissions committee, I knew that re-application would have been, indeed, futile.

I found out later that many of the students in the master's program, who had unsuccessfully applied to the doctoral program, received the same letter I did. We were all misled.

My advisor was also pessimistic about my chances of ever getting a job as a vocational rehabilitation counselor. Despite what they were teaching, social service agencies were hesitant to hire people with disabilities. A disability as severe as mine would make it virtually impossible to find employment in my field of choice.

I could only think, "Why am I even bothering to try?" Because I did not have an alternative, I decided to forge ahead with the semester. Fortunately, I was able to convince Teachers College to accept thirty credits from my Cornell master's program toward my degree at Columbia.

During my first semester at Columbia, I was still trying to develop a new thesis questionnaire for my Cornell degree. My new questionnaire, however, was rejected by my committee, as were my next few versions.

After about five different drafts, it was finally approved. It was pilot tested and then administered to more than a thousand students in Jim Maas's introductory psychology class, just before the semester ended in December. I received 471 completed questionnaires and spent much of my intersession coding them and going over the results.

Somehow, I managed to finish my first semester at Teachers College with a cume of 3.35.

◆ ◆ ◆

I registered to take sixteen credits for the second semester. That way, by completing seven credits of fieldwork over the summer, I would satisfy the requirements for my Master of Education degree in one year.

Five of my sixteen credits were for my practicum in vocational counseling. For that course, the students actually counseled people who came to the Teachers College Psychological Consultation Center. Because I was completing all of my requirements in just one year, I needed to do my practicum during my second semester. As a result, I was counseling clients at the same time I was taking the courses that had been prerequisites to the practicum.

Everything was supposed to be confidential. Just to bring a client into the interview cubicle, I had to get two different keys and go through two locked doors. Once there, my manual wheelchair barely fit into the room.

I was supposed to tape record each session. My poor clients! First, they were confronted with a counselor who was almost completely paralyzed. Second, my clients needed to wheel me into the interview room themselves and, once there, start the tape recorder. Third and most important, I had little idea what vocational counseling was all about. It was all terribly awkward and uncomfortable.

To protect client confidentiality, every session and final report had to be typed by me personally. Now even the paperwork was getting to me. I really had to question my career choice. After all that schooling, it looked like I might be in the wrong field, after all.

My first three clients did not return for a second session. I was convinced I was a terrible counselor and, in actuality, I probably was. Fortunately, my counseling skills improved a bit by the end of the semester.

In late April, I took and passed my comprehensive exam, which was required to graduate.

I completed my second semester with a cume of 3.55. Because no grade would be given for my fieldwork, my total cume at Teachers College was 3.43.

I arranged to do my fieldwork at the Bronx Veterans Administration (VA) Hospital. It began on Monday, May 17, 1976.

My first day at the VA, I was in my manual wheelchair. It was very difficult for me to begin counseling sessions, or even try to maintain any sort of professionalism, with an unhappy attendant wheeling me from place to place.

At the end of that first day, one of the psychologists at the VA suggested I use my electric wheelchair at the hospital. It was a good suggestion. Because I was not able to get in or out of my apartment building in my electric wheelchair, I had to travel back and forth to the VA in my manual wheelchair. Unfortunately, my van was not set up to accommodate both my electric wheelchair and me in my manual wheelchair at the same time. Upon arrival at the VA, I had to be transferred to my electric wheelchair, which I had to leave at the hospital.

I had hardly used my electric wheelchair since leaving Rusk, almost five years earlier. It took a lot of getting used to and was extremely tiring for my left arm, which still had to be supported by the BFO. As I traveled down the hallways, I usually had to stop and rest every few yards. I also had a lot of difficulty passing through a doorway with my arm sticking way out to the side in the BFO. By the end of each day, I was thoroughly exhausted.

One morning, just as I was entering a patient's room and introducing myself, I had a big muscle spasm. Because my hand was still on the control switch, the spasm sent me, and my wheelchair, flying right past the patient into a wall. Obviously, I still had a few problems of my own to work on.

A part of my fieldwork was doing supportive counseling with three patients on the spinal cord injury ward. Doing that, I felt I was acting more like a friend visiting, rather than a trained counselor. My three patients were permanently living in the VA hospital because they had no one to help them on the outside and no money to support themselves. They had no hope of ever being outside a hospital environment. It was very sad. It was also one of the situations that reminded me how fortunate I was to have family and friends who helped me.

I completed my 300 hours of fieldwork in eight weeks, finishing on July 8. I had now met all the requirements for my Master of Education degree.

During this time, I was still trying to complete my Cornell thesis. I put in a lot of hours at the typewriter. I typed three more drafts before my graduate committee was finally satisfied.

Knowing I would be completing my degree requirements at Teachers College during that summer, I drew up a two-page resume in June and began sending it out. On the second page of my resume, as well as in my cover letter, I stated that I was a quadriplegic. I felt that that would be an important piece of information for a potential employer.

I sent out more than 200 resumes in a ten-month period. To my dismay, I did not get much of a positive response.

My New York State Office of Vocational Rehabilitation counselor referred me to the Human Resources Center (HRC) in Albertson, Long Island, to receive placement assistance.

I went to the Center and met with a placement counselor. While not much came out of the interview, I was impressed with the Center, its physical layout, and wheelchair accessibility. For the first time, I saw many people with various disabilities actually working at a job site—although none with a disability as severe as mine. What a difference between that company and all the businesses in New York City I had visited while I was a patient at Rusk!

The Human Resources Center was comprised of three corporations: Abilities Inc., the Human Resources Research and Development Institute, and the Human Resources School, all devoted to either employing, helping, or educating people with disabilities.

Abilities Inc. was started in 1952 by Dr. Henry Viscardi Jr. as a facility run almost entirely by people with physical disabilities. Dr. Viscardi was born without legs. He became a leading advocate for people with disabilities, advising eight U.S. presidents on various issues related to disability.

I subsequently mailed my resume to the personnel department at HRC. My resume resulted in an interview with the personnel director, Mel Holtz, who informed me that there were no openings at that time.

About a month later, as a result of a recommendation by my Uncle Mel, I sent a resume to Marie Meier, a psychologist at Hofstra University. I spoke to her at length on the phone. She told me she also worked at HRC and that she would arrange a meeting for me with her friend Fred Francis, the Director of Vocational Rehabilitation Services there.

Fred and I immediately struck up a nice rapport. I really enjoyed talking with him.

A few weeks later, I had two more interviews at the Center for a public relations position that had opened. Only one left to go: an interview with Dr. Henry Viscardi Jr. That interview was scheduled for mid-December 1976.

Unfortunately, right before we were about to leave New York City to travel to Long Island, the condom leaked, not once, but twice. That meant I had to get back into bed and be changed two different times. As a result, instead of being a half-hour early, as I had planned, I was a little more than a half-hour late for my interview with Dr. Viscardi.

Fred was really upset I was so late, as was Dr. Viscardi. I was too embarrassed to tell either of them the real reason why I was late, so I told them we hit a lot of traffic driving in from the City, which was also true.

To make matters worse, my attendant had neglected to wipe off the Vaseline he had put on my face earlier that day to help with my dry skin. Dr. Viscardi, seeing my face covered with some kind of goop, and probably some perspiration as well, got up on his artificial legs and walked all the way around his desk just to wipe it off. I was terribly embarrassed, but grateful for his help.

Dr. Viscardi said he would prefer seeing me in a counseling position, since I had gone through two master's programs in counseling. Despite that, I was desperate to get any job, even if it was a job for which I was overqualified.

Shortly before Christmas, I learned that I hadn't gotten the public relations position. I couldn't believe it! And the Human Resources Center of all places, an agency devoted to helping people with disabilities. It sounded like even they felt I was too disabled to work.

On my brother's advice, I offered to do volunteer work at Human Resources Center. Steve and I hoped that, after showing what I could do as a volunteer, the Center would offer me a full-time position. But they would not even accept me as a volunteer. I couldn't give my services away!

I spoke to Fred Francis a couple of times on the phone after that. He wanted to see how my job search was going. Still, I was very surprised when he called me, in late April 1977, to say he had a position open on his staff in Rehabilitation Services and wanted to talk to me about it. He was offering me the job but wanted me to come in for an interview anyway.

That sounded almost too good to be true. I immediately made arrangements to be there the next day. To play it safe, I arrived forty-five minutes early. Fred couldn't have been nicer. He told me that I was to start work on May 3.

My salary at the Center, despite my having two master's degrees, was to be only $10,000, with the possibility of an increase to $12,000 after one year. To put those numbers in perspective, my attendant at the time was earning approximately $15,000, mostly covered by my father's major medical insurance. Still, I was thrilled to finally be offered a job.

Chapter 19

Making a Positive Difference

◆ ◆ ◆

Fred Francis, the Director of Vocational and Rehabilitation Services at Abilities Inc., put me in charge of a program to place disabled college students into jobs related to their academic major. The jobs would be either full-time positions during the summer or part-time during the school year. I would receive referrals for the program from the local New York State Offices of Vocational Rehabilitation (OVR), interview all the students referred to the program, and decide on an appropriate work experience for each one. I would then try to develop job placements for each student somewhere in the Long Island-Metropolitan area. Before placing the students, I would conduct job-seeking skills workshops for them, and, after placement, I would visit each student on the job to discuss the student's work performance with both the student and employer. I was required to maintain written correspondence with the OVR offices and I needed to stay in continuous contact with the employers.

My title was "College Work Orientation Program Coordinator." It sounded impressive. I needed Fred to repeat the title a number of times before I could remember it.

There was a problem though: I knew nothing about placement. My coursework in school never even touched on it. I had spent the past ten months looking for work for myself without success. Now, all of a sudden, I was considered an expert.

The prospect of taking on all the responsibilities Fred was giving me was daunting at best, but Fred felt my two masters' degrees were the perfect qualifications for the job. He even told me that I was not being hired on a trial basis. I had the job. Fred wanted me there and was convinced I could do the work. He had a lot more confidence in my ability than I had. I was already feeling guilty at the thought of letting Fred down, especially after he had placed so much faith in me.

Fred did everything he could to make starting on the job as easy for me as possible. He asked me what accommodations and modifications the Center could provide that would help me operate at my peak efficiency. He said that, at the Center, they were concerned about my handicap and they weren't concerned about my handicap. In other words, they would try to help me become the best worker I could be through accommodations, and then I would be expected to perform and produce as well as any other worker. I couldn't ask for more than that.

Making the adjustment to work full time was difficult for me. The eight-hour day seemed endless. During my first week, I was commuting from New York City. The Office of Vocational Rehabilitation arranged to have an accessible transportation company drive me back and forth from the City to Albertson, Long Island. To assure arriving on time, I had to get up at 5:30 a.m. I got very little sleep and, as a result, it was tough for me to keep awake during the day. I yawned frequently while in staff meetings and with the people I was counseling.

I arranged to leave my electric wheelchair at the Center. Even if I had been able to get out of my apartment building in the electric wheelchair, it would have been uncomfortable for me to travel sitting in it, because the back of the chair didn't recline or have a shoulder belt to keep me in place. With each stop or turn of the van my body inevitably would fall forward or to the side.

I usually arrived at the Human Resources Center before the other workers. That left extra time for me to transfer from my manual wheelchair to my electric one. As someone lifted the top part of my body, Fred would often assist by moving my legs. Fred was a bilateral above the knee amputee. For him to help transfer me, he had to get out of his wheelchair and balance on his stumps. I felt terribly guilty about him doing that but Fred insisted.

I was concerned about having my attendant at work with me. It would be difficult to maintain my professionalism, as well as my clients' confidentiality, with my attendant around.

Through Fred's encouragement, after my second day on the job, I tried to function without my attendant present at the Center. My attendant remained in the City, while I traveled back and forth in the van without him. Fred saw to it that someone would help feed me lunch and, if any problems arose during the day, they would be taken care of. Fred not only arranged to have people help transfer me back and forth between my manual and electric wheelchairs but also for someone to lift me off my buttocks a couple of times each day to let the blood circulate to help prevent bedsores.

During that first week, my father and Steve looked for an apartment on Long Island for me. They found a spacious two-bedroom in Hempstead, about a twenty-minute drive from HRC. They figured it would be a convenient place for me to live, and then, if need be, I could look for a better place.

Unfortunately, I was not able to get into the bathroom there. I washed my hair and shaved by the kitchen sink. Still, the Hempstead apartment was a big improvement from my apartment in New York City where, for two years, I couldn't even fit into the kitchen and I had to wash my hair and shave in the laundry room in the basement.

The first couple of days I worked at the Center, I felt completely useless. I didn't have my own desk yet, so I often just sat near a desk that was not accessible for me. I had a stack of folders on my lapboard in front of me but couldn't open or turn the pages.

A few days after I started, I was sitting in Jim Diffley's office, listening to him explain some of my duties. Jim had been the head of the College Work Orientation Program before me. He had been promoted to a new position, heading a permanent placement program. Jim was about my age, twenty-seven, and appeared to be a very hard and serious worker.

At some point during the meeting, Jim said to me, "We have to have a talk." He looked a bit frustrated.

I knew that I hadn't really accomplished much yet, but, after all, I had been there less than a week. I prepared myself to receive Jim's criticism. I thought I deserved it, too. I felt I had let Fred down, as well as my family. I didn't deserve the confidence they had placed in me. At that time, I didn't see myself lasting long at any job.

To my surprise, Jim said he was having a lot of trouble dealing with my disability and wanted to talk to me about it. I was so relieved. I couldn't believe how I had let my lack of self-confidence run away with me. I was also surprised at the strong affect my disability was having on Jim. After all, he was a rehab counselor, working at an agency for the handicapped. He had already dealt with a lot of people who had disabilities.

Jim, apparently, couldn't stop thinking about the fact that I had been a college athlete and was now almost totally paralyzed. Here we were, about the same age, and yet I had to deal with so many more obstacles than he and still managed to remain upbeat.

I was glad that my nervousness and uncertainty about my ability to handle the job was not obvious. More so, though, I was glad that Jim and others at the Center could not tell that I was still struggling to adjust and deal with my own disability and limitations.

Jim said that he admired my courage and motivation. It turned out that Jim was just a nice, caring individual, who truly wanted to help. I was so fortunate to have him as a coworker and later as a friend.

The Center was so well set up architecturally that it allowed me the independence and luxury of getting around in my electric wheelchair, unaided. There were even a nurse and a physical therapist, in a special medical wing in the facility.

When Fred initially asked what accommodations I would need, I really had no idea. I was just beginning to discover how I could function and work in an office setting. At that time, I still didn't know what else was out there to help me function more efficiently and independently. The only prior experience I had had was working for the Recreation for the Handicapped Unit, which hadn't gone very well.

I eventually designed my own workstation at the Center. I sat by a small table, two feet deep by two and a half feet wide. The table had a cutout on the left side to accommodate the control switch for my electric wheelchair and a cutout on the right side for my immobile right arm. When I wheeled under the desk, the cutouts left seventeen inches of workspace to put a book or file on. Had I not had the cutouts, the table would have had to have been higher to allow me to wheel under it. With the table higher, it would have been difficult for me to turn pages with my splints. It would not have been practical to keep the reading material in front of me on my lapboard. I needed that space for additional documents. I also didn't want to have anything on my lapboard in case I had to move around the Center.

I had two small tables to my left, where I kept a telephone and two Rolodexes. I had the telephone receiver attached to a bar that originally had been part of a "luxo lamp." The bar held the receiver near my ear. I used the Rolodexes to retrieve necessary information about the students and employers I was working with. That way, I did not need to ask a secretary to pull out a folder from the file drawer every time I needed a piece of information.

I was fortunate that the Center had Hans Krobath, a biomechanical engineer, on staff, to help with worksite modifications. Hans designed and made an attachment to my wrist splint that enabled me to write a little bit, turn pages of a book, and flip the cards on my Rolodexes, though certainly not without difficulty. In addition, he made other adaptations that enabled me to dial and answer the rotary telephone. Hans also extended levers on my tape recorder so that I could operate it by myself. Now, once in my electric wheelchair, I was more independent and self-sufficient at work. That was a great feeling.

Even if I were selling magazine subscriptions over the telephone, I probably would need these types of modifications to help me do the job.

It wasn't long before my responsibilities at the Center increased. In addition to my work with the college program, I was given a large individual and group counseling caseload. The counseling sessions involved vocational and career counseling as well

Ken with Jim Diffley and Fred Francis—spring 1978.
Photo by Michael Stanley.

as personal adjustment counseling. I was learning a tremendous amount about the work of rehabilitation services and the field of rehabilitation in general.

Some of my clients had been living with their disabilities for years, while others were newly injured or diagnosed. I had to make the transition from being the recipient of those same counseling services to now being their provider. I certainly could relate to my clients' problems and concerns. Sometimes, during the counseling sessions, I felt as if I was looking in a mirror, trying to advise myself.

Ken's workstation at Abilities Inc.—1977.
Photo by Michael Stanley.

The clients seemed to appreciate seeing me, someone with a severe disability, working and helping others. Perhaps as a result, many of them looked at me with admiration. It was probably one of the reasons I was hired. I felt I was doing important and much needed work. Finally, I could make a difference in other people's lives. Out of all the people we were trying to help, I was the one with the least movement and needed the most physical assistance.

Soon, I started helping Jim with one of the permanent placement programs. A good amount of our time was spent teaching job-seeking skills to individuals with severe disabilities. We were able to place a lot of people into full-time positions.

I was so impressed with the work ethic of many of the clients with whom I was now coming in contact. They didn't want handouts. They just wanted an opportunity to show that they still had value and could contribute.

One man who came to the Center for placement knew he would end up earning less money on the job we found for him than he would by continuing his disability benefits. He was a married man with children, who had emigrated from India. He told me that, in his culture, a man must work. He was desperate to get back into the work force, even if it meant losing money to do so.

I wondered, would I have made the same decision? I hope I would have. Working and helping others made me feel so much better about myself. Now, I not only understood his decision, I also better appreciated what went into it.

A constant concern for many of our clients was how their disability benefits would be affected once they finally got a job and started to earn a salary. There were many disincentives for someone with a disability to go to work. Many individuals were dependent on Supplemental Security Income (SSI) or Social Security Disability benefits. They absolutely needed Medicaid and attendant coverage. Many could not afford to go to work if it meant giving up those benefits.

While I never received SSI or Social Security Disability benefits, I was still very dependent on the attendant coverage provided by my father's major medical policy. My father's insurance company could have easily ended my medical coverage once I started work. Fortunately, because Mutual of New York was a private insurance company, my father convinced them to continue it.

In September, Fred asked me to appear on a panel, with others from the Center, to talk about architectural barriers and worksite modifications to employees at the Internal Revenue Service in Holtsville, Long Island. My talk went well and I was asked to reappear there again in October for another panel discussion. Soon I was sent out by the Center to give talks before groups on many different topics related to disability issues.

Fred jokingly said that the Center had been looking to hire "a good-looking quad who could talk." Apparently, the Center felt I fit the bill.

In mid-October, I received a call from Melba Tolliver of News Center 4 TV. She had a five-minute human-interest segment, aired at 5:55 p.m., during which she would do a story about someone in the New York area.

Melba Tolliver said that a representative of NBC was at a meeting during which a teacher from a high school for people who

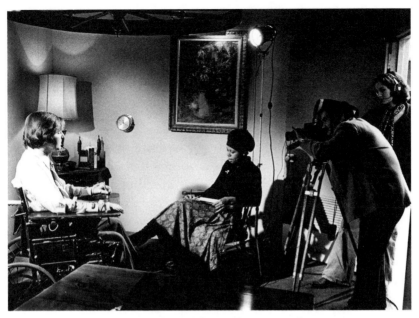

Ken being interviewed by Melba Tolliver—October 20, 1977.

had emotional problems talked about me. She had given her students an assignment to interview a person in a wheelchair. One of her students had spent two hours talking with me in August for that assignment.

On Thursday, October 20, Tolliver came to HRC with her film crew. I was surprised I wasn't more nervous. Probably as a result of the many newspaper and magazine interviews I had done in the past, I felt relatively comfortable and at ease.

On Friday, October 21, I spoke at a conference at the State University of New York (SUNY) at Farmingdale, concerning job placement for individuals with disabilities. A few other people were also supposed to speak on the same topic but, because they were nervous and not really sure what to say, I went first and did most of the talking.

Following my talk, I called in to work to see if there were any messages. During that phone call, I learned that my secretary

Diane, who had been helping me for the past five and a half months, had been given a different position at the Center. She would start on Monday. After hearing the news, I felt a bit upset. I had grown very dependent on Diane. A good deal of my ability to function at the office was a result of how well I worked with my secretary.

Diane knew exactly what I needed and was expected to do. I remember the first time I dictated a letter to her. I had to write a progress report to the Office of Vocational Rehabilitation concerning one of their clients whom I was counseling. I began:

Dear Ms. Smith,

Jane Doe is typing at twenty words per minute. She also is doing filing.

As I was dictating, I looked over and saw Diane writing and writing. I asked her to read back the letter so far.

Without hesitation, Diane began to read:

Dear Ms. Smith,

Thank you for referring your client to the Human Resources Center for vocational training. The following is a progress report on how she is doing.

Ms. Doe began her training on May 21, 1977. Her attendance to date has been perfect. She is extremely motivated and always maintains a pleasant attitude. Ms. Doe has improved many of the office skills necessary to obtain full-time employment. She is currently typing at the rate of twenty words per minute. In addition, she has become more adept at filing and other office work.

I had difficulty keeping a straight face. I told Diane the letter was perfect and she should continue to finish it. She was just what I needed. Everybody could use a "Diane."

Fred called to reassure me that they would be hiring another secretary to take Diane's place. While I didn't find much comfort in that at the time, it probably was good for me to work with other people and not be so dependent on one particular person.

I was learning a lot every day about what was required to be a professional. I still needed to develop more self-confidence though. I could do the work. I just needed to convince myself that I did not have to rely on any one individual for me do a good job.

On Monday, October 24, eight friends from the Center stayed after work to watch the Melba Tolliver segment with me. We wanted to videotape it off the TV, using some special equipment that was only available at the Center. It was called a VCR. I had never seen one before.

We were all happy with how my interview appeared on television. We then moved to my apartment to celebrate it more with some food.

On October 26, I received the Long Island Rehabilitation Association's (LIRA) "Rehabilitant of the Year" Award. There were about 250 rehabilitation professionals in attendance. I delivered a short thank you speech before many of the professionals in the area with whom I was now working. It was important to me that they come away with a good impression. It was my opportunity to assure that they would now treat me as a professional, rather than a client or just another individual with a disability. I received a lot of complimentary feedback from my coworkers at the Center, who were present at the award ceremony.

The next day, there was a short article in the Long Island newspaper *Newsday* about me getting the award. That really capped off a busy week, which had included the Melba Tolliver TV segment, the Farmingdale talk, and the LIRA award.

My social life had improved as well. Debbi, an instructional writer at the Center, and the organizer of the impromptu party after the Melba Tolliver segment, began to spend more time with me outside of work. Initially, I thought they were just friendly visits from a fellow worker but, fortunately, it was more than that. By Christmas Day, it had turned into a nice little romance.

Debbi was a popular, outgoing, and attractive young woman. More than anything else at that time, she was exactly what I needed. It had been four and a half years since I went out with Nancy. Just

Ken with Debbi—1978.

the thought that someone cared enough to go out with me, kept me smiling for days.

Debbi and I saw a lot of each other for the next ten weeks before our relationship turned into just a very good friendship. The extra attention and affection had felt great while it lasted. I hated to see it end. It reminded me, once again, of the impossibility of ever having a serious relationship.

◆ ◆ ◆

In addition to maintaining full responsibility for the College Student Program, I became more involved with another placement program run by Jim Diffley. I also did a lot of public speaking on behalf of the Center. It was nice to be so busy. It made me feel

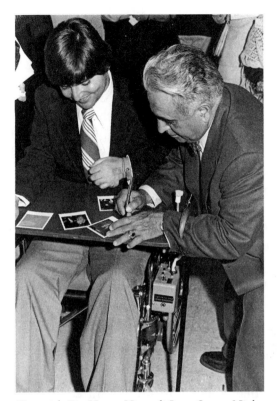

Ken with Dr. Henry Viscardi Jr. at Sports Night
at the Human Resources Center—May 17, 1978.
Photo by Michael Stanley.

important. I was not only being productive, I was making a positive difference in other peoples' lives.

May 3, 1978, marked my one-year anniversary working at the
Center—a real milestone for me. I had had so many self-doubts
before I started, as well as for the first couple of months after I
began working there. I was pleased to see the results of my one-
year review. For every category for which I was evaluated, Fred
checked either outstanding or superior. I was given a thirty percent
raise in salary.

My coworkers arranged for a surprise pizza lunch. I was very
touched that my one-year anniversary did not go unacknowledged.
It all made me feel very special and appreciated.

On May 17, 1978, I received the Human Resources Center's Celebrity Sportsman of the Year Award at their annual Sports Night Dinner. The Celebrity Sportsman Award was given to an employee at the Center who had a disability, had been involved in sports at some point, had made a significant adjustment to his or her disability, and was now helping others.

Sports Night was the largest fundraising event of the year for the Center. Approximately thirty famous sports celebrities came, talked, posed for pictures, and signed autographs. The event drew about 800 people, including my father, my brother, and Aunt Lorraine.

A fellow worker later told me that an executive at Grumman was standing beside him as I delivered my thank you speech. Grumman Aerospace Corporation was the largest corporate employer on Long Island. The Grumman executive remarked that if I weren't working at HRC, he would hire me at Grumman just to give speeches.

♦ ♦ ♦

During that spring, I finally submitted my completed thesis to my graduate committee at Cornell. A few weeks later, I was given the opportunity to defend the thesis over the telephone, while I was at work. I had now met all the requirements to receive my Master of Arts degree from Cornell, more than three years after I had finished my coursework there.

On Sunday, October 25, 1978, I went to a flea market near Roosevelt Field with Debbi. Debbi had left the Center a few months earlier and was now working for a firm in New York City.

It happened to be the same day that my brother was running in the New York City Marathon. At some point, I must have mentioned that fact to Debbi. I started talking about having watched Steve in court and that it looked like something I would enjoy doing.

When we returned to my apartment in Hempstead, I continued to talk to Debbi about how attractive the field of law looked to me. I thought about the many times I had spoken at conferences on behalf of the Center concerning affirmative action and nondiscrimination with reference to people with disabilities. Frequently after my talks, I would be asked questions about the topics. While I would certainly do my best to respond appropriately, I was always careful to caution the questioners that they should speak to a lawyer about their concerns. I suppose it wasn't long before I started to think there was no reason why I couldn't become that lawyer, or any other type of lawyer for that matter.

Working at the Center gave me the self-confidence to work as a counselor and be successful at it. I had proved to myself and others that I could do it. Now I was convinced there was still even more that I could do. I didn't feel I had reached my full potential. I knew I didn't want to work as a rehabilitation counselor for the rest of my life, nor did I want to remain in social services much longer. I knew there was a profession that offered higher salaries, better prospects for growth, and the opportunity to someday work for myself: LAW.

Debbi encouraged me to stop talking about it and apply to law school. At that moment, I made up my mind. I became so excited about it I could hardly wait for the next day, Monday, to come, so that I could call Hofstra Law School and request an application.

◆ ◆ ◆

Well before my decision to go to law school, I had arranged to take a six-hour test to become a Certified Rehabilitation Counselor (CRC). Being a nationally certified rehabilitation counselor was important if I were to continue working in the field. It also would enable me to supervise rehabilitation counseling student interns from Hofstra University and other graduate programs.

The test was to be given in New York City on October 28. I planned to spend the night before the test at my brother's house in Huntington Bay on the north shore of Long Island. Steve offered to drive me to the test, do the writing for me, and then afterward, take me to visit our grandmother in Jersey City, New Jersey.

I knew that Marcy, another employee of the Center, was taking the CRC test in the City the same day. Marcy had started working at the Center on August 1. Coincidentally, she sat at the same desk at which Debbi used to sit.

I asked Marcy if she wanted to drive into New York City with us. When she said yes, I became a little bolder and asked her if she would like to come to my brother's house for dinner the night before. To my delight, my invitation was accepted.

Marcy and I had a very enjoyable dinner and evening together. I spent a good deal of the night lying awake, thinking about her. While it was difficult for me to concentrate the next day, I still managed to pass the test, as did Marcy.

During the first week of November, I attempted to write an essay for the Hofstra Law School application, on: "Why I want to go to law school." I showed Marcy a draft of it. Fortunately, she didn't like it. Marcy spent a lot of time with me the next few weeks, rewriting it until it sounded like a work of art.

By the end of November, Marcy and I were seeing each other outside of work on a regular basis.

On January 16, 1979, I received my acceptance to Hofstra Law School.

♦ ♦ ♦

When I wasn't at work at HRC, I tried to do a lot of resistive exercises with my then-aide Joe Schultz, to strengthen the limited movement in my left arm. By March 1979, my left arm had gotten strong enough for me to feed myself, without my arm in the BFO. I asked a friend from work, Jim Cohen, if he could make a shorter handle for my fork, which had a swivel on the end. He did so, and on March 7, 1979, I fed myself without my arm being supported in a BFO for the first time since my accident. Jim made a few other attachments for my wrist splint, which increased my self-sufficiency. He also made me a lapboard out of Plexiglas, allowing me to see where my feet were so I wouldn't bump into things.

In the spring of 1979, an assistant of the Reverend Norman Vincent Peale, the bestselling author of *The Power of Positive*

Thinking, contacted me. A newspaper story about me had come to his attention and the reverend wanted to devote one of his one-minute nationally syndicated radio broadcasts, called "The American Character," to talk about how I was conducting my life.

They sent me a transcript of the text the reverend would say. It was a little corny but sounded great when the reverend actually said it over the radio. He ended his broadcast with the following words: "A quadriplegic overcoming great personal handicaps, Ken Kunken thinks only of rebuilding his life to serve others, in the American Character."

♦ ♦ ♦

On April 16, 1979, I spoke on a panel of four speakers at Adelphi University. The topic dealt with problems and needs of the disabled on college campuses and was part of the University's "Handicap Awareness Day."

The day before that talk was exactly eight years since I had testified before Senator Kennedy's Senate Health Subcommittee at Hofstra University. My public speaking ability, as well as my self-confidence, had come a long way since then. By now, I had developed decent skills speaking without notes. Since starting my job, twenty-three months earlier, I had delivered twenty-one presentations on various topics to different groups and organizations. This was to be my twenty-second, and my sixth in the past two months. The Center was getting their money's worth out of the "good-looking quad who could talk."

At the end of the Adelphi event, a few people remained in the room to speak to me individually. The last person sat very patiently in the first row, waiting until everyone else had left. He was well dressed, wearing a blue shirt, business suit, and a trench coat. Apparently, he had come into the room after I had finished speaking.

Burt Eckstein came up to me to say Hi, and we exchanged some small talk. Burt worked at Adelphi and resided in Oceanside. As Burt was about to leave, the man in the trench coat came up to the table next to me. Burt introduced his colleague from Adelphi by saying, "Ken, you know Tom Eyestone, don't you?"

The name sounded familiar but I couldn't recall when or where I had heard it before. I certainly did not recognize the man. Burt left and the man came closer. We were now alone.

The man spoke softly and almost apologetically, "I'm the person you tackled on Columbia."

You could have knocked me over with a feather. I was taken totally by surprise. I had broken my neck 3,089 days before. Yes, I had been counting the days. Now, for the first time, I was meeting the person I had tackled.

For the past eight and a half years, I had wondered what it would be like to meet him. Somehow, it was tough for me to imagine. Now here he was.

I told Tom that it was nice to finally meet him. We exchanged some small talk. It soon became apparent to me that Tom felt guilty about the part he played in my injury.

I emphasized that he shouldn't feel guilty at all. I had never blamed him for what happened. After all, I tackled him.

Tom said he really appreciated that but would always feel, at least somewhat, guilty.

It was sad listening to Tom say that. It was obvious he had spent a lot of time thinking about what had happened back in October 1970. It was clear that all those years had weighed on him emotionally.

Tom asked me what my recollection of the play was.

For some reason, I relayed more of what I heard from others and what I saw on film than what I actually remembered. Why, I don't know. Perhaps it was because, by then, I had watched the tackle replayed many times on tape, still trying to figure out why I was hurt.

I spoke almost in the third person and, surprisingly, with little feeling.

I told him it appeared he had just avoided a tackler and never saw me coming.

Tom did not remember avoiding a tackler. He said he was cutting to his right when I hit him. Tom said he couldn't believe how hard the impact was. He didn't think anybody on the 150s could hit that hard.

Tom said I hit him in the groin and he was in an awful lot of pain: "I was out for twenty minutes on my feet and was still feeling the effects a few weeks afterward."

I suppose I kind of felt a bit good hearing about Tom's pain. It just wouldn't have seemed right for me to break my neck and for him not to have felt anything.

Tom said he didn't find out until the Tuesday after the game how badly I was hurt.

We talked for a while. Tom had a wife and two children, a good job as the assistant director of admissions at Adelphi, and still looked in great shape. He would never let his kids play football though, only soccer. He said he hates football now.

Tom asked if I was able to drive a car.

I told him I didn't have enough movement. I then proceeded to show him the movement I did have and what I could do with my braces and splints.

Tom said he had helped raise money for me during the fund drive they organized at Columbia back in 1971. He remembered hearing that I was at Teachers College a few years ago. Tom said he had kept up with what I was doing by reading articles about me in the newspapers.

I told Tom I was sorry they had printed his name in the paper. There was no reason for that.

Tom was impressed that I had completed two masters' degrees and was going to start Hofstra Law School in August. He was happy I was able to accomplish so much, despite my disability.

I told Tom I was glad we talked. I repeated that I had never blamed him for what happened and that he should try not to feel guilty.

Tom thanked me again for saying this and for our little chat. Then, he stood up, walked out of the room, down the hall, and out of my life. Watching Tom walk away left me with some very strange and uncertain feelings. It is difficult to put those feelings into words. I still couldn't decide whether I felt happy or sad, good or bad, about our meeting. I was certainly all wound up.

Meeting Tom reminded me of so many things I wanted out of life but would never have. There would be no recovery from my injury, no wife, no children, probably no great career. Tom seemed to be fulfilling his dreams, while I couldn't even begin to dream mine.

It had taken a lot of courage on Tom's part to approach me but now his conscience should finally be clear. I know it wasn't Tom's fault that I was hurt. There shouldn't be anything for him to feel bad about. Tom should be happy. He should put his unintentional involvement in my injury behind him. Tom is a nice guy and I wish him well.

That evening I went out to dinner with Marcy and Tom Smith. Tom and I worked together at HRC and we both had applied to Hofstra Law School at the same time. That night, we were there to celebrate our acceptances.

As soon as I saw them, I started talking about my meeting with Tom Eyestone. I suppose I spoke about it for a good deal of the evening. Celebrating my acceptance to law school was almost an afterthought.

I got very little sleep that night. I lay awake in bed for hours, rehashing everything that had happened that day and during the past eight and a half years. I wonder how Tom slept.

♦ ♦ ♦

In May, I represented the Human Resources Center at a conference at the Institute of Rehabilitation Medicine (Rusk) in New York City, concerning the latest developments in environmental control units. Approximately twenty other rehabilitation professionals were in attendance. It felt strange to be wearing a jacket and tie at Rusk and attending a conference there.

I had the opportunity that day to try a wheelchair that could be operated by voice commands. Although it didn't work very well for me, I was amazed at how far technology had come. I could not help but marvel at where it would be in another few years. I would probably be able to do many more things, even if I did not get any more movement back.

Near the end of the day, I went down to the fourth floor to see my old room. While I was in the hallway, a female quadriplegic patient approached me and, out of the blue, said, "You look like you are going to be going to law school."

I was shocked. Did just putting on a jacket and tie completely change the way people saw me?

The woman's name was Conchetta. She had broken her neck in an accident while riding a motorcycle. She was going to be discharged soon and, coincidentally, had also been accepted to Hofstra Law School for the fall semester. Small world.

♦ ♦ ♦

My last day of work at HRC was on July 27, 1979. After I left, the Center not only hired a full-time counselor to replace me, it also had to divide additional duties I was doing between two other employees.

Chapter 20

Law School

◆ ◆ ◆

I began law school on Monday, August 20, 1979. Coincidentally, it was exactly eight years to the day I was discharged from Rusk.

The morning began with an orientation held across the street from the law school in a 300-seat auditorium in Monroe Hall. I sat in the very back, in an aisle, next to Tom Smith, my friend from the Human Resources Center.

During the orientation, one speaker after another welcomed us to Hofstra and then proceeded to tell us we were in for a year of pure hell. Every one of them told us that we would never have worked so hard in our lives as we would during this next year. It would be schoolwork morning, noon, and night.

Coming out of the auditorium, I saw Concetta. It had been almost three months since I first met her at Rusk. I thought it would be nice for both of us to go through our first year together but, unfortunately, Concetta dropped out after that first day. She decided she needed more time to adjust to her new physical condition and get her affairs in order. It had only been about two months since she had been discharged from Rusk.

I could certainly understand her decision. I had been out of Rusk for just eleven days before I traveled to Cornell to resume my studies in industrial engineering. Looking back, I was glad I had done that then and thankful it was now behind me. Eleven days was really too short a time, though. I would not recommend going back to school that quickly to anyone. So much adjusting still needs to take place for someone newly injured. I only did that myself because I didn't know any better.

During the first week of school only my Legal Research and Writing class met and that was for two hours in the morning and two in the afternoon. While everything in law school seemed like it would be hard for me to manage physically, I knew research and writing would be the most difficult.

As was the case with all my courses, I had homework assignments to do even before classes began. Virtually every law school course necessitated writing legal briefs. I had no idea how I was going to do that. I did the reading but just couldn't find a satisfactory way to write the briefs.

I didn't feel comfortable asking anyone to put carbon paper under his or her notes. I don't know what I intended, but I actually thought I might be able to manage by taking notes myself. That should have been an easily foreseeable failure.

I tried to write in a notebook balanced on my lapboard, while trying to keep my right arm from falling off the board. While my classmates appeared to be writing page after page, I ended up with just a few barely legible words, scribbled on a single piece of paper.

The next morning, I decided I would start going to class in my electric wheelchair. I didn't have a clamp, straps, or chains to secure it in the van at that time, so it was scary riding this way and probably wasn't safe. It felt like I was about to flip over at any moment. I made it to the law school, after a nerve-wracking six-minute ride, only to have my electric wheelchair stop working at the front door of the school. Apparently, the batteries were no longer good. I had to be pushed to class in that heavy electric wheelchair.

I had ordered a new electric wheelchair in July, about a month before law school started. Unfortunately, it still had not arrived. Rather than buy expensive new batteries for the old chair, I decided to just use my manual wheelchair until the new electric one came. I didn't know the new chair would not arrive until November.

As had been the case for years, every time I yawned or had a spasm, my right arm would fall off the lapboard. I yawned a lot during those classes. It was very uncomfortable leaving my arm dangling on the side of my wheelchair, but I didn't like asking a stranger to lift it back up onto my lapboard. As a result, I often just left it hanging there for more than an hour until the class ended and my attendant came to pick me up.

Eventually, I had someone drill a hole on the right side of my lapboard. I would then keep a wrist splint on my right hand and had a pencil sticking up from the hole preventing my right arm from falling off the board. It wasn't very comfortable but it seemed to help.

I finally mustered up enough courage to ask a young woman who was sitting at the same table in the front row if she would put a piece of carbon paper under her pad so I could get a copy of her notes. She agreed, but I hated asking her just the same.

My memory seemed to be failing me. I often didn't remember what I had read the night before. Fortunately, my research and writing class instructor only called on students if they raised their hands. At least she was not like Professor Kingsfield in the movie *The Paper Chase*. Professor Kingsfield embarrassed and grilled his students mercilessly. I had seen that movie in 1974 and was thankful at that time that I had chosen not to go to law school. The first year of law school looked absolutely brutal.

During my first week of class, we were assigned to write a six-page, triple-spaced, typed appellate brief. It was due that first Friday. Like most of the other students, I was completely lost as to how to do the assignment. I also was unsure how I was going to physically manage doing it, whatever "it" was.

My friend Tom Smith was not in my Legal Research and Writing class, but he was in my five other ones. Even though Tom was in another section, we had basically been given the same assignment, though Tom happened to be assigned to argue the opposite side. We decided we would do it together, writing out two complete briefs, one taking Tom's side and one taking mine.

We worked at my apartment both Wednesday and Thursday nights but were nowhere near ready to actually start writing our briefs.

It was relatively late Thursday evening by the time we started writing my brief. After struggling over every word, we finished it at about 1 a.m. Now we still had to work on Tom's.

We were both really exhausted but, after writing mine, Tom's was a little bit easier to tackle. We finished his at about 3 a.m., with me struggling the entire time to keep awake and be productive.

Now I had to type it. Tom set me up at the typewriter and then left my apartment. The typing seemed to take forever. I had to wake up my attendant each time I reached the bottom of a page so that he could put in a new piece of paper. He certainly didn't like that and made it known to me.

I finally finished typing the six-page paper around 8 a.m. As tired as I was, I really didn't want to miss class, but I was worried about getting bedsores from sitting up so long. I ended up skipping class, lay down, and slept for a few hours. I had my attendant, Joe, drop off the paper when class started in the morning because it was due then.

For the afternoon class, Joe dropped me off about ten minutes early. I was surprised that none of the other students had arrived yet. Nobody had told me that the class had been canceled. I ended up sitting there alone, for two hours, until Joe finally came to pick me up.

I thought a lot about the fact that I had already pulled one all-nighter. I was pretty much studying the entire day. I was having trouble remembering the material, and all this was for only one course. I still had to add five substantive law courses the next week. It didn't seem possible. There weren't enough hours in the day.

When I finally had a conference with the professor of my research and writing class, she told me that I wrote well and that my brief was one of the best papers in the class. Still, there were plenty of corrections. The professor said that my grade for the paper would be between a C+ and a B-.

During the second week of school, all six of my classes met. Four of my six professors put students on the spot by calling on them. It was difficult to sit back and relax in class, knowing that you could be called on at any moment and questioned in front of the other eighty students.

Because of the layout of the lecture rooms, I had to sit in front of the front row, off to the side. It made me that much more conspicuous to professors looking for a student to call on. I certainly didn't blend in with the crowd.

The first two days of the second week of classes, I asked Tom if he would take me to the library with him, between classes. I didn't feel like it was a great imposition because we were in the same classes and he was going there anyway. Tom, however, was very nervous about school, was not happy about pushing me, and told me so. I really didn't want to ask my attendant to come to Hofstra for a few minutes, just to push me from class to class. My attendant was already getting edgy about not having nearly as much time off as he had had when I was working all day at the Human Resources Center.

I couldn't believe that with all the things I had to contend with and adjust to, the two people whose help I was counting on the most, Tom and my attendant, were making it uncomfortable for me to even ask for help.

I still hadn't resolved the problem with writing briefs. The scratch marks I made in my books didn't nearly suffice. I ended up reading each case a few times and then tried to rely on my memory. Pretty soon, however, all the cases seemed to blend together.

One student offered to make a carbon copy of her class notes and briefs for me, but that only lasted a week and a half. It was difficult for me to manage holding onto copies of different briefs on my lapboard while flipping pages in the casebook. Due to the layout of the classrooms, which were in tiers, I had to sit in front of everybody so I couldn't even get help from a fellow classmate, even if I knew one to ask.

I went about two weeks without anyone giving me a carbon copy of his or her notes. I then asked a woman named Karen Murphy if she would mind making carbon copies of her notes. She ended up making them for me in every class for the entire year. Her handwriting was great and her notes were excellent. Karen even went back and recopied the notes I was missing. She was a tremendous help, and took a big burden off my shoulders.

It was still awkward and uncomfortable for me to try to find a student to push me from my class to the student lounge, and even moreso from the lounge to my next class. I would often spend the last ten minutes of each class, or my whole break between classes, looking for someone I could ask to give me a push. This made concentrating even more difficult.

The halls were crowded between classes and my inexperienced pushers often misjudged the length of my wheelchair. They would run into other people in the hall or bump my feet when they were opening a door or making a turn.

During the fifth week of classes, I developed a small bedsore, which caused me to miss one and a half days of classes. I got up for one, two-hour-long class, then returned to spend the weekend in bed.

That was especially frustrating because I was not able to read in bed. Hour after hour, I watched my valuable study time being wasted away as I lay in bed and stared at the ceiling. When I was able to get up to go to classes the next week, I had to lie down as soon as I got home to prevent my bedsore from reopening.

My second legal research assignment required me to research and write a six-page paper concerning the first three grounds for divorce in New York State. It meant having to do a lot of research in the law library. Initially, I had my attendant get me the books and copy the cases I was considering using. I would then take the copies home, and read and work on them by myself.

My attendant complained that it was too much work for him and that he needed more time off. The weekend before, my weekend attendant didn't show up at all. I spent that Saturday and Sunday at my brother's. I wasn't able to go to the library, as I had planned, and fell even farther behind in the assignment. Time was becoming a factor now. My attendant's complaining added to my anxiety and discomfort.

I spent a lot of time reading and rereading the enormous number of pages my attendant had copied. Then, I spent hours by the typewriter writing notes and organizing my thoughts. Finally, I spent even more time typing the paper myself. The entire report took an enormous amount of work and energy for me to complete. It also took a lot of study time away from my substantive courses.

At my brother's suggestion, I called the Hofstra Disabled Students Office to see if they could help me find someone to assist me with my research. The office was associated with Hofstra's Volunteer Office. They put me in touch with Martin Yazijian, a retired high school English teacher. It turned out to be a perfect match.

Martin and I would go to the law library together. I would tell him which books to pull from the shelves, and then he would copy the pages I wanted. I dictated a draft of the report to Martin, later dictated the finished copy to him, and eventually gave it to a friend to type.

Martin's help was invaluable and saved me a lot of time. Because of that, I was able to do a better job on my papers. I ended up getting an A for the course, which had been the one I had most dreaded before I started law school. Only two other students, out of the fifty in that class, got an A.

I knew I would be at a distinct disadvantage taking exams, because most of the other students wrote extensive outlines for each course. They used those outlines to study. They also relied heavily on them during open book exams. One student made me a copy of his torts outline, which was a big help. I was pretty much on my own for the other courses, though.

For exams, the administration agreed to allow me to go into a separate room with Martin and dictate my answers to him. They gave me as much time as I needed to complete the exams.

My Contracts professor, Monroe Freedman, gave the option to anyone in the class to take his midterm exam orally with him. I felt that, even though I didn't know the coursework very well, I should take advantage of the only opportunity I was given to take an oral exam. I was one of six, out of eighty students, who signed up.

I scheduled myself to be the first student to take the test, so that my attendant could catch a plane to Missouri to be with his parents for the holidays. As it turned out, he had to leave the night before. I, therefore, had to arrange to spend the night at Steve's house, an hour's drive from Hempstead. Steve had to drop me off at school by nine in the morning the day of the exam.

Juggling care coverage for me when I didn't have an attendant was always challenging. The plan this time was that, after the exam, I would meet Martin and we would go to the law library. My friend Marcy would then pick me up on her lunch hour, around 12:30, to take me back to my apartment. Martin would join me there and stay until 4:45, when my Aunt Betty would pick me up to take me to New Jersey for a few days.

If that sounded complicated, it got worse. Right at the end of the exam, the condom leaked. I tried calling my brother to see if he could take me home and change me but he was in court. I later had Martin call Steve's office and left a message for him to meet me at my apartment on his lunch hour. Fortunately for me, Steve did. I finally got into some dry, non-smelly clothes at about 1 p.m.

The Contracts oral exam was little more than a written exam, with the professor writing down everything I said. I thought I had really lucked out when I saw the exam was just a one-question test, basically asking what contract remedies the state would have if one of its contractors broke the nondiscrimination clause. I had dealt with nondiscrimination clauses at my job at the Human Resources Center.

I gave what I thought was a pretty good answer but it earned me only a C. Professor Freedman was a really tough grader. He said that, to him, C meant "competent to practice contracts." The average grade in his class was between C- and C.

My grades for the first semester were actually pretty good. I got an A- in Property. It was one of only ten, out of about eighty students, that Professor Silverman gave. He didn't give any As.

In torts, I got a B+. There were only four A-'s, so I felt pretty good about that as well. The two grades that actually went on my transcript were a B in Criminal Law and an A in Legal Research and Writing. They were each for three credits and were only one semester long. The other four courses continued for the full first year.

Judging by the grades of the other students I saw posted, after the first semester, I was probably in the top ten percent of the class.

♦ ♦ ♦

Once again, I had to spend a lot of time looking for a replacement for my attendant. Joe, at least, had given me plenty of notice that he would be leaving.

I ran ads in the newspaper for weeks. I interviewed a total of twenty-five not-very-good candidates. It really took a lot of time away from my studies. It also was happening during the time I had to work especially hard on my moot court brief. As a result, I fell quite a bit behind in my schoolwork and never caught up as much as I would have liked.

About a week and a half before Joe left, I had him train a man named Charlie. I could see from day one that hiring Charlie was a big mistake, but I really didn't want to advertise again until after my exams.

Charlie, among other things, was an alcoholic. He often left me alone in the apartment to go drinking at a bar across the street. A number of times, I had to call the bar to tell Charlie to come home. There were many unpleasant scenes and I was very glad to finally replace him after three long months.

Aside from falling behind in my work for the reasons already given, I had to also miss a full day of classes because the elevator at Hofstra wasn't working. That was especially frustrating.

♦ ♦ ♦

The most time-consuming project for the spring semester was working on my appellate brief for moot court. I had to write a lengthy brief arguing that a prosecutor had a legal obligation to disclose to the defense his office's plea-bargaining guidelines. It was an interesting assignment based on a real case. After completing the brief, I had to present and defend my case in front of a panel of three judges.

Thanks to my work at the Human Resources Center, I felt comfortable being bombarded with numerous rapid-fire questions from the judges. My experience teaching job-seeking skills really paid off. Part of that teaching had involved being able to answer any questions put to an applicant during a job interview. That certainly was good preparation for moot court.

My oral presentation went well. Steve, Nicky, my father, his wife Betty, my cousin Ronnie, Martin, and my attendant Charlie all attended.

I finished the year with a 2.71 cume. That probably ranked me in the middle of the class. It was quite a letdown after all the work I had done to prepare for the exams. I had put in about sixty hours per week for the three weeks preceding the tests.

All in all, though, I pretty much enjoyed the year academically. I really liked the law and law school. Each day I was learning a lot. It was very challenging in a good way. I knew I could compete in this field and do well.

♦ ♦ ♦

During the summer, I worked as an intern for the Hempstead Town Attorney. Hempstead Town Hall, where I did my internship, was just two blocks from my apartment. It took about ten minutes for me to go to the office, riding in my electric wheelchair in the street while my attendant walked on the sidewalk beside me. The street was heavily traveled almost all the time. I could not use the sidewalks along that road because, despite my having written a letter to the Village of Hempstead, which went unanswered, there were no curb cuts. A number of times, my spasms propelled me dangerously close to moving cars.

My law internship involved research and writing. Those were the very things with which I had the most trouble. Plus, I did not have my own desk, phone setup, or secretary for that matter. It reminded me of the two summers I worked for the county, when I wasn't able to do anything. During those summers, I had felt helpless and totally dependent on my attendant, who had stayed with me at the office the entire time. I couldn't believe that, after my work experience at HRC and one year of law school, I was once again back to square one.

I felt strongly about not having my attendant with me this time. I didn't think it would be fair to subject the office to another person, who would probably just sit there doing little or nothing, or, worse, wander around. Realistically, though, he probably should have been with me.

There were thirteen attorneys in the Town Attorney's Office. That summer they had five other interns, in addition to me. All the interns usually just sat at a long table in the law library and did their work there.

The condom leaked embarrassingly often. It usually necessitated me going home to get changed and then returning to the office. Unless it was almost lunchtime, I needed someone to call my attendant to accompany me home. As a result, I felt I always had to announce to the people in the office that the condom had leaked and I was now sitting in a puddle of urine. The strong odor and the discoloration of my pants probably gave me away anyway.

♦ ♦ ♦

On July 15, 1980, I turned thirty. I suppose everyone's thirtieth birthday is significant; for me, though, that birthday was significant for different reasons. Turning thirty meant I had spent virtually my entire twenties in a wheelchair. As far back as I could remember, I had thought that the best time of my life would be when I was in my twenties. If it were going to be downhill from here, my future would be bleak at best. I thought a lot about my previous nine birthdays.

I was still a patient at Rusk when I turned twenty-one. I will always consider that my most unhappy birthday. It was then that I first started thinking, "I'm not getting better, just older!" Still, I had gotten to speak to Betsy that day, for the first time.

I spent the evening of July 14, 1980, sitting outside on my patio in Hempstead, thinking about my life. The condom had leaked three different times that day. What a way to end my twenties!

For my thirtieth birthday, I went out to dinner with Marcy. The evening felt very strained. We had stopped dating about nine months earlier and it was the first time I had seen her in over a month.

Thirty was now here to stay. It did not seem to hold much promise for a change for the better. How far had I come those past ten years? It didn't seem very far to me, certainly not far enough. On July 16, the condom leaked again. Some things never change. It looked like another tough decade ahead.

On August 9, I went to Betty's cabin in Great Barrington, Massachusetts, for a five-day vacation with Steve and Nicky.

On Wednesday, August 13, we went to Williamstown, Massachusetts, an hour drive from Great Barrington, to see the play *Whose Life Is It Anyway?* I had heard bits and pieces about the play from a few people. It was about a quadriplegic who decides he doesn't want to live anymore. Certainly, it was a story I could relate to.

When we arrived, the people working at the box office were not sure they could accommodate someone in a wheelchair.

Betty convinced them that we could handle getting me, and my wheelchair, to a suitable space inside the theater, out of the way. My brother pulled me up the six steps that were in front of the entrance. How typical that, even when they put on a show about a person with a disability, they made it almost impossible for a person with a disability to get into the building to see it.

The play was a déjà vu for me. The lead character's name was Ken. He had a spinal cord injury, having broken his neck at the fourth cervical. It was as if I was watching my life unfold before me, with hundreds of people sitting in the audience intruding upon my privacy.

Seeing that play made me question whether I should actually write this book. After all, I really do value my privacy, and certain feelings and experiences might be better left unshared.

On the other hand, I could be in a crowded room and still feel alone because very few people know what I am going through, what I am thinking, and what I am feeling. Maybe my story needs to be told, even if only to bring more people into my world, or into the world of other people with disabilities.

Coincidentally, Nicky recognized one of the actresses during the first act. That actress had actually sold Nicky and Steve their house in Huntington Bay. Nicky sent a note backstage during the intermission, indicating that we would like to talk with her after the show.

After the final curtain, my brother hurried backstage and told the actress that I was very moved by the play. Steve asked her if I could meet Richard Dreyfuss, who played Ken. When Richard Dreyfuss heard that I had a spinal cord injury, he agreed to meet with us. So, after I was bounced down the six steps in front of the theater, I was bounced down another six steps, to get backstage.

Richard Dreyfuss was very nice and seemed eager to talk with me. He asked me how I found the play and how I got hurt.

I could see that, when I told Dreyfuss I got hurt playing football, it really moved him. Just imagine how he felt when I told him that my name was Ken, that I had also broken the fourth cervical in my neck, and that I had actually experienced so many of the things he portrayed in the play. Suddenly, his character became a real person to him.

The play, the evening, and more so, the past ten years, kept that question nagging at me: "Whose life is it, anyway?"

The rest of the vacation in Great Barrington was great. It was always good to be with my family and away from my attendants for a few days. There was a huge difference between the care I received from Betty and Steve and the care I received from my attendants. In Great Barrington, I felt like a real person again.

Chapter 21

Becoming an Attorney

◆ ◆ ◆

My law school classes began again on August 28. I signed up for four courses, totaling fifteen credits. The workload was heavy, but it was my personal problems with attendants and my health that put me far behind.

On September 5, my attendant Bill told me that he would be leaving on September 19, no matter what. However, on September 12 Bill quit, giving me only a few hours' notice.

Every one of my attendants always agreed that they would stay until I found and trained someone new. Then, one by one, they would all break their promise and leave me in the lurch.

Now, before I could find a suitable replacement, I had to scramble to get someone immediately. I decided to try an eighteen-year-old named John. I had interviewed John shortly before September 12. During the interview, I learned that John was on probation for committing a burglary. That alone should have been a reason to disqualify him. Unfortunately, now I had little choice. Either I hired John or I called my brother or Aunt Lorraine to see if they could pick me up and take care of me for who knows how long.

I decided to give John a try.

John came Friday night, September 12, and stayed for the weekend. I asked my weekend aide, Alan, to try to train him.

Hiring John was an obvious mistake from the beginning. It was quickly apparent that he was not trustworthy. John was constantly lying to me. He even had the nerve to invite over two of his friends from jail that first weekend.

I still hoped that maybe I could make it work for a day or two, until I either found someone else or made arrangements to go to my Aunt's.

I spoke to John, my new attendant, about some of my concerns regarding his behavior so far. I told him I would still give him a chance, though.

John waited until my weekend attendant, Alan, left and then John told me he quit and would not even stay the night.

Fortunately, Aunt Lorraine and my cousin Ronnie were able to come and pick me up. When they started packing my things, I found that all the money I had in my wallet, $40, had been stolen. It really wasn't an uncommon experience for me. My money had a way of disappearing around my attendants.

As I was to do a lot that year, I traveled back and forth between my apartment in Hempstead, Aunt Lorraine's house in Oceanside, and my brother's house in Huntington Bay. I was constantly trying to interview and try out new attendants, while still getting rides back and forth to school and attempting to squeeze in some studying.

Rob Passarelli, a fellow student who had been very helpful to me during my first year of law school, became an even closer and truly invaluable friend. Rob drove me back and forth to school when I needed a ride, whether I was at my apartment in Hempstead or at my aunt's house in Oceanside. He would lift me up during the day, to try and prevent bedsores. He fed me lunch at school, and if I didn't bring lunch with me Rob would give me half of his.

Rob made me carbon copies of his notes for one of the classes and helped me study for exams. He wheeled me around school wherever I needed to go. Rob played a major role in getting me through the first two years of law school.

About a week before finals, I developed another case of bronchitis. Between Aunt Lorraine, Steve, and my attendant, I needed to receive a lot of postural drainage to help cough up the phlegm that was filling my lungs again. It was a really difficult three weeks.

I was up the entire night before my Evidence final, coughing constantly. The exam took me close to eight hours to complete, agonizing over answers, while struggling to breathe. I was lucky that Hofstra gave me as much time as I needed to take my exams.

Somehow, I made it through the semester. My cume was only 2.22. I was just glad that I passed and could breathe again.

♦ ♦ ♦

I spent Christmas weekend at Betty's. Whenever I went there, More Mom, who lived in Jersey City, would come over as well. This time, however, despite numerous attempts, we had trouble reaching her. On December 26, we were finally able to get More Mom on the phone. She had taken a bad fall in her parking lot. Somehow, she had managed to get back into her apartment, but was in terrible pain.

Betty would not leave me alone to go to help her mother. She was finally able to get one of her friends to stay with me while she went with More Mom, by ambulance, to the hospital. My seventy-nine-year-old grandmother had broken her hip.

That day, I felt more helpless and frustrated than any day I could remember. More Mom was more like a mother than a grandmother to me. From the day my mother died, all through my hospital stays and rehabilitation, More Mom had always been there for me. She was the rock of the family. I desperately wanted to help her but there was nothing I could do. Not only could I not contribute one iota, I was taking away from the help of others.

♦ ♦ ♦

In January 1981, I took an intensive two-week course at Hofstra in Trial Techniques. The course went through just about every aspect of a trial. We even conducted two complete mock trials.

Not being able to write, it was particularly difficult for me. Virtually everyone taking the course wrote out all of their questions for direct and cross examination, as well as their opening statements and summary arguments. I had to rely almost totally on my memory and my ability to think quickly and logically "on my feet."

I also needed to be able to talk in front of a group without getting nervous or flustered. Despite my experience with public speaking, it was still very difficult for me. To add to the pressure, I was videotaped seven different times during those two weeks for critique purposes.

My two mock trials went well, and I found them challenging and exciting. That course in trial techniques convinced me I would like to do at least some trial work in my future practice of law.

◆ ◆ ◆

I was hoping that the new semester would at least be better than the last.

A scar from one of my old bedsores had gotten very red. I was concerned that it would break down again. I spent a week in bed, and then got up only sparingly, but the sore was still red. I then spent another two weeks in bed. As a result, I fell far behind at school.

I did some heavy cramming for exams but finished the semester with disappointing grades. My semester cume was only 2.39. My class rank was now 134 out of 248.

◆ ◆ ◆

Shortly before my final exams, More Pop, who had been ailing with Alzheimer's disease for quite some time, became drastically worse. He was virtually in a coma when Steve, Betty, and More Mom brought him to the hospital. Pop remained in the hospital for about a month.

Despite poor care, which had also resulted in Pop developing a bedsore and skin rash, he improved just enough to be discharged. He died at home a week later, on June 14.

Pop was the most incredible person I ever knew. He came to the United States from Russia when he was seven years old. He

More Pop, the day he received his Master's degree from
Columbia University—1963.

was the first in his family to go to college. He put himself through
school, graduating from Yale in 1919 with a degree in engineering.

Reading was his passion. He was a scholar when it came to
religion, but seemed to know a lot about everything. He even had
three patents. Pop loved learning so much, he returned to school
and earned his master's degree in Jewish history from Columbia
University when he was sixty-five years old. Pop will always be my
role model.

Pop's life, gradual decline, and finally his death had an enormous impact on me. Words cannot begin to describe it. All I can
say is that I will try to live my life as Pop lived his. I will greatly
miss him.

♦ ♦ ♦

After my second year of law school, Steve suggested I do a
summer internship at the Nassau County District Attorney's
Office in Mineola. I submitted my resume and went for an interview there in March. That was my first job interview since teaching

Ken with Nassau County District Attorney Denis Dillon—summer 1981.

Job Seeking Skills at the Human Resources Center. I got accepted for the internship, though it was unpaid.

I spent June 17 through August 11 working in the Nassau County District Attorney's Office. I sat in on trials, pretrial hearings, and court conferences. I also observed the assistant district attorneys interviewing and preparing their witnesses for court. The internship included field trips to the Nassau County Police Headquarters, the Nassau County Jail, and the Medical Examiner's Office, where I sat in on an autopsy. It all was interesting and exciting.

In addition, I got to see Steve almost every day, since his office was across the street from the courthouse.

♦ ♦ ♦

On Wednesday, August 12, I went to Great Barrington, Massachusetts, for our usual family week vacation at Betty's.

Betty's cabin was in the middle of the woods, approximately seventy-five yards from Lake Buel. There was a dirt path, filled with rocks and tree roots, that ran from her cabin to the lake. It was a difficult and bumpy path to navigate in my manual wheelchair.

On Friday morning, August 14, Betty pulled me in my wheelchair down to the lake near the dock. The lake was fairly shallow in the area where the dock was. Betty had to return to the cabin and told me that Steve would be down shortly.

Betty had left me in the shade. I was anxious to get into the sun to warm up. In order to be in the sun, though, I needed to be wheeled onto the floating part of the dock.

The only other person with me at that time was my twelve-year-old cousin Matthew. I was tempted to ask Matthew to pull me out onto the floating dock, but I decided to play it safe and wait for Steve to come. That decision may have saved my life.

When Steve finally came down, he pulled me, backward, across the stationary dock to the floating dock. Because the floating dock was about eight inches higher than the stationary dock, Steve needed to tilt the wheelchair back, into a wheelie position, to pull it up onto the floating dock.

As we approached the end of the stationary dock, we seemed to be leaning farther and farther to the left. I didn't know what was wrong, but it was clear to me that I was about to tumble into the lake, wheelchair and all. At the last possible moment, I took in a deep breath of air.

Suddenly, I was lying on my side in the mud, at the bottom of the lake, strapped to the wheelchair. My head was about eighteen inches under water. The stationary dock had collapsed.

Fortunately, Steve was able to straighten up the wheelchair. I gasped for air. While I didn't panic and tried to remain calm, I don't think I could have held my breath much longer. My lung capacity had been greatly reduced since my accident. What seemed like an eternity under water was probably only a few seconds.

I recognized that a lot of problems could cause my health to deteriorate and, perhaps, hasten my demise. Not being able to breathe always seemed to me like the worst way to go. And to think that I used to love being in or near the water when I worked as a lifeguard ...

◆ ◆ ◆

My summer internship at the Nassau's District Attorney's Office convinced me that I wanted to work there full time when I graduated from law school.

First, I enjoyed criminal law and felt comfortable working for the prosecution.

Second, working at the DA's Office would give me the opportunity to gain trial and courtroom experience. That was the type of experience I most wanted.

Third, the DA's Office would probably be the best place for me to work, considering my physical limitations. My office would be in the court building. I would not have to travel from an office to the courts. There would be plenty of other people on the staff to help me, if needed, because, in addition to other ADA's, there would be student interns, paralegals, investigators, and secretaries.

Fourth, the DAs Office provided Civil Service benefits.

Fifth, the DA's Office was in an ideal location for me. It was in the middle of Nassau County, two and a half miles from my apartment. Steve worked in the same court complex and his office was right across the street.

I sent the DA's Office my resume as soon as I finished my summer internship.

My first interview was set for September 11, 1981. Part of the interview process involved delivering an opening statement. The DA's Office sent a fact pattern of a case, in advance, to every applicant. That way, the interviewer could get an idea how the applicant might comport themself in the courtroom.

I delivered my opening statement, without notes, before the Administrative Assistant ADA, Pat McCloskey. Mr. McCloskey was the main person in charge of hiring. Marty Saperstein, the Deputy Bureau Chief of the Appeals Bureau, was also present and proceeded to interview me after I finished with Mr. McCloskey.

I could tell from the expressions on their faces they liked my opening very much. Two weeks later, on September 25, I received a letter telling me I had made it through the first set of interviews.

My second and third interviews with high-level executives also went well. Following the third interview, while I was waiting by the courthouse steps to meet Steve for lunch, Dennis Dillon, the District Attorney of Nassau County, walked by. Mr. Dillon stopped and spoke with me for a minute or two, asking how I was doing.

The next day, at about 4:30 p.m., Pat McCloskey called. At the time I was lying in bed, suffering with a bladder infection. Mr. McCloskey said that Mr. Dillon had told him to offer me the job. I accepted the offer right then and there. I was the first person they offered a full-time position to that year.

♦ ♦ ♦

The most difficult part of my third year of law school was fulfilling the upper-class writing requirement. I missed a lot of class and study time for my other courses in order to work on the paper. Because of all the time I spent on it, my substantive courses suffered terribly. I ended up finishing the first semester with the cumulative average of only a 1.998.

When I graduated, my cume was 2.441. My final class rank was 191 out of 238.

Although I was disappointed with my grades, I was still proud of the fact that, despite all the problems, I had managed to graduate in the standard three-year period, with my full-time dream job waiting for me.

Although I did not participate in the graduation ceremonies for either of my master's degrees, I was particularly proud of making it through law school, so I was looking forward to attending this one at Hofstra. The Law School held its graduation ceremony outside on the lawn. Many of my family and friends came to celebrate with me. It was a beautiful, warm, sunny day.

It was difficult wheeling my electric wheelchair on the grass with the rest of the graduates. One by one, each graduate proceeded onto the stage to receive his or her diploma. Because there was no ramp set up, I was asked to wait until the end and then

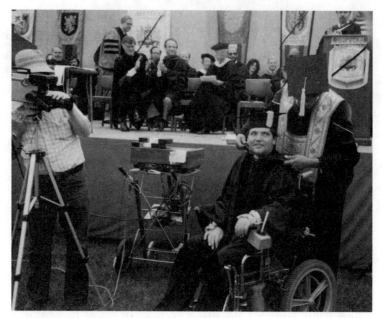

Ken's graduation from Hofstra Law School—May 30, 1982.

move in front of the stage to receive mine. There was a long standing ovation after my name was called.

Now all I had to do was to pass the bar exam.

I arranged to take the exam at Fordham Law School in New
York City. It was given on July 27 and 28, 1982. I did not want to
risk having to depend on an attendant for anything during those
two days, so I asked Steve to stay overnight in the City with me.

I had petitioned the bar examiners for extra time to take the
test. They only agreed, however, to allow me to start earlier than
the rest of the test takers each day. I had to finish at the same time
as every other student taking the exam.

That really did not give me much extra time. It takes about
two hours to get me bathed and dressed in the morning. Even if
I were to start getting ready at 5:45 a.m., I would have difficulty
getting to the testing facility before 8 a.m., one hour before the rest
of the students.

Early Tuesday morning, Steve and I walked to the Law School, where I met the woman assigned to do the writing for me. It is always difficult and time-consuming to dictate my answers to a stranger.

Years later, additional accommodations for people with disabilities have been provided, allowing them to take the exam over the course of four days rather than two—twice the amount of time.

Steve came into the room once in the morning and once in the afternoon to give me a drink of water and stretch my arms and legs. At the lunch break Steve and I had a sandwich on a bench in an open area across the street from the Law School.

The second day was much like the first. It was a long and grueling two days.

I would not get the results until the first week in December.

Chapter 22

DAs Office, District Court

♦ ♦ ♦

On August 2, 1982, I began my employment at the Nassau County District Attorney's Office. On that day, I met and became friends with Peter Shapiro, one of the new assistant district attorneys (ADAs). He remembered hearing about my injury while he was a senior at Columbia University the year I was hurt.

We were part of a group of twenty-six newly hired ADAs. We began our employment with an intensive four-week training program, which taught us all aspects of trial techniques from a prosecutor's perspective. The training program was conducted in two small courtrooms on the first floor of the West Wing court complex in Mineola. An unexpected problem immediately arose. My wheelchair wouldn't fit through the swinging doorways inside the courtrooms to get to where the lawyers sat. I needed to have one of the swinging doors, along with its screws and hinges, removed for me to fit through. Unfortunately, that was a problem I encountered in every courtroom in the complex.

Pat McCloskey, the Executive Administrative Assistant District Attorney who had interviewed me for the ADA position almost one year earlier, was one of the two instructors. The first time we had to perform in front of the other new ADAs was when we were practicing *voir dire*. *Voir dire* is the name used for the process of picking a jury. The exercise was new to most of us. It would take a lot of practice to get it right.

I was accustomed to the question and answer format of the *voir dire*. Again, my experience teaching job interview techniques at the Human Recourses Center paid off. Many of my fellow ADAs-in-training told me I was one of the best in the group for that exercise. From that moment on, I felt I was treated with a lot more respect from the ADAs in the program. Still, I learned later that the other training instructor questioned why I was hired, because, as he put it, "He can't even write." It took a while, but he eventually changed his opinion after observing me in action.

All the new ADAs were constantly in close quarters, which provided me with a few embarrassing moments. On more than one occasion the condom leaked. I was certain the other ADAs could smell the urine in which I was now sitting. To make matters worse, one day I had a bowel movement. I couldn't even get to a phone to call my attendant to pick me up. Those accidents would continue later, when I was working in the District Attorney's Office. A number of times they happened while I was actually on trial.

The training program provided us with a good background in trial techniques. It ended on August 31. The next day, I began my first assignment. It was in Traffic Court, which was located on the second floor of a neighboring building.

My friend Russ Canan happened to be visiting from Washington, D.C., at the time, and had stayed over in my apartment the night before. Russ went in the van with me, along with my attendant Ron, to take me to the building where the Traffic Court was.

As luck would have it, the elevator there was broken. We were told that I might be able to enter the building from the rear, which was the freight entrance. When we went to the back of the building, entering from there did not look very promising. I had to first get onto a hydraulic lift just to get up to the first floor. Then I had to travel to the other side of the building, where there were a number of steps to get to the next level. We recruited a few court officers to help and, together with Ron and Russ, they pulled me, in my heavy electric wheelchair, up the steps.

I began my first day of actual work as an Assistant District Attorney by trying to conference plea offers with a large roomful of people who had received traffic tickets. Each conference necessitated flipping through lengthy sets of computer printouts to see what that particular individual's motor vehicle record looked like. I then needed to refer to other papers to figure out what our office's plea-bargaining guidelines were. It was extremely difficult for me.

Three of the other new ADAs started there with me. We all tried to help each other but ended up relying mostly on two paralegals, who were familiar with the workings of Traffic Court.

A short time later, I moved to another room where I was to do my first traffic trial. It was in front of Judge Medawar, who recently had become a judge.

I had a few minutes to speak with the police officer who issued the traffic ticket. With only the traffic summons in front of me, I began to prosecute someone for going through a red light. My direct testimony of the police officer went fine. Then the defendant took the stand. He testified that the light was yellow when he went through it.

I asked a number of questions, but the defendant kept insisting that the light had been yellow. I asked the defendant if he had the radio on. He said no. I asked him if he was talking to a passenger riding with him at the time but he again said no. I asked if he'd looked up at the light when he went through it to be certain it was still yellow. He responded that he had. I finally ran out of questions, and the judge found him not guilty.

So, there you have it. I lost my first trial.

How was I going to convict murderers if I couldn't even convict someone for going through a red light? I had had only one trial and had already lost my perfect record.

My brother reminded me later that my record was, in fact, still "perfect." After all, I had lost every case I had tried up to that point.

I had three more traffic trials that day. They all involved speeding. Those three trials resulted in convictions.

At the end of the day, I felt uncomfortable having to ask the court officers to carry me, in my wheelchair, down the steps. To add to my discomfort, Judge Medowar, who took a liking to me, volunteered to help the court officers. The judge, before whom I had just appeared, was carrying me down the steps. How awkward.

I spent two more days in Traffic Court, one in the conference part and the next day in the trial part again. I had two more trials during that time. Once again, I got a conviction for speeding and an acquittal for going through a red light.

I decided to be proactive about getting the elevator repaired. I took it upon myself to call the General Service Administration for Nassau County to try to fix the problem. Within a short period of time, I received a call from Pat McCloskey, telling me that I should not have made that call myself. I should have gone through channels.

Pat then told me that, because they did not know when the elevator would be fixed, I would be transferred to our District Court Bureau on Tuesday, September 7. That was the day after Labor Day. All told, I spent just three days in Traffic Court. I suppose you could say I received my first promotion in the DA's Office because the elevator was broken and no one knew when it would be fixed.

Unfortunately, within two days of being transferred, I came down with bronchitis and was out of work from September 9 through September 14. It was not a good way to start my new position.

The DA's offices in District Court were located in the basement of the West Wing, in very cramped quarters. All the ADA's offices there were small. Most had room for only two ADAs to squeeze into, although two offices could squeeze in three. I was put into the one office that could fit only one.

My office was located in the back corner. It had no windows. Although that office had one desk in it, it was not one I could physically use. I needed to bring in the small cutout table I had used for my desk at the Human Resources Center.

♦ ♦ ♦

When I was not engaged in a hearing or trial, I was expected to go to court to handle the daily calendar call. The DA's Office handled thousands of misdemeanor cases a year. On a typical day, more than fifty were scheduled on each judge's calendar.

A case might appear on the calendar for trial, pretrial hearings, sentencing, violations of probation, or a plea-bargaining conference. There was a separate file for each case. The file often had a lot of papers and documents, which the ADA needed to be aware of and familiar with. The paperwork included police forms, supporting depositions, accusatory instruments, motions, notes made by the ADAs who had handled the case in the past, and the defendant's criminal record, just to name a few.

I was not physically able to take the papers out of the file to look at or make notes for. There were far too many cases on the calendar for me to memorize what each was about. To make matters worse, the next day there would be fifty different cases on the calendar. It didn't help that I still couldn't fit through the swinging doorways in the courtroom to get to the prosecutor's table. I had to sit in front of the railing that separated the judge's bench from the lawyers. There wasn't enough room for me to even face forward toward the judge. I had to have my wheelchair face sideways.

While sometimes I would be doing the calendar call with another ADA, other times I would be alone in court and expected to handle it all by myself. Doing the calendar call was torture for me. I always felt it was just a question of time before a case would blow up or that the judge would become exasperated at me for taking too long to do everything, especially with a crowd of defendants and their attorneys waiting for their cases to be called.

I tried to have my attendant help me in the office the night before and morning of calendar call, going through all the files and taking notes on Rolodex cards, which I could, hopefully, turn by myself once in the courtroom. Even if I could do that, I still had to take notes about what happened on each case and what each adjournment date was. I frequently had to rely on the court officers for help.

I found it to be much easier to be engaged on a trial or a pretrial hearing than handling calendar call. On the days that I was doing litigation, I only needed to be familiar with the facts of one case, rather than more than the fifty on the calendar that day.

Whenever I was preparing for a trial, I had someone photo-copy the important pieces of paper from the file and staple them together. That way, with a lot of effort, I could, sometimes, turn the pages myself with the pen attachment inserted into my wrist splint. It took me more than a year before I realized it was easier to punch holes in copies of the paperwork and put them into a three-ring notebook. Unfortunately, when the notebook was open, the cover was too big to fit on the limited work space on my lapboard between my immobile right arm and the joystick on the left side. I needed to have someone cut off a few inches from each side of the cover. Still, even turning pages in the notebook to get to where I needed to be was difficult and time consuming.

On September 30, 1982, I conducted my first bench trial. A bench trial is a trial without a jury. The judge, rather than the jury, decides the verdict.

Another ADA had given me the case the day before. The defendant had been in a car accident. Instead of giving his license and registration to the driver of the other car, the defendant had assaulted the individual and chased him into a nearby bank.

The defendant was charged with leaving the scene of an acci-dent, as well as harassment. Both of those counts were not even crimes. One was a traffic infraction and the other was a violation. The case was particularly interesting because the defendant was both hearing impaired and unable to speak.

The defense attorney was about seventy years old. He had the lyrical name, Ben Menn. Ben himself wore a hearing aid and seemed even more affected by his hearing limitations than the defendant was by his. At least the defendant had a sign language interpreter. Ben, on the other hand, needed almost every question and answer repeated because he couldn't hear them.

I presented two witnesses on my direct case. Direct case refers to the portion of the trial where the prosecutor presents his evi-dence, whether by witnesses, documents, or both. I later needed to cross-examine the defendant, who testified with the assistance of the sign language interpreter.

The trial ended with a conviction on both counts. The defen-dant wasn't a very nice person so I did not feel as bad as I had thought I would. Still, it was awkward telling my friends at the

Human Resources Center that the first defendant I prosecuted had a significant physical disability.

My second District Court trial began on October 13. It took place before an irascible judge named Marchese. The ADAs referred to him as "Crazy Charlie Marchese."

When I arrived at the courtroom, the judge told the defense attorney and me that the jury was on its way.

At that point, the defense attorney said, "Judge, the defendant is YO."

The judge immediately started screaming at me, "Why did you have me call over a jury? The defendant is YO!"

So much for a judge treating me any differently than he would any other attorney. I had no clue what I did wrong. All I had done was enter the courtroom and announce the People were ready for trial. I had no idea what the judge was talking about and I was shocked that he was yelling at me.

YO means "youthful offender." I hadn't heard that term before. A defendant was considered a "mandatory youthful offender" when the defendant was accused of committing a misdemeanor, had never been convicted of a crime before, and was less than nineteen years old on the date of incident. Even if the defendant were found guilty, the conviction would be vacated and the record sealed because of the defendant's age. In addition, the trial in District Court would be a bench trial. There would be no jury.

I had never been told this during our training program. Still, the judge was furious with me and angrily said to me, "Now, what am I going to do with this jury?"

The judge finally calmed down. He apologized to the jury when they came over, for wasting their time, and then sent them back to Central Jury to await being called for another case.

The defendant in this case happened to be an eighteen-year-old girl who was accused of stealing a weed whacker from her previous employer because he hadn't paid her all the money she felt she was owed.

An off-duty police officer, who lived next door to the place of incident, had observed the defendant squeeze through the opening of her former employer's garage door and take the tool.

I presented two witnesses on my direct case.

I was surprised when, as part of the defendant's case, her attorney called the defendant's father to testify as a character witness. He was a particularly nice fellow who also happened to be in a wheelchair.

Before the trial had begun, I had seen him sitting outside the courtroom. I didn't know who he was but seeing him in a wheelchair, I struck up a conversation with him. I liked him. Now, I had to cross-examine him.

I tried to make it clear to the court through my cross that the father was not with his daughter at the time of the incident and that he had no direct knowledge of his daughter's whereabouts at that time, or what she had done. I did it as gently and respectfully as I could.

At that point, I could not help but think about how things had changed for me. I had worked for more than two years as a vocational rehabilitation counselor. I was working with and trying to help people with disabilities. On both of my first two District Court trials, I had to cross-examine someone who had a physical disability.

The judge wanted to see pictures of the garage from which the tool was stolen. Unfortunately, the garage had been torn down before I got the case.

Judge Marchese ruled that he had a reasonable doubt that the defendant could have squeezed through the supposedly locked door of the garage to take the tool. The judge found the defendant not guilty.

On October 21 and 22, I conducted my third trial. To my dismay, it was again before "Crazy Charlie Marchese."

When I arrived in the courtroom, Judge Marchese called the defense attorney and me into his chambers. Before I knew what was happening, the judge had his arm around the defense attorney and said to me, "This man is like a son to me."

I was on one side of the room and the two of them were on the other. The defense attorney then announced that he was waiving a jury. It would be another bench trial in front of Judge Marchese. I knew my case was in trouble.

The defendant was accused of driving while intoxicated. He had been out celebrating his birthday and drank too much. On his way home, the defendant had difficulty negotiating a turn on a street in Baldwin and crashed into a tree. The defendant later refused to take a breathalyzer test.

Just before I went up to the courtroom, I met with the arresting officer to go over his direct examination with him. It didn't occur to me, at that time, to tell the officer to spit out the piece of gum he was loudly chewing. I just assumed he knew that you don't chew gum while you are testifying on the witness stand. Apparently, I was wrong to have made that assumption.

The moment my officer began testifying, I knew it was going to be a fiasco. Judge Marchese started screaming at him to take the gum out of his mouth. The judge soon started screaming at me for asking a question, which the judge felt wasn't worded properly. At one point, my witness became argumentative with the judge and the judge started screaming at both him and me.

When we finally broke for lunch, I went outside behind the courthouse to get some fresh air. I wanted to relax and clear my head. I remember trying to think if there was any way I would not have to return to the courtroom that afternoon to continue with the trial. I couldn't come up with anything.

What had I been thinking, leaving my nice comfortable position as a rehabilitation counselor, where everyone was nice to me, for a job in a courthouse, where it felt like everyone was screaming at me? I still didn't even know what I was doing wrong. I was just trying to make it through the day.

During the second day of the trial, the defendant took the stand. I cross-examined him about not stopping at the stop signs, that had been facing the defendant, one of which was huge. The defendant didn't even remember seeing them.

The judge found the defendant guilty of the lesser charge of driving while ability impaired by alcohol. That was a common verdict when the defendant did not take a breathalyzer test.

◆ ◆ ◆

Sometime during the fall of 1982, a representative from the Mutual of New York Life Insurance Company (MONY) came to my office to speak with me. He wanted to see how I functioned on the job. MONY had been covering my medical and attendant expenses since my injury. They were still covering me under my father's major medical policy because I had been under twenty-one at the time of my injury.

MONY could have stopped my coverage once I obtained full-time employment. That had been a big concern for my father and me when I was hired as a rehabilitation counselor at the Human Resources Center a few years earlier. My father had convinced the insurance company, back then, to continue my attendant coverage, and give me the opportunity to try to work and, possibly, one day become financially independent.

MONY had increased the cap on my insurance a number of times already. Probably as a result of my father being such a long-time valued employee, the company was extremely generous in my situation.

By 1982, MONY had been covering my attendant expenses for close to twelve years. During that time, I had obtained four college degrees and worked for two years as a rehabilitation counselor. I now not only had a law degree but also was working full time at a prestigious job as an Assistant District Attorney. While I did have medical coverage through my job, my employer would not cover any attendant costs.

MONY had the opportunity to stop my attendant coverage, with good reason. If they continued it, they would probably be on the hook to pay for my attendant costs for the rest of my life. Because I was only thirty-two that might amount to a sizable sum.

My starting salary at the DA's Office was $19,800. It was still less than my attendants were being paid at that time. I couldn't see not working for the rest of my life just to keep my attendant coverage. However, I also couldn't afford to work and live without that coverage. Once that coverage was gone, I would never be able to get it back.

I spent a nerve-wracking morning with the insurance company's representative. I could tell that the representative appreciated the effort I was putting into trying to make something of my life.

After that meeting, my father, once again, was able to convince the Mutual of New York Life Insurance Company to continue my attendant coverage. I will always be grateful to my father for that, and to MONY.

◆ ◆ ◆

Now my mind shifted back to worrying about whether I had passed the bar exam, which I had taken at the end of July. The DA's Office had a policy that, if you failed the exam, you could continue to work at the office until you took it again in February. If you didn't pass the exam on the second attempt, you would be let go. All the new twenty-six ADAs were on pins and needles, awaiting the results.

A number of my colleagues received their results in the mail on December 2. I did not. That meant I would almost certainly receive them on Friday, December 3.

My attendant at the time was a woman named Kathleen. She was my fiftieth attendant by then. She took her work seriously and was very concerned about my well-being. She truly cared about me and was anxiously waiting for the mail to be delivered that day. Kathleen was not supposed to open the envelope, though. She was just to bring it with her when she came to pick me up.

Kathleen, however, couldn't control herself. When the mail arrived, she opened the letter immediately. I was in court at the time, in Judge Steinberg's chambers. Kathleen was not able to reach me because I was not at my desk, so she called my brother instead and told him the results. He immediately came to the courthouse to try to find me, and soon joined me in the judge's chambers.

Steve told me that Kathleen had called him and needed to speak to me. The judge allowed me to call Kathleen from his chambers. There were a number of other lawyers in the room at the time.

Steve dialed my home phone number and held the phone to my ear. With everyone's eyes on me, I nervously asked Kathleen what she needed to talk to me about.

Kathleen first apologized for opening my mail. She told me that she just couldn't wait. Then she said, "You passed!"

I couldn't even pretend to be mad at her. It was actually a great way to receive the news. I let out a sigh of relief, which was soon replaced with a big smile. Everyone congratulated me.

Judge Steinberg seemed to be one of the happiest people in the room. The judge told me that he too was very nervous waiting to hear about my results. He then had a nice short celebration for me in his chambers.

Unfortunately, five of my fellow ADAs did not pass.

◆ ◆ ◆

District Court was an incredibly busy place to work. It was a challenge for me to keep up with investigating cases, determining the right plea offer, if any, and preparing cases for hearings and trials. The prosecution always has to be mindful of time constraints because if the prosecutor takes too many adjournments, the case might be dismissed for speedy trial reasons. Therefore, we always had to be ready on many different cases, any one of which might potentially go to trial. The first case that I spent a lot of time preparing for trial was adjourned. I quickly had to prepare to pick a jury on a different case.

My bureau chief called me into his office before my first jury trial. He thought we should discuss how I was going to handle my disability in front of the jury. He indicated that the jury would certainly be surprised to see someone in my condition as the prosecutor. He felt I should talk about my disability during jury selection to get it out of the way.

Initially, I wasn't sure how I was going to handle my disability in front of the jury. I thought about it for quite some time and, ultimately, decided not to discuss the subject at all.

Why talk about the obvious? I wanted the jury to treat me the same way they treated any other lawyer. I did not want sympathy or any special consideration. I was confident the jury would not base their verdict on my inability to walk but, rather, on how I conducted the trial and presented the evidence. I believed that, once the jury saw me in action, they would forget about me being in a wheelchair.

After my first jury trial, I was convinced I was right.

♦ ♦ ♦

Our District Court Trial Bureau had the responsibility of having an ADA cover arraignments 365 days a year. Arraignments usually occur within twenty-four hours of the defendant's arrest. At arraignments, the court takes jurisdiction of the case, the defendant is formally informed of the charges against him or her, and bail, if any, is set.

We had a couple of ADAs assigned to do arraignments during the week. On weekends and holidays, though, the rest of the ADAs in the Bureau took turns covering the part.

I was scheduled to do my first "weekend arraignments" on Saturday, January 8, 1983. My cousin Jeanie, who was nineteen at the time, agreed to help me, since she was on her winter break from Cornell.

Arraignments were held in the same building as Traffic Court, in Mineola. By that time, the elevator had been fixed.

Jeanie drove me to Mineola and sat at the prosecutor's table next to me, in the front of the courtroom, just to the right of the judge.

Forty defendants were to be arraigned that day. Unfortunately, when we arrived at the courtroom, none of the files had been organized or even put together. On the prosecutor's table was a pile of police forms and supporting depositions, a pile of rap sheets, and a separate pile of accusatory instruments. There was no rhyme or reason to the order of any of the three piles.

The arraignment judge that day was Judge Barbieri. He had a reputation for "moving the calendar" very quickly so that he could be done as soon as possible.

As each case was called, Jeanie scrambled to find me the appropriate paperwork, hurriedly flipped through the pages for me to read, and then showed me my Office's plea bargain guidelines, so that I knew what amount of bail to request. Jeanie and I did all this while the judge, the court officers, the defendants, and all the spectators were staring at us.

It seemed like we had papers flying all over the table. It was extremely challenging gathering all the appropriate documents together on each case and making a bail recommendation, without slowing up the process and looking incredibly incompetent at the same time. To add to the pressure, Judge Barbieri followed all my bail recommendations. Most judges don't. Because it was my first time doing arraignments, I wasn't sure I knew what I was doing.

Jeanie did a great job, under the circumstances. After arraigning all forty defendants, Jeanie and I stayed an extra hour and a half in the courtroom, organizing the paperwork and re-writing notes about the bail that was set.

I handled "weekend arraignments" three more times while I was in District Court. For those last three, Jeanie's brother Ronnie helped me. He was twenty-two years old and home on breaks from Syracuse University.

♦ ♦ ♦

During the late fall and early winter, I was getting all the necessary paperwork together to be submitted for admission to the New York State Bar. It was a tedious process. When it was finally completed, there was just one more hurdle for me to overcome. I had to go before the "Character Committee."

I received a call from an attorney on the Character Committee, to arrange for the interview. The attorney indicated that, to make it easier for me, he would come to my office. He would be the only person on the Committee to interview me.

I asked my brother and his wife, Nicky, who was also a lawyer, what I should expect. They basically told me it shouldn't be a problem. The Committee would be concerned whether I had ever been in trouble with the law, had any unpaid traffic tickets, or had done something to reflect poorly on my character.

I was relieved to know that it was basically a pro forma process. To play it safe, I decided to run a motor vehicle check on my old driver's license to make sure no problems showed up. I was able to do that right in the DA's Office in the courthouse.

I was shocked to see that the motor vehicle printout listed my license as suspended. The printout showed I had numerous unpaid traffic tickets, all occurring after 1975. How could that be?

I examined the printout closely. It had the correct spelling of my name and date of birth. I then saw that the printout listed my height at six feet, four inches tall. I am five feet, eight inches. It also listed a Suffolk County address. I quickly realized that my former attendant, Kris, whom I had let go in 1974 after he had broken his wrist in a fight, had been using my license. He had had the height and address changed.

I called the police immediately to report this. I told them I had pictures of Kris, his social security number, and his address.

The police told me, though, they couldn't do anything to Kris, unless they caught him in the act using my license. I had my interview scheduled for the next day with the Character Committee. Now what?

Fortunately, I was able to show the attorney from the Committee some paperwork indicating I had been a quadriplegic since 1970. I explained to him that my former attendant had apparently used my identity to get a driver's license in my name and then received a number of tickets he never paid. The interviewer understood. Afterward, he congratulated me on my upcoming admission to the Bar.

On the morning of February 9, 1983, Steve, my father, and Aunt Lorraine all went with me to Brooklyn for the swearing-in at the Appellate Division in Brooklyn.

♦ ♦ ♦

On Tuesday, August 2, 1983, I completed my first year at the DA's Office. When I'd first started, I had had many questions as to whether I would be able to function there at all. During the eleven months after I left Traffic Court, I had conducted four pretrial hearings, two bench trials, and picked five juries. I learned that I had passed the New York State Bar Exam and was admitted to the Bar. I also was admitted to the Southern and Eastern Districts of the Federal Court.

During that year, I had missed thirteen days of work while suffering with bronchitis, and three days of work because of a urinary tract infection.

All things considered, it had been a very full and eventful first year work-wise. I gained a lot of confidence in my courtroom abilities.

♦ ♦ ♦

Soon after I did my first bench trial in District Court, Steve left his position with the Legal Aid Society, where he had worked for ten years, to take a job with a private law firm in Freeport, New York. Instead of Steve's office being right across the street from mine, it was now twenty minutes away. Although my brother still wasn't far, it really changed the dynamics of my situation.

Before he changed jobs, I had been able to see Steve every day and occasionally have lunch with him. While I still saw him in the courthouse frequently, I didn't have the same secure feeling I had had when Steve had been across the street.

On September 19, 1983, my nephew, Charlie, was born. It was wonderful to see my brother hold his son. I had always known that Steve would be a great father. He loved kids and enjoyed spending time with them.

I knew that my relationship with Charlie would be as close as I would ever get to having my own son. It seemed as though being an uncle was the next best thing. I was certain I was never going to get married or have a family of my own.

It was frustrating not being able to hold Charlie or to physically help with any of his needs. Despite that, I really appreciated that Steve and Nicky included me in so many of their family activities. It meant a lot to me.

♦ ♦ ♦

Between September 26, 1983, and January 6, 1984, I conducted eight pretrial hearings and three jury trials. I became a fairly competent litigator.

Because of my performance in District Court, I was promoted to our County Court Trial Bureau before most of my colleagues.

Chapter 23

DAs Office, County Court

♦ ♦ ♦

I arrived at my new office in the County Court building shortly before nine o'clock in the morning on January 16, 1984. Although the building was right next door to the District Court building, the move seemed like a major milestone.

County Court handles felonies. Felonies are crimes punishable by more than one year in jail. By their very nature, every County Court case is more serious than the cases I had been handling in District Court, which were misdemeanors punishable by no more than one year in jail.

My new assignment would be especially challenging. With the exception of homicides and sex crimes, I would be handling some of the most serious cases in Nassau County. I wasn't sure I was ready to take on that responsibility. I had so many doubts.

♦ ♦ ♦

I had my own felony caseload to manage, which usually ranged from thirty to fifty cases at any given time. I had to attend daily calendar calls, present cases to the grand jury, and conduct trials and pretrial hearings.

Every judge was assigned his or her own caseload. The actual courtroom was referred to as the judge's "part." Each ADA was assigned to cover a "part."

My last trial in District Court had been a petit larceny, meaning the defendant stole property that was worth less than $1,000. My caseload in County Court included a shooting, a kidnapping, a jewelry theft totaling more than $100,000, residential burglaries, and sales of narcotic drugs, just to name a few. It seemed overwhelming.

While I was in District Court, I had become confident in my ability to remember everything about a case when I went to handle it in court. In County Court, however, the stakes just seemed too high to rely totally on my memory. The felony files were far more extensive as well. They often included not just more police paper work but hundreds of pages of grand jury and pretrial hearing minutes.

I was not familiar with the procedures involved in moving a felony from arraignment, through grand jury presentation, trial, and, hopefully, sentence. Much of the terminology was new to me. I had never dealt with most of these penal law charges before.

Even the County Court courtrooms were intimidating. They were about four times the size of those in District Court. They also had very high ceilings, which meant I had to speak much louder just to be heard. Unfortunately, the one similarity was that the swinging doorways were too narrow for me to pass through in my electric wheelchair.

On January 24, 1984, eight days after I was promoted to County Court, I presented my first case to the grand jury. Grand jury is a very secretive proceeding. No one other than ADAs is permitted to come into the grand jury room while it is in session. Usually, the only people in the room are the twenty-three grand jurors, the court reporter, the witness, and the ADA who is presenting the case. I could not bring in a secretary, a paralegal, or a student intern to assist me. I was totally on my own.

In the grand jury, the ADA acts not only as the prosecutor but as the judge as well. Grand jurors are permitted to ask questions of the witnesses. When an improper question is asked, the ADA must intercede and direct the witness not to answer. The ADA must also "charge" the grand jury on the law and answer any legal questions that arise. It can be overwhelming for a new ADA.

Fortunately, my first grand jury presentment was not a complicated one. The defendant was accused of possessing stolen credit cards when he was apprehended in the parking lot of the Massapequa Mall. I only needed to call one witness.

I had all my paperwork organized in a three-ring notebook on my lapboard in front of me. My notebook included not only the police and court paperwork but also the appropriate sections of the Penal Law that I would have to read to the grand jury when I "charged" them on the law. I did not have any of my questions written out beforehand, as almost every ADA has.

The presentation went well. Still, even on this simple case I had to turn a lot of pages in my notebook just to read the one charge and all the elements and definitions of the crime I was asking the grand jury to consider. I made it through without any mistakes. The grand jury returned an indictment, which meant that the grand jurors found there was reasonable cause to believe the defendant had committed the crime. It felt pretty good.

Two days later, I presented my second case to the grand jury. I was starting to gain a little bit of confidence in my abilities.

On February 21 and 22, I conducted my first felony pretrial hearing. The hearing would determine whether certain evidence would be admissible at trial. It was in front of a different County Court judge than I had been appearing before. His name was Judge Delin, and he was strict and impatient.

The victim had been shot in the wrist. He had a lengthy criminal record and was shot while he was running to a car, probably to get his own gun. By the time the case went to trial on April 23, my victim was in jail, having been arrested on a new charge, and the defendant was out of jail on bail.

At the conclusion of the pretrial hearing, the judge ruled that the evidence of the prior out-of-court identification of the defendant, as well as his oral admission, would be admissible at the trial.

The trial took place from April 23 through April 26, 1984. Judge Delin's courtroom, like most of the others, was not very accessible for me. I had to enter by the judge's chambers. To do that, I had to wheel past all the courtrooms, to the end of the building. I then had to have a court officer open a locked door and then I needed to wind through a bit of a maze to get to the back of Judge Delin's courtroom. Usually, by the time I got there, Judge Delin was waiting to enter by the courtroom door. Delin was another irascible judge and I did not relish the thought of spending even a few seconds alone with him as we both entered the courtroom.

I organized a copy of my entire case file into a large three-ring notebook. I created a separate section for each witness's prior testimony and supporting depositions. I had separate sections for police forms, medical records, information concerning the defendant, the indictment and accusatory instruments, and a large section for miscellaneous papers and documents. The notebook was very full, and it was difficult and time consuming for me to turn the pages to the appropriate spot.

Before jury selection began, the potential jurors were given questionnaires to fill out. As each potential juror entered the jury box, I was given a copy of that juror's completed questionnaire. The judge filled the jury box with fourteen people. We would be picking twelve jurors and two alternates.

Shortly before it was my turn to question the potential jurors, I was given fourteen questionnaires for me to juggle on top of my book, read through, and decide the appropriate questions to ask. I asked a court officer to try and force the questionnaires into the rings of my notebook. Unfortunately, once that was done, it became even more difficult for me to turn the pages. The judge had set a strict time limit for our first round of questioning.

During my first round, the judge had a court officer pass me a note indicating I had five minutes to go before I must stop and then he told me when my time was up. I politely thanked the judge and told him I had just a couple of more questions left.

Judge Delin immediately shouted at me in front of the jury, "Counselor, your time is up!" He made me stop. Clearly, he wasn't going to give me the slightest bit of slack.

When the time came for the attorneys to approach the bench, my wheelchair barely fit through the narrow space between the judge's bench and the railing in front of the prosecutor's table. I had to face sideways and turn my head at an awkward angle to look up at the judge. Because the jury was so close to us, we had to keep our voices low. Often, I couldn't hear what the judge was saying. To make matters worse, Judge Delin happened to be hard of hearing and had a difficult time hearing what I was saying.

Before the victim took the stand, I reviewed with him how important it was to describe his injury in detail to the jury. When the victim had been in my office, he'd indicated that, when he was shot, he felt a burning sensation and that "blood was spurting out like a water fountain."

When I asked the victim in front of the jury about his injury, however, the victim looked right at the defendant and, in as defiant and macho tone as he could muster, he said, "It didn't hurt. I didn't even know I was shot."

Not the answer I was looking for.

During the cross examination of my victim, when the victim was asked by the defense attorney to describe the person who shot him, the victim, again, looked defiantly at the defendant and said, "Fat, black, and ugly!"

The defense attorney objected to the answer but the judge overruled the objection and said, "You asked him, Counselor."

I called four witnesses, including a police detective. The defendant testified and presented two additional defense witnesses.

My Deputy Bureau Chief, Pat McCormack, sat in the back of the courtroom to watch my summation. As usual, I delivered it without any notes. Unfortunately, it did not go as smoothly or as well as I would have liked. I was dreading having to appear before my supervisor for his criticisms.

To my surprise, my supervisor loved it. From that moment on, I felt that he treated me with a lot more respect.

The jury found the defendant guilty of assault in the second degree and reckless endangerment in the first degree. I had won my first felony trial. That trial was a turning point in how I felt working in County Court. After more than three months of questioning my ability to handle such serious cases, I finally convinced myself I could do it.

After the jury left the courtroom, the judge turned to me and asked for my recommendation on bail.

The question took me by surprise. I hadn't thought about that before. At that point, I was just happy that the jury convicted the defendant.

I thought I was playing it safe by saying I would rely on the judge's discretion concerning bail.

The judge continued the present bail status and allowed the defendant to walk out of the courtroom. The judge then started yelling at me for not requesting the defendant be immediately remanded. To remand means to take into custody. He said I had put the judge in an awkward position by not asking him to change the bail status. Sentence was adjourned for six weeks to allow the probation department to conduct their presentence investigation.

Judge Delin then asked me how I was going to feel if, during the time before the defendant had to return for sentence, the defendant sought revenge on the victim and killed him. For the next six weeks, I lived in fear of that happening. I also started to worry every time I went outside that I would run into the defendant.

I would be such an easy target if a defendant ever encountered me outside the courthouse. I had always been concerned about that. Obviously, my physical condition made me stand out.

Once, not long after I was promoted to County Court, an individual approached me on a street by the courthouse. He stood before me and said, "Remember me?" Those are the words most ADAs do not normally want to hear when they are away from the courthouse.

My mind was racing but I could not place him. He then said, "You're the DA, right?" I knew I couldn't say no because I was the only trial Assistant District Attorney in the county in a wheelchair.

He then said, "My name is _____. You had me for two DWIs [driving while intoxicated] in District Court. I just wanted you to know that that was the best thing that ever happened to me. I entered into a program, got the help I needed, and am now doing well. I wanted to thank you." He then walked away.

"Phew!" That was quite a relief!

Interestingly, a few years later, after convicting a defendant for possession of an unloaded handgun, on my way down to the courtroom for the defendant's sentencing, the defendant suddenly got into the elevator with me. I was alone at the time. The defendant said that he had a proposition for me. If I didn't ask the judge to send him to jail, the defendant would agree to work as my attendant for a year. Apparently, the defendant thought working as my attendant for a year would be punishment equivalent to going to jail for two to four years. I wonder how many of my attendants felt that same way. I politely declined the defendant's offer. A few minutes later, he was sentenced to two to four years in an upstate prison.

♦ ♦ ♦

After living in my Hempstead apartment for seven years, I moved into a condominium in Rockville Centre on May 19, 1984. One of the advantages of owning a condominium, as opposed to renting an apartment, was that I could modify the inside to suit my needs. After making one of the bathrooms accessible, I was finally able to take a shower for the first time since I was a patient in the Rusk Institute, thirteen years earlier. This time I didn't pass out. It was great!

The condo in Rockville Centre proved to be an ideal location for me. It was within a twenty-five-minute drive to work, and only a mile and a half from Aunt Lorraine's house. It was walking distance to both the villages of Rockville Centre and Oceanside. I no longer needed to get into a car to travel to restaurants or movie theaters. The condo was also within walking distance of a bus stop and train station, which was useful for my attendants, who often needed to use public transportation to get to and from my place.

Rockville Centre had very few curb cuts, though.

When I was at Cornell, I convinced the university to put in a ramp by my dorm and some ramps by a few curbs. When I was in New York City, I convinced the City to install two curb cuts and the management of my apartment building to build a portable ramp. In Hempstead, I got the management of my apartment building to build a small ramp by the one step in the back of the building. Now, I set out to convince the Village of Rockville Centre to make the sidewalks more accessible throughout the Village.

I contacted numerous Village officials. I made many calls and wrote a few letters. I found it more difficult to convince the local Rockville Centre officials to make accommodations than I had the bureaucracy in New York City. I was persistent, though, and finally got the Village to agree. On October 17, 1985, I received a letter indicating that, beginning in the early spring of 1986, the Village was going to construct forty-seven curb cuts. As a result, almost the entire business district of the Village of Rockville Centre would be made accessible for people who used wheelchairs. Once again, this was well before the Americans with Disabilities Act took effect.

♦ ♦ ♦

On a number of occasions, I spoke to classes of high school students who were visiting the courthouse to learn more about our criminal justice system. On August 3, 1984, I had the pleasure to speak to students visiting from the Human Resources School. I had spoken to some classes at the school when I had worked at the Human Resources Center as a rehabilitation counselor. This was the first time I addressed them in my position as an assistant district attorney. I know they were very impressed and, on August 6, the Human Resources School sent a nice note, addressed to Denis Dillon, the District Attorney, specifically thanking me.

My life was relatively uneventful during this time, with the exception of being extremely busy at work. Between January 1985 and December 1987, I presented fifty-nine cases to the grand jury, conducted twenty-one pretrial hearings, and prosecuted nineteen trials. I had two bouts of bronchitis, as well as an additional upper respiratory infection. I missed six days of work with a urinary tract infection. All things considered, my health wasn't too bad.

♦ ♦ ♦

On April 24, 1987, I switched to Judge Boklan's part. I picked up a new caseload from an ADA who had been assigned to my new judge's part but had then left the Office. For me, that meant copying approximately fifty case files, many of them thick; organizing them into sections and notebooks; reading them, usually more than once; and speaking with all of the witnesses on those new cases. It was a tremendous amount of work but it had to be done. I was fortunate to have a very helpful and congenial secretary as well as a number of student interns to help with the paperwork.

In addition to my new caseload, I kept some of my indictments from Judge Baker's part. I had already put so much work into them that I wanted to see them through to their conclusion. Most of the rest of my cases went to the ADA who took my place before Judge Baker. That ADA was Dan Looney.

Dan had been working in the Bronx District Attorney's Office since the summer of 1981. At the time Dan left that office, he had been assigned to their Major Offense Bureau, where he had been handling homicides. April 24 was Dan's first day in our office.

I went over all of my old cases with Dan. I was a bit concerned he would not treat them as being as important as they were for me because he was used to prosecuting far more serious crimes.

Dan was just the opposite of what I anticipated. He had no ego, was eager to learn how we handled cases in Nassau County, and was one of the hardest workers and most dedicated individuals I had ever met. Dan's father had previously been the Police Commissioner of Nassau County. Many of Dan's relatives had been members of police departments. Dan is the epitome of what a public servant should be. He truly wants to help people and do the right thing every time.

My first trial in front of Judge Boklan began on July 22, 1987, and didn't finish until July 31. It was the most serious case I had handled up to that time, because it involved an armed robbery with shots fired at close range toward the victim. The case had originally been assigned to one of our ADAs in the Major Offense Bureau.

By the time I got it, the case had been indicted and pretrial hearings had been done. The file was really thick. I presented seventeen witnesses on my direct case at the trial.

That was the most witnesses I had ever called to testify in a case to that date. The jury convicted the defendant of robbery in the first and second degree, as well as reckless endangerment in the first degree. The judge sentenced the defendant to ten to twenty years' incarceration.

The jury was very complementary about my handling of the trial, and especially of my one-hour summation. The jury specifically commented on my ability to give my summation without any notes in front of me.

Not long after that, I was assigned a criminal mischief case. Not just any criminal mischief case, either, but the criminal mischief case from hell. The defendant was accused of putting the weed killer paraquat into the spray tank of a coworker at a lawn care company. That worker had thought he would be spraying an insecticide. The worker then sprayed the paraquat mixture on fifty-three lawns throughout Nassau County, destroying the lawns and causing more than $300,000 worth of damage. It was front page news on Long Island when the incident happened.

On December 14, 1987, I spent the day in the grand jury. I presented seventeen witnesses. To complete the case, I also had to admit into evidence notarized depositions from the homeowners and numerous other papers and documents. It was a logistical nightmare for me. Papers were all over the place and witnesses were anxious to get in and out of the grand jury as soon as possible.

When all was said and done, the grand jury returned a 109-count indictment. My job didn't end there though. I then had to fill out and complete a lot of paperwork to enable the grand jury secretaries to make sense out of all the charges, so that they could type up the indictment. For me, that involved constantly juggling, cutting, and pasting a lot of papers to properly organize and present them for typing.

On September 23, 1988, I conducted the pretrial hearing on the paraquat case. Because my judge, Judge Boklan, knew one of the homeowners, she recused herself and the case was reassigned to Judge Baker.

By the time the case came to trial, I had twelve notebooks filled with depositions, prior testimony from witnesses, scientific test results, police reports, literature on weed killers, as well as other documents.

To make matters more difficult, around the time that I was preparing for the paraquat trial, I was having a lot of health problems.

In January 1988, I had developed such a bad bedsore, I had to remain in bed and out of work from January 13 through February 22. I missed twenty-four straight days of work as a result. Apparently, I got back up in my wheelchair too soon because in March I had to miss seven more days because of the same bedsore.

After I missed another day from work in May 1988, Pat McCloskey asked if there was anything that could be done to help me avoid getting a bedsore.

I told Pat it would probably help if I were lifted more often because I am supposed to be lifted many times throughout the day to give the blood in my buttocks the opportunity to circulate. Sitting in one spot for any length of time limits, if not eliminates, the blood flow to the area. When I was first in the hospital, they told me I should try and relieve the pressure on my buttocks at least once every hour and even more frequently when possible.

This not only was impractical, it was just not doable in the office without my attendant remaining with me the entire day. Peter Shapiro, the ADA who had become a really good friend, had been lifting me at least once a day, in addition to feeding me lunch, when Steve was not around.

Pat posted on our County Court bulletin board the following memo:

To: Personnel, Second Floor, County Courthouse

From: Patrick L. McCloskey, Executive Assistant District Attorney for Administration

Date: June 2, 1988

Subject: Ken Kunken

As I indicated to a number of you on an informal basis, it is essential to Ken Kunken's continued good health that he be lifted from his chair 2 or 3 times a day. The entire procedure takes less than a minute. A copy of this memo is being placed on the County Court Bulletin Board. If you are willing to help, please sign your name on the bulletin board memo. Kenny will then be able to contact each of the volunteers on a rotating basis.

Thank you.

VOLUNTEERS:

To my amazement, in addition to Peter Shapiro, eighteen people signed up to lift me, including some of the top assistants in the office. The page was filled and I am convinced even more people would have signed up if there had been more room on the page. I was extremely touched by everyone's offer to help me. I never took them up on it, though, and instead continued relying on Peter and my brother. Still, the offer was greatly appreciated and never forgotten.

One of the problems with me being lifted was that, whenever I was lifted, there was more of a chance the condom would leak. In addition to the lifting pulling on the condom, my pants would bunch up, making it more difficult for the condom to drain.

When the condom leaked, I often had to stay in wet, urine-soaked clothes for hours before I was brought home to be changed. That was the worst thing for my skin. The urine would eat away at it, causing more bedsores to develop. Thus, ironically, lifting me was often counterproductive.

Unfortunately, all the precautions I took didn't save me from having problems with bedsores during the course of the year of 1989, when the paraquat case was to go to trial.

From August 1988 through April 1997, I had to miss thirty-six days of work because of bedsores. On one of those occasions, I missed fifteen straight days; on another, nine days; and on two other occasions, more than six days. During those times, I would have to spend the weekends lying in bed as well.

The paraquat case was supposed to start in early May 1989. I composed a form letter, which I sent to more than sixty witnesses, informing them of the status of the case. I enclosed a simple form with the letter for the witnesses to send back to me, telling me the dates and times that would be the most convenient for them to appear in court to testify. I also inquired if there were any dates during the summer when they would be away on vacation. Needless to say, trying to arrange dates and times for fifty-three homeowners, thirteen landscapers, numerous police detectives, workers from a lawn care company, as well as laboratory technicians, a toxicologist, and a weed science expert, was no easy task.

After I had all that organized and all the appearance dates for everybody arranged just so, the judge's law secretary told me the judge had decided to conduct a different trial at that time and my case was being postponed for a few weeks. I then had to re-contact all my witnesses, cancel their scheduled appearances, and, a few weeks later, re-contact them all to reschedule.

The case finally went to trial on May 31, 1989, and lasted until June 15. I managed to bring in and present forty witnesses on my direct case. On one morning, I called nine witnesses. I had to prepare each of them and go over their testimony before I could put them on the witness stand.

To my surprise, the defense attorney decided not to cross-examine any of those nine. As a result, my witnesses that day finished their testimony by 11:30. Judge Baker was furious with me for not having more witnesses to fill the entire morning. I couldn't believe that after all the work I had done to bring in those nine witnesses, prepare them, and get them on the stand, I was being yelled at for not having more witnesses that morning. Such is the life of a trial attorney.

As if the bedsores were not enough, in the middle of the trial I developed a respiratory infection and really struggled to make it through to the end.

The respiratory infection started to creep up on me over the weekend, during the second half of the trial proceedings. It would be a disaster to get sick now, with all the scheduling having already been done twice.

After my direct case, the defense attorney presented eight witnesses. I was still feeling pretty sick at the time. I had to pull myself together and cross-examine all eight of them. I then gave a lengthy and detailed summation.

The defense attorney complimented me immediately after my summation and asked if I would consent to the defendant remaining free on bail if the jury convicted him. Apparently I had even convinced the defense attorney the jury was going to find his client guilty.

Unfortunately, the jury found the defendant not guilty on every count of the indictment. There just wasn't enough evidence connecting the defendant to the crime.

Sitting through the verdict was torture for me, hearing the jury repeat the words "not guilty" over and over again.

Regardless, my supervisor at the time, Toby Kurtz, wrote a glowing critique of my summation:

> Without the use of any notes, and with no pause to collect his thoughts, ADA Kunken gave one of the finest summations I have ever heard.
>
> In spite of the substantial evidence detrimental to the People's case, ADA Kunken effectively led the jury to focus on one question, "Who put the paraquat into the spray truck?" He then fit all the People's evidence into his answer, "the defendant."
>
> Without ever repeating any point, he spoke for an hour in a perfectly organized fashion. During that hour I was never bored, despite the fact that there was nothing exciting about the evidence itself. The jurors appeared as mesmerized by ADA Kunken as was I.
>
> It was only because of this superior summation that ADA Kunken had any chance at a conviction in this case.

The judge's law secretary told me the day after the verdict that the jury raved to the judge about me, my summation, and the way I conducted the entire trial. One juror even said I was the most intelligent person she had ever encountered.

Still another comment was that my summation so clearly laid out the evidence and the issues before the jury that it made it easier for them to return the "not guilty" verdict. That was certainly a comment I did not like to hear.

I missed some work just after the trial because of bedsores again.

Between bronchitis, bladder infections, bedsores, and frequent excruciating shoulder pain, it was extremely challenging to concentrate on my work and keep on top of my cases. When I had to lie in bed, I was not able to read or do any work. It was extremely frustrating, just as it had been in college and law school.

When I have bronchitis, I breathe better sitting up in the wheelchair than lying flat in bed. I frequently spend the entire night in the chair. This was a particularly big problem when I was struggling with a bedsore. Sitting up on a bedsore all night is the worst thing for it. I had no choice, though; it was the only way I could breathe.

◆ ◆ ◆

Halloween fell on a Wednesday in 1990. I spent the day at work. I certainly couldn't concentrate on anything. All I could think about was that it had been twenty years. How depressing.

Steve arranged to take me out for dinner that night. After dinner, we went to a theater in Rockville Centre and saw the movie *Goodfellas*. I might have been the only person in the theater who didn't enjoy it.

◆ ◆ ◆

On May 28, 1991, I began the trial of a defendant accused of committing three bank robberies.

The trial had come at a particularly busy time in my schedule. I had just completed a seven-day pretrial hearing on a three-codefendant drug case. That hearing took place over a two-week time span. I had to stay in bed with a bedsore one day during the middle of the hearing. That bedsore was still a constant concern and I had to lie down at the end of each day, as soon as I returned home from work. That, of course, meant I could not put in as much time preparing for the hearing or trial as I would have liked.

It was particularly challenging keeping all the facts of the many cases I was working on in my head, and trying to organize my hearings and trial presentations without any notes. As had been the case throughout law school and my career as an ADA, I had to rely on my memory.

One night during the trial, I suffered excruciating pain in my right shoulder. It was so bad that I went to the emergency room at South Nassau Hospital in Oceanside. I had been having problems with severe pain in that shoulder for a few years by then. I had seen a number of different doctors and therapists concerning it and had had MRIs done on both shoulders. I had received diagnoses of bicepital tendinitis, bursitis, and subluxation of the shoulder. This time, the emergency room doctor told me I had a torn rotator cuff. He put my right arm in a sling.

I thought it would look strange, after having conducted half the trial, to suddenly appear in court with a sling on. I felt uncomfortable being seen by the jury that way. Besides, I looked disabled enough without it. It was also extremely difficult for me to operate my electric wheelchair or turn the pages of my trial notebook with my right arm in a sling. I could not keep my balance. So, I continued the trial without wearing the sling, with my right arm in a lot of pain, resting on my lapboard.

The defendant was convicted for all three bank robberies. He was sentenced to ten years to life on my case, to be run consecutively with an additional seven years he was still serving on a federal conviction.

Chapter 24

Life Outside the Courtroom

◆ ◆ ◆

On December 18, 1989, I was invited to participate on the Hofstra Law School's Dean's Alumni Advisory Council. Not long after, I was asked to participate on the New York State Advisory Council for Vocational and Educational Services for Individuals with Disabilities, as well as to speak on a panel at Hofstra Law School dealing with disability issues. I was surprised at the high regard others had for my expertise and input.

In January 1992, I was asked to be one of the guest faculty on the Hofstra Law School's National Institute of Trial Advocacy's Program. I helped teach the law students trial techniques for two days that year and one day a year every year, for many years after that.

I would have liked to have had more time and energy to devote to helping others, but with all the work I had to do at the District Attorney's Office and all the health problems I had been dealing with, it just was not possible.

◆ ◆ ◆

On Friday May 28, 1993, my ninety-two-year-old grandmother came to my apartment to visit for the Memorial Day weekend. My Aunt Betty and her husband Jay were heading to Great

Barrington for a few days and it was best not to leave More Mom alone in East Brunswick, New Jersey, without a relative nearby.

More Mom, although still living alone in her apartment, was in the early stages of dementia. Despite that, I enjoyed spending whatever time I could with her. We loved each other's company and always had a lot to talk about.

On Saturday, May 29, around midnight, as I lay on my side in bed waiting for a suppository to induce a bowel movement, my then attendant, Darek, came into my room and told me that More Mom was sitting on the toilet, complaining that her left arm was hurting her. I was not able to get up to go to her or speak to her at all. Thinking she might be having a heart attack, I called 911.

Two members of the Rockville Centre Police Department soon showed up at my door. Darek brought them first to speak with More Mom but it was soon clear to them that she was not very coherent.

The police came in to my room to speak to me about her. I could barely see them, as I was still lying on my right side, facing away from the door. I heard one of the officers tell his partner, "This is the District Attorney's home." I soon realized that that officer had been a witness for me on one of my trials.

The officer asked whether my grandmother had some cognitive issues, and when I indicated she did, he felt it best to call for an ambulance, which arrived quickly. As they were taking my grandmother out, I told the paramedics to tell my grandmother that I would meet her at the hospital as soon as I could.

I felt terrible that I was not able to provide any help to More Mom. I could not even be by her side as the strangers took her away.

I was also extremely frustrated and embarrassed that I was lying in bed in the middle of my bowel routine when the officers arrived. In addition to the unpleasant odor in the room, the officers must have thought I was a very unfeeling and unconcerned grandson because I didn't even roll over, let alone get out of bed, while my grandmother was having a heart attack.

As soon as the bowel movement was cleaned up, Darek got me dressed and into the wheelchair and drove me to the emergency

Ken with More Mom—1990s.

room at South Nassau Communities Hospital in Oceanside. More Mom was on a bed in the middle of a large room. I put my hand on hers and stayed by her side, trying to reassure her. I spent the rest of the night with her in the emergency room.

Betty and Jay immediately left Great Barrington and headed for the hospital, a three-and-a-half-hour drive, in the middle of the night.

I called Aunt Lorraine first thing in the morning and she quickly joined us at the hospital. Betty and Jay arrived shortly thereafter.

Betty and I stayed at More Mom's side pretty much around the clock the next five days, only leaving late at night to sleep in my apartment. More Mom lingered until the early morning of June 5, when she passed peacefully. It was very sad.

My grandmother had been a tremendous source of love, support, and strength for me from the day I was born. It was hard for me to conceive of her being gone. I felt as if I had just lost a mother for the third time.

♦ ♦ ♦

I took my usual one-week vacation at Betty's summer cabin in Great Barrington. On the afternoon of July 5, 1994, Betty and I went to Bash Bish Falls State Park.

When we first entered the park, we began walking up a path to the left of a creek, on the same level as the water. The rising path would eventually come to an end near the top of a waterfall.

The previous time Betty went to the park, she did not realize, nor had she noticed, the many rocks, ruts, tree roots, and obstacles along the way. That was not unusual. Most able-bodied people never notice those things.

Betty and I soon became convinced that no one in an electric wheelchair had ever navigated that path before. It was so rocky and bumpy we debated whether we should continue to try and conquer what seemed like Mount Everest, or just turn back. We decided to continue. It was a difficult hike but we finally made it to the top.

By the time we reached the summit, it was close to 5 p.m. and the park was about to close. Betty and I then started on our return trip down. On our way up, the path was angled so that the right side was a little lower than the left. At that angle it was easier for me to maintain my balance when I raised my left arm to operate the wheelchair. On the way down, however, the left side of the path was lower than the right. That made it far more difficult for me to keep my balance when I raised my left arm.

At one point, we came to an area that had a large water run-off. I stopped and told Betty I was not sure I could get by it but she assured me that I could. She was wrong!

As I raised my arm to move the joystick on my wheelchair, my upper body started to fall to the left. The wheelchair then turned perpendicular to the path and was now facing the edge of the cliff, overlooking the water. I was leaning part way out of the chair on a severe angle and could not control the wheelchair anymore.

The path under the wheels was filled with gravel. The chair was gradually sliding closer to the edge.

Betty was desperately trying to hold on to the wheelchair and turn it around. It was a seemingly impossible task, and no one was around to help.

We were now almost at the edge of the path and within seconds of going over what was about a seven-foot drop, straight down. Fortunately, at the last possible second, Betty hooked her left wrist around the joystick and was able to push it until the chair turned back parallel to the water. We both breathed a big sigh of relief.

Later that month, I was scheduled to undergo a surgical procedure in Miami that would remove pressure from my spinal cord and nerves. My neck would then be re-fused with a metal plate and screws and a bone graft from a tissue bank.

I was told that the surgery could offer the possibility of some more movement in my right arm. In addition, without it, if I was in any type of accident, or received a severe jolt to my neck, there would be a greater chance of further damage to my spinal cord.

Had I fallen off the edge in Bash Bish, perhaps I would have broken my neck again, or something even worse. My planned surgery took on even greater importance now.

I had the surgery on July 19, 1994, in Jackson Memorial Hospital in Miami, Florida. In hindsight, I don't know if I got any more movement back in my right arm, which was my goal for the surgery. Later, many people who knew me before the surgery told me I seemed to have more movement in my left arm. People also said I seemed to be more "animated" in my upper body. Fortunately, afterward, I did have less pain in my right shoulder, which had been bothering me for years.

By a strange coincidence, I was discharged from the rehab center in Miami on August 20. That was exactly twenty-three years to the day I had been discharged from the Rusk Institute and fifteen years to the day that I started law school.

I was very pleased with the attitude of the doctors, nurses, and therapists in Miami. They seemed a lot more hopeful and encouraging than the medical personnel had at Rusk in 1971.

Most of the Miami patients were young. I was glad to see that the Miami Project tried to educate them about their new physical condition. The rehab center had a number of meetings and lectures for the patients. During those sessions, the nurses and therapists talked about catheters, bowel routines, sex education, and other topics. I felt that was important and helpful. However, I was dismayed seeing patients with spinal cord injuries being discharged after just three months. That was all many insurance companies paid for now. Three months was too short a time for a newly injured person to adjust to his or her new physical condition, and to learn how to adapt to it. The nine months and twenty days I spent in the hospitals and rehab center had not been nearly enough for me.

In addition, a significant emotional adjustment needs to be made. That takes time and cannot be rushed. I worried about those young people's future. I was concerned about what would happen to them after they were home, away from the hospital and the rehab center's support system.

When I was injured in 1970, I did not know of anyone who had a high spinal cord injury who had gone on to do something productive with his or her life. There might have been people who had, but I never heard about them. There were no role models that I could look to for inspiration, or even to give me some hope that life was still worth living and that someone in my condition could make a positive impact on others.

So, while I was in the Miami rehab center, I tried to offer whatever encouragement I could to some of the newly injured patients. I shared with them, as well as with their families, some of the lessons I had learned during the past twenty-four years and tried to convince them that there was still a lot they could do.

Nevertheless, being back in a hospital was depressing for me. Whenever I hear about a new spinal cord injury, I am shaken to the core. I dread the thought of anyone having to go through what I went through.

I was especially upset when I learned of Christopher Reeve's accident, which happened on May 27, 1995.

I watched his interview with Barbara Walters on September 29, 1995, and was very impressed with his attitude and outlook. I was especially pleased to hear that he had become active in the American Paralysis Association. I was certain that having "Superman" as a spokesperson would raise awareness about spinal cord injuries and make a tremendous difference in the lives of a great many people. I was right about that.

I was so saddened by his death in 2004. He is and will continue to be sorely missed.

◆ ◆ ◆

During my first fourteen years in the District Attorney's Office, I prosecuted seventy-six trials, sixty-five of which were felonies. I conducted 118 pretrial hearings and presented 252 cases to the grand jury. My numbers were consistently among the highest in the County Court Trial Bureau each year.

On September 16, 1996, I was promoted to the position of County Court Trial Supervisor. I was used to doing litigation on serious cases and frequently gave advice to less-experienced assistants. I knew that they respected my knowledge, experience, and judgment. Still, it was strange having more than twenty ADAs coming to me for help.

Ken Kunken, Deputy Bureau Chief.

Working with Dan Looney.

On May 15, 1997, I was promoted once again, to the position of Deputy Bureau Chief of the County Court Trial Bureau. Soon, there was a line of ADAs at my door, seeking grand jury and plea bargain approvals on their cases. Apparently, they preferred coming to me rather than to the other supervisors.

Three days after my promotion, I drove to Washington, D.C., where I joined a number of other attorneys from Nassau County to be admitted to the United States Supreme Court. The Nassau County Bar Association sponsored the event.

In the morning of May 19, we went to the United States Supreme Court. Everyone with the Nassau County Bar Association sat in a group on the right-hand side of the courtroom. Because I was not able to sit with them, I sat off to the left, away from everybody else.

The admitting ceremony was very formal. Ira Warshawsky, a Nassau County Supreme Court Judge, requested the Court admit us to practice before the U.S. Supreme Court. As Ira read each person's name from our group, that individual would stand up. Ira read all the names fairly quickly.

When Ira reached my name, he said my name and told the Court that I was sitting off to the side, to the left of everyone. Ira turned his head and nodded to where I was sitting.

At that moment, all nine Supreme Court Justices turned their heads and shifted their gaze to focus on me. It was an incredible feeling. It seemed as though the Justices looked at me for a long time. In hindsight, I suppose it was for no more than a few seconds but it certainly felt a lot longer. Many of them smiled and nodded at me, as if to say, "Congratulations."

As I sat before the nine Supreme Court Justices, I was struck by the irony that the next day, May 20, I was to be one of the speakers at the fiftieth Anniversary Celebration of the Rusk Institute in New York City. The Rusk Institute was the rehab center in which I had been a patient twenty-six years earlier, the institution in which the medical personnel had seemed to think that the best I would ever be able to do was to sell magazine subscriptions over the telephone. I couldn't wait to tell the people at Rusk about my day at the Supreme Court.

When I was a patient at Rusk, I probably was not considered one of their success stories. After all, I did not regain much movement nor was I able to do many of the activities of daily living. While they did print a full-page article about me in their yearly magazine the year after I was discharged, I doubt Rusk's staff had been using me as an example to their other patients as to what a quadriplegic could still do or accomplish. And yet, here I was, twenty-six years later, being asked to be one of the speakers to help celebrate their fiftieth anniversary.

During my brief talk there, I told the audience what I had done with my life since I left the Rusk Institute. I told them how important it was for them not to impose limited expectations on their patients. I hoped my message would resonate. After all, apart from a few former patients, the audience consisted of therapists, doctors, and administrators currently working at Rusk. They needed to encourage patients to set high goals for themselves.

People with disabilities can accomplish almost anything they set their minds to. So far, I had.

The room was pretty crowded. When I finished talking, the audience was very receptive and complementary. It felt good returning to Rusk to share my message with them. That was the first visit to Rusk I had not dreaded. I actually came away feeling uplifted.

Chapter 25

Love, at Last

♦ ♦ ♦

Despite most people's limited expectations regarding my prospects, my professional life was quite successful. I was now a supervisor, and as such, I had stopped doing my own litigation in the courtroom. While my responsibilities in the office had increased, I actually had more free time to work on my personal life.

I tried to push myself to go out more and do fun things with the Danises, Steve, or my Aunt Betty. In January 1995, I went with the Danises to St. Thomas in the U.S. Virgin Islands in the Caribbean for five days. In addition to a few days in Great Barrington every summer, I would also spend a weekend every six to eight weeks with Betty at her house in New Jersey.

I loved going gambling with my Uncle Jay. We drove to Atlantic City a couple of times a year and every Christmas Day since 1987. It became our tradition. In early December 1995, Betty and Jay even took me on a vacation to Las Vegas.

Most weekends, though, I would just stay in my apartment, reading or watching television.

I was lonely and depressed a good deal of the time. I did my best not to show it. I tried to put on a relatively happy face in public. With the exception of Steve and Betty, few people knew how I actually felt.

Ken with Aunt Betty and Uncle Jay about to take a small plane ride
over the Grand Canyon—1995.

I was still in my forties, but I could see that, because of my
spinal cord injury, my body was aging faster than my contempo-
raries'. I had already suffered some significant bone loss, the begin-
nings of osteoporosis. Despite wearing a corset, my posture was
getting worse. My right shoulder was considerably higher than my
left. Often, I experienced back and neck pain in addition to my
shoulder pain.

I seemed to be constantly tired and was having trouble concentrating and remembering things. I thought I might be developing Alzheimer's disease or some other type of dementia. I was
worried. After all, if I could no longer rely on my memory, how
could I function at work, or at home for that matter. As bad as my
physical condition was, it would be far worse if I were to lose my
mental abilities as well.

My bladder no longer seemed to be emptying on its own
when it got full, so not long after my surgery in Miami I started to
employ intermittent catheterizations. I would refer to it as "doing

the catheter." I needed my aide to insert a catheter to empty my bladder about six times a day, depending on how much I drank. If I wasn't catheterized when I needed to be, I would break into heavy sweating and my blood pressure would go sky high again. The one positive note of not having to rely on "condom drainage" was that I no longer had to worry about the condom leaking and me ending up sitting in a puddle of urine. As a result, I had fewer problems with bedsores.

♦ ♦ ♦

The middle of April 1999 found me, once again, advertising for a personal care attendant. At least this time I only had to look for a weekend aide.

Since the late 1980s, whenever I needed to hire a new attendant, I put an ad in the *Polish Daily News*. That ad usually attracted better-educated and more serious candidates than my ads in *Newsday*. A young Polish woman named Anna responded to my current ad.

Whenever a female responded, I always asked her how tall she was. I knew that unless she was at least five feet, seven inches tall, she would have difficulty lifting me from the bed to the wheelchair. Most female callers were between five foot two and five foot five.

Anna told me that she was 184 cm. I quickly did the math in my head: 184 cm was almost six foot one. In addition, on the phone, she had a beautiful voice with a lovely accent. While Anna had no prior experience providing the type of help I needed, I knew I had to meet her.

I normally interviewed prospective attendants at my office in Mineola. That way I could screen most of the applicants, and only have the candidates I was seriously considering visit me at my apartment in Rockville Centre. I also hoped that telling prospective attendants that I worked at the District Attorney's Office and would be interviewing them there might cause some of the less trustworthy applicants not to show up.

Anna was studying English as a second language in New York City and had classes every weekday. The only time she could come for an interview was on a weekend. I arranged to meet with her at my home during the early afternoon on the following Sunday.

When Anna arrived, I was immediately struck by her appearance. She had long, light brown hair and blue eyes. She had perfect posture, which made her seem even taller than her six-foot, one-inch frame. In fact, Anna was positively statuesque. Her voice was incredible and sounded even better in person than it had on the phone.

During my interview with her, Anna told me that she had a master's degree in marketing and management from a Polish university. She had worked for a few years as a promotional specialist and marketing manager. Anna said she had come to America to improve her English.

Anna was staying in Garwood, New Jersey, with her Aunt Regina. Every day, Anna commuted to Manhattan to take classes in English at the New York Language Center. She was looking for something to do on weekends that would help improve her English-speaking skills, since she spoke only Polish when she was at her aunt's.

I explained to Anna what my physical needs were. She assured me she could handle them. As with every prospective attendant, I had to make sure that that person was physically able to lift me in and out of bed. If the person could not do that, I would not hire him or her. Anna was able to lift me without much of a problem. I must also say it felt great to have Anna's arms around me.

I was ready to hire Anna right then and there, but thought it more appropriate to continue with our interview and then check her references.

I called Anna a few days later and told her I would like to train her the next weekend to teach her everything involved with my care.

My weekday attendant at the time, Eugene, stayed for the weekend to help train Anna. The first night, while Anna watched, Eugene demonstrated how to take care of me. The second night, Anna took over my care, while Eugene was supposed to supervise and correct her. By the second evening though, Eugene was so tired, Anna decided not to disturb him when he fell asleep. She did everything by herself without Eugene's assistance. Anna was an incredibly fast learner. She had a gentle and caring touch and was an absolute pleasure to have around.

Well in advance of hiring Anna, I had made plans to spend a weekend in late May in Atlantic City with some friends from work. We had arranged to stay overnight at the Tropicana Hotel. Although Anna had been with me for only a couple of weekends by then, I felt confident enough in her ability to manage my care to travel 150 miles away from home with her.

My friends met us at the craps table in the hotel's casino. I had often played craps with Uncle Jay rolling the dice for me. This time, I relied on Anna. It was her first time in a casino. Thanks to Anna's winning rolls, I won $1,200. There is a lot to be said for "beginner's luck"!

We all went to an Italian restaurant at the Caesars Hotel for a late dinner. It was wonderful. I felt as if I was out with friends, with a beautiful date by my side, rather than with an attendant.

Following dinner, we returned to the craps tables at Tropicana to do more gambling. We finally retired to our rooms at two in the morning.

When Anna was getting me ready for bed, she jokingly told me that this would be the first time in her life that she was going to spend a night alone in a hotel room with a man.

Of course, everything was very proper and innocent. Still, I know I fell asleep with a big smile on my face.

In the morning, Anna and I joined my friends for breakfast and some more gambling. By that time, I actually wanted to spend more time just walking on the boardwalk with Anna than playing craps. Don't get me wrong, I was still feeling lucky … just in a different way.

Not long after the Atlantic City weekend, my father came for a visit.

My father and his wife Betty had moved to Orlando, Florida, a number of years earlier. Initially, my father came to New York at least once a month to continue working in his life insurance business. Near the end of the nineties, he retired full time. He still came to New York, usually alone, to visit with the family. Whenever he

Nicky (Steve's wife), Steve, Ken's dad, Bobby Leshansky (Meryl's husband), Meryl, and Ken holding Jeffrey Leshansky.

did, he stayed with me in my apartment. By now, Steve had two sons and my sister Meryl was married, with three sons.

One day, while my father was resting in my apartment, Anna and I decided to go to the Long Beach boardwalk to take a long walk. Following that, we sat on a bench and talked for hours.

We talked about ourselves. We talked about our families. We talked about our past jobs. We even talked about our plans for the future. The time went by very fast. It was obvious we really enjoyed each other's company.

At one point, Anna told me that one of the reasons she left one of her jobs in Poland was that her boss had made unwanted romantic advances toward her. She followed up that statement by warning, "Don't fall in love with me."

I didn't know it was that obvious.

As part of my daily routine, my aide would do range of motion exercises on me, twice a day, to keep my joints loose. This weekend, Anna seemed to take an especially long time doing them. In fact, she seemed to be touching my hands, shoulders, neck, and hair quite often throughout the two days. It made me think, "Who is falling for whom?" I didn't complain, mind you. It felt great.

The weekend went by too quickly. I couldn't wait for the next weekend to come so that I could see Anna again.

The next Friday, as usual, I let Eugene leave an hour early and waited alone for Anna to arrive.

To my delight, as soon as she entered she put her bags down and, while looking straight into my eyes, put her arms around me and gave me a long, passionate kiss. She said, "I couldn't stop thinking about you."

Unfortunately, Eugene didn't catheterize me before he left. By the time Anna arrived, my bladder was overflowing and I was sweating profusely.

Anna soon noticed my condition and without missing a beat, did the catheter. In some ways, it was an awkward reminder of my first date with Betsy. Anyway, it was an almost perfect start to a great weekend. It wasn't going to be just another lonely weekend spent with just an attendant. Anna was there with me!

The following weekend we had our annual family barbecue. This time it was at my cousin Jill's beach house in Amagansett and would be the first time most of my family met Anna.

I enjoyed having my family around but this time couldn't wait for an opportunity to be alone with Anna. No one knew that Anna and I had feelings for each other and we certainly weren't ready to tell anyone. In fact, we were not sure ourselves what those feelings actually were.

I remember being wheeled onto the beach in my manual wheelchair. The only other thing I remember about that weekend was how great Anna looked in a two-piece bathing suit.

Anna and I spent most of the summer weekends alone, watching movies on tape, talking, and occasionally walking on the Long Beach boardwalk.

Anna's thirtieth birthday, on August 2, fell on a weekday. She skipped her English classes and met me near my office in Mineola for the occasion. We went out for a nice lunch at the Bar

Association. It was wonderful to be out with Anna in the middle of a workday.

◆ ◆ ◆

Normally, my attendant slept in the second bedroom. When I needed assistance in the middle of the night I would have to yell loud enough to wake him or her up. I tried an intercom system but it often buzzed or made annoying noise, so I stopped using it.

Anna was worried that if she stayed in the other bedroom she would not wake up when I called her. So, every weekend night, Anna slept on a chair by the side of my bed. At some point, Anna noticed that I stopped breathing at times during the night.

After sleeping in a sleep lab on August 9, 1999, I learned I had a severe case of obstructive sleep apnea. The doctor recommended I use a CPAP machine.

On the nights I am able to sleep with the CPAP machine on, I see an enormous difference in how I feel. I can, once again, concentrate and remember things. Maybe I am not getting dementia after all and I just need more good nights' sleep.

◆ ◆ ◆

In September, my father came from Orlando for the Jewish New Year, Rosh Hashanah. We always celebrated that holiday at my Aunt Lorraine's house in Oceanside.

Anna and I walked to Aunt Lorraine's during the early afternoon. My father joined us there a short time later. While waiting for everybody to arrive, my father insisted on taking a picture of Anna and me. I was surprised when Anna put her arms around me, with her face against mine, for the picture. My father appeared equally surprised. It was our first picture together.

Every week, after Anna left my apartment on Sunday evening, I couldn't wait for the next weekend to come. I really missed her. I found myself smiling all the time, just thinking about Anna. I was surprised nobody asked me why I appeared so happy.

First picture with Anna—September 11, 1999.
Photo by Leonard Kunken.

I had dated a few other women in the past. The last time was almost twenty years earlier when I was in my twenties. Now, I was almost fifty. I was in love with Anna, but I never told her. It just didn't seem right to say it out loud.

I continually tried to bring myself back to reality. I knew that my relationship with Anna could not possibly have a future. Soon after I was injured, I had decided that as long as I needed to use a wheelchair I would never get married. I didn't think it would be fair to the woman. I remember telling that to my Aunt Betty and her telling me that there was no reason for me to feel that way.

Betty had said, "You have a lot to offer and there are many women who will probably fall in love with you. You can't decide what is best for them. Only they can make that decision."

I was adamant, though, and would not let myself even consider the possibility. I stated my feelings about marriage to Anna early in our relationship.

Christmas happened to fall on a weekend in 1999. As usual, I went to Atlantic City with Betty and Jay. Jay and I spent Christmas

Eve and Christmas Day losing money at the craps tables, a far cry from my last trip to Atlantic City with Anna.

Anna celebrated Christmas Eve with her relatives in New Jersey.

The following weekend, Anna and I were, again, not supposed to see each other. Traditionally, I spent New Year's Eve and Day, without an attendant, at my brother's house. Steve would help me on those days, to give my aide that holiday off.

However, we were about to begin a new millennium. This particular New Year's Eve would be memorable. I wanted to spend it with Anna. I missed her and knew that she had no special plans for New Year's Eve. I called her and invited her to spend that evening with me at Steve's.

We had a wonderful New Year's Eve with my brother and his wife. We were also supposed to spend the next day at Steve's and return to Rockville Centre on Sunday. However, the weather reports were predicting a large snowfall. I decided to return to Rockville Centre before it started. In addition, it gave me an opportunity to be alone with Anna again.

The next two months were wonderful. It was the most enjoyable winter I had had since my accident twenty-nine years earlier. It was about to end, though.

In February, Anna met a man named Franklin at her school. Franklin came from Ecuador, and had been living in the United States on and off for the past six years. He pursued Anna aggressively.

Anna told me about Franklin. She initially seemed amused by the whole situation but, by the next weekend, it got serious. With tears in her eyes, Anna told me that she couldn't help falling for Franklin.

Without really meaning it, I told Anna, "If he is a nice guy and if you think it could develop into something special then, by all means, you should go out with him."

We both believed our relationship was never going to get more serious than it already was. Just like with my previous girlfriends, there would never be anything permanent between us. Anna and I could never be more than just friends. I wanted Anna to be happy and to meet the perfect man. Perhaps Franklin was that person.

Anna started dating Franklin. Their relationship progressed quickly—too quickly, if you ask me. The closer Anna became with Franklin, the more distant she became with me. I felt terrible about the change in our relationship.

Anna told me a lot about Franklin. The more she talked about him, though, the more convinced I became that she was making a big mistake. Somehow, whenever Anna was trying to tell me something positive about Franklin, a lot of negatives seemed to slip out. Anna really didn't seem that happy.

She continued to help me during the next few weekends. Because we no longer had the same close relationship, our conversations became less personal. I certainly didn't want to talk about Franklin. It always made me very upset. Does anyone ever want to hear their ex-girlfriend talk about her new boyfriend?

Sometime in March, Anna told me that she was going to marry Franklin. She had already moved into an apartment in Staten Island with him. She also told me that I should start looking for a new weekend aide. She said she would continue to come to me for the next six weekends to give me time to find a replacement.

One evening, while Anna was massaging my shoulders, she told me our friendship was very important to her. She did not want anything to interfere with it, even her present relationship with Franklin.

Then Anna dropped a bombshell on me. She said that if I had asked her to marry me a few months earlier she would have said yes.

I was shocked. It took me totally by surprise.

I had made my feelings known to Anna, as well as to everyone else, that I would never get married as long as I was paralyzed. I remained convinced that my limitations would hold a woman back from too many things. I was certain a woman would be better off with someone who did not have the severe physical limitations I had.

Now, for the first time, I started to rethink that. I was convinced that Anna would be better off with me than with Franklin, even with me being totally paralyzed. I had to try to get Anna back.

That evening, for the first time, I said to her, "You know that I love you."

Anna hugged me tightly, but didn't say anything.

♦ ♦ ♦

The following weekend, I told Anna that while I was still a patient at Rusk, I had started writing a book about my accident and the events that followed. I had let very few people read it, but I was ready to share it with her. I wanted her to know me better. In addition, I didn't want to talk about Franklin any more.

For the next couple of weekends, Anna and I sat side by side in the living room, with me reading the rough draft to her. Anna turned the pages for me and occasionally asked questions. At that time, the book covered my injury and the following twelve years. There were many references to the problems I was having with unreliable attendants and how they often left me with little or no notice.

After spending the March 26 weekend with me, Anna called and told me she couldn't come the next weekend. In fact, she probably couldn't come any more. Franklin was sick and needed her. Anna said she couldn't leave him alone.

So, a few weeks earlier than she had said she was going to leave, Anna would stop coming, and I still hadn't found a weekend replacement. Anna was really leaving me in the lurch, as my prior attendants had often done.

Despite the hardship on me, I was more concerned about Anna. I felt she was making a terrible mistake.

Tom, my weekday attendant at the time, stayed with me for the next twenty-six straight days, until I was finally able to find a new weekend aide. Anna's replacement was a Polish man, who like Anna, had never done this kind of work before. Unlike Anna's, his care left a lot to be desired.

For weeks, I didn't hear anything from Anna. Finally, at the end of May, she called. She wanted to come to pick up her stuff.

We engaged in some small talk on the telephone. She asked how my weekend aide was. As it turned out, that aide had previously arranged to travel across country for a few weeks. He had left in the middle of May and was to return sometime in June.

I was not aware of his plans until a short time before he left. Fortunately, my aide, Tom, was able to stay with me the first weekend.

When Anna learned that I was, once again, without a week-end aide, she volunteered to come for the next two weekends to relieve Tom. Franklin was feeling better, so there was no reason for her not to come if I needed her. I was really looking forward to spending some time with Anna.

When the next weekend finally came, Anna appeared depressed and tired. She cried frequently, especially after Franklin's late-night phone calls. I didn't know what was going on with them because Anna stopped talking about Franklin to me. By that time, I really hated the guy. After all these years, I suppose I still do.

After the first two weekends, Anna told me she could come every other weekend, if I would like. She also tried to arrange to be with me on the weekend of July 8 because on that day Steve and Nicky were having a large party to celebrate my fiftieth birthday.

The party would take place at the pavilion by the beach, across the street from my brother's home in Huntington Bay. That facility would not be available on July 15, my actual birthday, so they scheduled it for the Saturday before. Steve and Nicky invited about seventy-five people.

Saturday, July 8, was a beautiful, warm, sunny day. Anna found a black T-shirt in my drawer for me to wear. It was perfect for the occasion. Written on the front of the T-shirt was: "How the hell did I get this old."

I had lost some weight, so the T-shirt fit me perfectly. I suppose I hadn't had much of an appetite during the past three months.

In the late morning, Anna and I took a walk to a bagel shop in town. We had gone there together many times in the past. Anna bought two flat sesame seed bagels with cream cheese. We decided to eat them in our usual spot, on a bench outside the senior citizen center, one block from my apartment.

Anna and I started to talk and the time just seemed to fly by. It felt like it used to.

Ken with his Oceanside friends, Dave Gilbert, Russ Canan, and
Rich Gilman, at Ken's fiftieth birthday party—July 8, 2000.

At one point, I said to Anna, "Let's skip the party and go away
somewhere." I was only partly joking when I said it.

Anna seemed to be ready to go along. If the party had been
for anyone else, we might actually have done it.

Anna drove my father and me to Steve's. Almost everyone
invited showed up. The pavilion was packed with my family and
friends.

Betty had organized a Jeopardy game. All the questions were
about my life. Kendra Crook, the daughter of my former nurse,
Barbara, won the game. She seemed to know everything about me.
After the game, my cousins Emily and Alan handed out lyrics to a
song they had composed about me. Everyone joined them in singing it. Many people then gave nice tributes to me. Anna was right
by my side throughout the evening. It was wonderful.

We finally arrived home around 11 p.m. Anna and I stayed
up past 1 a.m., reading cards and opening gifts. I was sorry when
the day finally ended.

On Sunday evening, Anna told me that, if I wanted, she would come back every weekend. Of course, I said yes. My birthday actually fell on the next weekend. It was great to celebrate that day with Anna as well.

At that time, Anna was no longer attending the New York Language Center, having finished the program. She seemed uncertain whether to attend a different school, go to Ecuador with Franklin, or return to Poland.

In any event, Anna was anxious to go back to Poland to visit with her family.

On top of that, Anna's visa was expiring soon and she didn't want to stay in the United States illegally. If she stayed illegally and at some point left the States, she would not be able to return. Anna told me her biggest worry was that she would never be able to see me again.

That summer, I had arranged to take a few extra days off after my usual Great Barrington vacation to do some sightseeing in Washington, D.C.. I had hoped that if Anna was in the United States, she would go there with me. It would keep her away from Franklin longer, and perhaps spending some time away with me would rekindle the relationship we once had.

Anna went to Poland for eight days. I met her at the airport when she returned. She greeted me warmly and appeared rested and happy. Her trip to Poland had been a good one. The next day, Anna and I left for Washington, D.C., just like I had hoped.

On our way, we stopped at Anna's apartment in Staten Island to drop off one of the bags Anna had brought back from Poland. The apartment was a second-floor walkup. It was not accessible to me, but I would have stayed in the van anyway because Franklin was there.

Anna asked if I would like to meet Franklin. I said no. Anna remained in the apartment for about fifteen minutes before she finally returned to the van, alone. Apparently, according to Anna, Franklin didn't want to meet me either. How dare he!

We crammed in a lot of activities while in Washington. We toured the FBI building, the *Washington Post*, and the Holocaust

Ken and Anna in front of Smithsonian Castle in
Washington, D.C.—August 2000.

Museum. We saw a play at the Kennedy Center, went to the top of
the Washington Monument and visited all the memorials on the
Mall, twice. We spent some time in the Air and Space Museum
and visited other parts of the Smithsonian as well.

Anna had brought back a photo album from Poland filled
with pictures of her growing up. She never seemed to be smiling
in any of them. I was determined to get new pictures of Anna,
showing her beautiful smile. Wherever we went, I would grab a
passerby and have him or her take a picture of Anna. I had to beg
her to smile for the camera. She didn't make it easy.

We spent five enjoyable days together, but soon after we
returned, Anna went back to Staten Island and Franklin. Oh well,
at least I'd tried. I remained terribly frustrated.

Anna's beautiful smile in Washington, D.C.—August 2000.

Anna continued to come each weekend, but seemed to be more and more subdued. She didn't seem to be her old self. We usually just stayed in my apartment and watched movies or went out for long walks, with neither of us saying much. We didn't talk about Franklin but I could tell things were not going well.

Perhaps, I thought, if Anna and I did some fun things together, it would take her mind off Franklin. So in September, she and I went to New York City to see the play *Phantom of the Opera* and then out for a nice dinner. It was the first time Anna had been to a Broadway musical. For the occasion, she was elegantly dressed in a long gray skirt and button-down blouse. She looked more beautiful than ever.

In early October, Anna and I went to the Meadowlands in New Jersey to watch the New York Jets play. Needless to say, it was Anna's first time going to a professional football game. I don't think she enjoyed it quite as much as *Phantom of the Opera*.

When Anna arrived in my apartment on Friday, October 27, she told me that Franklin was moving out that weekend. Their relationship had ended. She did not tell me much more than that. I wondered if I still had a chance.

Dinner with Anna after seeing
Phantom of the Opera—September 2000.

◆ ◆ ◆

I wanted to do something special on October 31, the thirtieth anniversary of my injury. Gambling in Atlantic City seemed like a good way to get through the day without dwelling on the past thirty years. I went there with Steve, my father, my father's wife, and my current weekday aide.

The day in Atlantic City probably would have been more fun had I been there with Anna. My father was no substitute. He didn't approve of gambling. In addition, whether we were in the casino or a restaurant, he continued to treat me like a child. Being fifty years old, it embarrassed me no end.

During the following week, I called Anna to check on her. She was pretty much a basket case, crying while talking to me. I convinced her to come to Mineola the next day to meet me for lunch at the Bar Association. She started to finally open up to me about the previous few months with Franklin.

According to Anna, her trip to Poland, and her trip with me to Washington, D.C., ended any plans she and Franklin had concerning marriage, or any relationship for that matter, beyond friendship.

The end of that affair left her with no plans for the future. Ecuador was out of the question and staying illegally in the United States was not an option. Anna would probably just go back to Poland before her visa expired in January.

That seemed to be it. Anna would leave me again, this time forever. I would not be able to pursue her in Poland, not in a wheelchair. I was losing any chance to get her back, even without Franklin around.

Ever since she had told me she would have married me if I had asked her, I could not stop thinking that maybe I should consider the possibility. After all, I really did love her. It would be great to spend the rest of my life with her. Anna knew very well what living with me would entail. A year earlier she had been ready to do it. Maybe if we had more time together, the subject would come up again.

Sometime in November, I convinced Anna to convert her tourist visa to a student visa again. That way she could continue her education and stay in the United States legally. I offered to be her sponsor. As such, I would guarantee that she would be able to pay her tuition, have a place to stay, and be financially secure while going to school.

Anna and I discussed what she would like to study. She loved both computers and art, so she chose graphic design. Nassau Community College offered a program in that field. That college was located in Garden City, about eight miles from my home in Rockville Centre.

I suggested that she live in my apartment while attending school, but she declined. Instead, she rented a room in Hempstead. It was affordable and located close to the bus terminal, which she could use to go back and forth to school.

We completed the necessary paperwork for my sponsorship and sent it out. Anna was scheduled to start classes in January 2001.

As always, I was dreading the beginning of winter. I suggested to Anna that we spend two weeks in Florida together. She had never been there before. She agreed to go with me. The last time I had been to Florida was in March 1998, with my attendant Darek. He enjoyed the trip so much, he ended up moving to Orlando with his family.

I was looking forward to showing Anna some of Florida's attractions. The trip would, hopefully, also take her mind off her breakup with Franklin.

On Saturday morning, December 2, Anna and I left for Florida. We planned to spend some time visiting with my father and his wife Betty in Orlando and take in some of the theme parks in the area.

Sea World had always been one of my favorites. At the end of the day there, Anna took her first roller-coaster ride. She loved it and I loved seeing her face lit up when she came back from the ride. She finally smiled and looked like she really enjoyed the experience.

On Thursday, Anna and I left for Fort Myers. We spent Friday exploring Sanibel and Captiva Island. On Saturday, we moved on to nearby Fort Myers Beach. We stayed in a suite overlooking the Gulf. By then, I just wanted to enjoy the Florida weather without Anna having to pack and unpack every other day. We stayed in Fort Myers Beach for three nights.

On Sunday morning, Dave Paldy, a friend from the DAs Office, called us on Anna's cell phone. Dave knew that Anna and I were going to vacation in Florida around the same time that he would be there, so we had exchanged our phone numbers well in advance.

Because we had a suite, I invited Dave to stay with us for a couple of days. Dave came that same day and, after he settled in our living room, we all went out for a bite.

Dave, Anna, and I spent the evening on a pier. As we watched the sunset, Anna put her arms around me. She had done that the previous night as well, but now Dave was with us.

As we were walking to lunch the next day, Dave asked me if there was something going on between Anna and me. I wanted to say, "I'm working on it," but instead said that we were just friends.

Dave left later that day.

On Monday, December 11, Anna and I learned that there was a movie theater nearby that served dinner during the show. We decided to try it. We saw a movie starring Russell Crowe and Meg Ryan, called *Proof of Life*. It was about a kidnapping in Ecuador.

Just before the movie started, while we were still eating dinner, Anna said that she would like to visit Ecuador someday.

That comment set me off. I could not stop thinking that, only a few months earlier, Anna had planned to move there with Franklin. The thought that she might still have feelings for that guy enraged me. I was so upset I didn't talk to her for the rest of the night.

When the movie ended, I drove my wheelchair so fast that Anna was not able to keep up with me. I was well in front of her when my chair got stuck in the sand off to the side of the road. I had no choice but to wait for her to pull me out.

I sat out alone on the balcony of our hotel suite until late at night, fuming with jealousy. Anna knew me well enough by now to just let me stew for a while. She seemed to understand.

On Thursday, December 12, we left Fort Myers Beach and headed for the Keys. I was still angry with Anna so I did not speak to her at all until we got to the Everglades, where we took a boat tour. I tried to put Franklin out of my mind, and hoped Anna did as well. In any event, I became a better traveling companion.

We stayed at the Hawks Cay Resort in Duck Key for the next two nights. I enjoyed watching Anna gliding effortlessly through the water in the pool. She looked even more gorgeous in a bathing suit than she had the first time I saw her in one.

After a relaxing lunch, Anna and I drove to Key West. It was a beautiful sunny day, without a cloud in the sky. We drove over many bridges and had breathtaking views of the aquamarine water. During the afternoon, we took an enjoyable stroll. Anna just seemed to glow. We spoke very little the entire day, not because either of us was upset, but rather because we were feeling relaxed and comfortable being there with each other.

We had a quiet dinner near the water, saw acrobats perform on the pier, and then watched the sun set, with Anna's arms wrapped around me.

When we returned to the hotel Anna gave me a long passionate kiss. It was the only time she did that during the entire trip. It was wonderful but, at the same time, frustrating and disappointing. I could tell that she still had strong feelings for me but, for whatever reason, wasn't ready to express them just yet. I was hoping for more, but I didn't want to push it.

I'm not sure the trip made a difference in our relationship but I, at least, enjoyed the time we were away together.

As usual, I planned to spend Christmas with Betty and Jay in Atlantic City. That year, Christmas Eve fell on a Sunday. Anna indicated that, rather than spending the holiday with her family in New Jersey, she would like to be with me, even if it meant spending Christmas in Atlantic City.

After a nice dinner at the Tropicana Hotel on Christmas Eve, Jay and I spent some time at the craps tables. While we were gambling, Anna took a long walk. She found a Catholic church a few blocks from the casino and planned to attend midnight mass there. I was supposed to gamble with Jay well into the night. However, I didn't want Anna to walk to the church by herself or be alone on Christmas Eve, so I offered to go with her. The church was crowded and the atmosphere was warm and festive.

We returned to our hotel room around 1:30 a.m. and Anna got me ready for bed. We didn't talk much. It was strange, especially after all the warmth we felt during the Mass just an hour earlier. I thought we both needed some of that warmth back. I asked Anna to come closer so I could kiss her. She didn't say anything, but she did move closer. Before we knew it, it was 5:00 a.m. and we still hadn't gotten any sleep.

I got Anna back!

Chapter 26

Found and Lost, Again

♦ ♦ ♦

In January 2001, Anna started her classes in computer graphic design at Nassau Community College. Despite the fact that she was taking a full load of courses, she was still able to give me a lot of attention. We managed to see each other almost every day.

In February, Anna's brother Greg came from Poland. Greg is nine years younger than Anna, and they have always been very close. Like Anna, he wanted to improve his English-speaking skills and see the country.

Sławek, my full-time aide at the time, announced in the late spring that he would be leaving me at the beginning of June. Anna suggested that she be my full-time aide, including during the weekends.

Having Anna with me seven days a week would be great. It would give me the opportunity to be alone with her every night and every morning. Since Christmas Eve, our relationship had been getting closer and stronger. I missed Anna when she was not around. My apartment felt empty without her. Fortunately for me, she felt the same way.

I knew how demanding taking care of me could be. Most of my previous full-time aides had complained about not getting enough sleep. They would nap during the day to catch up. During Anna's summer break, she might be able to manage doing everything but during the school semester, I worried, it would be

346 ◆ I Dream of Things That Never Were

too much for her. She told me she was confident she could do it. She just wanted to spend one night a week in her rented room in Hempstead, to be assured of having at least one full night's sleep. To make things easier for me, she convinced her brother Greg to take over my care during that one night.

Anna moved in with me on June 7. She quickly settled into a routine for her schooling and my care. When it was time for us to eat, Anna would give me a bite of food then she would take a bite. She became so adept at it she could practically do it in her sleep. One afternoon, though, when I wasn't feeling well and she was particularly tired, I asked her to give me two aspirin. She went into the next room and came back holding aspirin in one hand and a water bottle in the other. She put the aspirin in my mouth, then drank the water and walked away. Clearly, she needed more sleep.

That summer, during my two-week vacation, Anna and I managed to squeeze in a couple of nights at my cousin Jill's beach house in Amagansett as well as a short trip to Boston and a number of days in Great Barrington for our annual family weekend at Betty's.

It was her first time in Great Barrington. She got to meet many relatives from my mother's side of the family. They had heard a lot about her from Betty, who had met Anna the year before and had kept everybody informed about how happy I was since I met her.

We drove to the Berkshires on August 9. Throughout the last half of our drive, Anna kept talking about how much the mountains reminded her of Poland. She mentioned a few times how much she enjoyed hiking and camping with her sister in the Polish mountains. Sometimes her eyes became teary talking about it. She clearly missed it a lot.

I felt badly for Anna. Not only was she separated from her family for long periods of time, she was also separated from the country in which she had grown up. I saw then that she would really like to return to Poland someday. I could never move to Poland or replace her family. I couldn't even go hiking. The closest I had ever come to hiking had been with Betty at Bash Bish Falls—and that had almost ended in disaster. So I did my best

Ken and Anna at Tanglewood, Lenox, Massachusetts—August 2001.

to make this vacation especially enjoyable for Anna by introducing her to many local attractions, including museums, theater, and an outdoor concert at Tanglewood. We traveled really well together.

During the second week of September, I again came down with bronchitis. I stayed out of work on Monday, September 10, and didn't return to the office for two weeks.

On Tuesday morning September 11, 2001, I was watching *Good Morning America* on WABC Channel 7, when the first plane hit the World Trade Center. Anna's brother Greg was with me at the time. I continued to watch the events of the day unfold as I struggled to breathe with my respiratory infection.

During the late morning, Aunt Lorraine came to be with me so Greg could leave to pick Anna up from school. Because of the day's events, her classes had been canceled. As soon as she came through the door, she dropped her bags and rushed over to hug and kiss me. Clearly, she was affected by the tragedy. It was good for us to be together on that day.

When Anna went into the next room, Aunt Lorraine commented that Anna must have had really strong feelings for me. Aunt Lorraine was both surprised and pleased about that. It was the one bright spot in that terrible day for her.

A few days before Thanksgiving, my father came from Orlando to spend the holiday with the family. As usual, he stayed with me. At some point, he started talking to me about how much insurance I had left to cover my attendant costs.

At the rate my expenses were increasing, it looked as if I would only have enough insurance to cover the next seven years. It appeared my insurance would run out before I turned fifty-eight. It was a conversation we had had many times in the past, but this time we were within earshot of Anna.

My father, Anna, and I spent an enjoyable Thanksgiving Day at Steve's. Anna and I then returned to my apartment, while my father remained in Huntington Bay with Steve until Sunday.

When Anna and I were alone on Saturday morning, November 24, she asked me how exactly my attendant insurance coverage worked. She wanted to know why my father was so concerned.

I explained to her that I was covered under my father's major medical policy because I had been considered a minor when I got hurt. The insurance company could have ended my coverage once I was gainfully employed. Fortunately, however, they continued to cover me despite the fact that I worked, first at the Human Resources Center and then in the District Attorney's Office. My father had convinced them that it would be better for me to work than to sit at home for the rest of my life in fear that my insurance coverage would be stopped. Representatives from the company visited me at my jobs to review my situation and had always agreed to continue my coverage. Still, the coverage had a cap and, although it had been extended a number of times, it was now rapidly approaching its limit.

I told Anna I was fortunate to be fifty-one years old, working full time, living in my own apartment, and yet still able to qualify for coverage under my father's major medical policy. It would be extremely difficult, if not impossible, for me to be self-sufficient without that coverage.

By way of example, I told her that if we were ever to get married, my father's major medical policy would not pay her to take care of me. She then asked, "Would you like to marry me?"

My heart jumped. I responded, "Yes!"

Anna didn't say anything for a few minutes. I assumed that her silence meant she did not really want to marry me and the whole exchange was only a conversation about insurance.

She finally said, "Do you know that you just proposed to me?"

I said, "Yes, but you didn't give me an answer."

"Yes, of course I want to marry you!" she replied.

That is how we became engaged. To this day, we still cannot agree as to who proposed to whom.

When we had a chance to think about what we had just agreed on, Anna asked me how I thought our families would react to the news of our engagement.

I told Anna I was sure my family would be thrilled. I was also fairly sure her family would not. Would anyone's parents be happy that their Catholic daughter would be marrying a Jewish man, nineteen years older than she, and that they would be living 3,000 miles away from them? Did I mention that that future husband was paralyzed from the neck down and totally dependent on their daughter for his care?

Anna tried to put a positive spin on it. She said that her mother's biggest concern would be that Anna would never have children, never experience motherhood. Then, after a minute or two of silence and some cuddling, she asked how I would feel about trying to have children.

I told her I was very happy spending my life with just her. I didn't think I could be a good father.

Anna said that, judging by the way I was around my nephews and nieces, and how much they respected and adored me, she was sure I would be a great father. She then reminded me that the Miami Project was having some success with in vitro fertilization for people with spinal cord injuries. She asked me again if I would consider trying to have children. She said, "I would love to see a little Kunken running around."

I was skeptical that it would even be possible in my case. I had been paralyzed for more than thirty years and was already in my fifties. However, I knew that having children was incredibly important to her and her family. I wanted her to be happy and feel that she was living as full a life as possible, even if that life involved being married to me. So, on the spot, I agreed to at least try.

Anna then asked whether, if I couldn't father my own child, I might consider adoption. I told her I would.

At that point, I told her that if we were serious about having a child, we should have at least two. I thought it was important for a child to have a brother or a sister. Because Anna was very close to her siblings, as I was to mine, she agreed.

Thinking about it now, I realize that Anna, in a span of minutes, had talked me into not only marrying her but also having children. My quiet life was about to be turned upside down.

We decided not to tell anyone about our plans just yet. However, when my father returned from Steve's on Sunday, out of the clear blue he asked me, "Did you ever consider marrying Anna?"

I was surprised by his question and its timing. Because he asked so directly, I decided to tell him. I said that, as a matter of fact, Anna and I had actually become engaged the day before. Now it was my father who was surprised. He was also very pleased to hear the news.

I asked him not to say anything to anyone. Anna and I wanted to be the ones to tell people, at the appropriate time. In any event, my father was the first to know.

Now we had to decide how to break the news to Anna's parents. I knew it would not be feasible for me to call Kazik, Anna's father, and ask for his permission to marry his daughter. He didn't speak English, and my Polish was very limited.

Plus, I was fairly certain Kazik would say no. A letter announcing our decision, delivered by Anna, seemed to be the best way to break the news to her parents.

As fate would have it, on December 6, Teresa, Anna's mother, was in a serious car accident in Poland. She shattered her knee and injured her neck. She had to have surgery on her leg and then needed a lengthy period of rehabilitation.

The situation was very upsetting for Anna. She was in the United States, taking care of me, when her mother needed her most. Her father had been providing the assistance Teresa required, while also working full time. Anna felt that she should be the person to care for her mother, especially now, since she was so adept at caring for my needs.

I knew she really wanted to be with her family. In addition, she still hadn't told her parents about our engagement. The upcoming Christmas holiday seemed like the perfect time for Anna to go to Poland.

There were no tickets available to fly to Poland for Christmas, though. The best she could do would be to get a flight right before New Year's. She would have to return to the United States in ten days because her next school semester would be beginning.

There was also the issue of my care. At the time, only Greg was available to take care of me during the ten days Anna would be away. Thankfully, he agreed to take over, with my brother on call if an emergency arose.

On the afternoon of December 23, Anna and I drove to Betty and Jay's in East Brunswick, New Jersey, to spend the holiday weekend with them. As we were sitting down to dinner, Anna and I decided to tell them our news. I wanted her to be the one to tell them, but she felt it should come from me. I didn't do it very well.

I asked Betty if she would help me write a letter to Anna's parents, telling them about our relationship.

Betty anxiously asked, "What exactly is your relationship?"

I broke into a broad smile as I said, "We're engaged!"

Betty and Jay could not have been happier.

Betty said, "I knew something was going on between the two of you. I could tell from all the hand holding."

A flurry of questions soon followed, "How did it happen?" "What plans have you made?" "When are you going to get married?"

During the conversation, I told Betty that she had played a big part in our getting engaged. She was the one who had told me I should not rule out marriage if the right woman came along. Betty was thrilled to hear that.

Betty asked what I would like to say in the letter to Anna's parents. I said I wanted to explain, in detail, who I was. I would describe my physical limitations but would stress what I had done with my life since my injury. I would talk about my accomplishments and how I had not let my injury keep me from achieving so many things. I wanted to tell her parents that I loved Anna very much and would do anything to make her happy.

The next day, Anna left to spend Christmas with Greg and their New Jersey family. Anna didn't tell them our news. She wanted to make sure her parents did not hear about our engagement from anyone but her.

Betty, Jay, and I left for Atlantic City on the morning of the December 24, for our usual overnight Christmas Eve to Christmas Day stay. While Jay and I were playing at the craps tables in the casino, Betty started to work on a draft of the letter. The three of us went over the draft and made some changes. Before it was finished, Anna joined us in East Brunswick. She gave her approval to the final draft.

Anna planned that during her plane ride to Poland she would translate the letter into Polish, and then she would read it to her parents on New Year's Eve.

Greg drove Anna to the airport on December 29. He still didn't know about our engagement.

On New Year's Eve, Anna stayed home with her parents. Because of Teresa's limited mobility, Teresa almost never left her bedroom, so a couple of hours before midnight Anna asked her father to come to the room. Anna then read my letter to both of them.

December 25, 2001

Dear Mr. and Mrs. Błażejczyk,

It has been more than two and a half years since your wonderful daughter, Anna, came into my life. We enjoy our time together and do so many wonderful things. We eat out often and go to movies, plays, and concerts. We enjoy spending time by the ocean and going for long walks and car rides. We go to museums, parks, sports events, and parties. We have vacationed in Washington, D.C., Florida, the Berkshire Mountains, and the city of Boston, Massachusetts. We have full and active lives. Yet there is still time for Anna to attend school and for me to spend long hours at my job.

While I know Anna has told you many things about me, I would like to share a part of my life with you. I am now fifty-one years old. In 1970, when I was twenty, during my junior year at college, I suffered a spinal cord injury while playing football for Cornell University. The injury was very serious. While my head and mind were not affected, I was paralyzed, leaving only a little movement in my left arm. I was determined, however, that, despite my physical limitations, I would make the most of my life.

I spent the next nine and a half months in various hospitals and rehabilitation facilities. I worked hard to maximize the movement that I did have.

Eleven days after being discharged from the last rehabilitation facility, I returned to Cornell University where I completed my degree in Industrial Engineering. I went on to earn a Master's Degree in Education at Cornell University and, the following year, a Master's Degree in Psychology from Columbia University.

My first job after my injury was as a vocational rehabilitation counselor at the Human Resources Center on Long Island, a very well-known and respected rehabilitation institution.

After my injury I did a good deal of public speaking, including testifying before a U.S. Senate Committee on National Health Care, chaired by Senator Edward Kennedy. There were many articles about me in newspapers and magazines. I was interviewed and talked about on radio and television, focusing on having and achieving goals in spite of disabilities.

After working for more than two years as a counselor, I was ready for a new challenge and entered law

school to become a practicing attorney. I graduated from
Hofstra Law School and passed the New York State Bar
Exam on my first try. I was hired as an Assistant District Attorney (ADA) in Nassau County on Long Island
where I have been working for almost twenty years. I have
received a number of promotions and am currently the
Deputy Bureau Chief in our County Court Trial Bureau.
I supervise twenty-two other ADAs. I have been recognized for my achievements, including an award for being
an outstanding ADA and for being one of Hofstra University's distinguished alumni. I was included in a recent
edition of "Who's Who in American Law" and am being
considered for a listing in "Who's Who in America."

I have given you this list of accomplishments, not to
be boastful, but to give you some sense of my abilities and
to show you that my injury has not limited me.

Anna has made an incredible difference in my life.
My world is more complete with her and I know she feels
the same way about me. We would like to spend the rest
of our lives together.

There may be many issues for you about our relationship. I am sure, however, that, when you get to know
me and see how happy we are together, you will understand our decision.

Our plans, at this time, are for Anna to continue
her education over the next two years, at which time we
would like to marry. In the meantime, I want to assure
you that no one will ever love her and cherish her more.

I hope we will be able to meet soon, and close wishing you a Merry Christmas and Happy and Peaceful New
Year.

Sincerely,

Ken

I was concerned Anna's father would be offended that I had
never even tried to ask him for his daughter's hand in marriage.

So, after she read my letter to her parents, she apologized, on my behalf, for not doing so.

Seeing the changes in Anna since she met me and how happy she was, her parents had known it was coming. Nevertheless, it was hard for them to be happy about Anna's decision. Everything that they knew about me that was good was overshadowed by the amount of care I needed every day. They didn't want that hardship for their daughter.

Kazik asked if there would be a full-time attendant to help with my needs. Anna explained that she didn't want to have attendants in our home, unless it was absolutely necessary. She wanted us to have some privacy. Anna stressed to her parents that it was her decision, not mine.

Teresa and Kazik were not happy that Anna would be living so far away. In addition to missing her, they were worried that if something happened and Anna needed their help, they would not be able to provide it. I was certain her parents had far more concerns and reservations than just the geographical distance.

There was also the question of her ever having children. As Anna had predicted, her mother felt that that was the most important part of a marriage. She did not want Anna to miss out on it. According to Teresa, a marriage could not survive if there were no children.

Anna told her parents about the discussion we had had concerning children on the day of our engagement. We would try to have our own through an in vitro procedure.

Because Anna's mother was a devout Catholic, Anna wasn't sure if pursuing an in vitro procedure would upset her mother. In vitro was frowned on by the Church in Poland.

Anna's parents were surprised it was a possibility, but were encouraged by the news that there was at least a remote chance that Anna might someday be a mother.

I called Anna every day while she was in Poland. When we spoke on New Year's Day, Anna described the atmosphere in her home as "very tense." She knew her family was not happy about our decision but hoped that, over time, they would at least be supportive.

Only Alina, Anna's sister, was enthusiastic about our engagement. Alina was confident Anna knew what she was getting into and she trusted Anna's judgment. Alina was looking forward to meeting me.

Anna's parents started to ask more questions. They wanted to know about our wedding plans. They also started to ask what they could do to help.

Anna wanted them just to be there with us at the wedding.

Anna was supposed to return to the United States on January 7. Before that, however, because she had changed her tourist visa to a student visa while in the United States, Anna needed to go to the American Consulate in Poland and have the consul issue a visa under the new classification and attach it to her passport. Without that she could not re-enter the United States.

Anna had done this once before, in 1999, when she was studying English at the New York Language Center in New York City. She had had no problem doing that back then. After just a few questions, the consul had issued her an official new student visa.

On January 3, 2002, Anna traveled by train to the American Consulate in Kraków. It was a three-and-a-half-hour ride from Wrocław. There was a lot of snow throughout Poland and it was extremely cold.

Anna's papers seemed to be in order but, nevertheless, the consul started to question her. The consul's main concern was the change in her visa status, which had been made in the United States. According to the consul, that change of status was now illegal.

That didn't make sense because it was the U.S. Immigration and Naturalization Services that had changed her status. Nothing else had changed with respect to her status from the time Anna had gone through the same process two years earlier, with the exception of the events on 9/11.

In addition, the consul wanted to know more about me and why I was sponsoring her. She was hesitant to answer any questions about me. Certainly, she did not tell the consul we were engaged. I still hadn't told most of my family about our relationship, so Anna was not about to share it with a stranger.

Since 9/11, U.S. Immigration and Naturalization authorities were questioning everything and suspicious of everyone. The consul believed Anna was not being forthright. That, coupled with the change in her visa status, provided the consul with a reason both to deny Anna a student visa and to cancel her tourist visa as well.

Neither Anna nor I ever anticipated there would be a problem renewing her visa. Now what?

Anna texted Greg with the news and he immediately called her. Greg put the receiver to my ear so that I could talk to Anna. It was still early in the morning our time, so I hadn't left for work yet.

As soon as I heard Anna's voice, I knew something was terribly wrong. She told me what had happened at the Consulate. I asked Anna to get me the Consulate's telephone number so that I could call the person she had spoken with to straighten the matter out.

Anna had never gotten the name of the person and didn't have the telephone number of the Consulate. She didn't have any specific information as to why her visa had been denied.

I told her to try to relax and not worry, that I would take care of it. I was confident that if I could speak with the consul on the telephone I would be able to explain Anna's visa status and allay any concerns he might have.

After I hung up with Anna, I called my brother Steve and asked for his advice. He suggested I speak with Howard Brill, an immigration lawyer he knew.

I called Howard and quickly explained our problem. I then arranged to see Howard at his office to discuss it in person. Instead of going to work, I went directly to Howard's office that morning.

Howard asked if Anna had a written document from the Consulate stating the reason her visa had been denied. He said she was entitled to that. It was important to get that document so that we would know exactly what the problem was and what needed to be done to resolve it.

I called Anna from Howard's office. She said she did not have such a document.

Howard told Anna she needed to go back to the Consulate and have them give her a form specifically stating the reason for their denial. He told her that, while she was with the consul, she should answer whatever questions he had about me. Perhaps Anna could convince him to grant her a visa by answering all of his questions. After all, her student visa paperwork specifically listed me as her sponsor.

I told Anna that while she was with the consul, if he still wouldn't grant her a visa to call me so that I could speak to him.

Anna said the Consulate had a rule that, after the denial of a visa, twelve months had to pass before the applicant could reapply. Nevertheless, because she trusted me, she agreed to try again the next day.

Early the next morning, Anna traveled back to Kraków. Again, she had to wait in a long line before she got to speak with another consul. This consul not only denied Anna her student visa, he told her she could not reapply for ten years!

Anna texted Greg and we immediately called her. She sounded very down. She was not surprised that the consul didn't change the decision of the previous day. She said it was hopeless to even try. I was afraid that she was just going to give up. I, on the other hand, did not consider giving up. I desperately wanted Anna back.

I told her not to lose hope, and assured her that I would get her back to the United States.

I spoke to Howard Brill again. Howard indicated that I would need the support of someone who had political clout to intervene on Anna's behalf.

I went to Congresswoman Carolyn McCarthy's local office in Hempstead, Long Island. The congresswoman happened to be in Washington at the time but I was able to speak at length with her aide, Eileen Fitzpatrick. Ms. Fitzpatrick seemed genuinely interested and wanted to help.

I was very open and honest with Ms. Fitzpatrick. I told her that initially Anna had worked for me as my weekend aide but when she had applied for a student visa the previous winter, I became her sponsor. I then showed her the immigration form indicating my sponsorship. I also told her that Anna and I had recently become engaged.

Ms. Fitzpatrick said she would speak with Congresswoman McCarthy and assured me they would try to help us.

I then went to my office and met with my boss, Denis Dillon, the District Attorney. I told him about my relationship with Anna and the problems we were now facing. I asked Denis if there was anything he could do. I knew he would help if he could. As a result, Denis spoke to Congresswoman McCarthy on my behalf.

Congresswoman McCarthy sent a written communication to the Consulate in Poland, vouching for Anna. She probably thought the request was not such a big deal.

The Consulate sent back a scathing reply, indicating that the Consulate believed Anna was not trustworthy and had been deceptive with them. The reply also indicated that they believed Anna's brother Greg intended to remain in the United States in violation of the terms of his visa.

While none of that was true, Congresswoman McCarthy was clearly embarrassed about vouching for Anna and upset with me for putting her in that position. Her office no longer took my calls. They didn't even give me the opportunity to refute the Consulate's allegations.

My friend Peter Shapiro happened to call me at that time to say hello and chat. After I told Peter about Anna's immigration problems he suggested I find an American to marry her.

I told Peter I had already found one: me!

Peter said he was serious.

I told him so was I!

Peter still didn't believe me.

I finally started telling other people that Anna and I were engaged. I am not sure if any of them believed me either.

I don't think Anna's family had any confidence in what I could do about her immigration problem. From their perspective, it was useless trying to fight the American government. Despite that, I told Greg, "I won't stop until I get Anna back."

I called everyone I could think of to help Anna get a visa.

In addition, I got in touch with Senator Edward Kennedy's office in Washington and explained our predicament. I told his

Ken with Greg—2002.

assistant I was sure the senator would remember me because I had testified in 1971 at one of his Senate Subcommittee hearings on health care. I told her that Senator Kennedy had even written about me in his book *In Critical Condition*.

The assistant indicated she would speak to Senator Kennedy and would get back to me within a few days. She called me back later in the week and told me that the senator remembered me and was prepared to help Anna get a fiancée visa. It would take up to six months before she could return to the United States and, under the terms of that visa, when she did return, we would have to get married within sixty days.

It was comforting to know that, as a last resort, I would be able to get Anna back in six months. But six months was a long time. Would our relationship last if we were apart for that long? It would certainly give Anna's family a lot of time to convince Anna to change her mind about marrying a quadriplegic.

I spoke with Anna's teachers at Nassau Community College and explained what was happening. They understood. Most of them had some experience with students who were in Anna's position. Some of those students had not been permitted to come back from their home country following their vacations.

Even the president of the college was very supportive. He wrote a letter to the American Consulate in Kraków on Anna's behalf.

Pressure was mounting, however. Nassau Community College had already started its spring semester. The vice president of the college told me that if Anna missed more than the first two weeks of classes she would not be able to stay enrolled for the spring semester. If that were the case, she would no longer be eligible for a student visa and would not be able to return as a student.

I continued to call everybody I could think of. I spoke with people in the U.S. Justice Department as well as in the U.S. Immigration and Naturalization Services. I called lawyers, judges, and people in every profession I thought might have any chance of helping.

With seemingly no other viable option, Steve suggested that he and I go to Poland to try to get Anna back. Betty and Jay offered to go with us as well.

Once in Poland, we planned to go to the American Consulate with Anna and meet with the consul in person. We were advised by Howard Brill, the immigration attorney, however, that even if we did manage to meet with the consul, it probably would be a fruitless effort.

Steve and I then discussed my marrying Anna while I was in Poland and trying to bring her back as my wife. Howard discouraged that as well. He said that even if I were to marry Anna in Poland they still might not let her back into the United States.

I spoke with Anna by phone every day, sometimes a few times a day, to let her know what was going on. I didn't tell her about half of the things I was doing that had, so far, been unsuccessful. I didn't want her to lose hope.

One of Steve's close friends, Jeff Haas, was friends with Frank Tauches Jr., who had worked for both Senator Chuck Schumer and Senator Hillary Clinton. Jeff got in touch with Frank on my behalf. Frank was the former mayor of Garden City and Chairman of the Water Authority of Western Nassau County. He was also the president of the Marine Corps Reserve Officers Association and knew Carolyn McCarthy personally. Frank was willing to speak to the aides of both senators and the congresswoman on my behalf.

I believed that at that late date, when time was certainly of the essence, Congresswoman McCarthy was still our best hope. I was convinced that, if I could just meet with her in person, I could get the congresswoman back on my side and persuade her to help Anna. Unfortunately, Congresswoman McCarthy was still refusing to even take my calls.

Congresswoman McCarthy had forwarded the Consulate's scathing letter to my boss, Denis Dillon. Dillon was clearly not happy with the position I had put him in with the congresswoman. I knew it was important for me to explain to Dillon that the Consulate's email was filled with inaccuracies, false accusations, and assumptions. I needed to speak with Dillon in person. I wanted him to know that I had been honest with him and the congresswoman.

I arranged to meet with Dillon at the end of the workday. I knew I had an uphill battle on my hands. I went through the Consulate's letter with Dillon, line by line, explaining why each and every one of the Consulate's accusations against Anna was not true. I also showed Dillon the letter from U.S. Immigration and Naturalization Service indicating that I was Anna's sponsor.

I convinced Dillon that I had been honest and straightforward with him. He was now once again on my side, but he wasn't sure whether Congresswoman McCarthy would help me anymore.

The only hope I had left was to have Jeff's friend, Frank, convince Congresswoman McCarthy to meet with me. However, once Congresswoman McCarthy's office became aware that Frank wanted to speak with the congresswoman on my behalf, her office stopped taking Frank's calls as well.

Frank learned that one of the congresswoman's aides was supposed to appear at some type of function connected with the Marine Corps. Frank went to the event and was finally able to persuade the aide to have Congresswoman McCarthy meet with me.

Frank called me immediately. He told me that the congresswoman would see me first thing Monday morning, January 21.

If we didn't get Anna back by the following week, she would have missed two weeks of school and it would then be too late for her to get a student visa.

I thought it would be best if I had Steve with me during the Monday meeting. I knew it would not be a good idea to meet with Congresswoman McCarthy with Anna's brother Greg by my side. The congresswoman might still have had questions about Greg's violating the terms of his visa, even though Greg had had a ticket to fly back to Poland for months by then and had never overstayed his visa or even planned to do so. Just like Anna, he didn't want to risk staying in the United States illegally. He wanted to, someday, come back here for another visit.

When our meeting with Congresswoman McCarthy began, I thanked the congresswoman for meeting with us. I told her all about Anna and then went through the letter from the Consulate, line by line, explaining all the inaccuracies.

Steve told Congresswoman McCarthy a lot about me, as well as about my relationship with Anna. He became emotional while talking about us and how Anna had changed my life.

It took a while before we convinced Congresswoman McCarthy to go to bat for us, once again. She told us, though, that even if the Consulate granted Anna a student visa, there was no guarantee she would be allowed to enter the United States when she arrived at Kennedy Airport.

Steve and I put together a package containing my sponsorship form, a letter from Congresswoman McCarthy, a letter from the president of Nassau Community College indicating how well Anna was doing at school, a letter from Anna's father saying that her parents were hoping that Anna might someday build a house on land they were giving her in Żórawina, Poland, and a letter from Steve. We then faxed the package to the Consulate in Kraków.

A couple of days later, the U.S. General Consulate in Kraków finally agreed to grant Anna the student visa!

I was now able to call Anna and tell her the good news. I asked her to go to Kraków for the third time. I arranged for her to receive the same fax we had sent to the Consulate, including Congresswoman McCarthy's letter, so that Anna would have everything with her for her meeting in Kraków. I also wanted Anna to have it with her for her meeting with the immigration officer at the airport upon her arrival in New York.

Anna went to Kraków on January 24. This time, there were very few questions. It was just a formality.

Once Anna returned to Wrocław, she started looking for a flight back to the United States. The closest airport at which she could get a flight on such short notice was in Berlin, Germany, approximately 220 miles from her parents' home. Anna's father and her sister Alina drove her there.

According to Anna, most of the four-hour drive to Berlin was made in silence. Everyone was too emotional to talk. It was a bittersweet trip for the three of them. Kazik and Alina knew that once Anna left she would not be able to return to Poland for a very long time.

On Tuesday afternoon, January 29, Greg and I anxiously awaited Anna's arrival at the airport. I was growing more and more concerned the longer we waited.

As we had all feared would happen, an immigration officer at Kennedy Airport detained Anna. Information indicating that Anna had been denied a student visa during her visit to the Consulate on January 4 remained in the computer system, even though she had been granted a new visa by the American Consulate in Kraków on January 24.

Anna was held in a pen with other passengers who had immigration problems. There was still a real possibility that she would be sent right back to Poland.

It took more than an hour before she was able to speak with an immigration supervisor. The supervisor questioned the legality of her visa. It was a good thing Anna had with her all the documents I had faxed. She showed the supervisor Congresswoman McCarthy's letter, which explained everything. That did it! Anna's passport was finally stamped. She was now free to get her luggage and meet Greg and me.

When I saw Anna, she seemed cold and distant. She never had been one to show much affection in public. Still, I wasn't sure if her feelings about me had changed. She told me that she was

Ken and Anna, together again—2002.

extremely upset with the treatment she had received in the airport. The stress of the previous weeks was weighing heavily on her as well. She looked exhausted. I knew I had to let her unwind. I had to be patient a little longer.

Fortunately, after Greg left my apartment the next day, and we were finally alone, Anna made it "clear" that her feelings toward me hadn't changed. Our relationship quickly resumed the way it had been, perhaps even better.

Chapter 27

In Sickness and In Health, Rain or Shine

◆ ◆ ◆

Over the next few weeks, Anna shared with me some of her parents' concerns about our plans to marry. I thought it appropriate to send them the following letter:

February 19, 2002

Dear Mr. and Mrs. Błażejczyk,

I am writing to tell you how wonderful it is for Anna and me to be together again.

I really appreciate the support and encouragement you provided throughout the stressful weeks during which we were working on the renewal of Anna's visa.

It is exactly three weeks since she flew back to the States and our lives have finally returned to normal. Anna continues to do extremely well in school. I am able, once again, to give full attention to my work in the District Attorney's Office, and we are enjoying our leisure time together.

I miss Greg, who I have come to regard as a friend, and am truly grateful for all his help while he was in this country.

Anna and I continue to hope that you will visit us in the United States sometime soon. I look forward to meeting and getting to know you. I am certain that, when we are able to spend some time together, you will feel comfortable giving our relationship your blessing ... something that is very important to both Anna and me.

I hope that Mrs. Błażejczyk continues to progress in her recovery and will be able to resume full activity very soon.

My very best wishes,

Ken

◆ ◆ ◆

Months after our engagement, we still hadn't told most of our friends and family about it. Many didn't even realize that Anna and I were in a relationship other than her being my aide.

In June 2002, my father came to Long Island to celebrate his eightieth birthday and Father's Day with the family, which happened to fall on the same day that year. Jill offered to have a party for him at her new house in Amagansett. At the party, almost in passing, my father mentioned something about Anna and me getting married. Not everybody present knew about it, so the news made quite a stir.

My father's reveal during his party pushed us into a more serious planning mode.

First, Anna and I had decided that our wedding would take place sometime in June 2003, after Anna's graduation from Nassau Community College. We would have more than a year to think through all the plans.

Second, Anna found a Polish priest to perform the ceremony. She was certain that her parents would appreciate that. The priest, Robert Kuźnik, resided in a parish in Baldwin, which was only a few miles from our home in Rockville Centre.

Anna arranged for Father Kuźnik to come to our condo to speak with us. When I first met him, I was not very impressed, to say the least. He arrived dressed in blue jeans and looked about as far from a priest as I could imagine. I asked him some questions about his background and learned that before he went into the priesthood he had worked as a car mechanic. Now while car mechanics are highly skilled in their field, I had trouble visualizing one officiating our wedding.

Furthermore, during our conversation Father Kuźnik told us that while he had been studying in the seminary, one of his fellow students, a quadriplegic, had needed a lot of physical help. Father Kuźnik went on to say he had quickly grown tired of providing assistance for his paralyzed colleague. He felt it was an enormous burden. I couldn't believe the priest was saying this to me, and in front of Anna, no less.

Once we had arranged for the priest, Anna and I began speaking with my family about where and when our wedding should take place. My brother suggested that we hold our wedding reception outdoors, in a tent next to his house in Huntington Bay. The reception could take place in a large field, across the street from the bay. That sounded like a great idea.

My friend Debbie suggested holding the ceremony at the Interfaith Chapel at CW Post College in Brookville, with her cantor, Herb Strauss, participating along with the priest.

We decided our wedding would take place on June 14, 2003.

◆ ◆ ◆

That fall, as Halloween was approaching, Anna said that, rather than me continuing to get depressed every year on that date, we should do something nice together to celebrate it instead. After all, if not for my injury, Anna and I never would have met. So, on October 31, 2002, we went to see *Les Miserables* on Broadway.

We took a train to Penn Station and then walked to the theater. I have never liked spending time in New York City and this day only confirmed my long-held beliefs that there are a lot of crazy people there. I saw one group of strange looking individuals after another. I couldn't believe how they were dressed. It took me a while before I realized that many of them were dressed in Halloween costumes. I had forgotten what day it was. I guess Anna's attempt to take my mind off the date was working.

♦ ♦ ♦

For the first time in fifteen years, I did not spend Christmas in Atlantic City. Clearly, it was time to recognize that my fiancée was Catholic and preferred not to celebrate the holiday at the craps tables.

Anna bought a Christmas tree and put it up in the corner of our apartment. My sister Meryl and my nephew Jeffrey came over to help decorate it. Being Jewish, they had never had the opportunity to do that before. They really enjoyed it and had even brought over some new ornaments for the tree. I suggested having holiday music playing, as I remembered Betsy had during the Christmas I spent with her family in 1971. It was a wonderful way for everyone to get into the spirit of the season.

Anna missed celebrating Christmas the Polish way, so she decided to prepare Wigilia, the traditional Polish Christmas Eve dinner for family and friends. Counting Anna and me, we had thirty-two people over that first Christmas Eve. That included Betty and Jay, who decided to forgo Atlantic City to celebrate with us. Somehow, Anna was able to pull off having a sit-down dinner in our apartment.

We decided to still visit Betty and Jay in New Jersey a few days later. Jay and I managed to squeeze in a quick day trip to Atlantic City to uphold our special Jewish celebration of the Christmas holiday.

In January 2003, Anna and I traveled to Florida to attend my friend Dave Paldy's wedding. We visited with my father in Orlando and spent some time in Key West.

While in Orlando, my father showed me my mother Judy's wedding ring. It was a beautiful platinum ring, with a rectangular design on the outside and the inscription inside: "LYK to JMG June 29 1947." LYK were my father's initials, Leonard Yale Kunken, and JMG were my mother's, Judith Mae Goldblatt. My father suggested I give my mother's wedding ring to Anna as her wedding ring.

I was very moved by his gesture.

I was surprised that my father had kept that ring for more than fifty years. I had never seen it before. I hadn't known that he still had it. Only now did he decide to part with it.

Anna felt especially honored to be able to wear my mother's ring. We later had a jeweler squeeze in the additional inscription, "KJK to AB, 6-14-2003," inside the band.

Staying in Key West with Anna was like an early honeymoon. One evening it became particularly chilly, at least for me, so I wore my down vest, two neck warmers, a winter hat, and mittens. I was, without a doubt, the only person in the Keys dressed that way. Anna and I dined outside at a nice casual restaurant. I must have looked very strange and out of place, all bundled up, surrounded by tropical flowers. Anna sat beside me, feeding me a delicious seafood dinner.

A man sitting at a neighboring table watched us the entire time. We tried not to pay much attention to him. When he finished his meal and paid his check, he came over to us, smiled, and said, "This must be what unconditional love looks like."

Anna and Ken in Florida—January 2003.

I guess it was hard for anyone to comprehend how a beautiful woman such as Anna could love somebody in my condition. He could tell by the way Anna fed me and by the way we looked at each other. Only unconditional love could account for it.

Our second Florida trip together was very different than our first one three years earlier had been. The biggest difference was the change in our relationship. There was absolutely no tension. Anna trusted me and I trusted her. There was a certain magic, a certain chemistry between us. It seemed like a match made in heaven. The man who made the comment in Key West saw that as well.

♦ ♦ ♦

Two weeks before the wedding, I developed a small bedsore. I stayed in bed from June 3 to June 6, hoping it would heal before the big day.

On one of those days, Anna and I tried to write our marriage vows. We were having a lot of difficulty with it. Finally, Anna took out a small book that I had given to her for her birthday the year before. It had a lot of nice quotations in it. We went through the book a number of times, and found many appropriate lines that either Anna or I could use in our vows. After a lot of cutting and pasting, we each came up with something meaningful to say.

Anna's parents and brother came to the United States a few days before the wedding. My first meeting with Teresa and Kazik was very formal, but it went about as well as I suppose it could be expected to. Anna and Greg took turns translating. I was nervous and uncomfortable. I knew that no matter how open-minded Anna's parents were, it would be hard for them to be happy about their daughter marrying me.

On June 14, we arrived early at the Interfaith Chapel to have pictures taken. It was the first time I saw Anna in her wedding dress. She was gorgeous. The dress was beautiful too.

Shortly before the ceremony, Anna and I went outside so that her father could give us his blessing. Clearly, it was very meaningful for both Kazik and Anna. To me, it meant that Kazik accepted

Teresa, Anna, Ken, Kazik, and Jill in Montauk, a week after
the wedding—June 2003.

and approved of our marriage. From that moment on, I was an
integral part of the Błażejczyk family.

However, I desperately needed to be catheterized. I was sweating profusely from my full bladder and already feeling miserable.
I couldn't find Steve or my current attendant, Jarek, to help me.
I needed Anna, in her white wedding dress, makeup and all, to
catheterize me as soon as possible.

There was no private accessible room for me inside the chapel
though. The only area in which Anna could do the catheter was

just to the left of the chapel entrance, which was awkward because our guests were still arriving. I turned around so that at least my back would be to the parking lot. I had 1,000 cc of urine in my bladder. I don't know why it did not burst.

It had rained every day for two straight weeks prior to the event but the sun actually shone brightly during the wedding ceremony, which was performed in three languages: Polish, English, and Hebrew. The cantor and the priest worked together very well. Despite my having some concerns about our Polish priest, he impressed me not only with his speech about marriage but with his professionalism in general.

I read my vows from two pieces of paper, which were stapled to a folder Steve held for me, then Anna read hers. In the middle of it, Anna became very emotional. We were later told that most of the guests were tearing up as well.

The cantor was about to end the ceremony when I reminded him that I still needed to break the glass. Breaking a wine glass during the wedding ceremony is part of the Jewish tradition. Usually, the groom stomps on the glass with his foot. Instead, I rolled my chair over a light bulb wrapped in a bag. The sound of the bulb shattering was clear and loud, an effective ending to our ceremony.

The entire event was very moving for us, as well as for the 200 guests in attendance.

When you hold an event outdoors, you always run the risk of bad weather. Two straight weeks of rain had made the grounds in and around the reception tent into a mudhole. On the morning of the wedding, one of Steve's neighbors went to the village of Huntington and bought all the flip-flops he could find. He put two big baskets full of them next to the entrance to the tent. Many of the women took off their beautiful high-heeled shoes and wore the flip-flops during the reception, which worked out very well. The flip-flops have been a source of conversation every time someone talks about our wedding.

We had a great five-piece band playing that afternoon. We asked them to play "A Love Until the End of Time" for our first dance. They learned it especially for our wedding. For the dance,

First dance—June 14, 2003.

Anna sat on my lap and I wheeled both of us around the dance floor. I was told there was not a dry eye in the house.

Unfortunately, Anna had no opportunity to dance with her father that day. She has always regretted that.

A lot of people made toasts and, at the end, I delivered mine in Polish. Everyone was surprised, including Anna, who had no clue I was going to do that.

In the middle of the reception the skies opened up and it poured. Regardless, everyone said it was "the wedding of the century." In spite of the rain and a few mishaps caused by it, it was perfect.

Mr. and Mrs. Ken Kunken—June 14, 2003.

Chapter 28

The Miracle of Science

◆ ◆ ◆

Anna and I were now ready to tackle our biggest challenge: making a baby!

Back in September 2002, Anna had attended the Miami Project's annual research update at the Waldorf Astoria in New York City. She had wanted to learn more about their fertility program for people with spinal cord injuries. The Project offered some hope that even a man in my condition could still father a child.

After learning more, Anna and I decided to pursue in vitro fertilization (IVF).

I spoke on the phone with a woman at the fertility clinic in Miami. She sent me some information about sperm retrieval, as well as the names of a few male fertility doctors in the tri-state area, one of whom was Dr. Bruce Gilbert, a urologist very well known in that field. He had an office in Great Neck, approximately forty-five minutes from our home.

Anna and I had our first appointment with Dr. Gilbert on December 16, 2002. The doctor went through my medical history, did a physical examination, took a blood sample, and asked me to provide a urine sample. During that initial visit, I met Dr. Gilbert's nurse Tom, who was very adept at assisting the doctor. The two of them exuded a sense of confidence that made Anna and me feel encouraged about our chances.

I was concerned that, as a result of my numerous past urinary tract infections, the passageways might be clogged permanently and there would be no way for the sperm to be released. The doctor told us that, if viable sperm could not be retrieved through electro ejaculation, it could still be collected directly from my testes by way of a minor surgical procedure. All that is needed to fertilize an egg is one healthy sperm, he said. After examining me and reviewing the test results, Dr. Gilbert was optimistic about my chances of fathering a child.

Anna and I had decided to wait until after we were married to go through with the procedure. It just didn't feel right to try to conceive a baby before our wedding.

In addition, it would give Anna and me more time to enjoy each other's company and make whatever arrangements we needed to make. We didn't really know how long the entire process would take.

More than six months passed between our initial meeting with Dr. Gilbert in December and our next visit. It gave me the opportunity to think a lot about the whole business of starting a family.

While I knew Anna wanted to have a baby, and Anna's mother really wanted Anna to experience the joys of motherhood, I would have been content to keep things the way they were—just Anna and me. For the past four years, I had been happiest when Anna and I were alone together. Why change that? I knew that once we had a child, everything would be different. I would have to share Anna with someone else, even if that "someone" would be the cutest baby ever.

In addition, just like my original reservations about marriage, I felt it would be unfair for a child to have a severely disabled father who could do very little physically with him or her. I would never be able to have a catch with my son or dance with my daughter. I would not be able to hold him or her when he or she cried, or protect my child in times of danger. In essence, Anna would have to raise the child practically by herself. What kind of parent could I possibly be?

While I had many questions and reservations about being a father, I had no doubts that Anna would be a great mother. I wanted that to happen, so I was ready to try, if not for my own sake, to make Anna happy. It didn't take long before I, too, started to become excited about seeing a little Kunken running around our home.

With the exception of her family in Poland, Anna and I decided not to tell anybody that we were even thinking about having a baby, much less that we were actually in the process of trying to make it happen. We did not want to raise anyone's hopes or run the risk of having anyone try to diminish ours.

I decided to have the sperm retrieval procedure take place on my birthday, July 15. After all, what better present could I hope to get on that day?

Early in the morning of the 15th, Anna and I went to Dr. Gilbert's office. Anna and Tom, Dr. Gilbert's nurse, laid me on the table. An IV was inserted into my arm in case I needed medication to regulate my blood pressure. I was turned onto my side and a special device was inserted into my rectum. An electric current was then applied. It soon became very uncomfortable. My blood pressure must have gone sky high. The current finally caused me to ejaculate.

Tom took the specimen to their office laboratory and examined it under a microscope. Sure enough, there were some sperm, but they were not motile enough to fertilize an egg.

Despite the outcome, Dr. Gilbert remained optimistic. In time, he said, my body might actually start producing new, hopefully viable, sperm.

Anna and I were very excited when we left the doctor's office. It was great news that my sperm could still be extracted. We were convinced that our next attempt would be successful.

Dr. Gilbert suggested that we wait a week and try electro ejaculation again, but to do the next procedure in North Shore Hospital in Manhasset. The doctor was concerned that I would get dysreflexic and that my blood pressure might go dangerously high. That condition could be more easily controlled in the hospital.

On July 21, I was even more anxious before the procedure in the hospital than I had been in Dr. Gilbert's office. Now, it was feeling more like surgery.

The electro ejaculation was repeated. This time, after examining the specimen under a microscope, Tom said that the retrieved sperm was not motile at all. I was disappointed. I had been expecting more positive results.

Dr. Gilbert told me not to worry. He was still sure he could retrieve viable sperm through surgery. I asked if we could try the electro ejaculation one more time. If it was not successful, I pleaded, then we could do the surgery. Dr. Gilbert agreed.

I certainly did not want to have surgery on my scrotum unless it was our last and only hope for success. Although I do not have actual sensation below my chest, harsh contact with my scrotum and testicles is still extremely painful and causes violent spasms.

However, I was determined to do whatever it took for Anna to get pregnant. I am sure that, when most husbands think about "making a baby," they daydream about a romantic experience that both partners enjoy in the moment and recall later as having been blissful. So far, I had gone through two very uncomfortable procedures, was about to go through a third, and probably was going to end up under the knife. Not exactly my dream.

The procedure, and possible surgery, was scheduled to take place at the outpatient surgical unit of North Shore Hospital. While Anna had been present with me for the other two procedures, on August 1, she would not be permitted inside the operating room. It felt strange for me to do my part without Anna even being in the same room.

One of the nurses asked Anna to remove my wedding ring, in case the IV caused my finger to swell. I asked to keep my ring on so that I could, at least, feel that part of Anna present with me. The nurse hesitantly agreed and let me keep it. Once inside the room, electro ejaculation was tried for a third time. Unfortunately, no motile sperm was retrieved.

Dr. Gilbert and I had previously discussed whether I would need anesthesia for the surgery. Anesthesia could be dangerous for me because I had a severe case of sleep apnea. I could simply stop breathing. I did not want to be put to sleep unless it was absolutely necessary. I also did not want to take the risk of being intubated.

An IV was inserted into my arm. Dr. Gilbert applied some topical anesthetic to my scrotum and soon began cutting along the seam. My body started spasming like crazy. The spasming was incredibly painful. It felt as though a strong electric shock was being applied to my genitals.

During the surgery, Dr. Gilbert was able to extract some sperm-producing tissue from the testes. He then stitched the scrotum back together and applied a dressing. The procedure itself was not that difficult for the doctor, but for me it was brutal. When it was finally over, I was totally drained.

Now, I anxiously awaited the results.

Tom analyzed the tissue right away. There was plenty of viable sperm, enough to fertilize more than one egg. I was very relieved.

For now, though, the sperm would be kept in Dr. Gilbert's freezer. When I heard that, I started to worry. What if there was a power failure? The doctor assured me that, even in the event of a power failure, the sperm would remain frozen for at least a month. Therefore, according to the doctor, I had nothing to worry about. I worried nevertheless. I didn't want to go through that surgery a second time.

With the exception of a short vacation in Great Barrington, Anna and I had spent most of August focusing on me healing and planning for our upcoming honeymoon trip: driving across the country to California and back. We decided to wait until after the trip for Anna to go through her IVF procedure.

Now was the time for us to enjoy ourselves. We intended to use every minute to make as many great memories as possible. If Anna were to get pregnant right away, it might be a long time before we again had the opportunity to go away.

Anna and I had been living together for two years. Because I was working full time, I would go to the office every day during the week. As a result, during part of each day Anna and I were apart. We had a chance to do our own thing and miss each other. Not a bad arrangement in a relationship. Now we were going to

Beginning of our cross-country trip—August 30, 2003.

spend an entire four weeks together, cramped in a van most of that time. What if we got tired of each other's company after two weeks?

As it turned out, Anna had the same concerns. What if we discovered, during our honeymoon, that we didn't like spending that much time together? What if, somewhere in Arizona, we found that we had absolutely nothing left to talk about? The whole trip might turn out to be one big fiasco.

On the other hand, I knew that, ever since I had met Anna, I had wanted to spend as much time alone with her as possible. So far, I couldn't get enough of her company. I missed her terribly while I was at my office. I was still hopelessly in love.

Once the trip started on August 30, my worries evaporated. Just having Anna beside me in the car was reassuring enough for me that I felt safe and happy.

We traveled through twenty-two states, driving 9,101 miles, and wished we had even more time to explore the country. Some-day, hopefully, we would be able to go back on the road, with a

At the Grand Canyon—September 12, 2003.

child in the back seat. We knew that the destinations then would be very different.

♦ ♦ ♦

Anna decided to have her part of the IVF done at the Center for Reproductive Medicine and Infertility in New York City, which was a part of the New York Presbyterian Hospital–Weill Medical College of Cornell University.

Choosing that group guaranteed there would be no co-payments for most of Anna's procedures. However, there was a $25,000 lifetime spending limit for the fertility treatments. That limit would be enough to cover no more than two IVF cycles.

Anna scheduled an initial visit with Dr. Goldschlag, one of the doctors associated with Weill Medical College, for October 8, 2003. Dr. Goldschlag had a second office in Hewlett, about fifteen minutes from our home.

During that first visit with Dr. Goldschlag, Anna underwent some routine examinations. A series of tests were then scheduled.

On February 10, we met with Dr. Goldschlag's nurse for an hour-long lecture concerning all aspects of the procedures Anna was about to undergo. The whole IVF process seemed overwhelming to me. There were so many different things Anna would have to do, and, unfortunately, I would not be able to help her with any of them. She needed to keep track of many different components. There were medications she would have to inject herself with, sometimes at very precise times. The dosage of the medications would be constantly changing. The nurse completely lost me about two minutes into her lecture. Fortunately, Anna did pay attention. Later she explained everything to me as she was going through it.

For the first few weeks of her IVF cycle, she went to Dr. Goldschlag's Hewlett office to have her blood drawn. Sometimes they would also do a sonogram. The same afternoon, Anna would receive a phone call from the nurse with instructions about the dosage for the next hormone injection and the plan for the next day.

Starting on May 31, hormone treatments became more intensive. She had to go for more frequent blood tests and sonograms of her ovaries. She started to feel the effects of the treatments. She became weaker, lost weight, and was tiring more easily.

In June, Anna was told that she had to go to the Center for Reproductive Medicine in Manhattan for her daily checkups. She had to get me up very early every day so that she could get to New York City before 9 a.m. She was still giving me a shower every morning, after which my attendant, Jarek, would come and finish dressing me. Jarek would then take me to work while Anna would drive to the City in our spare van.

Not everything went smoothly. One day, after Anna received her daily phone call, she called me at my office and told me her hormone levels were too high. The doctors were afraid they were overstimulating her. That could cause problems in the future.

A nurse advised Anna to significantly change the dosage of the hormones she was injecting herself with. If her hormone levels did not improve by the next day, she was to stop her IVF cycle altogether.

That would mean that the last month of grueling treatments had all been for nothing. Anna would then have to take a break for about three months and start a new cycle from the beginning, including sonograms, blood tests, injections, and daily trips to Hewlett or Manhattan.

Who would have guessed that we might not be able to have our own biological child because of Anna's fertility problems, not mine?

Maybe it was our positive thinking, or just that Anna's doctors were more skilled than we thought, but the next morning, her hormone levels stabilized, giving her the green light to continue with the present cycle.

While all of this was going on, Anna was getting our second bedroom ready for the baby's arrival. The room needed a fresh coat of paint. Unfortunately, Anna was not as strong as she had been before the hormone treatments began. While painting the room, she developed a cold, and possibly strep throat, but decided not to take any medication to treat it. She worried it might affect her fertility treatments. The infection, on top of the hormone treatments, had a strong effect on her.

One afternoon, Anna took a load of laundry from the drier to our bedroom to fold. I was set up with the TV remote in the den. Sometime later I heard sobbing. I called Anna, but she didn't respond. I went to the bedroom and found her crying uncontrollably. She couldn't even explain what was bothering her. She was inconsolable.

I knew she needed a hug and a shoulder to lean on, but Anna was sick. If she were to get too close to me, I might get sick as well, which would make things even more difficult for us. So she clung to my legs instead and continued to sob for the next twenty minutes or so.

I had never seen Anna fall apart. I tried to stay calm and not make the situation worse. I kept assuring her that it was probably just her sky-high hormone levels that were affecting her.

Ken's father and sister just learned Ken and Anna were planning
to become parents—June 6, 2004.

Later, after Anna finally calmed down, she was embarrassed
about losing control. She said she had felt so miserable that she just
could not stop crying.

It never happened again, at least not in front of me.

Near the end of May, my father came to visit. As always, he
stayed with us in our condo. We decided to share the news about
our plans to have a child with my father and my sister Meryl at the
same time. When Meryl came to our condo on June 6, I told them
both what we were up to.

They were surprised, to say the least. Like most people, they
hadn't believed it would even be possible for me to father a child.

Meryl was very excited for us. Right from the start, my sister
asked if there was any way that she could help. At the moment,
there was none.

As happy as my father was that I might be able to have a
child, he kept asking if the baby would really be mine. He then

started asking questions about who would take care of me if Anna got pregnant. As always, he worried about finances.

♦ ♦ ♦

On June 7, Anna's sister Alina came from Poland to visit. I had never met Alina before. She wasn't able to come for our wedding, having given birth to her second son only six months earlier.

The following day, Anna told me that from that point on she would not be able to continue taking care of me as she had before. Weeks of hormone treatments had taken a toll on her. Lifting me into the wheelchair or giving me a shower would no longer be possible, at least for the time being.

The treatments made her produce more eggs than typically would occur during her menstrual cycle. Instead of just a few eggs in different stages of development, her sonograms were showing more than thirty "ripening" eggs there, all big and almost ready to be fertilized. Although Anna lost some weight, her belly was bigger and more tender than usual due to her enlarged ovaries. It was very painful when anything pressed against it.

My aide Jarek had been with us since 2002. He spent one night with me every week so that Anna was able to have at least one good night's sleep. After the end of 2003, Jarek took care of me two days a week.

Normally, on Tuesdays Jarek would pick me up from my office to begin his two-day shift. Now we asked him to help me full time, for at least the next couple of weeks.

On Wednesday evening Anna's injection needed to be done at a precise time, which would determine when the eggs retrieval would take place. The next day, June 10, 2004, we went to Cornell Weill for the procedure.

Anna was given general anesthesia for the retrieval. She doesn't remember much about the experience, other than feeling nauseous and uncomfortable. While we were driving home on the Cross Island Parkway, Anna told Jarek to pull over as soon as possible. Jarek stopped the car on the side of the busy highway. Anna quickly got out of the van and threw up. She then lay down on the grass by the van, feeling very dizzy.

A police car pulled off the road and an officer asked what was going on. Jarek spoke with him and the policeman left.

I felt terrible not being able to help Anna. I knew that the whole process was very hard on her even though she had tried to make it look easy up to that point. I hadn't fully realized how miserable she actually felt. I didn't like seeing Anna go through that ordeal. Maybe having children was not such a good idea for us.

We had to wait until the next day, June 11, to find out the results of the retrieval procedure. Anna stayed home, resting. She got a phone call from a nurse at around 3 p.m. and promptly called me at my office to tell me the news.

Twenty-six follicles (eggs) were retrieved from Anna's ovaries, sixteen of which appeared to be ready to be fertilized. Soon, though, four of those sixteen were no longer viable. The fertility team tried to fertilize the remaining twelve. Of those, only six continued to develop and multiply in a Petri dish in the lab.

I was very excited to hear that. We hadn't expected Anna to have so many follicles. When we learned the fertility team had fertilized six of them, we were confident that at least one would result in a pregnancy. I was hoping for twins. I did not want Anna to have to go through this whole process again, even if it meant that our baby would not have a sibling.

The date on which the embryos would be implanted hadn't been set yet. It would depend on how well they were developing. It might be three or even five days after the retrieval took place. We later received a call telling us that the implantation would take place on the third day.

On Sunday, June 13, we went to New York City so that Anna could undergo the procedure. We sat in the waiting room with other couples that were scheduled to have the same procedure done that day. At some point, we started to talk with one of those couples. It turned out that they had gone through the IVF cycle six times already, without getting pregnant.

Just before the procedure, Dr. Goldschlag took Anna and me aside, saying that he needed to talk with us. I was worried that there was already a problem with the embryos.

Dr. Goldschlag told us that everything was fine. He said three of our six embryos had developed enough to be implanted. Usually they do not implant more than two at a time but, in our case, Dr. Goldschlag recommended that we implant all three. He indicated that there was no guarantee that even one of them would "take." Implanting three would increase the odds that at least one would succeed.

Because we had been hoping for twins, implanting three seemed to make sense. Dr. Goldschlag told us, though, that it was possible that all three might take but that the odds of that happening were very small. He also said that, once the embryos were implanted, they could conceivably split. We might actually end up with six, although the odds of that happening were minuscule.

I resented the fact that Dr. Goldschlag hadn't given us much time to decide. He'd confronted us with that big decision just minutes before the implantation.

Dr. Goldschlag stood right beside us as Anna and I looked at each other, bewildered. We agreed to implant all three embryos, still hoping for twins.

Anna was then ushered in to an adjacent room. I was told to go back to the waiting room. It didn't feel right to me. I wanted to be with my wife while she was trying to get pregnant.

After a long fifteen minutes I joined Anna, who was lying in a bed, holding a picture in her hand. It was a photo of the three embryos that had just been implanted in her uterus.

It felt strange to look at them. Each embryo was made up of no more than six or seven cells. They didn't look like much of anything. It was hard to imagine that one of those small clumps of cells might actually become our son or daughter. I certainly didn't feel any attachment to them at the time.

The next day, June 14, our first wedding anniversary, I took the day off from work. In the morning, after Jarek left, I spent a couple of hours alone in the den, while Anna was in her room.

When she finally joined me, she was holding a sheet of paper in her hand. She had written a letter to me as a present for our wedding anniversary. In the letter Anna expressed her appreciation for everything I had done for her during the past year and for all the wonderful things we had done together. Not surprisingly, going through my sperm retrieval and her IVF procedures were at the top of the list.

The embryo implantation was the culmination of a long, and not always pleasant process. We had given it our best shot and now could only sit back, wait and hope.

As luck would have it, Anna and I were scheduled to conduct our interview with the Immigration and Naturalization Services concerning Anna's application for a green card, two days after the implantation procedure.

All the interviews took place on the second floor of an office building in Garden City. The building did not have an elevator. We were told that we had to wait until an immigration officer was able to come downstairs and interview us in one of the back rooms on the first floor. We were kept waiting for over an hour before a female officer finally came down.

As soon as we entered the interview room, the woman told us that she would not be able to make a decision that day. Apparently, there was a second immigration file on Anna somewhere in the system, which the officer did not have access to.

My heart dropped at the news. I knew the immigration officer was referring to the file Immigration had had on Anna when the American Consulate in Kraków would not grant her a visa in January 2002.

I could not believe that two and a half years later that was still going to be a problem. I had hoped it had all been resolved when Congresswoman Carolyn McCarthy had intervened on our behalf. Apparently, once there is an issue it remains in the system forever.

The immigration officer then proceeded with her questions.

We left the interview disappointed that there were still more hurdles to overcome for Anna to get a green card. We also had no idea how much longer it would take before we would get another interview, if there was going to be one.

◆ ◆ ◆

The blood test to check whether Anna was pregnant was scheduled for July 1. After the pregnancy test, Anna and Alina went to the Brooklyn Botanic Garden.

The nurse promised to call Anna in the afternoon with the results. Anna had planned to be out of the apartment the whole day, so she asked the nurse to call her cell phone.

At some point, I decided to check the messages on our home answering machine to see if the nurse had left a message there. I called home, dialed the code, and a message came up.

A nurse from Cornell Weill Medical Center, very matter-of-factly, left a message for Anna stating that her test was positive.

I was fairly sure, but not absolutely certain, that the message meant that Anna was pregnant. I was very excited and called Anna with the news. When Anna answered the phone, I said, "Congrat-ulations, you are pregnant!" I heard Anna say something to Alina and then heard them both started screaming.

Now that we knew we were pregnant, the question in both our minds was, "Pregnant, but with how many?"

Chapter 29

Pushing the Limits

♦ ♦ ♦

On July 9, Anna was scheduled to have her first sonogram since we had learned she was pregnant. This would be the first time I would see a sonogram performed, and it would tell us if *we* were, hopefully, pregnant with twins.

I stayed close to Anna but directed my attention to the monitor.

Almost as soon as Dr. Goldschlag began, he said, "Here is a sack."

Apparently, a sack meant a baby. It was very strange to be looking at something so small and thinking that this would be my child.

Within seconds, the doctor said, "Here is another sack."

"Jackpot!" I thought, "Twins!"

Almost immediately, the doctor said, very matter-of-factly, "Here is another sack."

"Oh, my God, triplets!"

As I was about to congratulate Anna, I saw the doctor was still moving the device around. It suddenly became clear to me that he was looking for more sacks.

My mind immediately started racing back to the day of the implantation. Dr. Goldschlag had warned us then that the embryos might split and we could conceivably end up with six.

I wanted to tell him to stop—three was plenty. I was relieved when he finally did. It was definite. We were pregnant with triplets. Our life would never be the same.

Anna and I looked at each other incredulously. Was this really happening?

I hesitantly asked Anna how she felt about it.

"Great!" she replied.

I was sorry I had agreed to go to work immediately after the visit, instead of spending the rest of the day with Anna.

While we were in the van, we called Steve, my father, Aunt Lorraine, and Aunt Betty. Every one of our conversations went something like this:

"We just finished the sonogram. We are having more than one."

They each excitedly said, "Twins?"

"Keep going." I replied.

There was dead silence, followed by, "What do you mean?"

"Triplets!" I exclaimed.

Everyone was speechless.

My father immediately started raising concerns and questions about the pregnancy and how we were going to manage. I was not surprised, although I had been hoping for a more positive reaction. Quite frankly, I hadn't the faintest idea how we were going to manage. I couldn't picture what it would be like to have triplets. I had never even seen triplets before.

◆ ◆ ◆

It was a high-risk pregnancy. According to Dr. Goldschlag, anything might happen. Anna could lose one or more of the babies early on. There was the possibility of ending up with none.

For now, we decided to take it one day at a time. We still hadn't told most of our family and friends that Anna was even pregnant. We wanted to make sure Anna made it through the first three months without any complications.

There were so many things Anna and I had to think about. We immediately needed to arrange for a full-time attendant for me. It was an absolute necessity now.

Fortunately, Jarek, who had another job during the day working at a pharmacy, promised to stay with me every night for as long as we needed him. He wanted to earn extra money, so this would be a good situation for him as well. He assured us he would let us know if it became too difficult.

Suddenly, our spacious condo seemed too small. How were we going to fit three babies, my aide, and Anna and me in our two bedrooms? We immediately canceled the new couch we had recently ordered. There would be no way we could fit the couch and three cribs into the second bedroom.

I started reading the book *What to Expect When You're Expecting*. In addition, Steve gave me a book about becoming a dad.

By this time, I was looking forward to becoming a father. I felt frustrated though, because I was unable to do anything to help Anna during the pregnancy. What would I be able to do to assist her after the babies were born?

During the next two weeks, I did not see any physical changes that would even hint Anna was pregnant. I expected her to start having morning sickness, showing a bit of a baby bump, and gaining weight. If anything, she lost weight. I was starting to worry. Maybe she had lost the babies sometime after the last sonogram. She did have a glow about her though, and looked more beautiful than ever.

We had another visit scheduled with Dr. Goldschlag on July 23. During that visit, we heard the babies' heartbeats for the first time. They were strong and beating rapidly. It was thrilling. All three babies were still there, and healthy. Thank goodness!

Near the end of that visit, Dr. Goldschlag told us that his involvement would now be ending. We needed to look for an OB/GYN group that specialized in high-risk pregnancies.

Anna made an appointment for August 5 with the Division of Maternal Fetal Medicine in Great Neck. We met with Dr. Smith-Levitin, who talked to us for an hour about all the risks and dangers of carrying triplets. There were many.

Anna's health, as well as her life itself, could be put in serious jeopardy. As a result of possible complications, she might become permanently disabled.

Even if Anna was fortunate enough to carry all three, triplets were always born prematurely. That would also increase the risk of birth defects. And Anna's age was a factor as well. She had turned thirty-five three days earlier.

If everything went perfectly and Anna gave birth to healthy triplets, there would still be plenty of problems caring for them. There would be more babies than Anna had arms. Because I would not be able to help physically, we would always need additional help. Obviously, the costs of raising triplets would be extremely high, right through and including college.

Dr. Smith-Levitin told us we should seriously think about reducing the pregnancy. Anna and I both sat there, listening in silence. At the end of the hour-long lecture, the doctor left us alone for a few minutes so that we could talk about what we had just heard.

I told Anna I would support her in whatever decision she made but I felt it should be her decision. It was her body, her health, and possibly, her life. I also told Anna that concerns about money should not be a factor.

I was worried about Anna. I loved her more than anything in the world and, to be perfectly honest, at that point I did not feel the same connection to the three babies growing inside of her.

Anna looked at me and smiled. She said she wanted to have all three. She said that she was strong and healthy and was prepared to take whatever risks were necessary. We never discussed it again.

We told the doctor what our decision was.

I was thankful that we at least had a choice. I certainly did not want to reduce, but I would have been very upset if we had no say in the matter.

Deciding to have triplets was, again, pushing the limits. No one had expected us to get married in the first place, let alone pursue having our own biological children. However, based on our history, Anna had come to believe that everything we did together would somehow be extraordinary. So far, she was right.

The doctor recommended that we go for genetic counseling and testing, in addition to chorionic villus sampling (CVS), which was a relatively new procedure back then and could be done earlier than amniocentesis. Considering the fact that I was in my fifties and had numerous physical problems, and Anna was already thirty-five, genetic testing did seem appropriate. That is not to say that based on the results we would do anything differently, but it would certainly ease our minds for the duration of the pregnancy if we knew what to expect.

The doctor then did a sonogram on Anna and, fortunately, all the babies were healthy and thriving. From then on, the doctors, as well as the technicians, referred to our babies as Baby A, Baby B, and Baby C.

On August 12, Anna and I went to North Shore Hospital for CVS testing. A week or two after the procedure, Anna got a phone call from a nurse who told her that the tests didn't detect any genetic disorders.

At the end of the phone call, the nurse asked Anna if she wanted to know the sexes of the babies. Anna said yes.

Anna immediately called me with the news. First she told me that all the babies were healthy. That was a huge relief.

Then she told me the sex of the babies, one at a time.

"Baby A is a boy."

"Baby B is a boy."

"Baby C is a boy."

"*Jackpot*, again! Three boys!"

So far, we had agreed only on names for girls. Now, we had to start all over.

◆ ◆ ◆

I tried going with Anna to as many of her doctor visits as I could. In fact, I missed only one, when I was sick with bronchitis. The whole process fascinated me. Initially, I couldn't wait to see the sonograms. It was incredible observing our boys grow and develop. I particularly enjoyed it when I could see the whole baby on one screen. Once they got bigger, it was difficult to know exactly what I was looking at.

As time progressed, I became more and more apprehensive before each sonogram. It had been great seeing my babies developing. However, it seemed as though every examination now was focusing on potential abnormalities. I held my breath before each new image appeared on the screen.

On one visit, a technician whom we had not met before was doing Anna's sonogram. When she focused on Baby A, she said that everything looked good. When she focused on Baby B, she repeated that everything looked good. When she focused on Baby C, she stopped, turned to Anna and asked, "Did you have genetic testing done?"

I felt like my heart stopped.

"What's wrong? We had the testing."

"Nothing" she said, "I was just curious."

I aged twenty years in those five seconds.

◆ ◆ ◆

During the first few months of Anna's pregnancy, I tried to get her to rest more but it was virtually impossible. My attempts to get Anna to take it easy probably sounded as if I was talking to a pet dog, "Anna, sit." "Anna, stay." "Anna, lie down." It was exhausting trying to make Anna rest.

When she finally started experiencing morning sickness in the middle of August, she was throwing up every day, several times a day. I had wanted to see some signs that she was actually pregnant. A baby bump would have been sufficient.

As her pregnancy progressed, I no longer had to convince Anna to slow down. She spent most of each day lying on the couch in the den.

Later on, she was not able to eat much. The babies were pushing on her stomach, not leaving much room for food. In addition, nothing seemed to taste good. Sometimes we would sit together in the den and Anna would try to have some tapioca pudding. Despite me encouraging her to eat, she would just end up feeding me the pudding. As a result, I gained weight, Anna didn't. I was the one who had cravings, felt bloated, weak, and uncomfortable. I started to feel sympathy pains and cramps. I couldn't wait for "our" due date.

We continued to talk about potential names for our boys. Anna suggested the name Franklin but I immediately vetoed it. Franklin was the name of her last boyfriend. While I was fairly sure she was just teasing me, I wasn't one hundred percent certain.

Finally, after a lot of deliberation and discussion, Anna and I decided that Baby A would be named Joseph Benjamin. Joseph was the name of my paternal grandfather. The middle name, Benjamin, would be after my paternal grandmother, Beatrice.

Baby B would be named James Lawrence. The J in James was to honor my mother, Judy. The L from Lawrence would be to honor my maternal grandmother (More Mom), Lillian. My brother's oldest boy had been named Charles, after my maternal grandfather (More Pop). So, now, between Steve and me, we were honoring all four of our grandparents, as well as our mother.

Baby C would be named Timothy Francis, to honor Anna's side of the family. It was the perfect name. Anna's mother's name is Franciszka Teresa. Anna's maternal grandfather's name was Franciszek, and her maternal grandmother's name was Teofila.

I loved the thought of referring to our three boys as Joey, Jimmy, and Timmy. Those names sounded a lot better than Baby A, Baby B, and Baby C.

Remembering the lecture Dr. Levitin had given us concerning the dangers of the triplet pregnancy, we made sure to have our legal documents in order before Anna went into labor. We had many decisions to make. Most of them were relatively easy. The most difficult one concerned end-of-life care. Who would make the decision to "disconnect the machines" if necessary? We agreed I would be the one to decide about Anna, but Steve would decide about me. I felt that Anna might have become too emotional in time of crisis. Anna agreed. In addition to the end-of-life care issue, we both had wills drawn up.

♦ ♦ ♦

On Friday, January 21, Anna's condition changed significantly. She was extremely short of breath. The babies were now pushing on her diaphragm, leaving little space for her lungs to expand. I watched Anna get up and try to go to the bathroom. She had to stop halfway, hold onto the wall, and catch her breath. When she came back to the couch, she was breathing heavily, totally exhausted.

When we went for a checkup that afternoon, Anna seemed to be slightly better. Despite her difficulty breathing, Anna still did not want to go for the C-section.

"Just a few days longer," she said, "Let them grow a bit more."

One of my many fears was that Anna would go into distress or labor in the middle of a big snowstorm. Even in good weather and with no traffic, it took us forty-five minutes to drive to North Shore Hospital. As luck would have it, on Saturday, January 22, the forecast predicted more than a foot of snow.

That Saturday, Anna was very short of breath again. I called the doctor's office and told them it was crucial for Anna to stay in the hospital that weekend. They agreed and told me to bring her over.

Anna packed her bag and Jarek drove us to the hospital. Snow flurries were already starting to come down.

When we arrived, a nurse gave Anna a brief examination. Fortunately, everything was still fine.

While Anna was waiting for a room, she encouraged Jarek and me to leave for home. By the middle of our long and difficult drive back, we were in blizzard-like conditions, with visibility close to zero at times. There were between twelve and fifteen inches of snow on the ground by the next day. I was just thankful that Anna was safe.

On Monday morning, January 24, Anna had a sonogram that showed a significant difference in the amount of blood going to Baby B through his umbilical cord than to the other two. Dr. Rochelson, one of the doctors in the Division of Maternal Fetal Medicine, recommended to go ahead with the C-section that day. Because Jimmy was experiencing some problems, Anna finally agreed. She was thirty-four weeks and five days into her pregnancy.

Anna called me at my office from the phone in Dr. Rochelson's office and said, "Today is the day."

Chapter 30

The Triplets Are Here!

◆ ◆ ◆

"Today is the day!" I was bursting with excitement. I couldn't wait to get to the hospital to be with Anna.

I called Jarek and told him to pick me up at my office. I then called Steve, who said he would meet me at the hospital. I asked him to bring a camera.

I called Aunt Lorraine, Meryl, and my father, who was in Orlando. Anna contacted her side of the family.

It was frustrating waiting for Jarek to arrive. It felt as though it took forever. Staring at the clock did not help the time go any faster.

◆ ◆ ◆

It was the first time I had seen Anna since Saturday. She seemed calm and upbeat. She was on the delivery ward, connected to three different monitors, one for each baby. A chorus of beeps was coming from the machines. It was not a reassuring sound for me. Sometimes, the cadence of the beeps changed, making me more concerned that something was wrong.

I had been so worried about Anna's health throughout her pregnancy. I was particularly worried about Anna's difficulty breathing during the past week. My own breathing problems have always been the hardest thing for me to deal with.

I was also worrying about the babies Anna was carrying. They were no longer just small clumps of cells on a picture. They were no longer letters "A," "B," and "C" to me. They were Joey, Jimmy, and Timmy.

At one point, Anna got out of bed to use the bathroom. She needed a nurse to disconnect the many machines she was hooked up to. I worried not just about Anna falling but also about Joey, Jimmy, and Timmy not being monitored—for even a few minutes.

I hoped that when Anna returned the nurse would wheel her right into the delivery room, but that was not the case. Two emergency C-sections needed to be performed before the staff would be able to prepare Anna for surgery. It was nerve wracking, watching and listening to the baby monitors for the next few hours.

Steve, Meryl, Aunt Lorraine, and my niece Lauren soon joined Anna and me. I really didn't feel like talking, but the others were chattering away.

Finally, Dr. Rochelson came in. He asked all our visitors to go to the waiting room so that he could talk with Anna and me alone. He told us that because we were delivering three premature babies, there would be a lot of nurses and doctors in the room. The staff needed to make sure that all three newborns received the proper care throughout the delivery and immediately thereafter. He indicated there also would be a nurse there specifically assigned to assist me, in case I needed anything.

I appreciated being allowed in the delivery room and having my own nurse. I now started to worry about how I was going to handle the delivery, for instance, whether I might pass out or get sick to my stomach. In addition, if there was any problem with Anna, Joey, Jimmy, or Timmy, I would be beside myself and probably lose it altogether.

When Dr. Rochelson finished explaining the procedure, he asked if either of us had any questions.

Anna had one: "Would the incision be horizontal or vertical?"

The doctor replied, "Horizontal."

"Good," Anna remarked. "Does that mean that, if I decide to have another baby, I could have a natural delivery?"

What did she just say? I could not believe my ears. Was Anna really thinking about having another baby while she was about to give birth to triplets?

Anna said it would be nice to have a girl next. And she said that so matter-of-factly! We were in big trouble if Anna wanted to go through all the IVF again, while having three babies and me all in need of her attention.

After Dr. Rochelson left the room, Anna turned toward me and realized how petrified I was that she would even consider getting pregnant again. At this point, she just burst out laughing. It was not funny to me at the time but, later on, it became a running joke between us.

It was a few more minutes before a nurse came in. Anna, now serious again, was lying on her side, holding my hand. We didn't do much talking. We knew we were spending our last moments alone together before our lives would change forever. If all went well, there would soon be five of us.

Anna was disconnected from the monitors and taken into the delivery room by a nurse. I wished her luck.

A few more minutes went by and then a different nurse finally led me to the doorway of the delivery room. She put a gown on me, inserting my arms in the sleeves. She then put a cap on my head, covering my hair, and a mask over my mouth and nose. I could have passed for one of the surgeons.

Suddenly, I started having trouble breathing. Although the mask was not really blocking my airways, I felt I wasn't getting enough oxygen. I was worried that I would start to hyperventilate, but I knew I had to keep the mask on to be allowed into the delivery room.

When the door was finally opened, I saw Anna on a bed in the middle of a large room. There was a big curtain across her chest, blocking her view of what was about to take place. The room was filled with doctors and nurses.

I wheeled inside and stopped to the right of Anna, next to her head. I put my left hand out for Anna to hold with her right hand. While I could not feel her hand, I hoped it would be some comfort for Anna to feel mine. We remained that way throughout the

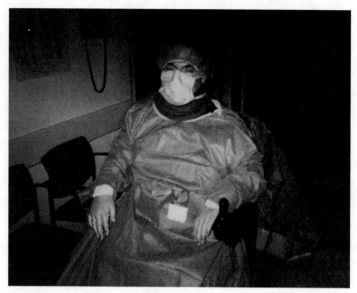

Ken about to enter the delivery room—January 24, 2005.

delivery. I was thankful that the curtain was so large that I couldn't even accidentally see what was happening on the other side.

Dr. Rochelson explained that as he took each baby out Anna would feel some pressure but that it shouldn't be painful. Once they got started, the deliveries would be very quick.

My eyes were focused on Anna's face. She looked calm and gorgeous as usual. I was very proud of her.

At 5:25 p.m., Dr. Rochelson told Anna she would feel some pressure. In an instant, Joey was born, and within seconds we heard him cry for the first time. What an amazing sound! Anna and I looked at each other and our eyes welled up with tears.

The doctor told us the baby was fine, held Joey up above the curtain for us to see and then passed him to a nurse from the Neonatal Intensive Care Unit (NICU) to clean him up. Anna, unfortunately, was not able to see Joey as the doctor held him up.

I had just gotten my first look at my son. He was not the beautiful baby I had been expecting. In fact, it felt to me as if I was looking at E.T.

At 5:26 p.m., Jimmy was born. It took a few seconds before we heard his first cry. The doctor then said that the baby was fine, held him up for me to see, and quickly passed Jimmy to a nurse.

My son Jimmy was gorgeous. What a relief! I immediately exclaimed, "Anna, he is perfect! He is absolutely perfect!"

At 5:27 p.m., Timmy was born and let out his first cry. The doctor told us everything was fine, held up Timmy for me to see, and then passed him to another nurse.

Timmy was smaller than the other two and, to my dismay, looked even worse than Joey. We now had two little E.T.s and one gorgeous baby.

There was still a lot of activity going on. Everyone was busy. The staff were conducting medical tests on each baby, while Dr. Rochelson remained focused on Anna. Everyone seemed healthy and was doing well.

Shortly after that, the nurses brought the babies over for Anna to see. By then, they were cleaned up and swaddled in blankets. The nurses piled all three babies on Anna's chest. I didn't think they were being very careful carrying my boys. Didn't they know how delicate my babies were? How could they be so nonchalant?

It was incredible seeing all three boys on Anna's chest as she looked at them for the first time. My nurse took some photos, and then Joey, Jimmy, and Timmy were whisked away to the NICU.

I was asked to leave the room so the staff could finish suturing Anna's incision and get her ready to be moved to the recovery room.

I told Anna she did great, and that I loved her, and would see her soon. I then left her in the medical staff's hands.

Once I was in the hallway, the nurse took off my cap, gown, and mask. I could finally breathe again.

The entire event had been surreal. No words could adequately describe it. Hearing Joey's cry had been probably the most exhilarating experience of my life. The sight of my three children resting on Anna's chest, with Anna looking at them, will be forever engraved in my mind as the most incredible moment I have ever witnessed.

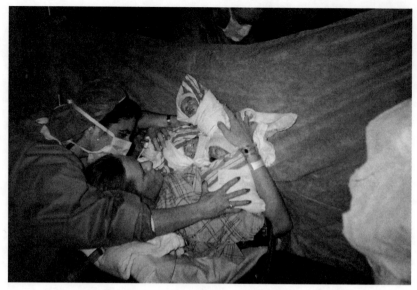

All three boys on Anna's chest—January 24, 2005.

I quickly wheeled down to the waiting room and announced to Steve, Meryl, Aunt Lorraine, and Lauren, "I am a father. We have three beautiful boys!" I didn't tell them that we actually had one beautiful boy and two little alien babies. I figured there would be plenty of time for them to find that out for themselves.

We then all went down to the cafeteria. After about a half hour, Steve and I went back upstairs to join Anna in the recovery room. We were not permitted to see her yet, but we could see the boys. We were allowed into a secured area outside the NICU, where we looked at the triplets through a large window. The babies were in separate incubators, in a room with other newborns, also in incubators. I could just barely see my boys' faces. If the nurse hadn't pointed out which babies were mine, I would never have known.

Steve and I then joined Anna, who looked weak and tired. I asked her how she was. She replied that she felt "so empty inside."

I immediately became concerned that Anna was experiencing postpartum depression. I had read about that in the baby books but didn't think it could start so quickly. Anna never mentioned that empty feeling again, though.

Steve and I stayed with Anna for another half hour. When Jarek arrived to pick me up, I said good-bye to Anna, and then Jarek and I drove home—just the two of us. When I got home I felt more alone than I ever had in my life. Although I had been warned well in advance that Anna and the children would remain in the hospital for some time after the delivery, just as Anna did, I felt "empty inside." I couldn't wait to see them all again. Needless to say, I got little sleep that night.

Unfortunately, throughout this time I was having problems with the catheter. Jarek could no longer insert it into my bladder, which needed to be done a few times a day. My urethra had been damaged and it was bleeding. Early the next day, Jarek drove me to my urologist's office. The doctor inserted a Foley catheter, which had to remain inside me for a few weeks to give the area time to heal.

It seemed that right after I had reached an all-time high with the birth of my three boys, I was brought down to earth again, having to deal with my own chronic medical problems.

I went straight from the doctor's office to the hospital. Anna was in bed, looking very unhappy. She desperately wanted to see the babies but was not allowed to leave her room. She was too weak for that.

Jarek went with me to see the boys. The NICU was kept very secure. To get in, I had to show a bracelet, which a nurse had put on me the day before, that identified me as one of the fathers.

The NICU comprised four different nurseries. Each baby's room would be determined by how well he or she was doing that day. Our boys were in two or three different rooms during their stay there. To visit them, I had to go from room to room.

The first time I visited the NICU, I felt like a bull in a china shop. Trying to maneuver my oversized wheelchair through the tight access between the machinery that was stacked around each incubator was a real challenge. I worried that I was going to injure or damage someone or something.

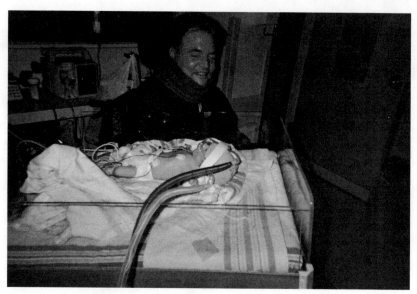

With Jimmy in the NICU—January 25, 2005.

Our boys had been born five weeks prematurely. At birth, Joey weighed three pounds, fourteen ounces; Jimmy was three pounds, eight and three-quarter ounces; and Timmy was three pounds, two and one-quarter ounces. As preemies, they needed to stay in the NICU until they showed they could breathe, regulate their body temperature, eat, poop, and pee on their own, like a full-term baby. They also needed to be a certain weight, or at least show they were gaining weight at a good enough pace, in order to go home.

As a precaution, on the first day of their lives Jimmy and Timmy had machines pumping air into their lungs. Joey didn't need that. Our boys were in separate incubators, most of the time swaddled tightly in white and blue hospital blankets, with very small blue hats on their heads. They were connected to a range of monitors and their rooms were very noisy, with loud beeps and buzzers going off constantly.

The boys appeared to be truly fragile and delicate. I really appreciated all the care they received in the NICU and could not imagine how Anna would ever be able to take care of them at home, even with help. It seemed overwhelming.

Before Anna's pregnancy, I had never dreamed that I would someday become a father. I had been content to be just "Uncle Ken" to my many nephews and nieces. In fact, I was so used to being called Uncle Ken that the first time I spoke to one of my sons I started to say, "Joey, it's Unc ..." I caught myself in the middle of the word "uncle" and stopped. I felt a huge smile come across my face. As my eyes welled up with tears, I said for the first time, "It's Daddy."

Anna, still very weak and sore from her surgery two days earlier, was finally allowed to go to the NICU. We entered the ward together, me leading the way, with Anna pushed in a wheelchair by Jarek.

As soon as I saw Anna picking up and holding our babies, I knew she would be a terrific mother. The nurses in the NICU gave her some basic instructions and she was ready to go. Unfortunately, after a short period of time, Anna started to feel dizzy. Her pain had come back and she had to lie down. With sadness in her eyes, she reluctantly returned to her room.

I went back to work two days after the boys were born. To my surprise, upon entering the DA's Office I was greeted by signs posted all up and down the hallway, announcing "THE TRIPLETS ARE HERE." My secretary had made sure the whole world knew that I had become a father. She also listed each boy's name and weight on a flyer posted on the door of the secretaries' room and my office.

I visited Anna and the triplets at the end of every day. I was not able to concentrate at all during those next few weeks. I spent each day staring at the clock, anxiously waiting for the small hand to hit five. I couldn't imagine not being with my boys every day, even if all I could do was look at them and talk to them through the glass of the incubators. There was also something especially beautiful about watching Anna taking care of them.

Anna was discharged on Friday, four days after giving birth. She needed a lot of rest to recover from the delivery but insisted on

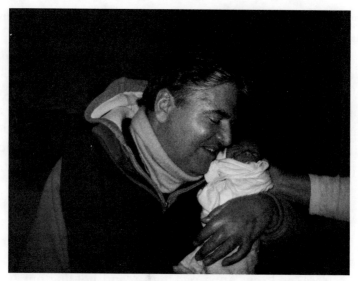

Ken holding one of the boys—February 5, 2005.

going back to the hospital the next day, and every day after that, as long as the boys were in the NICU.

Before I left for work each day, Anna and I would get a phone call from a NICU nurse, with a report about our children. That way, we knew if anything significant had happened since we'd left the hospital the previous night and what to expect during the coming day.

Joey was soon moved to a room for babies who were almost ready to go home. We expected him to be the first to leave the hospital, after about a two-week stay. All he needed at this point was to demonstrate that he could gain weight at a steady pace. He seemed to pass every test with flying colors.

Jimmy was also doing great, despite his low birth weight. Fortunately, he had been gaining weight steadily and was expected to come home second, after about three weeks.

Timmy required the most attention. He was small and delicate. He looked like a little old man in a tiny hat. Anna and I gravitated toward his incubator more than to the other two. Timmy was expected to stay in the hospital for at least four weeks.

Ken by Joey's incubator—February 5, 2005.

Near the end of the second week, we received a call from a nurse telling us there was blood in Joey's stool. They were concerned he might have a perforated intestine. Being a preemie, his intestines might not be sufficiently developed to handle food. According to the nurse, his condition might be serious. Anna and I raced to the hospital.

When we arrived at the NICU, the doctor told us that as soon as the bloody stool had been discovered X-rays had been taken to check for leakage from Joey's intestines. Leakage might cause a life-threatening infection, which might necessitate the removal of the infected parts of the intestines. His condition could turn worse at any time, the doctor said, so we gave our consent for surgery, well in advance.

Joey's X-rays showed that his intestines were inflamed. As a result, the doctor decided to stop feeding him by mouth. Instead, he was fed intravenously. In addition, a small tube was inserted through Joey's nose into his stomach. The tube was attached to a sucking device, which was removing stomach acid. Because there was no milk going in, the acid in the stomach could, potentially, destroy the lining of it. The goal was to give Joey's intestines time to rest and heal, with the aid of an intravenous antibiotic.

Joey was moved to the NICU room reserved for more serious cases. Beeping machines surrounded him again and he had needles stuck all over his small body, including his foot and arm. A splint-like device on his arm kept the IV from moving.

That day, since there were so many wires and IVs connected to Joey's little body, the nurses discouraged Anna from taking him into her arms. She was only allowed to stroke his leg or hold his hand, the one that had no needles in it.

While Anna was with Joey, I spent time with the other two. Fortunately, Jimmy and Timmy were doing fine. One of the nurses would take the boys from their incubators and hold them by my face so I could kiss them and feel them against me. I don't remember ever touching anything so soft in my life.

Once I was convinced the other two boys were okay, I returned to Joey's room. I sat there and talked to my son while Anna was attending to the needs of Jimmy and Timmy or pumping her breast milk. When she was not with the other two boys or pumping, she would return to Joey's room and we would just sit together beside his incubator.

I had been a father for only a couple of weeks and already could not imagine my life without that tiny baby in it. It was excruciatingly painful for me to think about what Joey was going through or what might happen to him.

After a day or two, Anna was finally allowed to hold Joey in her arms. She would cradle him for hours. When I came from work, I would take over watching Joey.

♦ ♦ ♦

Well in advance of having children, we had decided that Anna would take over their spiritual education, which meant raising them Catholic.

Teresa, Anna's mother, was concerned that Joey might die before he was baptized. Usually, the baptizing ceremony would take place in a church, with a priest pouring holy water onto a baby's head. There would be parents and godparents present, as well as the rest of the baby's family.

Teresa strongly suggested that Anna baptize Joey herself, using just regular water. All that was required was an independent witness, who could later confirm that the child was a Catholic at the time of his or her death so that the child could be buried in a Catholic cemetery. Teresa also believed that sometimes just baptizing alone could be helpful, especially if there was nothing else anybody could do.

Anna had never seemed very religious to me, but when it came to her first-born son she was ready to do everything and anything. With Jarek as a witness, we gathered in Joey's room. Anna said, "Joseph Benjamin Kunken, I am christening you in the name of the Holy Father, Jesus Christ, and the Holy Spirit, Amen." Anna then sprinkled some water on Joey's forehead and kissed him. That was it.

A few days later, we received good news from a nurse during the morning phone call. X-rays showed that the damage to Joey's intestines was healing properly, so the doctor had decided to remove the tube leading to Joey's stomach.

That afternoon I couldn't wait to get to Joey's bedside. As soon as I arrived at the NICU, I asked the nurse at the desk if the doctor had removed the tube from Joey's nose. The nurse told me that he had. I rushed into Joey's room, expecting to see him with fewer wires and probes around him. I became very upset, though, when I saw a tube still sticking out from the baby's nose, just like the night before.

I immediately complained to the nurse in the room, "They told me they had taken the tube out of Joey's nose and now I see that it was put back in. What happened and why was that done?"

The nurse looked at me and in a very calm voice said, "That is not your baby. Your baby is over there." She pointed to an incubator on the other side of the room. They had moved Joey because he

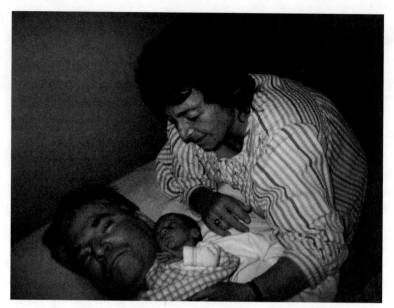

Aunt Betty bringing Jimmy to Ken—February 15, 2005.

was doing better. I had been sitting beside an incubator containing a little baby girl, wearing a pink hat. How embarrassing ...

After ten days, Joey's X-rays were looking better. Despite being big enough to leave the hospital, though, he needed to remain in the NICU a while longer.

While Joey was going through his problems, Jimmy seemed to be thriving. The doctors decided to release him from the hospital before the other two. My Aunt Betty volunteered to stay with him in our apartment while Anna spent most of the day in the NICU taking care of Joey and Timmy.

On Jimmy's first night home, Betty brought him into my bedroom while I was lying in bed and put his face next to mine so I could feel him against my cheek. He smelled great, a mixture of milk, baby oil, and something else that was his own scent. How good it would be to hold him in my arms and smell that wonderful scent forever!

♦ ♦ ♦

Timmy now seemed to have his eyes open every time I was in his room, as if he had been waiting for me, so I tended to spend more time beside his incubator. There was a big difference between just watching a sleeping baby versus watching a baby who was looking straight at me intently.

The nurses said that Timmy would benefit from close contact with his parents. "Cuddling with Daddy" therapy was recommended. During one of my evening visits, Anna unbuttoned my shirt, pulled up my T-shirt, and put a diapered but otherwise naked Timmy against my chest. He snuggled there for a while, with Anna holding Timmy close to my skin. It was incredible to feel his small hands touching me. It was wonderfully strange to feel him moving against me.

One day, a NICU nurse who didn't know me very well thought it would be great if I held Timmy by myself. I was apprehensive but figured the nurse knew what he was doing. He assured me he would remain close by. He then put Timmy, bundled in a blanket, in the crook of my left arm. Timmy was very small but still weighed more than three pounds. My left arm had gotten stronger over the years, but supporting Timmy's weight for more than a few seconds was a huge effort for me. I didn't even have my lapboard to rest my arm on.

As soon as the nurse put Timmy in my left arm, I knew it had not been a good idea. I was scared to death that my arm would fatigue and I would drop him. Within a few seconds, I told the nurse to take Timmy away. I didn't want the nurse to think I didn't want to hold my son. I would have given anything to be able to do that for hours, but I knew my limitations.

I recognized that my role as a father would be limited physically. I would never be able to pick the boys up when they cried, or change their diapers, or give them a bottle. I would have to find different ways to be helpful. My role was to be exclusively that of provider, and I worried I wouldn't even be able to do that adequately.

As soon as we had found out we were expecting triplets, I couldn't stop thinking about the expenses it would involve. During many long, sleepless nights, I tried to come up with different ways to pay for the help Anna would need. I thought about every possible way to use my financial resources to the best advantage. No matter which way I approached the problem, though, I still seemed to fall short.

Anna pointed out that my role of "provider" was very similar to the role my father had assumed after my accident. He never really provided me with any physical help. Instead, he focused on making sure money was there to pay for the help I needed. I desperately wanted to care for my sons but I obviously could not do so physically. I started to better appreciate my father's concerns about finances.

I also started to realize how awful my father must have felt, back in 1970, when he received that first phone call about my injury. My three sons were only a few weeks old but already I could not imagine my life without them. I didn't like even the thought that they may be in any pain or discomfort.

We brought Timmy home on Saturday, February 19, and Joey the next morning. Betty had to return to New Jersey the day Joey arrived at our condo. Fortunately, Anna had arranged to have Sue, a baby nurse, stay with us for the next nine days. How were we going to survive after that?

Chapter 31

Full House

◆ ◆ ◆

On Sunday, after Jarek left in the morning, Anna was so busy with the boys, she barely had time to attend to my catheter.

Feedings were fascinating to watch. Sometimes I would go into the babies' room, sit in the only free space between the cribs, and just watch in awe.

Jimmy and Timmy constantly fidgeted while eating. Whoever was feeding them needed to maintain a firm grip on their bottles. Joey was different though. He drank like a champ. In fact, he did it so well I was actually able to feed him. Anna would lay Joey on a pillow on my lapboard, with his bottle propped up on my left hand. It was wonderful for me to feed Joey by myself, to watch him and watch him watching me. I would talk to him, smile, and make faces to keep his eyes on me. I wanted to do that with all three boys but, unfortunately, only Joey would cooperate.

It was frustrating that I couldn't help more with the boys. In fact, often I felt like I was in everyone's way.

Pumping breast milk, feeding the boys, doing laundry, cooking, shopping, cleaning, and helping me, especially during weekends, kept Anna extremely busy. She often had one boy strapped into the baby carrier in front of her and another in the crook of her arm while she stirred something on the stove with her free hand. I still do not know how she managed.

Ken feeding Joey—March 12, 2005.

It was too expensive to keep the baby nurse for long. Anna had to start looking for a suitable nanny, so she posted an ad on a Polish website. Many people who were not Polish used this site for their job searches as well.

One of our first interviews was with a nice woman who came to our apartment with her husband. She was Muslim and was wearing a beautiful headscarf. She appeared to be in her sixties.

As she was holding one of our boys in her arms, the baby spit up all over her headscarf. I was mortified. I thought the woman would get upset but, instead, she smiled and said, "It is a blessing." That convinced me that this woman would be the right person for our boys.

She told us she would need some time every day to stop what she was doing and pray. I was a bit conflicted for a moment or two, thinking about having a Muslim woman praying a few times

Ken with the triplets (from left to right:
Jimmy, Timmy, and Joey)—April 30, 2005.

every day in what was left of my Jewish home, keeping in mind, of course, that my wife and children were Catholic. But if that woman considered my baby's spit-up "a blessing," she should be the "chosen" one.

Unfortunately, the woman's husband called the next day and said it would be just too hard for his wife to work for us.

A few days later, a Polish woman came for an interview. Her name was Zuzanna.

Zuzanna arrived just before feeding time and helped give one of the boys a bottle. She was in our apartment for less than an hour. As soon as Zuzanna left, Anna turned to me and said, "She is the one."

Apparently when Zuzanna was holding one of our boys, Anna saw tears in her eyes. Anna told me, "She has a lot of love to give. We will be very lucky if our boys are the ones to receive it." The next day, Anna called Zuzanna and offered her the nanny's job.

My personal care attendant, Jarek, was trying to become a doctor in the United States. He had completed medical school in Poland and recently passed his medical exams here. Jarek wanted to start his residency in a U.S. hospital. It would be impossible for him to do that and continue working with me. He had been helping me every night since June 2004, with the exception of one night before the last of his exams.

Anna was still too weak to take over my care. It could jeopardize her health if she tried to lift me too soon after her C-section. In addition, she was way too busy with the triplets.

I ended up hiring a young Polish man who had some experience as a physical therapy aide.

Not long after Easter, Teresa, Anna's mother, arrived. This would be Teresa's first time seeing her three new grandchildren. It was always fun for me to observe people's reactions upon seeing our triplets. Teresa was not able to decide which baby to marvel at first. She was completely blown away.

Teresa with Joey and Jimmy—May 11, 2005.

Teresa had not fully recovered from her 2001 car accident. Her knee was often swollen and painful. Despite that, she always seemed to be in a good mood and got along beautifully with Zuzanna and Anna. Often Teresa would sit on the couch with a cold compress or special therapeutic lamp, treating her injured knee while holding one of the boys. It was especially cute to see her in the morning, lying on the couch cheek to cheek with a sleeping baby.

As Anna had predicted months before, my needs seemed to be less important now. When our boys were crying, I had to put aside whatever discomfort I was experiencing at the moment. Whenever I needed something, I had to be patient and wait my turn. Anna did her best to help me, but it took some getting used to on my part to no longer be number one in her life.

♦ ♦ ♦

By late April, Anna and I were busy making preparations for the boys' baptism. I wanted my children to grow up with the same values and beliefs that made their mother the incredible person she is. If that meant bringing my boys up in the Catholic religion, then so be it. The baptism itself did not have a strong religious meaning to me but clearly it did for Anna and her family.

Anna told me we needed six responsible Catholics to serve as the boys' godparents. I was still not familiar with the role of a godparent, nor did I understand how important that person would be in each of our boys' lives. The image of Marlon Brando in the *Godfather* movie was something I could not get out of my head. However, Anna explained that if anything should happen to a child's parents the godparents would assume responsibility for the child's receiving a proper Catholic upbringing. I thought my brother Steve would have been perfect—except for the "religious" thing.

The boys were baptized on May 22. Following that, we tried to attend church services every Sunday. When the weather was nice, we walked the mile to St. Agnes Cathedral in Rockville Centre, with Anna wheeling the boys in their stroller and me trying to keep up with them.

The ramp to get into the church was situated on the side of the building, near the altar. As a result, we usually sat in front of most of the other congregants. I felt that I was particularly conspicuous sitting there, probably the only Jewish person in the building, sitting closer to the altar than the hundreds of Catholics in attendance. I couldn't help but feel they were all staring at me. Of course, I still seemed to attract attention wherever I went.

When the boys got a little older, I would keep one or two of them on my lap during the service, sometimes taking turns with Anna holding a different boy every fifteen minutes or so. It was a great opportunity for me to have them up close for an hour and give them an extra dose of kisses.

The same people usually sat near us every time we went. Over the years, they watched our boys grow, week by week. Anna was always receiving compliments that noted how remarkable she was to be taking the boys to church every Sunday, especially at their young age, and how well behaved they were. People were constantly congratulating me on what a beautiful family I had. I never got tired of hearing those words. On one occasion, a woman told us she might have to stay for the next Mass because she had spent the entire service marveling at our boys instead of praying.

Quite often, a priest or another individual would make a special effort to offer me communion. At every Mass I would have to make early eye contact with them and shake my head vigorously from side to side, to indicate that I didn't take communion.

One Sunday, Bishop Murphy approached me. Despite my shaking my head, he leaned forward and asked why I didn't want to take communion. I was taken aback by the bishop's persistence, and finally blurted out, "I am Jewish." The look of surprise on his face reminded me of Nancy's reaction when she realized why I didn't know the words to "Noël, Noël."

Since that day, the bishop always acknowledged my presence with a big smile and nod.

♦ ♦ ♦

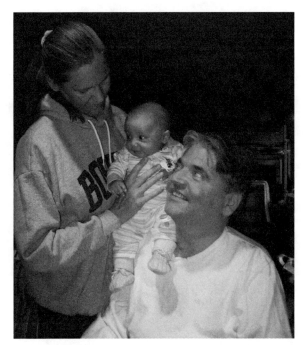

Ken with Anna and Joey—May 12, 2005.

Ken with Timmy—June 29, 2005.

Anna and Ken with Teresa the evening before she returned
to Poland—June 24, 2005.

The time finally came for Teresa to go back to Poland. It was
very hard for her to leave Anna and the boys. It was a sad goodbye
for all of us. We were not sure when Teresa would get to see her
new grandchildren again.

In June, I replaced my male attendant with a young Polish
female medical student named Joanna.

Joanna was as tall as Anna and very pretty. It was funny to see
Anna actually concerned about my hiring such an attractive aide.
Anna seemed to be jealous of Joanna!

I was surprised that Anna felt so insecure about my feelings
for her. Of course, she had nothing to worry about. In the summer
of 2005, after Anna had given me three beautiful sons as well as a
happy and wonderful life, I could not have been more in love with
her. In addition, she looked absolutely gorgeous, before, during,
and especially after her pregnancy. What more could a guy want?!

On the other hand, because she had been so extremely busy
with the boys and everything else going on in our life, any close-
ness between us at that time was almost nonexistent. I missed the
intimacy but I knew that I had to be patient.

On June 14, the day of our second anniversary, Anna managed to write me another wonderful letter. The letter reminded me not only how incredible my wife was but also what a truly special relationship we had.

♦ ♦ ♦

Anna and I often went with the boys to the Long Beach boardwalk on weekends. I sometimes carried one of the boys in a papoose-type carrier strapped to my chest. Although it was extra hard to operate my wheelchair this way, it was great to feel a small warm body so close to mine. It was also fun to see people stealing looks while passing us.

Some parents of triplets didn't like the extra attention from strangers. I had no problem with that. I could talk about Joey, Jimmy, and Timmy all day long to anybody who would listen. I felt so proud saying, "These are my children." Many times, though,

On the Long Beach boardwalk—June 19, 2005.

Ken carrying Jimmy on the Long Beach boardwalk—July 2, 2005.

a well-meaning person would approach me and say, "You must be a very proud grandpa!" Oh, well . . .

◆ ◆ ◆

Near the end of September, my aide Joanna returned to Poland to resume her medical studies. Anna then took over my physical care. It was great being in her loving arms again.

Zuzanna was terrific with our boys. She clearly loved them, and treated them as if they were her own grandchildren. Sometime in the fall, Zuzanna's husband Krzyś joined us as well. Our apartment was extremely crowded, but the atmosphere of love, warmth, and laughter made our home a place I looked forward to returning to every day.

More than ever, though, we needed a bigger place to live.

Fortunately, we heard of a ranch house that was for sale just four blocks from our condominium. It needed a lot of work and was quite expensive, but it had a large back yard that would be

Taking a family picture was a challenge (from the left: Joey, Timmy, and Jimmy)—September 19, 2005.

perfect for the kids, so we decided to buy it. As fate would have it, we closed on our new house on October 31, 2005, exactly thirty-five years to the day of my injury. Finally, I had something to celebrate on that day.

Nevertheless, as Halloween was approaching, despite Anna's best efforts it was difficult for me not to think about my accident and all the events that had followed from it. I still got depressed whenever I saw a pumpkin.

In the summer of 2005, though, someone gave us a onesie outfit that had orange pumpkins all over it. Anna dressed Joey in it and placed him on my lap for a picture. Joey was smiling and looked gorgeous. From that day forward, every time I saw a pumpkin I thought of Joey's smiling face instead of my accident. Halloween was, once again, becoming a day I could look forward to. I couldn't wait to go trick-or-treating with the boys.

♦ ♦ ♦

In August 2005, I received a phone call from Fred Kunken. Fred's father, Milton, was my father's first cousin. Fred was the head of the Pediatric Dentistry Department of North Shore Hospital in Manhasset, Long Island.

During our phone conversation, Fred told me that every month at North Shore University Hospital/Long Island Jewish Hospital they devoted an evening to topics related to medicine. Doctors and medical residents attended those lectures. Fred was in charge of arranging all of them and for November 8th he had scheduled a program concerning stem cell research. Fred had invited Dr. Wise Young to deliver a talk on the topic. Dr. Young was the head of the Spinal Cord Injury Project at Rutgers University in New Jersey. He was one of the world's leading doctors working on spinal cord injury cure research.

Fred thought that, after Dr. Young's talk, it would be interesting to have someone with a spinal cord injury speak, to put a human face on the subject. Fred asked me to be that speaker. He told me the topic of my talk would be: "What Stem Cell Research Means to Me."

I accepted Fred's invitation. It would be great to meet and speak on the same stage as Dr. Young and to have the opportunity to try to influence the medical community's approach to this line of research. I had tried to follow the latest developments in the search for a cure for a spinal cord injury and it was clear to me that the most promising paths to follow led to stem cell therapy.

I delivered my talk without notes. After describing my injury and the challenges I had faced, I concluded with the following:

> On January 24th of this year, my wife Anna gave birth to triplets. We have three beautiful baby boys: Joey, Jimmy, and Timmy. I cannot begin to tell you how much we love them.
>
> What does stem cell research mean to me? It means that someday I will actually be able to hold my babies. It means that I will be able to lift them up and comfort them when they are crying. It means that I will be able to help my wife with their physical care. It means that I will

be able to get down on the floor and play with them and do so many other wonderful things that fathers do with their children.

I thank and applaud Doctor Wise Young and all the other researchers for the great work they are doing. They are making incredible progress. It is nice to no longer have to ask the question, "*Will* there be a cure for spinal cord injuries?" and replace it with the more optimistic question, "*When* will the cure come about?"

We have come so far. We need to increase funding for stem cell research. More work needs to be done but please, Doctor, try to speed up the process. My children are getting impatient.

Every time I practiced the talk, I had trouble getting through the part about my children without becoming emotional. Fortunately, I made it through all right. The audience, however, was moved to tears.

I was still on a high when I got home that night. After getting settled, Anna turned on the television to watch the local election results. To my surprise, I learned that Denis Dillon, the District Attorney for whom I had been working for the previous twenty-three years, was losing in a close race to Kathleen Rice. When I awoke the next morning, the results were official. My boss had lost.

For the first time since I had started working in the District Attorney's Office, I worried whether I would still have a job in January. The possibility of suddenly being unemployed was unsettling to say the least. I was married, was the father of young triplets, had just closed on a house, and had a huge mortgage to pay.

Chapter 32

Publicity

◆ ◆ ◆

While Anna was managing the chaos at home, I was worrying about my job and future in the DA's Office. I still had not even met Kathleen Rice, the newly elected District Attorney.

ADAs serve at the whim of the DA. Denis Dillon had been the DA in Nassau County for thirty-one years. Everyone who worked for him felt secure in his or her job as long as Dillon remained the DA. He ran a nonpolitical office. It did not matter to him whether you were a Republican or a Democrat. In some other DAs' offices, however, your party affiliation could be the determining factor as to whether you kept or lost your job.

Because we had 174 ADAs in the Nassau County office, I knew it was unlikely, and would be not very practical, to replace the whole staff. It was very common, though, for a new DA to bring in his or her own supervisors, people that shared his or her vision and would be totally loyal to the new DA. Unfortunately for me, I was now a supervisor.

In December 2005, Kathleen Rice told many of the supervisors in the office that they would not be part of her new staff in January. The number of people that were being let go totaled nearly twenty, and more of us were still being looked at to determine whether they would be allowed to keep their jobs. Many of those people had been in the office for more than twenty years.

In January, after Kathleen Rice had been officially sworn in, she held a meeting for our entire office. At that meeting, DA Rice indicated that in the next few months she was going to try to meet with every ADA, individually. It was left unsaid, but we all knew those meetings would determine who was going to stay and who was going to be let go.

DA Rice also said she would have all the offices and hall-ways renovated. They had been in disrepair for many years. She indicated we would be getting new furniture, new carpeting, and would have our individual offices painted.

Many people approached me, both in and out of the office, asking me about my job status. Was I safe or was I in danger of losing my position? I told them I didn't know. I would say, only half-jokingly, "I am not looking for a pat on the back or even a comment that I am doing a good job. All I am looking for is for someone to ask me, 'What color would you like your office painted?'" That would mean I was staying.

Kathleen Rice began meeting with the ADAs sometime in February. A couple of months went by before I was scheduled to meet with her in April. When my time finally came, I waited patiently outside her office, while she was in a meeting with others. After half an hour, I was told the DA was running late and would have to reschedule my meeting. After another couple of months, it still had not been rescheduled. It was stressful.

Before my injury, I had been able to relieve stress and work out many of my frustrations on the athletic field. Now I have to deal with these issues mentally rather than physically. It is one of the "non-visible challenges" most people never realize I have to handle on a daily basis.

Since our boys were born, however, my best stress relievers were Joey, Jimmy, and Timmy. They always managed to divert me from my worries and the discomfort I felt every day. One look, one smile, one hug was enough to brighten my mood.

When they were toddlers, they loved sitting on my lap as I drove around the condo or on the sidewalk. I was eventually able to go outside with one boy on my lap without Anna walking beside me. That was a lot of fun and a wonderful time for me to

Ken with the boys in the house—October 29, 2007.

bond with each of my children individually. While I was walking with them, I would talk to them, direct their attention to different things, and tell them what they were: fire hydrant, sewer, airplane, stop sign, and so on.

By the spring of 2006, our boys were all over our condo. They were crawling or walking everywhere, so it was challenging to be around them. I needed to know where all three boys were at all times, to be able to move safely and not run over them. I could not see behind me, or my sides, because of the limited range of motion in my neck.

Observing Joey, Jimmy, and Timmy was like watching a wonderful, heartwarming, never-ending movie. It was fascinating to see the way they approached different problems and interacted with each other, as well as with other people.

Every day, when I returned from work, the boys would greet me at the door and try to climb up on my wheelchair onto my lap. It was the greatest feeling in the world. I couldn't wait to come home.

Ken riding with the boys around the neighborhood—May 10, 2008.

Watching my children reminded me how much was at stake if I were to lose my job. For example, apart from the financial security that came with my position in the DA's Office, there was also the issue of potentially losing medical insurance for all of us.

♦ ♦ ♦

Sometime in late May, Dr. Bruce Gilbert, the urologist responsible for my becoming a father, contacted me. He was now involved in a philanthropic program called "Sharing the Dream." That program assured access to sperm banking for financially challenged men who had been diagnosed with cancer or other medical conditions, treatment for which might impair their future fertility. Dr. Gilbert indicated that North Shore Hospital was going to have some media coverage concerning that program to coincide with Father's Day weekend. The hospital's public relations representative thought it would be beneficial to have some of Dr. Gilbert's former patients present at a press conference.

Dr. Gilbert asked if Anna and I would be willing to be interviewed during the press conference and pose for pictures with our three boys. We readily agreed to help in any way we could. We hoped that spreading the word about Dr. Gilbert's program would help other couples benefit from medical advancements in the fertility field.

Dr. Gilbert gave my name to Michelle Pinto, the public relations director at North Shore Hospital. Michelle called me while I was in my office during the second week of June. She told me Dr. Gilbert had given her some information about Anna and me but she still had a few more questions. She proceeded to interview me over the telephone.

It seemed that, after almost every one of my responses to her questions, I heard Michelle exclaim, "Oh, my God!" and sometimes she would add, "Oh, my God! This is a story!"

On June 15, when Anna and I opened the door to Dr. Gilbert's waiting room, we saw it filled with reporters, television cameras, and photographers.

Anna put Joey and Timmy on my lap, while she held Jimmy on hers. Dr. Gilbert sat to the right of Anna. The cameras began filming and reporters started asking questions. They began many of their questions by saying, "The press release said ..." I had no idea what press release they were referring to.

At the conclusion of the interview, I mentioned that I had not seen the press release but would like to. Someone gave me a copy. I was surprised to read the title: "Miracle Dad Shares His Family's Story in Celebration of Father's Day." It wasn't until then that I realized why everyone was focusing the press conference on me instead of on Dr. Gilbert.

The next day, as we were about to get into the van to go to work, Anna unfolded our copy of *Newsday*, which had been lying on our driveway as usual. There was a big picture of me with our three sons on the cover. There was also a large article inside about me and our family, which I didn't have a chance to read because I didn't want to be late for work.

As soon as we arrived at my office, Kathleen Rice, smiling from ear to ear, rushed into my office holding her copy of *Newsday*. She said the pictures and the story in the newspaper were wonderful. She added, "It is great to see a DA on the front cover of a newspaper for something good for a change." The evening before, she even saw one of the TV news segments about us and thought that was terrific as well.

DA Rice gave me her copy of the newspaper. I later learned she kept a second one in her office. She told me she would love to see the triplets in person, and asked if I would bring them in. She could not have been nicer or more enthusiastic.

For weeks after that, we were local celebrities. People stopped us on the street and told us how much they liked the story. Some even stopped their cars in the middle of traffic when they saw us walking, just to say hello.

A few weeks later, we received a package from Michelle Pinto containing a copy of the *Newsday* article, an article that had appeared in the *New York Daily News*, and one from another newspaper. Michelle also sent us a VCR tape with all the TV news segments about us. As it turned out, seven TV stations had covered the story. Even Telecare, the Long Island Diocese's Catholic TV station, ran it.

The afternoon the article appeared on the cover of *Newsday*, Barbara Thomas, the secretary in administration who was responsible for refurbishing our offices, approached me. Her first question was, "What color would you like your office painted?"

I never had that interview with DA Kathleen Rice. I guess her coming into my office with the copy of *Newsday* to talk about the triplets was enough for her.

Chapter 33

Full Circle

◆ ◆ ◆

Our daily living expenses were high. Anna was busy taking care of our home, the triplets, and me. She was not able to bring in any additional income. I spent many sleepless nights worrying about how we were going to afford to put our boys through college. My cousin Jill suggested that public speaking might provide an opportunity to earn some additional money.

At first I resisted the idea. While I had done some public speaking in the past, I was not comfortable doing so for money. I still didn't think that I had done anything so unusual that strangers would want to hear about it, let alone pay for the privilege. Besides, it was torture for me to come up with something to say and then a struggle for me to deliver the talk in front of an audience. Still, many people were encouraging me to do so now.

A short time after that, Anna asked me what I thought about the idea. As we talked, it became clear to me that as far as she was concerned it was not about money, but rather to motivate others by using me as an example. Anna strongly believed I had the power to move people. In fact, she said that I should pursue motivational speaking because it was the "right thing to do."

Soon, Anna and I started to brainstorm about what my motivational talks might address as a topic. The discussions took place during those rare times when I had Anna's full attention, like during our drives to and from my office and during the routine of getting me up in the morning and ready for bed in the evening. Sometime in November, Anna and I started to write a draft.

My first paid talk was on February 19, 2007, in New York City. My cousin Roy, who was now one of the top people at a large wine distribution company, asked me to deliver a motivational talk at his company's annual meeting to business owners from throughout the nation.

When Anna and I had completed the final draft of my talk, we rehearsed it so we could refine it. We also needed to synchronize the Power Point presentation, run by Anna, with me speaking.

Every time I reached the part about my boys being born, I would start to tear up. No matter how many times I practiced, I always lost it there. Making it worse, Anna had the same reaction. She told me that she got a lump in her throat just thinking about it.

There were approximately 120 people in the audience. I could tell by the looks on the faces in front of me that everyone was hanging on my every word. I must say, no one was more surprised about this than I was. At the end, I received a long and loud standing ovation.

After my talk, Roy told the audience that I was his cousin, and a little more about our relationship over the years. The audience loved it.

Roy later forwarded me many complementary emails sent to him about my talk, along with inquiries about the possibility of my speaking to some of the companies that were represented at the meeting. Maybe there actually was a future for me doing motivational speaking.

♦ ♦ ♦

I often reflect on how much I enjoyed my job as a rehabilitation counselor at the Human Resources Center. I am very proud of the work I did there and of the mission of the Center itself. I remember Dr. Viscardi fondly, and the important role he played in my life. I have absolutely no doubt, though, that I made the right decision to leave when I did to go to law school.

Over the years, I encouraged many people to visit the Center to see what a great place it is. In 2001, I took Anna there. We even had the opportunity to talk with Dr. Viscardi. By then he was semi-retired although still very much a presence in the Center, which, at that time, was called Abilities!

Dr. Henry Viscardi Jr. died at the age of ninety-one, on April 13, 2004. It was altogether appropriate and long overdue when, in 2012, Abilities! officially changed its name to the Viscardi Center.

In the fall of 2008, I was asked to become a member of the Board of Directors of Abilities Inc., one of the corporations comprising the Center. I was both surprised and honored by the request. It had been twenty-nine years since I had left. Many years earlier, Abilities Inc. was the only employer willing to give me a chance to show what I could do. Now they not only remembered my contributions to the Center but also felt I could be a valuable member of their Board of Directors. On January 29, 2009, I joined the Board.

Programs run by Abilities Inc. included the evaluation and training of adults who had been forced to change jobs or look into pursuing a new occupation because of changes in their health or physical conditions. In the spring of 2009, I was the keynote speaker at the graduation ceremony for those training programs.

Later that year, I had the opportunity to speak to the students of the Henry Viscardi High School. I talked informally to them and then answered questions.

The students at Viscardi are comprised mostly of boys and girls who have been born with significant disabilities. In addition to mobility problems, many of them have issues with their speech and are often difficult to understand.

While I was describing the obstacles I had overcome, I found myself thinking that some of those students were so physically limited they would never be able to accomplish many of the things I had managed to accomplish after my injury. It wasn't until I finished thinking about it that I realized my perceptions of those young people were probably no different than peoples' perceptions of me had been, thirty plus years earlier.

In 2022, Ken's cousin Roy Danis became Chairman of the Board of Directors at the Viscardi Center. To the right of Ken is John Kemp, who was president and CEO of the Viscardi Center from 2011 to 2022—December 1, 2016.

It really made me think. Why did I have this reaction and what can I do to change that mindset, in me as well as in others? Some people still believe that a person with a disability cannot do anything productive or even think intelligently. Am I so different?

After I became a Board member, I tried to attend the Henry Viscardi High School graduation every year. When our boys turned eight, Anna and I started bringing them along. I wanted the boys to feel comfortable around other people with disabilities and not to prejudge anyone. I wanted the boys to expect all kids, wheelchair bound or not, verbal or not, to strive to be the best they could be, well beyond the expectations of others.

In 2015, I was asked to deliver the commencement address to the Viscardi graduating high school class. This time, I talked about how times had changed since I went through my college years, completed my education, and looked for a full-time position.

The community's perceptions of the students' abilities at Viscardi have been changing as well. In 2014, a Viscardi High School graduate, Robert Pipia, was elected to serve on the Nassau County District Court bench.

At the commencement, I stressed the importance of keeping their expectations high. I urged the graduates not to listen to naysayers or people who say "you can't do it" or that it is "just too difficult." I told them that, while they needed to be realistic, they should try new things, experiment. Paraphrasing President John F. Kennedy, I reminded them that sometimes they should choose to do something not because it is easy but, rather, because it is hard.

If I had listened to the many people who told me I would never be able to do certain things and probably shouldn't even try, I never would have accomplished what most people thought was impossible.

I know that some of the Viscardi students may never be able to live independently but I am heartened by the fact that three-quarters of those students actually do go on to college. The remaining twenty-five percent continue their education in other ways.

We all have to deal with our own limitations and learn the best way to function to our optimum potential. It takes a lot of effort, as well as a lot of trial and error, to figure out the best way to do that. The teachers at the Henry Viscardi High School deserve enormous credit for their skill, ability, and patience in bringing out the best in their students. One needs to look no further than the administrators, teachers, workers, and students at the Center to find future role models.

♦ ♦ ♦

Anna was issued her green card on January 8, 2005, but it took until July 6, 2009, before she finally became an American citizen. Ever since we'd had to deal with her problems returning from her trip to Poland in 2002, I had worried about Anna being deported. I knew it was unlikely because she had never been here illegally, but getting her citizenship papers made me less anxious about losing her. I probably wanted Anna to become an American citizen more than she did.

Timmy, Joey, and Jimmy on Halloween—October 31, 2009.

Timmy, Jimmy, Ken, and Joey on Halloween—October 31, 2010.

♦ ♦ ♦

On October 31, 2010, forty years to the day after I was injured, I went trick-or-treating with my three boys, this year dressed as pirates. They spent hours knocking on doors throughout our neighborhood, laughing and smiling the whole time, just as I had done when I was their age. By the end of the evening, the boys had enough candy and chocolate to last them into the new year. Halloween was great—again!

On that crisp Halloween afternoon, I received many phone calls from family and friends. I also got a few emails that I didn't expect. One came from one of my former Lightweight Football teammates:

Dear Ken,

My first thought upon waking this morning was a strange and strong realization that it was forty years ago today that you suffered your life-changing injury. You may not remember me or even be aware that I was injured a few plays earlier with a concussion, and that you substituted for me. I don't remember the day at all. I do remember that it was my nineteenth birthday that very day, and my roommate at the time, John Magill who was also on the team, says that I was completely disoriented and confused after being laid out by the Columbia player. I have been told that it was just a few plays later, on kickoff coverage, that your injury occurred. I have carried an embarrassed sense of guilt for forty years with the thought that perhaps it should have been me and not you, and that "but for the grace of God ..." But apparently God had better ideas for you, and what you have done with your life has been nothing short of remarkable. You have made the Cornell community proud, and have been an inspiration to many, particularly to those of the 150 family.

I have often thought that there are two measures of a man that are most important—how he deals with adversity, and whether he leaves the world better than he

444 ◆ I Dream of Things That Never Were

found it. You have certainly proven yourself with the first, and what you have done to inspire, along with your legal successes are clear evidence that the world is a better place because of you. So, it is with great respect and admiration that I reach out to you to apologize for not writing sooner, to commend you on a life well lived and to wish you well. I hope to see you in Ithaca sometime.

All the best,

Mal McLaren

Cornell Eng'g '73

Yes, "but for the grace of God ..." I would not have been the one to make that tackle.

Much of what happened to me since my injury has been very difficult, both physically and emotionally. And yet when I look at my wife Anna and our sons Joey, Jimmy, and Timmy, and think about how terrific they are, and how much I love them, I am absolutely convinced that all the challenges that I faced in my life have been well worth it.

When numerous clergy had visited me in the hospital, I never found much comfort from anything they had to say. However, I do remember them saying, "Everything happens for a reason," and "God has a plan for you." For the first time I have started to think, "If God's plan was that I was to become so severely disabled that I would need Anna to take care of me, would then fall in love with her and have three beautiful children, then I guess it was a pretty good plan!!!"

I stopped working full time at the DA's Office on April 30, 2016, although I have continued to work there in a part-time capacity. I also still serve as a member of the Board of Directors at the Viscardi Center and occasionally deliver inspirational/motivational talks to various groups and organizations.

Most of my focus now is on my children's health, happiness, and well-being. What can I do to help them become the best they can be?

Ken's dad's eighty-eighth birthday: Ken's dad is holding Joey, Ken is holding
Timmy, and Anna's dad is holding Jimmy—June 16, 2010.

Ken and Anna with the triplets wearing their college T-shirts:
Joey, Cornell University; Jimmy, SUNY Morrisville;
and Timmy, Syracuse University—May 21, 2023.

I feel extremely happy and fortunate. I have the most wonderful, incredible, beautiful, caring, and loving family anyone could ever hope to have. And after all, isn't that what life is all about?

When I was twenty, I dreamed of leading a useful, productive, rewarding, and happy life. As I finish writing this book, I realize that despite needing to use a wheelchair for the past fifty-plus years, I am living my dream.

Afterword

◆ ◆ ◆

On June 14, 2023, Anna and I celebrated our twentieth wedding anniversary with our children. Nine days later, our triplets graduated from Oceanside High School, fifty-five years after I had graduated from the same school.

In August 2023, James began his freshman year at the State University of New York at Morrisville, studying renewable energy. Timothy started a dual major in the S.I. Newhouse School of Public Communications and the Maxwell School of Citizenship and Public Affairs at Syracuse University. And fifty years after I had graduated from Cornell University, Joseph enrolled in Cornell's College of Arts and Sciences.